Ours Once More

The Dan Danciger Publication Series

Ours Once More

Folklore, Ideology, and the Making of Modern Greece

By Michael Herzfeld

 University of Texas Press, Austin

First Edition, 1982

Library of Congress Cataloging in Publication Data

Herzfeld, Michael, 1947–
   Ours once more.

   (The Dan Danciger publication series)
   Bibliography: p.
   Includes index.
   1. Folk-lore—Greece. 2. Nationalism—Greece.
3. National characteristics, Greek. I. Title.
GR170. H47   398′.09495   81-10398
ISBN 0-292-76018-3   AACR2

Publication of this work has been made possible in part by grants
from the Andrew W. Mellon Foundation and the Lucy Maynard
Salmon Research Fund of Vassar College.

Contents

For my parents, C.T.H. – E.O.H.

Preface

Greece today confronts the visitor with a series of startling contrasts. The ruins and hints of the Classical past mix with the bustle of modern urban life, the warm hospitality with a sometimes overt suspicion of foreigners, the paraphernalia of a functioning national bureaucracy with the omnipresent evidence of patronage and favor trading. Like the early nineteenth-century philhellene, the present-day visitor may arrive in a haze of romantic expectations, only to be thwarted by the importunities of ordinary experience. Generations of travelers have arrived with their baggage of preconceptions about who and what the Greeks were, and many of them soon began to blame the Greeks for failing to fit these uncompromising images. Perhaps the most offensive aspect of this one-sided, soured philhellenism is the insidious conviction that Greeks generally lack any capacity for individual or collective self-criticism.

Yet the reason for these observers' misapprehension seems clear enough: the Greeks see little reason to share their sense of personal and national shortcoming with carping outsiders. Were these critics only privileged to hear the endless agonizing over what one local writer has dubbed "the misery of being Greek" (Dimou n.d.), they might reverse their judgment entirely. The point is, however, that they do not hear such things—not necessarily because they are bent on deliberate misrepresentation but often because they are predisposed to find a very different Greece and because their hosts know this very well.

Indeed, for the Greeks, the persistence of the Classical image in the West poses a painful dilemma: how far should they consciously try to live up to it? There are, after all, two competing views of Greece. One, built from the accumulated materials of European Classical scholarship, looks out beyond the national borders and appeals to those who have championed the Greek cause abroad or yoked it to the service of élitist interests. The other involves reflexive knowledge—a self-portrait that does not always flatter, a Greek's understanding of what it means in practice to be Greek. This second view is an introverted one: visitors may share some parts of it only by taking the Greeks

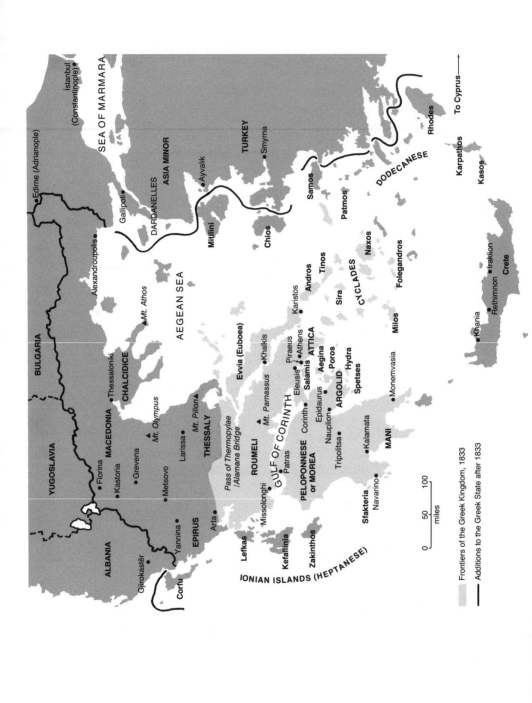

Istanbul (Constantinople)
Edirne (Adrianople)
SEA OF MARMARA
Gallipoli
DARDANELLES
ASIA MINOR
TURKEY
Ayvalik
Smyrna
Mitilini
Chios
Samos
Patmos
DODECANESE
Rhodes
To Cyprus →
Karpathos
Kasos
BULGARIA
Alexandroupolis
Mt. Athos
AEGEAN SEA
Thessaloniki
CHALCIDICE
MACEDONIA
Mt. Olympus
Larissa
Mt. Pilion
THESSALY
Evvia (Euboea)
Khalkis
Karistos
Andros
Tinos
Sira
CYCLADES
Naxos
Folegandros
Milos
Crete
Iraklion
Rethimnon
Khania
YUGOSLAVIA
Florina
Kastoria
Grevena
Metsovo
Pass of Thermopylae /Alamana Bridge
Mt. Parnassus
ROUMELI
GULF OF CORINTH
Patras
Corinth
Piraeus
Eleusis
Athens
Salamis
Aegina
ATTICA
Epidaurus
Nauplion
ARGOLID
Poros
Hydra
Spetses
Monemvasia
ALBANIA
Gjirokastër
Yannina
EPIRUS
Arta
Missolonghi
Lefkas
Kefallinia
Zakinthos
IONIAN ISLANDS (HEPTANESE)
Corfu
PELOPONNESE or MOREA
Tripolitsa
Kalamata
MANI
Stakteria
Navarino

0   50   100
miles

—— Frontiers of the Greek Kingdom, 1833
[shaded] Additions to the Greek State after 1833

literally on their own terms. Otherwise, were the visitors to insist on the old preconceptions as the price of their sympathy and support, the Greeks would presumably try to disabuse them of such notions only if the foreigners' support had ceased to matter or even to be particularly desirable.

Here, then, is the crux of the matter: we are dealing less with questions of fact (since both images have some claim to a factual basis) than with ideological formulations. Both images, the externally directed and the introverted, are "constructions" of history and culture, and both have become distinct idioms in the effort to delineate a national identity. Each is predicated on certain presuppositions about what makes a "correct" assessment or, in other words, on its own criteria of relevance. The supporters of the extroverted model, for example, point to the "survival" of linguistic and social traits from the Classical era, while their opponents are more likely to dwell on the traces of Turkish values in everyday Greek life. This is not a distinction between "ideal" and "real" so much as a contrast between two "realities," two notions of what matters in the attempt to define Greekness. All descriptions are saturated with presuppositions about what is relevant. To understand the clash of national images is thus to probe each aspect of these descriptions— ethnographic, linguistic, historic, literary—as we receive it, without any imputation of bad faith to the respective authors; it is to identify, not deride, the criteria which shaped both images in their sharply differentiated ways. The central theme of this book, then, is an examination both of the ways in which a sense of national identity was constructed in the young Greek nation-state and, more particularly, of the influence of competing ideologies on the selection of relevant ethnological materials. It is thus a history of history as well as an ethnography of culture theory.

This book also represents its author's shifting personal focus. No scholar can seriously claim to understand the culture of an entire nation in all its complexity. A gentler observation, however, may help put the present work in its proper perspective. I have "lived Greece," as the Greeks themselves express it, and have experienced both the novice's blend of romanticism and bafflement and the later, more reflective curiosity about the conflict of perspectives. As the latter concern became dominant, I tried to gain sharper insight from the many opportunities that came my way. First of all, there are the many Greek friends—urban and rural, scholarly and lay—who responded so generously to my persistent peering and prying. Then, there are the many teachers who guided me at all stages of my constantly intensifying interest in Greek culture. Not least among these were the several teachers of my adolescent years at Dulwich College, who first awakened that interest both through instruction in the Classical languages and literatures and through extracurricular activities that included a richly provocative visit to Greece. Among their successors, I would particularly like to mention the late David L. Clarke, restless critic of taxonomic systems in archaeology and related fields; the late George K. Spiridakis, who supervised my first lengthy acquaintance with academic folklore in Greece; Margaret B. Alexiou, sensitive guide to the literary context of medieval and modern Greek; Ravindra K. Jain, with his knack of constantly asking crucial questions and his infectious commitment to the anthropological study of oral tradition; and J. K. Campbell, whose guidance provided a royal road into the intricacies of Greek ethnography.

John Campbell is also among those whose specific criticisms and comments on versions of this book have helped give it whatever focus and insight it may possess; also influential were Dan Ben-Amos, Gareth Morgan, Loring M. Danforth, and Spyros Stavrakas. I am profoundly indebted to them all. Cornelia Mayer Herzfeld brought her special insight and good sense—an invaluable boon throughout— to bear on many a pertinent discussion as this project began to grow into a tangible entity.

To my former colleagues at Vassar College, I want to express my very real appreciation for a memorably lively anthropology-sociology colloquium at which, with their splendidly argumentative help, I began to hammer this assortment of ideas and materials into a greater semblance of unity. To the librarians of Vassar College—especially to Shirley Maul, presiding genius of their interlibrary loan service—goes much warm recognition of their rare patience and efficiency. And to Vassar College as an institution goes my profound gratitude for its extraordinarily generous financial assistance with the completion of the necessary research and, through its Lucy Maynard Salmon Research Fund, the publication of the present volume. Finally, these acknowledgments would be incomplete without warm thanks to Holly Carver and Suzanne Comer, for their remarkable patience and helpfulness, and to all of their colleagues at the University of Texas Press who helped turn the manuscript into a book.

The issues broached here continue to occupy me in various ways; they have ramifications many of which are barely hinted at in these pages. My personal interest in this cluster of topics has nevertheless already acquired, as in any student's work, certain contours and emphases of its own. That I have always been free to develop my academic interests in various idiosyncratic directions is to an immeasurable degree the gift of my parents. To them, in unstinting gratitude, I am happy at long last to dedicate this book, which is itself very much the child of that freedom.

Note on transliteration. In a book of this kind, it is virtually impossible to be consistent about the transliteration of Greek names and phrases. I have generally adopted a modified phonemic style, except where names are better known in some other guise. The titles of Greek works in the bibliography are given in English translation; these should be readily accessible to those who know Greek, while other readers will gain a sense of the topical coverage.

Ours Once More

Chapter 1
Past Glories, Present Politics

". . . the Europeans as mere debtors . . ."

Cultural Identity as Ideology

In 1821, the Greeks rose in revolt against the rule of Turkey and declared
themselves an independent nation. Their goal was far more ambitious than
freedom alone, for they proclaimed the resurrection of an ancient vision
in which liberty was but a single component. That vision was Hellas—the
achievements of the ancient Greeks in knowledge, morality, and art, summed
up in one evocative word. What was more, the new Greek revolutionaries
went one step further than their forebears had ever managed to do: they
proposed to embody their entire vision in a unified, independent polity. This
unique nation-state would represent the ultimate achievement of the Hellenic
ideal and, as such, would lead all Europe to the highest levels of culture yet
known.

Europeans in other lands, though largely receptive to the attractions of
Classical Greek culture, were not uniformly impressed by the modern Greeks'
claim to represent it. By what token could the latter-day Greeks portray
themselves as the true descendants of the ancient Hellenes? Even if they were
able to do so, had several centuries of unenlightened Ottoman rule not had
any effect on their intellectual and moral condition? Were they still, in any
sense that an educated European could grasp, the same as the Greeks of old?

In a strictly literal sense, of course, they were not. No culture remains
totally unaltered with the passage of time; as generation succeeds generation,
all kinds of changes occur, some abruptly, others imperceptibly but nevertheless with equal persistence. Thus, sameness must in reality be a matter of cultural similarity or continuity. These kinds of connection are unlike the absolute notion of sameness, however, in that they depend on the observer's
criteria of relevance—on a whole set of presuppositions, in other words, about
what traits really constitute acceptable or interesting evidence for some sort
of link. Clearly, then, a premise of cultural continuity cannot usefully be regarded as a question of pure fact. That it is often so regarded in practice is

some indication of the substantial political interests that are vested in it. When cultural continuity is quite obviously a political issue—and in Greece it was never anything else, since it provided the theoretical justification for creating the nation-state in the first place—the observer's personal politics are crucial in determining whether such continuity is admitted to exist.

This book is an attempt to show how Greek scholars constructed cultural continuity in defense of their national identity. It is *not* intended to suggest that they did so in defiance of the facts. Rather, they assembled what they considered to be the relevant cultural materials and used them to state their case. In the process, they also created a national discipline of folklore studies, providing intellectual reinforcement for the political process of nation building that was already well under way.[1]

In their attempt to project a particular view of the Hellenic ideal, moreover, the Greeks were acting no differently than the representatives of other, older European scholarly traditions. The selective character of their research was a well-established trait: Europeans of widely separated times and cultures had long been apt to reconstitute Classical Greece in the terms most familiar to them. The concept of Hellas was already a quicksand of shifting perceptions when the modern Greeks came to it in their turn, bringing with them their specialized nationalistic concerns. Even when Classical scholars could see how much "their" Greece differed from that of some other period or intellectual tradition, their deeper sense of perspective did not necessarily release them from their own time-bound and ethnocentric tastes.

A few examples of European scholarly attitudes will serve to make the point. The early medieval writers are said by one authority to have viewed the Greeks as "more simple-minded and devout, above all more romantic" than they were later to seem (Loomis 1906: 7-8). With the Renaissance, there came a greater respect for the Greeks' intellectual achievements; the influx of Greek scholars to Italy after the sack of Constantinople in 1453 (see Geanakoplos 1962, 1966) produced a rapidly increasing familiarity with Classical philosophy and a general reverence for the wisdom of the ancient writers. As Classical scholarship began to expand and to become more specialized, however, and as philological knowledge was joined by the emergent discipline of archaeology, alternative ways of looking at the ancient world proliferated. By the nineteenth century, Classical scholars had come to pride themselves on a remarkable degree of academic perfectionism, but their views were clearly as much a matter of intellectual fashion as ever. A frankly critical American observer of nineteenth-century European scholarship decried not only the English scholars' "limp Grecism," as evidenced in the excessively "scented, wholesale sweetness of the modern aesthetic school in England," but also the Germans' use of Greek "as a stalking-horse for Teutonic psychology" and their grave concern with minutiae. Scholars of the two nations resembled each other, he thought, "in but a single trait—the conviction that they understand Greece" (Chapman 1915: 12-13). Nor was this acid commentator entirely free of any such conviction about himself, to judge from the tone of these remarks. And so, presumably, it will go on. New truths will yield to still newer truths about the same basic idea, the vision of Classical Greece—the source, in a commonly held view, of the very practice of historical writing itself.

Such changes in perception are of interest here for two reasons. First, they show that through all the divergent interpretations there runs a common theme: the idea of Hellas as the cultural exemplar of Europe.[2] And, second, these same contrasts mark the progressive enhancement of that exemplar's authority, not its dissolution (as we might expect) in the bickering of the ages. Whatever Greece is or was, the *idea* of Greece—like any symbol—could carry a wide range of possible meanings, and so it survived triumphantly. Similarly, the concept of European culture, so stable at the level of mere generality, has undergone many transformations through the centuries. "Europe," like "Hellas," was a generalized ideal, a symbol of cultural superiority which could and did survive innumerable changes in the moral and political order. It was to this European ideal, moreover, that Hellas was considered ancestral. Such is the malleable material of which ideologies are made.

Folklore and History

It is as an ideological phenomenon that we shall treat the twin concepts of Hellas and Europe here. They provided the motivating rationale for one of the most explosive political adventures of the nineteenth century, an adventure which claimed thousands of lives and brought many more under the control of a nation-state that had never before existed as a sovereign entity. This adventure was the Greek struggle for independence of 1821 to 1833. Its eventual success was by no means certain in the early stages. The Great Powers were reluctant to commit themselves to the Greek cause until, forced by public opinion at home, by the Greeks' own successes, and by the fear of each other's intentions, they began to take a more active part in bringing the Greek State into existence. That the Greeks did eventually prevail, despite the enormous Turkish armies with which they had to contend as well as their destructive internal squabbles, is some measure of the evocative power of the name of Hellas among their European supporters. To be a European was, in ideological terms, to be a Hellene.

Yet the Hellas which European intellectuals wished to reconstitute on Greek soil was very different from the Greek culture which they actually encountered there, despite all the western-educated Greek intellectuals' efforts to bridge the gap. Nowhere were the contradictions more apparent than in the earliest attempts to provide the new nation-state with an explicit foundation in political theory. In 1822 a national charter, the so-called Constitution of Epidaurus, was promulgated in a language so archaic that few Greeks could fully understand it. This language was symptomatic of the idealism with which the charter had been conceived: it promised a statist democracy in accordance with the principles that were thought to have guided a very different sort of polity, the Athenian city-state of the fifth century B.C. Although this impracticable blueprint was soon superseded by other constitutions, it expresses nicely the paradoxical situation in which the new Hellas found itself.

The paradox, though not openly expressed so baldly at first, was a matter of immediate concern to the founders of the new state and may be crudely paraphrased in these terms: how could a modern nation-state survive on the premise that its citizens were the same as the long-lost inhabitants of the land?[3] Other, related questions followed in the stream of this first one. How, for example, could one be a "Hellene"—a term which had meant "pagan" in the early years of Christianity—while still a member of the Orthodox Christian faith? How could one be considered a Hellene when ordinary conversation was conducted in a language, Romeic, which was conceptually *opposed* to the ancient ("Hellenic") tongue? What, more generally, were Greeks to make of all the cultural traits which, though a familiar part of their lives, were now under attack by their leaders as well as by foreigners as "barbarous" and "oriental" and therefore as the very antithesis of Greek? Such difficulties threatened the coherence of the national ideology at the moment of its supreme political triumph.

From 1821 on, the intellectuals had to deal with a large rural population in the realm of practical politics. The unlettered peasantry presented a potentially embarrassing contrast to the idealized image of Greece which the European supporters of Greek nationalism—the philhellenes, as they are so aptly named—had entertained for so long. How were the Greek rural folk to fit into the grand design? They had almost no documented history which might connect them, however tenuously, to their ancient predecessors.

The study of folklore provided the most comprehensive answer—hesitantly at first, then with growing confidence as the methods and orientation of this (for Greece) novel discipline became more and more systematic. The concept around which the early Greek folklorists organized their enterprise was precisely that of cultural continuity. This specialized version of the commonly entertained conception of Hellas as the exemplar of all Europe shared with the latter a similar liability to wide-ranging and ambiguous definition. In its successive reformulations, it responded to many of the ethnological fashions which sprang up abroad, though often in forms adapted to Greece's special needs and preoccupations. Against the background of the Greeks' dependence on European patronage, moreover, the role of folklore in fashioning an acceptable external image for the country had political significance right from the start. If it could be shown that the peasants, the largest demographic element, retained clear traces of their ancient heritage, the fundamental requirement of philhellenic ideology would be satisfied, and European support for the emergent nation-state could be based on a secure foundation of historical justification.

An Externally Directed Ideology

For these reasons, folklore was not merely an abstruse academic concern in the early years of Greek independence. It addressed what were perhaps the most sensitive aspects of national identity, and its political implications were widely recognized. Foreigners as well as Greeks, politicians as well as scholars helped launch Greek folklore research on the path along which it was to travel for decades to come. This rise of academic folklore was generated in the interplay between local and foreign interests in the legitimation of the new state.

The nationalist scholar and ideologue Adamantios Koraes (1748-1833), a correspondent of Thomas Jefferson and a close observer of pre- and post-revolutionary France, both exemplified and initiated that process. Koraes could be highly disparaging of the vernacular culture: he once dismissed the Cretan Renaissance verse-romance *Erotokritos* as "the ugly handmaid" of Greek letters, for example (1805). Despite such attitudes, he encouraged Greek scholars to take an interest in vernacular studies and expressed warm admiration for Claude Fauriel, the French historian and compiler of the first substantive collection of Greek folksongs to appear in print (Sainte-Beuve 1870: 202; cf. Llewellyn Smith 1965: 54). Some of the songs in Fauriel's collection had apparently been supplied by Koraes himself, via the good offices of the Greek scholars Christodoulos Klonaris (1788-1849) and Nikolaos Piccolos (1792-1866) (Fauriel 1956: 2). Koraes' own attitude toward folk literature can perhaps best be gauged through his linguistic ideas. In contrast to the neo-Atticists, who wanted to restore the Classical Greek of Plato and the Attic tragedians to daily use, he was willing to retain certain vernacular forms as well as to draw on European traditions of grammatical codification. Whether or not Koraes' moderate stance was what enabled demotic Greek to survive the onslaught of extreme neo-Atticism (Babiniotis 1979: 4), his interest lay less in reviving the Classical glories as such than in locating in the modern Greeks a Hellenic essence which could be refashioned in the philhellenic idiom.

The development of folklore in Greece can be understood only against this background of an externally directed ideology, ever responsive to foreign

comment and criticism. Perhaps the greatest period of activity in the history
of Greek folklore began with the vehement denial of the Greeks' claims to a
Classical ancestry, articulated by the Austrian polemicist and scholar Jakob
Philipp Fallmerayer. But, while due regard must be paid to such foreign stim-
uli, the achievements of the Greek folklorists are not thereby diminished. On
the contrary, it was the Greeks' willingness to join battle in the first place
which allowed them to recover and preserve so vast a corpus of material;
without their efforts, most of it would have vanished long ago. Nor is there
any profit in laughing at their methods and theories, outlandish though many
of them may now seem. These were partly a reflection of ethnological thinking abroad, partly a response to local political conditions and ideological
trends. Above all, the Greek folklorists' methods were intended to guide the
earnest search for factual knowledge. These folklorists were actually dogged
empiricists, no matter how ambiguous their evidence may seem today. There
is nothing to be gained from looking at the early Greek folklorists as an assortment of charming eccentrics, even though the recent treatment of nineteenth-century philhellenes and nationalists (St. Clair 1972; Howarth 1976)
may suggest some such course. To understand them, we must instead relate
their ideas to the political, social, and moral universe in which they moved.

Toward a National Anthropology

How is such a task best approached? The Greek folklorists were attempting to
explain a national culture which they considered to be both internally chaotic
and corrupted by foreign influences of many kinds. Their notions about what
it meant to be Greek acted as a filter through which only "relevant" data
could pass. Indeed, these ideas were often translated into systems of classification. It is by treating such systems semiotically—that is, as a code which
embodied and expressed the folklorists' guiding assumptions—that we can
most effectively work back to the assumptions themselves.

Every cultural commentary—be it folkloric, historical, or anthropological—
is an attempt to convey to an audience of relative outsiders something which
already has its own internal forms of explanation and rationale. In the present
case, however, it is the commentators themselves that we are studying. The
Greek folklorists saw their nation's culture as a unity in which they were
themselves fully participating members. In order to examine their relationship
to the peasantry whose lore they studied, we cannot afford to accept that
assumption uncritically. On the contrary, it is just one of the many distinctive
traits of their culture within a culture, of the habits of thought which set
them apart from other Greeks. Their willingness and ability to think in terms
of *studying* folklore are some measure of the distance which actually separated them from the rural people. In that sense, too, this book is essentially

an "anthropology of anthropologists,"[4] whatever its wider implications with regard to modern Greek culture as a whole.

These Greek scholars were anthropologists of a special kind. Most of what they did was in some way a response to the ideological needs of their emergent polity. Indeed, they made a distinctive and important contribution to the making of modern Greece, no less than did the military and political leaders in their respective areas of competence. Their methods and assumptions are thus crucial to our understanding not only of the ideological development of Greece in its first few decades of independence but of the complexities of modern Greek culture as we encounter it today. All too often, our insights are restricted by the boundaries of current academic disciplines. Village-level ethnographies and studies of particular artistic and literary movements are valuable and interesting, but they address comparatively small and isolated segments of the national culture. By examining the Greeks' study of their own national culture, we can at least begin to gain some sense of how these various segments are connected in the national sense of identity.

Attractive though this framework of inquiry is, it does raise two serious difficulties which have to be discussed before we go any further. The first of these concerns the extent to which the folklorists exerted the kind of influence which may have caused the folklore itself to conform increasingly to their preconceptions. The second problem is both more general and more immediate: how can we be sufficiently confident of our own sense of Greek folklore to be able to make a critical examination of the original collectors' work?

The first question—that of the folklorists' influence on cultural change—is hard to answer with any real accuracy. There is no doubt that the folklorists did have some effect on the content of school textbooks, which in turn contributed to the partial dissemination of learned culture (see especially Beaton 1980: 190). Moral censorship, too, seems to have had some effect; what the folklorists permitted themselves to include in their collections may have had greater chances of survival simply because of this semiofficial approval. Yet we should be careful not to overstate the case here; the real difficulty is that our major source of information about the folk culture is precisely the body of material collected over the years by the local scholars, and in fact there is some evidence (e.g., Herzfeld 1979) that the more disreputable forms have survived remarkably well in some areas. Some of the scholars' linguistic emendations may have entered the folk repertoire as the spoken language moved increasingly toward standardization. Here again, however, it is not at all clear how radical the folklorists' influence actually was, and I have been extremely cautious about assuming that they were responsible for any of these kinds of cultural change. It is not necessary to presuppose such input on their part in order to argue that their scholarship represents a highly selective view of the country's popular culture; insofar as such input can be identified, it can only strengthen this overall picture.

As to the second question—the status of our own interpretations of Greek culture—these need not present a serious obstacle provided that we do not use them to "disprove" those of the local scholars whose work concerns us. This proviso, however, is vital. An anthropologist does not try to expose informants' "ignorance" of their cultural universe; it is only possible to say something about how they perceive and articulate that universe. In much the same spirit, our aim here is not to challenge the factual basis of early Greek folklore studies or to treat their motivating principles as somehow erroneous. Since we are treating the scholarly sources as "informants" out of the past, we should no more attempt to debate with them than we would consciously force a living informant to adopt a particular anthropological theory. Of course, there are factual errors aplenty in these sources, and one is sometimes tempted to mutter about poor standards or even fraud. But imputations of bad faith lead nowhere—especially when our aim is to discover why our "informants" thought as they did, rather than to assume the answer in advance.

This is a matter of suiting methods to the purpose of the study. It is one thing to reject an older interpretation as incompatible with current frameworks and interests, quite another to condemn it out of hand. Exactly the same is true of the charge of eccentricity—a word which in Greek means being "off-center." It is to our own conceptual center, not to that of their contemporaries and compatriots, that many of the early Greek folklorists seem marginal. In the context of their time and place, their views, which were by no means crudely uniform, made good sense.

The Premise of Cultural Continuity

The central tenet of cultural continuity provided an organizing principle for the collection, classification, and ranking of all ethnographic items. Although the folklorists' emergent discipline was mainly concerned with nonmaterial artifacts, they were unusually fortunate in the wealth of historical evidence to which they could turn. In many parts of the world, folklorists can often only guess at the stages through which their materials have evolved. In Greece, by contrast, a rich archaeological record enhanced an already surprisingly large assortment of scraps of oral literature preserved (or at least mentioned) in ancient and medieval writings.

The archaeological aspect of this historical perspective was extremely important; indeed, it provided the dominant model for the whole enterprise. Although the phrase "monuments of the word" was first applied to Greek folklore by Claude Fauriel in 1824, it has since enjoyed enormous popularity among local scholars. Apparently an invention of that German philosopher of national identity, Johann Gottfried von Herder (but cf. Nisbet 1969: 100 on Turgot's 1750 formulation), it was extensively used by the Grimm brothers, whose work was to exercise considerable influence on Greek folklore scholarship in the second half of the nineteenth century. The archaeological model is thus not a uniquely Greek concept, but it certainly suited Greek conditions exceptionally well, and it enabled Greek scholars to present their view of cultural continuity in terms to which their European colleagues could respond easily. In describing a present which was also a past, it harmonized with the political aims of a revolution which was also a resurrection.

Superficially, the Greeks were not very different from any other nascent European nation seeking the evidence of its collective character in folklore. Sounding very much like the Greeks on the subject of Turkey, the Finns, for example, contrasted their "European" culture with the "oriental barbarism" of the Russians (Wilson 1976: 148). The Finns, like the Greeks, used their folklore to validate both their national identity and their cultural status as Europeans. Unlike the Greeks, however, they did not speak an Indo-European language and so had even less claim than most European peoples to having "originated" European culture. Greek antiquity, by contrast, was scanned as a prototype for the modern folklores of such countries as Ireland (Dorson 1966: 293) and Finland itself (Wilson 1976: 172). No other country was ever accorded such a generative role in relation to the rest of Europe, and it is this above all which makes the Greek experience the reverse of that of virtually every other European country.

In order to justify their special ancestral status, the Greeks naturally relied heavily upon their archaeological model. Indeed, official endorsement of folklore studies partly rested on the assumption that they were of an archaeological nature. As recently as 1968, celebrating the fiftieth anniversary of the founding of the Folklore Research Center of the Academy of Athens, Academician Anast. Orlandos approvingly described the twin directions of early folklore research in Greece as, respectively, "literary" and "patriotic or archaeological" (1969: 6). A literary essayist might perhaps be a patriot; an archaeologist, by definition, could be nothing else.

Youngest State, Oldest Nation

Although Greece was conceptually the very source of Europe, it was politically one of that continent's youngest member states. As a result, when we compare the history of Greek folklore studies with similar intellectual developments elsewhere in Europe, the sense of inversion is enhanced still further. Before the establishment of the Greek nation-state, the existence of Greek nationhood was an intellectual and political article of faith; the process of ethnological justification, however, was really set in motion only *after* that event. Elsewhere, as in Finland again, folklore studies played an important part in creating a national consciousness long *before* statehood could be achieved. The Greek scholars were unusual in having folklore studies virtually forced on them by events.

There was no local tradition of folklore research as a systematic, autonomous discipline. In early Christian and Byzantine times, folklore attracted attention either as a persistent and subversive paganism, as in the writings of Saint John Chrysostom, or as a source of such curious illustrations as those in the exceptionally perceptive Homeric commentaries of Eustathius of Thessaloniki (cf. Koukoules 1950; Spiridakis 1966: 476-477). Later came rare collections of verbal curios: two fifteenth-century manuscript renderings of the song of Armouris (see Beaton 1980: 82-86), the fourteen song texts with musical notation preserved in a seventeenth-century manuscript from the Iviron Monastery on Mount Athos (Bouvier 1960), and the eighteenth-century compilation of proverbs by the Yannina monk Parthenios Katzioulis (Politis 1899-1902: xxix-xxxv, 69-132). An 1812 manuscript from the island of Folegandros carries a long text of the so-called swallow song, a children's carol that was probably sung on the eve of March 1 every year. But now we are on the threshold of independence.[5]

In general, the foreign contribution to the early stages of folksong research and publication was substantial. The French traveler André Guillet (La Guilletière 1676) had considered making a collection of songs from Greece, but nothing came of the scheme. Claude Fauriel's two-volume compendium, published in France in 1824 and 1825, was followed by the German historian Theodor Kind's shorter effort in 1827. The Greeks, embroiled in a desperate war, also lacked the equipment needed for producing books on their own territory. That matters other than academic publication preoccupied them at this time is quite clear from their unenthusiastic reaction to the gift of printing presses which some Benthamite well-wishers decided to foist upon them (St. Clair 1972: 146-149); it was not until the relative tranquillity of the mid 1830s that such ventures became generally feasible. There were, of course, Greek printers in Venice, where Niccolò Tommaseo published a distinguished collection of Tuscan, Corsican, Greek, and Illyrian folksongs in 1841 and 1842. But the Greek colony in Venice, which had been highly active in the dissemination of Greek learning during and after the Renaissance, was largely composed of literati and wealthy merchants who showed scant interest in the monuments of their rural compatriots' vernacular culture. Fauriel had poor luck hunting for Greek folksongs there (Colquhoun 1954: 173). Only in the Ionian Islands (the Heptanese) were singers and printers to be found in close proximity under conditions of relative peace. Even there, however, the rise of Corfu as the outstanding local center of Greek folklore studies did not begin until the middle of the nineteenth century; by then, the British were on the verge of ceding the Ionian Islands to Greece (1864), and a considerable amount of research had already been done on the mainland too. Thus, the eventual development of folklore studies in Greece seems to owe much more to political and ideological developments than to such purely circumstantial matters as the availability of printing presses.

Although publication was late in developing, the Ionian Greeks certainly showed an interest in folklore from the beginning. One of them, Andrea Mustoxidi, is generally credited with having been the first to voice the need— as early as 1820—for folklore studies in Greece. After the War of Independence, Greeks from many parts of the country became involved in this research, and their publications provided what successive national constitutions had not: a vibrant charter for their *Altneuland*.[6] Unlike, for example, the United States Declaration of Independence (see Wills 1979: 38), the stilted Greek constitutions had hardly served as a focus for allegiance, enthusiasm, and a new mythology. What was needed was a body of patriotic writing which could juxtapose grand ideals with cultural experience. Such a text was collectively created through the development of a national discipline of folklore—or, as some (e.g., Bryer 1976) prefer to call it in order to stress its distinctively local flavor, laography (Greek *laografia*).

Why laography? Ostensibly, folklore entailed the study of the *ethnos*, the nation, yet *ethnografia* has never been a very popular term in Greece. *Laos* denotes the people (cf. *Volk*), *ethnos* the nation qua inheritors of the Classical mantle.[7] In order to justify the creation of the state (*kratos*) in the terms of ideological philhellenism, it was necessary to show that *ethnos* and *laos* were one and the same thing, with the sole difference being that the *laos* did not include the educated élite (cf. Campbell 1976). This meant that there would have to be an independent discipline concerned with the *laos*—laography—from which it would be possible to prove that the common people indeed belonged to the Hellenic *ethnos*. The *ethnos* did not need a branch of study of its own: it was one of the eternal verities, an absolute moral entity against which the *laos* could be matched and measured. Laography was thus politically committed from its inception, and no study of it can ever be anything other than an excursion into ideology.

Quintessential Europeans

If foreigners were among the first to collect Greek folklore, and even to exploit its ideological potential on behalf of the philhellenic cause, they did so as part of a far more extensive commitment. From the outbreak of war in 1821, often at the risk of angering reactionary governments at home, European liberals came to witness and to fight for the rebirth of Hellas. Despite all the twists and turns of the struggle, dedicated foreigners continued to join the affray. Many died in Greece of sickness—like Lord Byron—or of wounds received in battle. Often, expecting to be hailed as leaders and saviors, they found their advice ridiculed or ignored by haughty local guerrilla "captains" who cared little for the much touted advantages of "European warfare" (St. Clair 1972: 75-77). Despite the example set by those who returned home in disgust, others were usually more than eager to take their place.

The Greek cause did not suddenly spring fully formed from the minds of nineteenth-century intellectuals. Among the Greeks themselves, as some authorities have argued (e.g., Vacalopoulos 1970; Xydis 1968), its roots can be traced back at least to the later years of the Byzantine Empire. It seems to have become a major political force only in the second half of the eighteenth century, however, as the rise of nationalist and liberal philosophies in Western Europe began to attract expatriate Greeks with some knowledge of Greek history. The expansion of Russian power in the Mediterranean during this period excited the imagination and ambition of local Greek leaders, who saw the Russians, Orthodox Christians like themselves, as natural allies against the infidel Turks. In 1770, Russia actively encouraged rebellions in western Crete (the revolt of Daskaloyannis of Sfakia) and the Peloponnese but allowed both uprisings to collapse ignominiously when it became evident that Russian interests would not benefit from a protracted involvement.

The Russians nevertheless continued to encourage anti-Turkish sentiment as a means of keeping the Turks damagingly busy in Greece (Kordatos 1972: 59), while the flourishing Greek merchant colonies in South Russia became centers of a swelling national consciousness. It was in Odessa, in 1814, that a group of Greek activists founded the Filiki Eteria ("Friendly Society"), a clandestine organization devoted to spreading nationalist propaganda throughout Greece; this group's work was a major factor in the development of national identity among the rural people.

France and Britain were slower than Russia to take an active role in Greek politics. Once the Greeks had risen in revolt, however, fear of each other's intrigues and of the predominance of the pro-Russian faction among the Greeks eventually forced their hand (Petropoulos 1968; Dakin 1973). The attitude of the Powers toward Greece was thus largely one of step-by-step opportunism, although it was invariably presented as a defense of the Greeks' best interests. The establishment of a monarchical system, designed in part to unite the warring Greek factions behind a disinterested ruler, became the focus of elaborate diplomatic activity on all sides; the eventual choice of Otto, second son of Ludwig I of Bavaria, was a compromise which brought home to the Greeks the impossibility of their taking any major political decision independently of the Powers' collective approval (Couloumbis, Petropulos, and Psomiades 1976: 19-20; Dakin 1973: 275-290). While the European Powers played no small part in the eventual consolidation of the Greek nation-state, their intention was to form an entity made in their own image and upon their own terms.

It is difficult to know what the rural population thought of these developments. Their scanty acquaintance with Classical culture made it easy for European enthusiasts and western-educated Greeks to promote the ideal of a regenerated Hellas over their heads. Some historians have argued that the rural folk preserved no knowledge or memory of the Classical past at all. The rural Greeks certainly seem to have been puzzled by the expectations which the philhellenes entertained of them, to judge from the accounts of those non-Greeks who returned to tell the tale. If this was the situation at the time of the War of Independence, it seems to have been substantially the same for several centuries before that. While the Marxist historian Yanis Kordatos may be oversimplifying by stating that, at the time of the Turkish conquest in the fifteenth century, "only the learned who of necessity left Constantinople and Thessaloniki and went to Italy and Western Europe spoke of the ancient Greeks and of ancient Greece" (1972: 56, n. 1; cf., e.g., Vacalopoulos 1970), it is likely that few rural folk had any *detailed* knowledge of the ancient culture at that time. Much the same state of affairs seems to have obtained at least until the late eighteenth century, despite the growth of centers of learning in Epirus and elsewhere (on which see Henderson 1970). It was the educated minority who thought in terms of Classical culture, and it was largely in the West that they found the encouragement to do so.

The partially western origins of their vision hardly dismayed the Greek intellectuals, for whom all European wisdom was Greek by definition and derivation. Apart from such rare exceptions as the philosopher Johann Georg Hamann, Herder's mentor, most European thinkers were in general agreement with this position. What they did not endorse quite so readily was the Greeks' nationalistic extension of it. An example of this special attitude is provided by the nineteenth-century Greek historian and folklorist Spyridon Zambelios (1813?-1881), a prominent figure in this account, who proclaimed that Westerners writing their own history "had only consequences to illuminate; whereas, for the Hellene, *consequences* have the lesser rank. His history occurs in an epoch of causes, as a gospel of the genesis and dissemination of ideas, the beginning of fatherland (*patris*) and faith, wisdom, and freedom" (1852: 14).

Half a century earlier, Adamantios Koraes, whose admiration for the French Revolution was tempered by a deep respect for the cultivated ideals of the *ancien régime* (Clogg 1976: 127), had already described the Greeks' cultural primacy in scarcely more compromising terms:

It is France which had the glory of seeing in her own bosom that meet-

ing of philosophers who were the first, in the middle of the past century, to lay the foundations of that vast edifice known by the name
of the *Encyclopédie*. The light which rebounded from that literary
revolution, following the same laws as physical light, had necessarily to
spread clarity far beyond its own environment, in any place where it
encountered no obstacles. We have already seen that, for the Greek
nation, these obstacles had to be large indeed; but we should also have
observed that they were counterbalanced by the sentiments on which a
considerable part of the nation is nourished. The Greeks, proud of their
origin, far from closing their eyes to the lights of Europe, considered
the Europeans as mere debtors who would repay with very great interest a capital sum received by them from the Greeks' ancestors.

(1803: 12)

This is a clearly stated view of cultural relationships, phrased in the language of a philosophical nationalism. Note, first of all, the strong emphasis on
the "natural laws" of human development. The light of the intellect obeys
the same laws as physical light: the poetic conceit serves as an ideologically
powerful metaphor. There is *necessity* in such laws; thus, Greece will find its
just reward. Europe was not entirely unprepared for such a message; indeed,
in the half century following the publication of Koraes' words, Lamarckian
evolutionism had the effect of enhancing still further the general tendency to
place the Greeks at the historical and moral head of human development (cf.
Goodfield and Toulmin 1965). Zambelios' theory of cultural cause and effect, though it owes much to a "historicist" tradition which grew up in opposition to the French natural-law school, converged with Koraes' argument on
this assumption of the Greeks' cultural primacy.

Both arguments, moreover, involve two basic assumptions: the Greeks
constituted a nation, and they had done so before. It is easy to argue (e.g.,
Holden 1972: 22-23) that the Greeks had never previously been united in a
single independent polity, but this misses the point. With their extensive
knowledge of Classical literature, contemporary Greek intellectuals were not
likely to overlook the difference, in scale at least, between Periklean Athens
and a modern nation-state.[8] On the other hand, the Classical Greeks had certainly conceptualized their cultural unity, in opposition to the barbarians
(who were not so much "savage" as, quite simply, "not Greek"). The Greeks
of 1821 likewise had a sense of common religion, language, and customs. Part
of the problem of determining what it means to say that the Greeks were, or
had been, a nation lies in the difficulty of distinguishing *in Greek* between
"nationhood" and "ethnicity." Some such distinction nevertheless has to be
made for present purposes, for, while a shifting sense of collective identity
seems to have existed among Greek-speaking Orthodox Christians long before

1821, it is much less clear how much this constituted a set of national aspirations. Some historians take a critical position. According to Kordatos, for example, the nation (*ethnos*) "is a phenomenon of recent years, a historical phenomenon which had its starting point at the end of the Middle Ages, when feudalism began to be disrupted and the bourgeoisie came into the ascendant" (1972: 33). Whatever the justice of this view in strictly political terms, it should not lead us to assume that other forms of collective identity did not bind Greeks together in the centuries between the Fall of Constantinople and the Greek War of Independence.

Certainly, the formulation of a Greek national identity in terms of cultural continuity was something of a novelty to the largely illiterate country people. No less an observer than Koraes has recorded certain revealing reactions to the Classical revival among unlettered Greeks. It had been only a short while before, he remarked, that "for the first time one saw Greek vessels bearing the names of the great men of antiquity. Until then, only the names of the saints had been known. Today I know of vessels bearing the names of Themistocles and Xenophon" (1803: 44). Koraes was well aware that "in a country where once the wisest laws of Solon . . . reigned supreme," ignorance of the past was now a cardinal problem for the cause of Hellenic regeneration (Clogg 1976: 118-119).

Folk culture, for Koraes, was less a source of proof that the people actively yearned to recover their ancient virtues than evidence of their potential (and need) for extensive reeducation. His own experience, in which a series of lucky chances made it possible for him to acquire some learning at an early age (Clogg 1976: 121-124), may well have influenced his thinking here: the Hellenic virtues could be acquired, given only native diligence and aptitude. That one had to turn to Western Europe in this endeavor was simply a matter of historical circumstance, of the fact that Europe had been the repository of Greek learning during the centuries of Ottoman rule—a time when the Greeks themselves had acquired a shamefully Turkish patina which now had to be scraped away.

Koraes is today remembered most of all for his leading role in the development of *katharevousa*, the neo-Classical form of the modern Greek language which, somewhat ironically in the light of his revolutionary principles, has become closely associated with the political Right and the foreign interests which it represents (Sotiropoulos 1977). *Katharevousa* was always something of a cultural appeal to the West for recognition, an attempt to demonstrate that the ordinary Greeks of today could speak a tongue which was undeniably their own yet no less clearly Hellenic. Such purism naturally demanded that all words of obviously Turkish origin be eliminated. A recent commentator's description of this deorientalization of the language as "beneficial" (Babiniotis 1979: 4) shows how successful Koraes was in establishing a moral standard by which all subsequent linguistic developments could be evaluated. Ideological criteria of culture, if they are to be judged successful, must in some measure become self-fulfilling prophecies—a theme which will recur insistently in the following chapters of this book.

The development of *katharevousa* was part of Koraes' wider, educative view of Hellenic regeneration. Culture, rather than physical descent, still seems to have been the main component of Greekness in his day. Educated people throughout the Balkans called themselves Hellenes; in the Romanian princess Dora d'Istria, we shall later meet one of the latest and most flamboyant embodiments of this conceit. It seems, moreover, that language was sometimes thought virtually sufficient to make people forget that they had ever been anything but Greek—in 1802, there appeared a quadrilingual dictionary published by the priest Daniel of Moskhopolis, exhorting "all who now do speak / an alien tongue rejoice, prepare to make you Greek" (quoted in Clogg 1973: 20). This attitude was to change significantly later on, after the establishment of the new Greek State, when greater emphasis came to be laid on an essentially retroactive claim to descent from the ancient Greeks. Such shifts in the ideology of culture are not uncommon: the United States apparently experienced a somewhat similar switch to a descent-based ideology, with a retroactive attribution of descent "from the same ancestors, speaking the same language" (John Jay, quoted in Jones 1960: 140; see also Lipset 1963: 29), at a comparably postindependence phase. But, while massive immigration into the United States eventually led to the displacement of such ideas by both the melting-pot concept and emergent minority movements, Greek ideology developed in a very different direction: Koraes' cultural proselytizing gave way to claims, in the later nineteenth and the twentieth centuries, of the Hellenes' "racial" predominance throughout the Balkan Peninsula.

One People, Two Histories

The first president of independent Greece, Count John Capodistrias, was assassinated in 1831 by disgruntled Maniat leaders; the ensuing civil strife was brought to an end only with the installation of King Otto by the Great Powers in 1833. The Powers' effective domination of the country's internal politics was in fact generally recognized, the three principal parties being known as the English, French, and Russian (or Napist) (cf. Petropulos 1968; Couloumbis, Petropulos, and Psomiades 1976: 19). Internally, too, Greece was subject to the views of outsiders, for the new king brought with him a group of largely German advisers on whom he relied extensively in the administration of the country.

Ironically, however, under the more peaceful conditions which came with externally imposed rule, the Greeks had more ample opportunity to reflect on the nature of their national identity. With the nation-state an accomplished reality, the intelligentsia now had to come to terms with the obvious discontinuities between Hellenic ideal and Greek actuality. Foreign observers had already shown great interest, most of it benevolent, in the traditions of the Greek countryside: Kind and Tommaseo had published their collections of folksongs to an enthusiastic response from European intellectual circles; Goethe had expressed particular admiration for Greek songs after meeting another collector, Werner von Haxthausen, in 1815 (Kemminghausen and Sonter 1935: 7); while C. B. Sheridan had compounded the dangers of translation by publishing his own English rendering of Fauriel's French! There was thus a receptive audience for Greek folklore in Europe, and the Greeks had a vital political interest in maintaining it. On it depended their ability to convince their benefactors, once and for all, that they were truly the Hellenes of the new age.

What of this designation of "Hellene"? In the traditions of the rural Greeks, it had hitherto played a restricted and ambiguous role. Even those Greek scholars who attempted to demonstrate its survival in the popular memory were unable to show that it had been used by the peasantry as a category of *self*-designation rather than as the name of a mythical race long since vanished from the face of the earth. Its survival was nevertheless of crucial significance to the nationalist ideology, which may usefully be dubbed the Hellenist thesis. To exponents of this ideology, the term's perseverance through the long centuries of foreign domination represented the persistence of the Hellenic ideal itself on Greek soil; it could thus now be cited in retrospect as a supreme symbolic justification for what had been accomplished politically in the shape of the Greek nation-state.

But the Hellenist thesis was not without its critics inside Greece, even in the early years of independence. Their counterargument can be called the Romeic thesis (see also Kiriakidou-Nestoros 1975: 217-234, 1978: 155). According to this point of view, the self-designation of the Greeks had long been that of *Romii*, a name which echoes the Byzantine (East Roman) Empire and hence also the Orthodox Christian tradition to which the overwhelming majority of Greeks still adhered; the Greeks ordinarily called their spoken language *romeika* ("Romeic"), a usage which was even adopted by some of the travelers who visited their country while it was still under Turkish rule. A form of the Romeic name had been applied to all Greeks, and in Asia Minor to virtually all non-Moslems (Dawkins 1916: 641; cf. also s.v. *Hellas*, p. 598), by the Turks.

Most discussion of the relative merits of the two words, Hellenes and

Romii, has been conducted in the terms of an extremely literal sense of cultural history. The choice lies between ancient pagan glories on the one hand and the more immediate and familiar attractions of Orthodox Christianity on the other. Both sides to the dispute claim a strictly factual basis for their respective positions—an excellent illustration, if we need one, of the selective nature of historical explanation and, as such, an ideal introduction to the theme of this book. From a critical perspective, however, the issue is not simply one of selecting a favorite period of history. The Hellenic-Romeic distinction has another role in Greek discourse, one less obtrusive (but cf. Leigh Fermor 1966: 106-115) but nevertheless fundamental to the ideological division in question: the difference between an outward-directed conformity to international expectations about the national image and an inward-looking, self-critical collective appraisal. The outward-directed model is precisely what we may call political Hellenism; the introspective image is the essence of the Romeic thesis.

When a Greek wishes to make an affectionate or a disparaging comment on some aspect of the national culture—in other words, on something very familiar—the object is appropriately described as *romeiko*; this is equally apt for the ills of the bureaucracy, the crafty antics of the shadow-theater antihero Karagiozis, or the stereotype of the sexually aggressive male. Again, the demotic language, *romeika*, is full of acknowledged Turkisms and familiar colloquial expressions.

The Hellenic image is conceptually opposed to all these things. It is not, strictly speaking, a resurrection of everything Classical, as the shade of Aristophanes discovered during the censorious days of the right-wing Papadopoulos regime. It is, rather, a response to the European image of Classical Greece, as this was interpreted by the modern Greek nationalists in their turn. Its linguistic domain is *katharevousa* (although latterly all forms of Greek have been called *ellinika*, "Hellenic"). The Hellenic image is avowedly antiquarian, in sharp contrast to the familiarity of the Romeic. What more eloquent expression of this contrast could there be than the rural Cypriot use of *anttika* (cf. Italian *antico*; Kiprianou 1967: 43) to denote ugliness? Reverence for the ancient past would seem, at least in part, to be an intrusive idea in the culture of rural Greeks.

The linguistic aspect of the Hellenic-Romeic distinction is perhaps the most accessible to analysis. The invention and cultivation of *katharevousa* were consistent both with early philhellenic idealism and, in consequence, with the "outer-directedness" (Sotiropoulos 1977: 27-28) of Greek statecraft. This is a logical expression of political Hellenism (pace Holden 1972: 265), being a way of presenting the nation in a light acceptable to the West. Thus, the Hellenists' academic attempts to burnish the image of the modern

Hellene were expressions of "national pride" (*ethnikos eghoïsmos*; see, e.g., Apostolakis 1929: 57), of a desire to conceal whatever a foreign-educated audience might consider unseemly.

Again, the concern with appearances is especially obvious in the realm of language. At the turn of the century, according to the November 3, 1900 *Spectator*, it was still thought necessary to switch from the vernacular and to conduct conversations, "at least when strangers were present, in a curious jargon modelled upon Xenophon with a strong flavour of Dumas." The writer of these words, a British enthusiast for the demotic language and lore, found the Greeks to have been "eagerly employed for more than a century in the patriotic task of destroying their national language and literature, in order to substitute brand-new articles 'made in Europe' and guaranteed pure and classical by eminent professors." Bitter words, perhaps, but they were echoed by Greek as well as foreign critics of the Hellenist ideology, and they point up the salient paradox of *katharevousa*: this supposedly autochthonous tongue was in fact, to a considerable degree, a response to imported ideals. Greece was unique among the new European nations in not using the vernacular as the language of its *risorgimento*, and this, more than any other aspect of its cultural history, underscores the country's beholden condition (Sotiropoulos 1977: 8-9).

The tension between these mutually opposed images is also reflected in the way Greeks still talk about Europe. They may use the term *Evropi*, either in its geographical or in its cultural sense, to include themselves. This usage carries implicit overtones of the Hellenist ideology, of the view that the Greeks are central to the European entity. When, as they often do, they use *Evropi* to *exclude* themselves, they are in effect expressing the Romeic dimension of their identity. Such oscillation between two models is not the result of some "constant inconstancy of the Greek character" (Holden 1972: 31) but a linguistic and conceptual adaptation to the conflict between an imported ideology and a nativist one.

Local Claims, National Interests

In addition to their ideological preferences with regard to the broad question of national culture history, Greeks also had to decide what kinds of events had been decisive in shaping their recent accession to statehood. To some extent, of course, these two questions are aspects of the same issue. Thus, at its crudest, the Hellenist view equated history with war and war with patriotic joy—a formula further reduced to virtual caricature in recent school textbooks (Frangoudaki 1978: 112-113). Other problems of historical "fact," however, seem to have been determined by ideological elements of a different

order. Such, for example, is the date on which the Greek Revolution is supposed to have begun. This may seem an entirely straightforward empirical
problem. Yet, although Greek historians agree on the year of the outbreak of
war, the day and month are the subject of fierce debate. Why should this
be so?

The date of a national revolution is a momentous symbol of collective
identity. Whether it is literally correct or not may scarcely be relevant to
those who celebrate it, and even a demonstrably inaccurate date may be accepted by those who were involved in the original event; this, to cite an
especially dramatic instance, was the case with Thomas Jefferson and the
signing of the Declaration of Independence (Wills 1979). We can hardly expect that the date of the outbreak of guerrilla warfare in a largely illiterate
and divided land would be any less problematical. The date of a battle, still
more of a protracted and uneven period of war, entails complex questions of
definition and context (cf. Goldstein 1976: 68-70; Austin 1975: 143-144).
As to the *event* which *began* the *war*, the potential ambiguity is enormous.

The date usually selected for the national celebration of this event is
March 25, which is also the Feast of the Annunciation (*Evangelismos*).
Whether by design or not, a parallel is thereby suggested between the regeneration of Hellas and the prophecy of Christ's birth and resurrection. The Greek
term for "revolution" (*epanastasis*), with its strong overtones of "resurrection" (*anastasis*), reinforces that parallel. Local ecclesiastical involvement may
have added still further to the force of the religious analogy, for, on March
25, 1821, Metropolitan Germanos of Old Patras led an uprising from the
Lavra Monastery.[9] Other towns of the Peloponnese were also implicated in
the revolt, however, and several of them claim to have been the place from
which it started, in some cases even earlier than March 25 (Paleologos 1977).
Nor was the social basis of the revolution at all uniform. Even the *kotzam-
basidhes*, wealthy landowners who so feared for their privileges in the event
of a national uprising that Capodistrias was to dismiss them contemptuously
as "Christian Turks," joined the fight for fear of being still more completely
identified with Ottoman interests (Dakin 1973: 60). Thus, many different
groups and motives were represented in the initial revolts, which were hardly
coordinated at all. Various local leaders sought personal gratification and
power, and localist sentiment ran high from the start.

Not only are such allegiances still represented in the competition over the
birthplace of Greek freedom, but they played a significant part—which will be
discussed in a later chapter—in the development of Greek folklore research.
Since they continue to affect the deceptively simple-looking issue of when
and where the Revolution began (Petropulos 1976a), their effects on the
more diffuse problems of folklore should occasion no surprise.

Revolution as Resurrection

Such localist rivalries are also evidence of a wider, transcendent unity. The folklores of various regions are set in competition with each other to determine which of them best approximates pure Hellenism. Local scholars seek evidence not only that their respective regions have proved the most loyal to the revolutionary cause but that they have preserved the ancient customs and values better than any other. Logically, in a revolution which is also a resurrection of the past, antiquarianism and revolutionary ardor go hand in hand; archaeological folklore is the intellectual expression of patriotism.

These associations belong mostly to the Hellenist model. The Romeic alternative was slow to develop; it was perhaps out of tune with the struggle for international recognition in those early years. Admittedly, the theoretical contrast between the two models had begun to develop long before the War of Independence, notably over the language issue (Henderson 1970), but the political implications of the Romeic model were hardly compatible with the country's extreme dependence on foreign support. The premise of cultural continuity—the Hellenists' principal article of faith—suited the times far better.

In the first century of statehood, which takes up the greater part of this book, the Hellenist model was thus dominant politically and academically. Since the Greeks were obliged to build their nation-state under the watchful eye of more powerful countries, circumstances clearly favored the externally directed model over the introspective self-view. By the end of the first century of independence, other events allowed the Romeic model to develop more freely. But by that time, too, ideological Hellenism had done its work, and the modern Greek nation-state had become an irreversible reality of world politics. What follows is an account of the folklorists' contribution to that achievement.

Chapter 2
Extroversion and Introspection

". . . a certain important law of history . . ."

Folklorists to the Cause: Beginnings

The Greek Revolution united only three-quarters of a million people under the new authority (Dakin 1973: 1). Athens, whose temporary recapture by the Turks in 1827 seemed for a while to kill all hopes for the Hellenic regeneration (St. Clair 1972: 317, 330), was a small, economically unimportant town at the outbreak of fighting, with a mixed Greek and Albanian population that was later to attract Fallmerayer's gleeful scorn. It was only after the departure of the Turkish garrison as late as March 1833 that Athens, in succession to Nauplion, became the capital of Greece. As a mercantile and cultural center, it was quite eclipsed up to that point by such places as Thessaloniki, Smyrna, Constantinople, and Yannina—all in Turkish hands—and by the Ionian Islands, most notably Corfu, which were only ceded to Greece by Britain in 1864.

Corfu, indeed, plays a seminal part in the present story. The Ionian Islands were ruled by Venice from various dates, beginning with Zakynthos (Zante) in 1482 until the collapse of the Venetian republic in 1797, when they were annexed by France. In 1800 they were given republican autonomy under the joint protection of Russia and Turkey, an unstable arrangement which led to a two-year renewed annexation by France and thence, in 1809 to 1810, to British control. These islands thus had enjoyed far longer and closer contact with the West than any other part of Greece, and they were the home of a flourishing literary tradition—the birthplace of Dionisios Solomos (1798-1857), author of the Greek national anthem, and also of Count John Capodistrias (1776-1831). The Italian connection never really lapsed, as many Heptanesians went to Italy to study; Capodistrias himself studied medicine at the ancient university in Padua. Venice remained the alternative home of many Heptanesian literati who felt as comfortable with Italian as they did with Greek.

If we begin the Heptanesian part of this story with a character who was not noticeably interested in modern Greek folksongs at all, it is because he epitomizes the mixture of Italian and Greek culture against the background of which some of the first Greek excursions into folklore research must be seen and also, more particularly, because he was taken as a literary exemplar by at least one of the early folklorists, Zambelios. Niccolò Foscolo was born in 1778 on Zakynthos, the son of a Greco-Venetian nobleman and a Greek woman. He grew up speaking both the local form of Greek and Italian. In 1792 he left Zakynthos for Venice, where his mother had already established herself. Three years later, he changed his first name to Ugo, and it is as such that he is still celebrated as one of the major romantic poets of Italy. His friendship with Capodistrias, then an envoy of the Russian court, eventually procured him a safe passage to England, where he fled as a conscientious objector from service in the hated Austrian army (Marinoni 1926: 53-60); there, in lonely exile, he died in 1827, the year in which Athens was recaptured by the Turks and while the outcome of the Greek Revolution was yet in doubt.

Not that Foscolo, who made his name strictly as an Italian poet, had ever shown much commitment to the Greek cause. He was ambivalent on the question of his origins, even going to the point of devising—and publishing— two quite separate etymologies for his surname, one aristocratic and Italian, the other poetic and Greek (Marinoni 1926: 2)! The Italian version, which linked his family with the patrician lines of the Foscari and the Foscarini in a common derivation, was included in his study of the constitution of the Republic of Venice; while the Greek derivation—from *fos* ("light") and *kholos* ("melancholy"), giving the sense of *splendida bilis* "exalted by Horace as the source of great poetry"—appeared, appropriately, in a literary periodical. Such a concern with imaginative etymology is worthy of Vico at his most fanciful, and in fact there is some evidence (e.g., Luciani 1967: 185) that Foscolo was an admirer and imitator of Vico. If indeed he was, his life makes a still more apposite backdrop to the rise of a Vician circle which included Fauriel and Tommaseo, both collectors of Greek folksongs, and which apparently culminated in the work of Zambelios as far as Greek ethnology is concerned.

Foscolo's ethnic ambivalence dramatizes the curious situation of the Heptanesian Greeks, especially during this period when neither the Italian nor the Greek independence movement had come to full fruition. His Hellenism was literary and antiquarian, rather than personal and activist. Indeed, when the Italian ex-*carbonaro* Count Salvatore Santarosa called on Foscolo on his way to join the war in Greece, he found the poet, shattered by poverty and an exceedingly messy love affair, unwilling to share more than his obsession with the problems of translating Homer into Italian. The following description comes from Tommaseo's far from friendly pen. Foscolo "was translating

Homer with very great care. . . . In his letters he forgot his sadness; in letters and sadness, he forgot his homeland (*patria*). Santarosa went to see him the day before leaving for Greece, [to inquire] whether he wished anything for Greece, the land where he, Santarosa, was going to fight. Foscolo scarcely replied; then—'Hear these lines of Homer, see whether you like them.' This wounded Santarosa's very soul. To hear someone tell the story now is still more moving, when you think that this unhappy Italian was at that moment saying his last farewell to the Greek, ready to die for Greece, while the Greek just kept on fitting Italian grammatical suffixes to a conceit of Homer's!" (1953: 75; cf. 1904: 120). Worse was yet to befall the poor count. The Greeks gave him a more than reluctant welcome, and, in May of 1825, he met a sordid and unnecessary death at Turkish hands in a cave near Sfakteria (St. Clair 1972: 256).

Foscolo's Classicism was certainly "literary" rather than "patriotic or archaeological." It served nevertheless to excite the interest of another revolutionary of Venetian-Greek stock, the Corfiote Emilio de Tipaldo, who put enormous energy into compiling Foscolo's biography; it was to Tipaldo that Tommaseo, in a letter of 1835, wrote his sour account of the poet's encounter with Santarosa. Tipaldo was one of a group of cosmopolitan Italians[1] interested in Vico, especially in the nationalistic filtration of Vico's historical philosophy through the teachings of the Neapolitan historian and revolutionary Vicenzo Cuoco (1770-1823). Among the principal figures of this coterie were the *risorgimento* poet Alessandro Manzoni (1785-1873), the Dalmatian Niccolò Tommaseo (1802-1874), and the Corfiote politician, historian, and bilingual poet Andrea Mustoxidi (1785-1860). Mustoxidi, who was Tipaldo's brother-in-law and fellow philologist (Traves n.d.: 74), incurred Manzoni's eventual dislike; Manzoni, somewhat in the style of Tommaseo on the subject of Foscolo, thought that Mustoxidi's ingratitude to Italy was typical of the Greek revolutionaries (Tommaseo 1929: 12-14). Despite such tensions, however, this group of scholars displayed a considerable degree of intellectual coherence and a common range of interests.

They also enjoyed a close association with Claude Fauriel (1772-1844), who was greatly admired as a historian by his contemporaries and who was sufficiently comfortable in Italian to write competent verse in that language. Fauriel shared with the three Italians an active commitment to the cause of revolutionary nationalism. Manzoni and Tommaseo were in constant trouble with the authorities at home and even, on one occasion, managed to get Fauriel into bad odor with the Austrian police. Not that Fauriel was a stranger to police persecution; in fact, he had experienced it from both sides of the fence. A Jacobin in his early youth, he had managed to escape the excesses of the Terror in France and eventually became personal secretary to the notorious police chief Fouché in 1802. He apparently gave up this position—much to Fouché's disgust—at the insistence of his mistress, the widow of the French philosopher Condorcet; and it was to assuage his grief over her death in 1822 that Fauriel buried himself in work on his celebrated two-volume *Chants populaires de la Grèce moderne* (Sainte-Beuve 1870).

The Greek revolutionary intellectuals had their own share of trouble with foreign authorities. Mustoxidi, who had returned to Corfu from Greece after the assassination of Capodistrias in 1831 and was shortly thereafter made official historian of the Ionian Islands protectorate, was dismissed from his post by the British only four years later on the grounds that he had been intriguing with Capodistrias' Russophile political heirs—an incident which, for a while, earned him Tommaseo's sympathy and admiration (Manesis 1860-61; Tommaseo 1953: 69). In a reverse movement, Andreas Papadopoulos-Vrettos fled to Athens in order to escape harassment by the British. The biographer of Capodistrias (1837) and Mustoxidi (see Tipaldo 1860), this scholar is important in the present context as the author of an early treatise on the persistence of ancient Greek cultural traits on the Ionian island of Lefkas (1825). He claimed to have identified such connections in dances, costumes, marriage and funerary rites, songs, and divinatory techniques as well as in such unlikely or unverifiable features as the veiling of women (which he claimed to have traced to a story recorded by Pausanias).

The activities of this circle suggest the intimate relationship between political interests and the emergence of a serious approach to folklore. Capodistrias himself may have sent folksong texts to Goethe through the good offices of Mustoxidi (Bees 1956: xii). Mustoxidi, again, instructed both Fauriel and Tommaseo in matters relating to Greek language and folklore. Tommaseo was perhaps somewhat guilty of the ingratitude which he was so ready to attribute to others, for, although he requested and received extensive advice on matters of translation (especially with regard to demotic words without obvious Classical Greek antecedents; cf. Lascaris 1934), he claimed that Mustoxidi had great difficulty in speaking Greek; that Mustoxidi could not write his own language, though he sneered at the Venetian dialect of Italian spoken in the Ionian Islands as "a language of harlequins"; and that he wanted to make Classical Greek the ordinary language of conversation in Greece (Tommaseo 1929: 12). Yet the obvious affinity between these quarrelsome friends may be seen in the fact that they both served as ministers of education in short-lived utopian revolutionary governments, Mustoxidi in Capodistrian Greece and Tommaseo in Venice (Petropulos 1968: 115; Tommaseo 1953: 69).

Manzoni was in many ways the dominant figure of this group. He was an ardent admirer of Vico's philosophy, although it has been suggested (Colquhoun 1954: 51) that his understanding of it was restricted; it may be that he was nevertheless able to communicate some of his enthusiasm to the philhellenes and Greeks who came under his influence. Tommaseo and Fauriel were more careful Vicians; the Neapolitan's emphasis on repetitive process in history, his famous *corsi e ricorsi*, must have seemed analogous to the concepts of *risorgimento* in Italy and resurrection or renascence (*anayenisi* or *palingenesis*) in Greece. Tommaseo, especially, devoted critical study to Vico's work and collaborated with Tipaldo on a biography of the philosopher. He also attempted to apply Vico's etymological concepts, particularly the idea of a latent meaning which transcends all later semantic changes of a more superficial kind, to a study of the Illyrian tongue (Croce and Nicolini 1948: 600), an exercise which paralleled in more systematic form what Zambelios was meanwhile trying to do for Greek.

Fauriel, although he professed admiration for Vico's thinking, wrote relatively little about him, but there is some evidence that he and Manzoni discussed Vico's aesthetic views at considerable length (Croce and Nicolini 1947: 485). It is certain, in any case, that this group of romantic nationalists and writers shared a broadly common outlook in which their interest in Vico was a perceived and unifying element. Nor, since Vico had stressed the importance of such ethnographic materials as song, dance, and vernacular language for the understanding of a people's history, is it unlikely that interest in his work should have contributed to the awakening of the nationalists' interest in folklore.

The collecting of folksongs was not unknown among philhellenes even before Fauriel brought out his volumes. The German Werner von Haxthausen (1780-1842) had assembled a collection as early as 1814. Haxthausen, however, kept putting off publication, and in the end it was nearly a century before the compilation appeared in print. It nevertheless circulated in manuscript form among German scholars and writers; when Haxthausen met Goethe in Wiesbaden in 1815 and showed him his collection, Goethe was galvanized into exploring modern Greek folksongs for himself. Haxthausen came to hear of Fauriel's collection, which was rapidly translated into German for publication, and apparently hoped to collaborate with him. But the interest which Haxthausen's collection evinced in Germany, notably on the part of the Grimm brothers, never sufficed to prod him into publication, and it seems that he hoped that others would take on the responsibility of doing something with his material (Kemminghausen and Sonter 1935).

Haxthausen's and Fauriel's collections share one aspect which would probably not be regarded with so much tolerance today: they showed that it was not really necessary to go to Greece itself in order to amass a substantial corpus. Haxthausen collected some of his songs from sailors whose ships docked at British ports; for other material, he turned to Theodhoros Manoussis (1795-1858), a distinguished Greek academic who was then living in Vienna and who joined the first faculty of the University of Athens in 1837

(Spiridakis 1966: 478; Kemminghausen and Sonter 1935: 6 and n. 19). Fauriel obtained his material from Greek exiles in Venice, who were mostly too sophisticated to be of much help, and from the Greek colony in Trieste, as well as from such luminaries as Piccolos, Mustoxidi, and the great Koraes himself. He was indebted to these men of letters for much more than mere materials; as he freely acknowledged, the idea for a collection of Greek folksongs had originally been broached by Mustoxidi in a letter to Dimitrios Skhinas of the Academy of Bucharest (Bees 1956: xiii). Fauriel professed to regard it as nothing more than good fortune which enabled him to be the first to publish such a collection (Fauriel 1824, 1956: 2). In the same antiquarian tradition, in which secondhand materials were perfectly acceptable, Tommaseo likewise included songs gained through his scholarly collections; many of his texts are taken from Fauriel's two volumes, although in such cases he did not consider it necessary to reproduce the Greek originals again. There was apparently a very free exchange of materials among these scholars—Mustoxidi's correspondent Skhinas even possessed a copy of Haxthausen's manuscript (Kemminghausen and Sonter 1935: 22).[2]

These early foreign collectors seem to have been extremely scrupulous in the care which they took over the accurate rendering and translating of their texts. Tommaseo's letters to Mustoxidi bear witness to his industrious determination to make no mistakes. In a passage which may echo his revered Vico in its scorn for the pedant and its respect for the folk poet, Tommaseo writes, "Whoever knows no other poetry than that of printed books, *whoever does not venerate the folk (popolo) as a poet and inspirer of the poets,* let him not rest his eye upon this collection, which is not made for him. Let him condemn it, let him scorn it: we will consider this praise indeed" (1841, I: 5; my emphasis). Later in the same passage, he explicitly denies himself the right to emend Tuscan folksong texts. To do so, he says, would be a "sacrilegious folly"; he was, according to Cocchiara (n.d.: 106-107), equally careful of the Greek texts which he published. Fauriel, too, appears to have left the texts very much as he found them, and his renderings were even used a century later (Apostolakis 1929) as a yardstick with which to measure the textual alterations of Zambelios. The transcriptions of Tommaseo and Fauriel may not be completely faultless, but it is an indication of their austere scholarship that they preferred to leave blank any uncertain passages of the Greek rather than attempt imaginative reconstructions. Of his Tuscan texts, again, Tommaseo wrote that he "would certainly not think of suppressing and condemning . . . any of the sweet wording" (1841, I: 14). As foreigners, Fauriel and Tommaseo perceived as pearls of primitive naïveté textual elements which local folklorists of Hellenist persuasion were to find embarrassingly inconsistent with their loftier view.

It is certainly possible that Fauriel and Tommaseo refused to print texts which they thought vulgar or bawdy, although their criteria were undoubtedly less stringent than those of their Greek successors. Expurgation (cf. Goldstein 1967) was a feature of Western European scholarship at that time, and academic detail surrendered more easily to prudery. Robert Pashley's response to some bawdy songs about the sexual antics of monks is at least honest: "Of such effusions of the modern Grecian muse, every Englishman, writing in the nineteenth century, must feel it difficult to publish specimens: and I cannot venture to transcribe those which I heard" (1837, I: 146). More's the pity, although Pashley does insure that we understand that there is a lacuna in his account at this point. Over the years, the cumulative expurgation and bowdlerization of folklore were to result in a massively unbalanced portrait of the rural Greek as a sexual innocent (e.g., Lee 1959), in accordance with the ideological requirements of the outward-directed model of the Hellenists.

Although there is no clear evidence on the matter, then, it is possible that Fauriel and Mustoxidi censored their own materials; it is nevertheless no less likely that their educated Greek informants exercised a certain discretion in the first place. There is certainly a "moral" aspect (Martellotti 1943: x–xi) to Tommaseo's classification of the folksongs under four thematic categories: love, family, death, and God. But this schema, while quite in harmony with the Hellenists' moral sensibilities, offered them no particular advantage in their search for antiquarian connections and was never adopted by them.

Despite the conceptual differences between Fauriel and Tommaseo, on the one hand, and the indigenous Hellenists on the other, all were agreed on the inherent virtue of the Greek cause. Tommaseo's indignation at the unpatriotic escapism of Foscolo is matched by the admiration which Fauriel, in the extensive introduction to his *Chants*, expresses for the newly resurgent Greeks. Fauriel had already published, in 1823, a translation from the Italian of a poem by Berchet about the flight of the Greek population of Parga, one of the saddest episodes of the period immediately preceding the outbreak of the Greek Revolution. Now, a year later, he enthusiastically declared that the Greeks' own folksongs "would make modern Greece loved and known and would demonstrate that the spirit of the ancients, the breath of poetry, lived there yet." And he urged the Greeks "to collect what has not already been lost of their folksongs. Europe will owe them gratitude for whatever they do to preserve them; while they themselves will one day be enchanted, because they will be in a position to acknowledge these products of a wise and cultivated poetry, these simple monuments of the spirit, history, and customs of their ancestors" (see Fauriel 1956: 86). With these solemn words, the concept of folklore as a repository of verbal *monuments* enters, at an early date, the intellectual apparatus of Greek folklore studies.

A Greek Reaction

In the eyes of their Greek critics, enthusiasm on the part of foreign observers was not enough. The academic tradition of Europe, so despised by Tommaseo, took root strongly in Greece as a source of legitimation for the Hellenist thesis. What both Tommaseo and Fauriel had presented in their studies was essentially the Romeic view of Greece—a view of the peasantry as it saw and expressed itself. This was difficult for the Hellenists to accept. For, if the Hellenists were outward-directed in terms of their audience, they held strict views as to what was suitable fare for that audience. It was time, they thought, to construct a truly national history of their own.

The first task was clearly to slough off the foreigners' interpretations of Greek history and culture. The philhellenic conceit was now turned against itself. Zambelios states the impassioned subjectivism which this entailed: "The past? Alas! we allow foreigners to portray it to us under the prism of their prejudices and according to the circumstance of their systems and self-interests. . . . Yes! And why should we hide it? Our fathers molded *truth*, a broadly based, vital, genuine truth; whereas we forge myths—myths, moreover, which are not in the least philosophical in the manner of our ancient and ancestral ethos, with suggestions of exalted significance, but foreign ones, disguised in ancient clothing, alien specters, introducing to us the deceptions and distortion of western silliness" (1852: 7-9).

A more extreme and distinctly *ad hominem* version of this attitude is to be found in the attack which George Evlambios launched on Fauriel in 1843. Evlambios' book, *The Amaranth: The Roses of Hellas Reborn*, is a collection of folksong texts evidently intended to supplant Fauriel's. Its title expresses the Hellenist view of Greece as an evergreen plant (*amarandos*) which nevertheless—the essential paradox again—was now undergoing resurrection. It also implies the usual thesis that whatever was good in the vernacular culture was but a resurgence of antique values. And its characteristic outward-directedness is evident in that it was published abroad, in Saint Petersburg, in a bilingual Greek and Russian text.

Even by the time Evlambios attacked him in this work, Fauriel had become firmly established as one of the brightest stars of philhellenic scholarship. The polemic is suitably muted at first: "The effort and labor of Fauriel are exceptionally worthy of respect. But Fauriel, as a foreigner, was not familiar with modern Greek life and was obliged to accept whatever was offered to him as a product of folk creativity. For this reason, in his collection we encounter alterations and distortions—if the expression may be permitted me" (1973: i). Evlambios then begins his specific argument with the criticism that Fauriel had included in his collection of oral poetry verses by Rigas and Solomos. This is patently unfair: Fauriel, far from pretending that these poems were from oral sources, acknowledged and praised their authors' patriotic sensibility (Bees 1956: ix). It is possible, of course, that Fauriel considered demotic poetry sufficiently close to the oral idiom to merit inclusion under the somewhat ambiguous heading of *traghoudhia* or *chansons*, both of which may be used for written verse; his compatriots, Voutier (1826) and Marcellus (1851), were to include many more such literary creations in their published collections.

Evlambios then directs his fire at Fauriel's lack of firsthand acquaintance with Greek customs. He begins by noting that Fauriel's collection of distichs lacks coherence between the texts. This criticism, which has some basis, is the best evidence that Evlambios can muster of his own more intimate knowledge of Greek folkways. Semantic continuity between distichs is considered essential to effective performance in many parts of Greece (Herzfeld 1981c), although only a few folklorists have bothered to explore it (e.g., Aravandinos 1880). It is to Evlambios' credit, and a considerable aid to his credibility, that he observed this characteristic.

But he descends anew into ill-considered polemic when he criticizes Fauriel's textual accuracy. Foreigners, he argues, should not attempt the impossible by seeking to penetrate the mysteries of Greekness—a frequently adopted position among the Hellenists. "I do not know," he observes early in the preface of his book, "whether a foreigner can ever assimilate the spirit (*pnevma*) of another people (*laos*) to the point of daring to correct and alter the people's creations, especially when the Greeks themselves—born and bred in their fatherland, and in contact from childhood on with their customs and language—do not give themselves such a right" (1973: ii).

This would be questionable criticism were it only for the fact that just one collection of folksongs, an anonymous volume produced in Nauplion in 1832 and known to Tommaseo, had so far been published by a Greek and in Greece. Evlambios could not foresee the extent to which later Greek scholars would accord themselves that forbidden "right" of textual emendation, it is true, and this was a habit which he was quite justified in distrusting; in 1865, for example, the scholarly journal *Pandora* published an entire set of folksongs which were later exposed as spurious (Politis 1973: lviii). But the specific complaint which Evlambios lodges against Fauriel in this connection is less than effective. Fauriel had published the text of a short song lamenting the death of the guerrilla leader Zidros (1956: 116-117). Since he thought the text incomplete (for in this respect he was as much of a literalist as any of his contemporaries), he added a fifth line—*in the French translation only*. The Greek text is presented, as far as it is possible to tell, exactly as he received it. Yet Evlambios excoriated this as a "creation of the author's Gallic imagination" (1973: xi). The charge is all the more curious in that Fauriel, who had wanted to print the Greek texts using a strictly demotic orthography (i.e., omitting terminal /n/ where it was not pronounced), had been persuaded not to do so by his scholarly Greek friends (1956: 2)—they were *katharevousiani*, linguistic Hellenists. Only much later (1854: 61) did he recover his self-confidence sufficiently to insist on the autonomy of the demotic forms.

Nor is this all, for the attack on Fauriel's intellectual honesty follows an equally bitter criticism of the French writer's failure to censor his own materials more effectively! Thus, "among many poetical verses," grumbles Evlambios, "the reader suddenly encounters prosaic phrases and even, finally, vulgarities—among the demotic songs are included worthless and coarse compositions. This curious mélange, ornamented with freshly concocted song titles, constitutes an ill-formed edifice, wherein marble ornaments are covered by piles of undressed masonry" (1973: ii). Such examples of "worthless" and "peasantish" folklore as Fauriel is charged with improperly including have since passed muster with folklorists in Greece, although, since they do not meet the canons of "European" poetics, they have attracted little study locally. In any event, Fauriel's alleged vulgarities (1825: 70, 150, 160) were not particularly offensive even by the austere moral standards of his time. In objecting to the use of invented song titles, however, Evlambios does identify a source of future confusion. Just like any other taxonomic device, single-text song titles presuppose that the reader will accept the collector's view of what the song is about and therefore tend to direct all subsequent interpretation (cf. also Herzfeld 1973).

Perhaps the most symptomatic part of Evlambios' diatribe, however, is the passage in which he attacks Fauriel's treatment of funeral dirges. Fauriel experienced some difficulty in obtaining specimens of this genre—not, perhaps, surprisingly, since villagers are still sometimes reluctant to conjure up the specter of death and misfortune for the inquisitive stranger. He did manage to secure one specimen (1825: 262), but, storms Evlambios, "very oddly, he considers that this imaginary dirge was performed by a Turkish woman" (1973: iv). Evlambios' disgust can be understood only in the light of his assumption that "the dirges (*miroloyia*) are the only exclusively Greek form of song" (1973: vi). If sustained, that essentially taxonomic assumption would of necessity either debar Fauriel's specimen from the category of dirges or discredit his attribution of it to a Turkish woman. Evlambios tries to achieve both ends, and it must be said that this was an entirely consistent procedure in the terms of his operative scheme of classification. Fauriel, however, explains quite clearly that the performer was Turkish in what we should today recognize as the broader Greek sense of being a Greek-speaking Moslem. Evlambios, by contrast, took the term in its literal or national sense, and this left him no option but to construe Fauriel's attribution as definitionally impossible. Yet his argument is a curious construction of events on the part of

one who claimed to be close to the folk: it entails the imposition of an absolute, literalist classification of ethnicity upon the vernacular idiom.

Evlambios' familiarity with folk customs seems not to have been geographically extensive. Fauriel's remark that his text was improvised by the
singer is in agreement with many reports now available (cf. Alexiou 1973).
But Evlambios, without the advantage of the accumulated materials which we
now have at our disposal, could not believe in the existence of such extem-
poraneous performances: "The dirges which *I* publish here show how un-
founded Fauriel's information is. Dirges were, on the contrary, *specific* songs
(*traghoudhia*) which were learned like other popular songs. . . . Upon the experience and the ability of the keener depended whether she might add something of her own to the dirge, something directly connected with the life of
the deceased. Those additions were no longer sung but pronounced in a grief-
stricken voice" (1973: iv, n. 1). Evlambios here overlooks the fact that vernacular usage makes a somewhat less rigid distinction between "speaking"
and "singing" than do *katharevousa* or the Western European languages.[3] His
tendency to generalize from restricted ethnographic data to a panhellenic
canvas is a logical consequence of the doctrine of Greek cultural unity.

In Evlambios' work, especially in his treatment of Fauriel, certain salient
aspects of the Hellenist thesis are apparent. Above all, it is taken as axiomatic
that an educated Greek will automatically possess the innate ability to speak
for and interpret the entire national culture. The connection with Classical
culture, moreover, is a matter of doctrine and, as such, overrides any apparent
discontinuities: "The Fates of the modern Greeks are *the same* [my empha-
sis] as the Fates of the ancients. Here are the names of today's Fates: *Mira,
Tikhi, Riziko*; the names of the ancient ones were *Clotho, Lachesis*, and
Atropos" (1973: cvi). What Evlambios does not point out is that both *riziko*
and *mira*, like the cognate Classical *moira*, are generic terms for fate; modern
villagers do not give personal names to the three old women who determine
their destinies at birth. *Tikhi*, on the other hand, was (and is) also a generic
term ("luck") but was personified as a minor deity (Tyche) in Hellenistic
times. To establish "sameness," Evlambios has had to give very short shrift to
the survival of such generic terms in order to make his case for the more
"mythological" survival of the three personified fates. This argument involves
an unusually high degree of special pleading to demonstrate some sort of
connection with the Classical past; we do not find it reproduced in the more
detailed analyses of the mythology of fate by Schmidt, Wachsmuth, or Politis.

But the most diagnostic feature, which Evlambios displays in an unusually
raw form, is the view that Greek folklore should be left to the Greeks. By
Evlambios' time, the fight to refute the theories of Fallmerayer was already
under way. Fauriel, however, seems a comparatively improbable target for

such attacks, unless it is borne in mind that the outward-directed ideology of the Hellenists logically debarred foreigners in general from prying into Greek culture on their own account. Not all Hellenist scholars adopted this extreme position, of course; Politis, in particular, drew upon the modern Greek researches of Schmidt and Wachsmuth, and other Hellenist scholars (e.g., Spiridakis 1966) have acknowledged the contribution of early voyagers' accounts. Yet Evlambios' more aggressive and xenophobic posture deserves sympathetic consideration. The philhellenes had fostered an idealized picture of the Greeks; it must have seemed capricious in the extreme that now, when an independent nation-state had finally been achieved, they should be prepared to contaminate that picture with their "Romeic" insights. For contamination is just what the "vulgarities" of certain songs imply, as does the idea that a "Turkish" woman might sing a characteristically "Greek" genre of song. The Greekness of the dirges, indeed, was soon to become a more elaborate tool of the Hellenist thesis in the hands of Zambelios. For, by the time that he took up his own pen, in his native Ionian Islands, a sophisticated and western-influenced version of the Romeic model was already in full swing from within.

The Pedant and the People

Corfu, capital of the Heptanese, had long been a center of intellectual activity when the toga-clad British philhellene, Lord Guilford, established his short-lived university there in 1860. Unlike Athens, where the overwhelming majority of scholars were committed Hellenists, many of the Corfiote intellectuals were demoticists. Their leading figure was the poet Solomos, a friend and associate of Manzoni, Tommaseo, and—for a while—Zambelios. Tommaseo includes some folksongs which Solomos had recorded in his native Zakynthos, and Solomos regarded folk poetry as a rich source of understanding and documentation for the systematic study of the demotic tongue. Solomos, indeed, advocated a conscious program of nation-forming literary activity, in which the demotic language would serve as the vehicle whereby the great works of foreign literature and philosophy would be introduced to the Greek people. He inspired many imitators and disciples, among whom Iakovos Polilas (1826-1898) was probably the most fanatical—as Zambelios, after his break with Solomos, was to discover to his cost.

Another member of Solomos' circle of friends was Andonios Manousos, whose collection of folksongs was published in Corfu in 1850. Zambelios' parallel but Hellenist venture appeared there in 1852. Since Zambelios' quarrel with Solomos—and thus with the entire demoticist camp—followed hard upon the publication of his own collection, the emergence of two distinct streams of folklore research, essentially the "literary" (demoticist) and the "patriotic or archaeological" (Hellenist), can be said to have begun in this period. Zambelios is often claimed by today's Hellenist folklorists as their first major intellectual ancestor (e.g., Spiridakis 1966: 485-487; Orlandos 1969: 6); Manousos, by contrast, is at best cursorily mentioned by them. Midcentury Corfu is thus a watershed in the historical development of two distinct ideological styles of folklore research.

Somewhat in the self-consciously antiacademic manner of Tommaseo, who explicitly denies himself the dubious pleasure of writing a formal introduction to his Greek songs, Manousos refuses to announce his collection with the kind of "methodological" prologue composed by Evlambios and Zambelios. Perhaps this refusal contributed to the relative obscurity into which his work has fallen. Certainly, his comments on individual texts are suitably patriotic and scarcely depart from the Hellenists' position. The references to a common Greek fatherland (*patridha*), the assumption that kleftic songs (i.e., songs of brigandage under Turkish rule) constituted a discrete category of patriotic texts (cf. chap. 3), the treatment of the guerrilla leader Odysseus' death as the result of his enemies' vindictiveness rather than of his own treachery (cf. St. Clair 1972: 190, 239; but also Petropulos 1976b)—all these devices are part of the Hellenists' position, except, perhaps, the charge that the "penpushers" (*kalamaradhes*) were to blame for Odysseus' demise. In Manousos' work, we see immediately that the dispute between the Hellenists and the demoticists was conducted on a considerable area of common ground through the medium of shared concepts and vocabulary. Yet the sharpness of his polemic against academic pedantry certainly does not suggest any sense of compromise.

Manousos' ideological preferences are made especially clear by his substitution of a dramatized discussion for the conventional introduction. This imaginary confrontation is conducted by a wordy pedant, the populace (*laos*), a friend of the author, and the author-editor himself. (It is perhaps significant in this context that Manousos chose to portray himself as an editor [*sindaktis*] rather than in the more actively interventionist role of author, since the point of the whole argument is to decry the excessive interference of pedantic scholars.) The contrast between the pedant's extreme *katharevousa* and the simple demotic of the other characters invests the scene with a piquant irony, foreshadowing a recurrent feature of future Greek scholarship in the humanities by the use of different language "registers" to emphasize ideological distance. The pedant, naturally, gets the worst of Manousos' lampooning. The speech of "your Four-times-secretarial-Penpushership," as he is unctuously addressed, is reduced to the most pompous neo-Classical posturing imaginable. The contrast thereby induced vividly conveys the tensions and confusions which could be generated by the *ghlossiko zitima* ("language question"), as it came to be called.

A clear connection is thus established between linguistic attitudes and the question of the scholar's position in Greek culture. Manousos' disclaimer of any right to emend the texts is phrased in terms of attitudes—particularly the peasants' expectation that the scholars will assert, rightly or wrongly, a privileged ability to explain rural customs—which the ethnographer may still encounter in the Greek countryside. The opening words of the tableau set the tone:

> *Member of the populace:* Excuse me, but would you print our songs?
> *Editor:* You mean that *I* should publish them in printed form? Why? Will you criticize me at all?
> *Another member of the populace:* Not at all! Does it look likely? We're illiterate (*aghrammati*)—that's no job of ours!
> *Editor:* You are mistaken, my friends. These are your own creations, the outpouring of your soul, and nobody can better hear them to correct their omissions and errors than yourselves.
> *Another:* It may be as you say. But we haven't come now in order to correct you but to do our duty and thank you for broadcasting and praising what [we do] in the sweetest hours of our lives, when our souls are at rest with a glass in one hand and love in the other, forgetting their toils and travails and finding comfort and pleasure in song.
> *Editor:* I accept your thanks, as a gift of kindness, not as a duty. The duty is not only my own but that of all Greeks who have had some sort of education and upbringing, who, if they love their nation (*ethnos*) wholeheartedly, must make a careful study of that nation, not leave its brilliant creations unstudied and on the brink of oblivion.   (1850: 3-4)

In a complaint which he shares to a remarkable degree with Zambelios, the editor then compares the sorry state of Greek folklore scholarship with the interest and enthusiasm which foreigners of many nations have shown for the songs of the rural Greeks. But Manousos, lacking the defensive selectivity of the Hellenists, does not at least display any disapproval of the foreigners' role; his criticism is all directed against his compatriots.

The demoticists' respect for the integrity of the oral texts was to remain a canon of their ideology, sometimes to the point where their accusations of meddling fell on dubious grounds (e.g., Apostolakis 1929). Manousos, in this early representation of the ideological choice which confronted an editor in folklore, brings to the reader's attention a besetting ambiguity of the editorial role. On the one hand, Manousos respected the oral character of the texts and said so; on the other, he wished to save them for posterity as a spiritual monument, a task which required that they be frozen on the printed page. As a scholar, he had to confront the peasants' self-abasement as "illiterates"—a term not necessarily meant in an absolute sense but indicating the contrast with his own erudition—yet he championed the superiority of the oral poet over the learned fool. Perhaps the funniest moment in his tableau comes when the pedant ironically praises the editor, in an archaizing style which lacks only the elegance of Attic Greek, for exhibiting "miraculous ingenuity in working with such . . . I dare to say virtually dead material" (1850: 6). The editor, pretending to toady to this overweening pedagogue, asks how he is to save himself from the consequences of such misguided enthusiasm for folk culture."Change the language!" recommends the pedant. The editor demurs: how can one change the language of one's fathers—the immediate, Romaic fathers, as it were? "Write, my dear friend," the pedant tells him, "in a manner totally devoid of meaning, and behold! the problem is solved" (1850: 8-11).

This is a conflict between histories. In the one, the forefathers are those who spoke the same language as the editor and who passed it on to him in turn. In the other, they are the long-dead Greeks of ancient times, whose speech must be pruned of all real significance in order—thought Manousos—to achieve a convincing sense of continuity with the pedantic *katharevousa* of the Hellenists. In the Hellenist view, of course, the "living" traditions must indeed be "dead," as the pedant makes them; in the neo-Classical utopia, they would have no appropriate context of their own. Here Manousos caricatures what he saw as the worst folly of the *katharevousiani*, and he was perceptive enough to realize that the issue had dimensions far wider than those of language alone.

But, in the sphere of language, Manousos makes it fully explicit that his quarrel is with Hellenism. In the concluding speech of the tableau, the editor summarizes the logic of his own argument: "But all those who babble that the Greek (*grekiki*) language becomes better *the more it approaches the Hellenic (elliniki)* seem to me to be doing the same as though they were scheming to correct a naturally beautiful and pretty young woman and to fix her face like that of an old dame so that she might appear to have the beauty she had enjoyed in her youth and no longer possesses" (1850: 14; my emphasis). It had long been usual to distinguish between modern demotic and Classical Greek as *romeika* and *ellinika*, respectively; Manousos' use of the slightly more obscure *Greki* for *Romii* is an Ionian dialect usage, possibly affected here, which hardly disguises the nature of the contrast which he was making. That contrast pitted against each other two cultural ideologies, two Greek languages, two readings of Greek history, two concepts of the Greeks' place in the world and of the Greek scholars' place among their people.

The Greek Past Regained: Zambelios

Manousos' espousal of the Romeic cause is explicit and unqualified. Hardly more compromising is the first major development in folklore studies of the Hellenist ideology by Spyridon Zambelios (1813?-1881), likewise a member of the circle around Solomos until projected into an adversary position by offended dignity and divergent views.

Relatively little is known of Zambelios' life, although what we can glean shows a cosmopolitan Heptanesian intellectual of distinctly hot temper. He was born on Lefkas, the son of a writer of neo-Classical tragedies, and was sent to study at various famous establishments of learning—it is not known which ones—in Western Europe (Zambelios 1902). He eventually inherited an Italian estate in the vicinity of Leghorn (Livorno), and it was here that he appears to have spent a considerable part of his mature life. His last known work, a discourse on the prehistory of the Greek and Latin languages, was published in Paris in 1880, and he died in Zug, Switzerland, the following year. He thus spent much of his later life outside Greece and his native Heptanese, perhaps soured by that failure to achieve recognition which had partially contributed to his break with Solomos (Valetas 1950: xxii). Zambelios seems, in fact, to have been a choleric and demanding person; for example, when his illegitimate son wanted to marry, Zambelios *père* decided that he wanted the young bride for himself, and when the son refused to cooperate the father disinherited him, leaving his entire estate to some Cretan philanthropic institutions instead (Kambanis 1920: 23-25). Similarly, he refused to forgive the equally truculent Solomos for calling him an idiot, although the insult was delivered when the poet was a patently sick man (Jenkins 1940: 196-197), but took up a lonely and embittered offensive against Solomos' reputation until well after the latter's death in 1857.

The initial occasion for their quarrel arose in 1853. In the previous year, Zambelios had published a monumental collection of folksongs, prefaced by an extremely long and solemn "Historical Study of Medieval Hellenism." This combination of archive and essay, probably Zambelios' most substantive work of scholarship, is notable both for the weight of detail adduced in support of the main argument and for its majestic claims of intellectual originality. Solomos, however, derided it for "putting Hegel into a slouch hat"—a strange remark, certainly, when we consider that it was addressed by a self-proclaimed Hegelian to a writer who later (1859) attacked *him* for his heavy reliance on the German philosopher.

Zambelios' indubitable pomposity and his often inaccurate handling of historical materials all too easily obscure the principal merit of his essay, for this work departed significantly from the embryonic tradition of historical writing which then existed in Greece. Its novelty lay in the frank admission, indeed the insistence, that a medieval phase of some importance in its own right connected the Greeks with their ancient forebears. Zambelios eagerly confronted the absurdity of virtually ignoring a millennium of history and pointed out that it was not necessary to do so in order to posit continuity between the Classical and modern periods. Instead, he maintained, it would be more useful to treat the medieval phase as the connecting link (*krikos*) between the ancient and modern cultures. Throughout the centuries of political upheaval, invasions, population movements, and foreign domination, as Zambelios' novel approach would show, the Greeks had retained all their ancient genius and had remained fundamentally unchanged in spirit.

Zambelios proposed to recognize three phases of Greek history: the modern, the medieval, and the ancient, each neatly self-contained. The medieval phase was a time of ethnic regression, during which many signs of an unquenchable Hellenic consciousness were nevertheless in evidence. The tension between the imperial throne of Byzantium and the Orthodox Patriarchate was described, in this connection, as a conflict between "Roman" (and therefore foreign) authoritarianism, on the one hand, and the democratic spirit of Classical Greece which the Greeks had perpetuated in the institutions of their church, on the other. For the defense of the Hellenist model, it was logically necessary to define the "Roman" or "Romeic" element as foreign and, therefore, undesirable. But Zambelios did not scorn peasants in the style of Manousos' pedant, and he did not in any sense dismiss popular lore as either dead or foreign. Instead, he saw folklore and the church as the two great repositories of the true Greek character, and he attributed the almost complete lack of a truly Hellenic documentary history of the medieval phase to the foreign rulers' egotistical control over the court chroniclers.

Zambelios' respect for the vernacular traditions, which contrasts with his own use of a strict *katharevousa*, is solidly evidenced by his very substantial collection of folksongs. These alone could supply the deficiencies of the "Roman" chroniclers, albeit only in a very general way; Zambelios does not elicit specific historical insights from each text separately, as others later tried to do. He also felt free to emend texts without indicating that he had done so, perhaps on the implicit argument that as a Greek he was a participant in the same culture as the singers. In this he made an assumption similar to that of Evlambios, but without the latter's self-restraint in the matter of textual alterations: a Greek was the best-qualified person to understand Greek folklore. He was also, it appears, convinced of his own poetic talents (Apostolakis 1929: 34).

The oral origins of the texts make it extremely difficult to ascertain exactly how much they have been tampered with. Since many of the songs have since disappeared from the living repertoire, there is little reliable material available for comparison. The "Romeic" folklorist Yannis Apostolakis

(1896-1947) attempted a detailed critique of Zambelios' emendations, but his openly avowed subjectivism raises legitimate doubts about his own critical acuity. It must be remembered that by 1929, when Apostolakis' criticisms appeared in print, the Hellenists must have already had a considerable influence on the shape and content of the rapidly dwindling folk repertoire, just as *katharevousa* was progressively infiltrating the demotic language. Apostolakis was also German-trained, so his claim to instinctive knowledge of the folk aesthetic is not wholly reassuring. In his exposition, moreover, there are occasional switches to a more Hellenist style of reasoning, indicating once more how difficult it was for the Romeic scholars to escape the theoretical framework of assumptions which the Hellenists had constructed.

Let us briefly consider Apostolakis' treatment of one of Zambelios' texts, in order to illustrate these points more fully. The song in question describes the departure of a young man for distant parts and his eventual temptation into forgetting his family. "Whereas the son bids farewell in the presence of his mother and his father, his mother at the end bids him not to forget her and her [other] children, while of her husband—his father—not a single word is heard. Such an omission is strange, if not indeed *unnatural*. Well known to us, *and we know on our own account*, are the respect and *tender love with which a wife was wont to look on her husband* in the *Hellenic home*" (Apostolakis 1929: 22-23; my emphasis). Such knowledge of rural conditions and conventions is partly derived from the song texts themselves, with all the editing and selection which they had previously undergone, and seems to conflict with some firsthand ethnographic observations (e.g., Campbell 1964: 151). The constraints which the early collectors set on subsequent perceptions are always, to some extent, inescapable.

Yet some of the evidence for textual interference is more convincing and serves to point up the magnitude of the problem. Apostolakis' criticism is at its most incisive when he finds Zambelios outdoing other Hellenists, rather than foreigners or demoticists, in the patriotic editing of a common text. An example is provided by a song celebrating a guerrilla raid on one of the Zagori villages in Epirus. In one version of the song—not Zambelios'—the robbers calculatingly interrogate their female captives:

> *They were taken and questioned, each in turn,*
> *as to whose husband would turn out to be the best touch for a ransom.*

Zambelios, however, saw these robbers as wild heroes of the national revival. In the text which he presents, no explicit mention is made of anything so despicable as a ransom, although it is a matter of recorded history that extortion of this kind did occur where villagers were wealthy enough to make it a worthwhile proposition:

> *They put them in the middle and questioned them again and again:*
> *which of them had the worthiest husband, the truly brave man?*
> *Angeliki, the daughter of Koumos' wife, has a truly brave husband—*
> *his legs are strong like a Hellene's, his chest like a lion's.*

Zambelios, according to his critic, here found a way to "exhibit the ethnic pride of the robbers and of the women, as well as his own." A text published at a *later* date by a scarcely less committed exponent of the Hellenist thesis (Aravandinos 1880: 87) explicitly spelled out the demand for a ransom, thereby casting serious doubt on the interpretation and perhaps also on the actual text offered by Zambelios (Apostolakis 1929: 57-69). Whether the last line is a forgery, as Apostolakis thought, is less clear; the Hellene may here be a perfectly genuine mythological giant rather than a national stereotype. Zambelios' omission of the ransom episode, by contrast, is more conclusive as evidence of his approach.

This is not to attribute bad faith to him. Zambelios' emendations may indeed have served to show Apostolakis "how peculiar . . . the ethnic self-regard (*ethnikos eghoïsmos*) of Zambelios was, and what misplaced and laughable thoughts it could bring the man to entertain" (1929: 57); but patriotic duty, though probably a sufficient justification in itself in Zambelios' eyes, is far from being the full explanation. Zambelios assumed that, as a Greek, he had a participant role in the shaping of Greek culture, and it is in all likelihood this assumption, so consistent with Hellenist ideology, that most effectively explains the alterations and suppressions of his folksong corpus. In the missionary view which he took of his task, he differed from Solomos in denying the usefulness of foreign learning; it is an ironical consequence of the Hellenist thesis that, although outward-directed, it should in practice be so much more xenophobic culturally than the Romeic. In his subjectivism, more specifically in his assumption that a Greek would necessarily know Greek culture best, he was again not very far from his detractors, particularly Apostolakis. But he differed radically from Apostolakis in the direction that subjectivism led him; and that difference was, in the final analysis, one of ideological orientation.

Tragic Genius Preserved

Zambelios' quarrel with Solomos confirmed the ideological rift. In 1859, two years after the poet's death, Zambelios took the offensive with a highly invidious comparison between Solomos and Foscolo, much, of course, to Solomos' disadvantage. Yet this critical diatribe actually forms a coda, in effect, to a discussion of the true nature of Greek poetry and song, under the cautiously academic title *Whence the Vulgar Word* Traghoudho? *Thoughts*

Concerning Hellenic Poetry. Zambelios' less personal aim in this work is to pursue the demotic term for "singing" back to its Classical origins and, in so doing, to establish the respectably Hellenic character of Greek folk poetry.

His thesis turns upon a linguistic curiosity. Why is it, he asks, that the Classical word *ado* ("sing") was displaced by an entirely different term, *traghoudho*, in the Christian era? Zambelios thought the value of such an abstruse inquiry to be quite beyond question, for, as he explains, "every word, whether living or in desuetude, encapsulates a historical fact which demands special investigation" (1859: 4).

And so he proceeds to a sweeping review of Greek thought and poetry through the ages. At an early date, the greatness of Homer lay in his exaltation of humankind. In Homer, the gods are a product of human creativity; and the heroic ideal is represented by none other than "the Hellene, gloriously fighting for Greece" (1859: 10)—a truly panoptic symbol replacing the petty jealousies of the first city-states. The development of literature in Greece thereafter pursued a progressive course down to the Periklean era: "Ancient Lyric poetry overlooked the earth and only looked up to heaven. Epic introduced into Poetry the element of nationhood (*ethnotis*). But Drama envelops heaven, fatherland, and society *within the mind*, within the heart of the individual" (1859: 13).

Homer did indeed celebrate the deeds of the Achaeans, as Zambelios notes, but the subsequent history of Greece shows how difficult it was to translate a sense of shared distinctiveness as Greeks into practical politics. Zambelios intended his readers to assume that the achievement of a sense of ethnic unity was a watershed from which there was no turning back and that the unification of the modern Greek polity was the culmination of an ideal which had been ever present in the national consciousness (*ethniki sinidhisis*; see chap. 3). He was not so ingenuous or poorly read as to pretend that there had literally existed an ancient Greek nation-state similar to the modern state of his own day.

To his list of literary achievements in the Classical era, Zambelios adds the work of the philosophers:

> It has been said that Christianity emerged among the Athenians in the Academy of Plato. I am of the opinion that it appeared among them still earlier, in the theater of Sophocles and Euripides.
>
> Socrates, Euripides, and Plato, three familiar and inseparable collaborators, stand in relation to the subsequent call of the disciples of Christ as the invention of the compass did to the later discovery of America. (1859: 15)

And he concludes:

> Christianity confirms the promise of Epic, of Drama, of Philosophy.
> In condemning the multiple tyranny of the gods, it makes man the ruler
> of an ordered polity. Established on the throne of this selfsame con-
> sciousness, man speaks forth as a god on earth.   (1859: 17)

Christ on the cross—"a miracle partaking of Epic but at the same time of
Tragedy ... proclaiming the blessed end of human struggles"—symbolizes this
ultimate achievement, of which the political dimension, the rebirth of the
Greek nation as a political entity on earth, is foreshadowed in the poetry of
the common people (1859: 17).

In his portrayal of this progression, Zambelios has drawn heavily on
Hegel's account of the development of aesthetic religion in Greece and of its
displacement by the absolute religion of Christianity. In some respects, Zambelios' schema closely resembles any outline of Hegel's (e.g., Mure 1965:
104-109). To adapt the Hegelian schema for his own essentially nationalistic
purposes, however, Zambelios had to make a number of changes, notably an
extended discussion of the "lyric" phase of Greek poetry and, most significantly of all, the yoking of Christianity to Hellenism. For him, Christianity
was not in any sense a displacement of one form of religion by another but
the ultimate synthesis of human understanding *in the minds of the Greeks.*
The ecumenical ideal of Christianity was thus represented as the Hellenization
of the entire world; the rise of Protestantism, which Hegel saw as the matura-
tion of revealed religion, was simply another of those secondary effects in
western history whose causes Zambelios attributed exclusively to Greece.
Thus, in the regenerated Greek nation, human understanding would now be
brought to its consummation.

To demonstrate this, it was necessary to show also that the Greeks had
never relinquished their special qualities. The traditions of Classical poetry—
the source from which both Hegel and Zambelios drew material for their respective schemata—had largely been eradicated or transformed by the theological requirements of the new religion of Christ. Folksong, on the other
hand, remained relatively unaffected, Zambelios thought, so specimens of it
from the Byzantine period "may be regarded as the sole evidence for the
sensibilities and sensitivities of the Hellenic people during that long and trou-
bled period of Christian metamorphosis" (1859: 26). It is thus to folksong
that one should look for evidence of continuity in the national character.

And Zambelios did precisely that. Explaining the transference of the Classical word for "tragedy" (*tragōdia*) to the semantic domain of song, he turned
his attention to the traditional dirges (*miroloyia*) for the dead as evidence of
an inherited sense of tragedy in the Greek spirit. It was an ill-advised move,
born of his comparative ignorance of his rural compatriots' terminological

usages, for, as has already been observed (Menardos 1921: 2), these dirges are not usually classified by the Greek villagers themselves as songs (*traghoudhia*). The latter term would, under normal circumstances, be inappropriate for dirges, except in a metaphorical sense (see Herzfeld 1981: 44-53). For *traghoudhia*, as joyful songs or verses, stand in polar and complementary opposition to *miroloyia*; and the corresponding verbs are similarly opposed to each other. Zambelios thus chose a perilously thin support for his argument. That he was almost certainly unaware of this can be inferred from the very considerable detail which he devotes to dirges in order to make his case.

He conceded that the chanting of funeral laments as such was not confined to Greek culture. (It would be somewhat invidious to see in this proof that Zambelios was a better observer than Evlambios, for Evlambios may have meant that the style and content of *miroloyia*, rather than funeral laments in general, were unique to Greece.) Zambelios' interest, however, was caught by a more subtle and, he maintained, distinctive trait:

> What is unique, not to say paradoxical, lies in the climax of lamenting for situations which call for anything but sorrow or grief: for example, in that most joyful of domestic ceremonies, the wedding celebration, that same occasion at which, everywhere else in the rest of Europe, harmony and rejoicing prevail.   (1859: 45)

Zambelios witnessed such laments for the bride's departure to her new household on some island, unspecified, in the Cyclades. He was overwhelmed:

> The uncontrived and spontaneous drama which I beheld before my eyes gripped my heart strongly. I confess that, before that dramatic aspect of the marriage, I too was overcome and could not restrain my tears. And yet how often have formal tragic performances left me unmoved!
> (1859: 49)

Thus did the son of a tragic dramatist join with his ideological enemies in lauding the popular over the pedantic. There is no logical reason, for that matter, why he should not have done so, for he saw in the folk laments the purest evidence of continuity with the Classical genius.

To this material, Zambelios added those traditional dance songs which, though outwardly cheerful in tone, are nevertheless graced with a refrain recalling the inevitability of death. These, too, he considered as distinctively Greek and as further evidence that the tragic sense had survived among his people.

Having disengaged the tragic spirit from modern folksong, Zambelios then turns briefly to the other repository of Hellenism, the ecclesiastical. In the Greek Orthodox funeral service, he finds the analogue of the *miroloyia* and is moved to exclaim:

Everywhere and forever is Death, beloved of the Soul. Life, Death, and the resurrection of the dead, inseparable.

Behold Hesiod, Theognis, Phocylides! Behold the poetry of Mimnermus! Behold the Gospel! Behold the hymns of the burial service! Behold, in like manner, the source from which there flowed, and from which still flows, everything fine and original in modern Greek poetry!

(1859: 50)

For Zambelios, cultural continuity was continuity of the spirit (*pnevma*), and the originality of an individual artist could be apprehended only within that context.

This continuity of the spirit provides the solution to the linguistic conundrum with which he began the essay. The essence of the art form, *tragōdia*, had been maintained by the common people in their *traghoudhia*, their poetry and song. The sterility of the Romeic, monastic learning of early Christianity could not quench the poetic inspiration of the Hellenes—for whom, what is more, Christianity "confirms the premonitions of Epic, of Drama, of Philosophy. Rejecting the multiple rule of the [pagan] gods, it makes man the leader of the rational polity. On the throne of the selfsame consciousness is seated man, proclaimed as God on earth" (1859: 17); and, since the new Christian ideal "is not simply Attic or at most Hellenic but entirely ecumenical" (1859: 18), Hellenism has finally, in this new and sublime embodiment, been brought to all humankind. This is the logical completion of Zambelios' 1852 answer to the eastern origins of so much of Greek culture: the assimilation and perfection of half-formed eastern philosophies, Christianity now included, were themselves definitive characteristics of the Greek genius. In a century when educated Western Europeans saw a precursor of Christ in Socrates and the essence of Christian religiosity in the writings of the Classical Greeks generally, when Oscar Wilde could seriously find satisfaction in the belief that Jesus' language had actually been Greek (Jenkyns 1980: 69, 91-93, 158-159, 229), such claims as those of Zambelios did not seem especially preposterous.

Zambelios in a European Context

Zambelios' 1859 essay on the etymology of *traghoudho* has not generally received the recognition which was accorded both his history of medieval Hellenism and an intermediate essay, published in 1856, on the Byzantine phase of Greek ethnicity. It is possible that this has something to do with its intemperate comments on Solomos, who was already coming into his own as the acknowledged national poet of Greece. Zambelios' remarks were countered in a sharp, satirical essay by Solomos' ardent disciple Iakovos Polilas only a year after they appeared in print (see Valetas 1950). Yet the linguistic aspects of Zambelios' essay, although extravagant by present-day standards, deserve a more generous hearing than they have been given so far. Not only are they a useful source for the development of the continuity concept, but they indicate something of the intellectual background of Zambelios and his Heptanesian peers, and they are not without ingenuity.

The essay is admittedly not of a kind where one can say that its author belonged to a single identifiable school of thought. Zambelios was careful to acknowledge no foreign roots and to condemn what he saw as the humiliating imitation of foreign philosophers by his contemporaries. He was, however, well acquainted with various aspects of foreign scholarship, and his Hellenism is palpably, and predictably, directed toward the refurbishment of the Greeks' *external* image. To have assimilated and perfected foreign teachings in his own mind, and to have labeled the result as both Greek and his own, would have been entirely consistent with his theory of Hellenic cultural primacy: the wisdom of the West was Greek by origin and by right, while that of the East could be valued only in its Greek distillation. If there are distinct suggestions of Vico in his writings, as well as of the neo-Platonic tradition, and if we also sometimes meet in them the ideas of Herder and Hegel, there is yet nothing to be gained by labeling Zambelios as a plagiarist or as a poor imitator. Whatever elements of foreign philosophy he absorbed were assimilated to an overall design of some originality, one which provided its own argument against acknowledgment.

Zambelios' references to national consciousness, moreover, do not necessarily reflect the direct influence of Herder or his German successors. The concept of *Volksgeist* was far from new when Zambelios appeared on the scene. Its connection with folk traditions, furthermore, had an alternative source in the writings of Vico, who was to exercise considerable influence on the development of folklore in his native Italy (cf. Cocchiara 1952: 278) and on the thinking of some of the Greek and Italian scholars already mentioned above. Zambelios must have had some contact with Vico's ideas, however indirectly, through the Heptanesian intelligentsia. His linguistic reasoning, moreover, does not recall the grammatical concerns of the Herderians' *Sprachsphilosophie* (cf. Berlin 1977: 170) so much as it does Vico's analyses of etymology.

Vico had argued, and tried to demonstrate by a distinctive combination of historical detail and intuitive guesswork, that etymology could be used to reveal the peculiar histories of cultural institutions. Zambelios' announcement of "a certain important law of history," whereby "every word . . . encapsulates a historical fact," sounds suggestively like a summation of several Vician formulas (see especially Vico 1744: nos. 154, 167, 354). Whether the connection between Vico and Zambelios was anything more than an indirect one, however, is an open question.

Certainly, Zambelios did not plagiarize the specific details of his disquisition on the etymology of *traghoudho* from Vico. There is no evidence to suggest that it was derived, at that level, from any other source. Tommaseo, in fact, came much closer to plagiarizing Vico when he adopted the Neapolitan philosopher's (probably accurate) proposal (nos. 910-911) of a connection between *tragōdia* ("tragedy") and *tragos* ("goat")—an indication, according to both Vico and Tommaseo, of the Dionysiac origins of the drama. In a passage which, without acknowledgment, more faithfully reproduces Vico's cyclical *corsi e ricorsi* than anything Zambelios wrote, Tommaseo notes that "*traghoudho*, from 'tragedy,' to the Greeks of today means cheerful song: almost returning to its origin in *tragos* and the Bacchic songs" (1842, III: 140, n. 3). And then Tommaseo properly notes that the term is contrasted in Greek usage with the word for funeral laments—the point which Zambelios evidently missed. This shows that Zambelios almost certainly did not take his Vician ideas, if such they are, piecemeal from Tommaseo but developed for himself a version which is more faithful to the methodology than to the examples of Vico's thinking.

Because of its assimilated nature, Zambelios' seeming Vicianism never emerges more unambiguously. There are possible hints of it in his treatment of Homer (although, unlike Vico, he accepted Homer as a single, real person), in his respect for folk traditions ancient and modern, in the correlation of symbolism (Vico's *fantasia*) with social changes, and in the acceptance of a divine Providence as the guiding principle of cultural evolution. But he differed from Vico in praising the institutions of democracy, just as he parted company from Hegel on the question of monarchy (Zambelios detested it). He also shows little of the cyclical sense of history that one expected from a committed Vician—not that he should be criticized for failing to adopt what Berlin has described as "the least interesting, plausible, and original" of Vico's theories (1977: 64).

The exact relationship between Zambelios and Vico is opaque. Zambelios did not represent his own ideas as derivative, but this may have resulted from a desire to avoid associating himself too obviously with foreign philosophies, especially after quarreling with Solomos on just that account. Opportunities for reading Vico must have existed both on Corfu and abroad, and Vico's ideas were current in the circles in which Zambelios tried to make his name. The obscure style of the *Scienza nuova* encouraged haphazard mining rather than systematic perusal, and Zambelios' use of ideas which may have come from that source certainly suggests a much more restricted range of interests. By Zambelios' time, much of Vico's thinking had been more generally diffused or, as with Herder, paralleled in the independent conclusions of others. But the resemblance between Zambelios and Vico is striking, to say the least, when we examine their approaches to etymological reconstruction. Zambelios' "important law of history" is well-nigh indistinguishable from the cardinal *degnità* ("axiom") of Vico's imaginative linguistics (cf. also Zambelios 1880: v).

Ecumenical Ethnocentrism

The argument that the modern Greeks' destiny was to perfect the philosophies of East and West carried certain responsibilities and consequences. To illustrate these, we conclude this chapter with an essay which, whether or not it was directly inspired by Zambelios, pushes his argument to its logical extreme. In this particular essay, the comparative lack of attention suffered by Greek folklore research in the wider European context becomes easier to understand—not because the essay is representative of scholarly standards in Greece but quite simply because it indicates, in exaggerated form, the isolating effects of a methodology and a philosophy that were clearly stated to be national rather than global in scope.

For Greek folklore remained, for the most part, a strictly national discipline. Even the term *laografia*, when it was eventually coined in 1884, denoted the material and the discipline more or less indiscriminately. And, since Greek folklorists were generally disinclined to take a sustained interest in the folklore of other lands, except insofar as it provided insights into their own (and not always then), the discipline itself rarely achieved more than purely domestic importance as a scholarly activity. In consequence, Greek folklorists are rarely given more than a passing mention in international studies of folklore epistemology. Cocchiara's wide-ranging historical study of European folklore scholarship (1952) does not name a single Greek folklorist, although it accords warm recognition to both Fauriel and Tommaseo for their Greek and other studies. It is not necessary to invert Zambelios' view of the cause-and-effect relationship between European cultures in order to perceive how radically the Hellenist ideology inverted the international perspective of ethnology and, thereby, prevented the Greek scholars from making a more ecumenical contribution to methodology. Such examples as Finnish (Wilson 1976), Russian (Oinas 1961; Sokolov 1950: 40-155), and Serbo-Croatian (Karadžić, in Cocchiara 1952) folklore studies also indicate that a language barrier cannot provide a sufficient explanation of so high a degree of isolation. The reasons for this isolation lie, rather, in the interests and presuppositions of the local folklorists themselves.

While later folklorists, working in the tradition of Politis, were at least prepared to use foreign materials in illustration of their Greek data, Zambelios and his immediate contemporaries, though often well versed in the literary works of other countries, were unwilling to do more than refer in the most general terms to their folk traditions. The result was to create an intellectual cul-de-sac in the midst of an already closed academic environment. Exemplifying the extreme development of this trend, at a time when Politis had already begun to publish his comparative essays on Greek folklore and world ethnology, is the disquisition which the Athens lawyer Stamatios Valvis published in 1877. This essay is an attempt to see in the dying words of one of the revolutionary guerrilla leaders a philosophical refinement which surpassed the best work of even the Classical Greeks or the modern Europeans. The argument, which particularly recalls Zambelios in its identification of the ancient literati with the largely unlettered population of the modern countryside, adds to this the more dynamic notion of an autochthonous spiritual evolution among the folk themselves.

Valvis' dissertation consists of twenty-three pages devoted, ostensibly, to the study of a single folk distich. The couplet in question is that said to have been uttered by Diakos when he was led off to execution after his hopeless defense of the Alamana bridge against overwhelming Turkish odds. To this day, it has remained a well-known verse with intense patriotic associations:

> But see what a time Death has chosen for taking me,
> now that the trees are blooming and the earth is sprouting grass!

But it takes Valvis slightly more than half his essay to come to the point of actually quoting the verse itself. The earlier pages are resplendent with philosophical musings on the admiration which sensitive human beings feel for nature and on nature's own insensitivity to the feelings of humans. Saint Matthew, Sophocles, Virgil, Goethe, and the modern Greek poet Alexander Soutsos are all quoted in witness against nature's callousness toward human pain. The ancient tragedians' words are held to be especially moving in this connection, partly because of "the serene beauty of nature in Greece": the contrast between human suffering and the serenity of nature is especially painful.

After finally quoting the couplet, Valvis declares his ideological focus:

> We may say that this couplet does far more honor to that much sung hero than his own Leonidian heroism, because it shows that that greathearted fighter had a sensitive and wholly pure heart, a heart which nurtured feelings such as those which stirred in the breasts of those noblest of men, educated in the highest of cultures, whose sentiments we have noted above.   (1877: 143)

Diakos, however, not only exemplified the finest of the virtues extolled in Attic tragedy and Holy Writ alike but actually surpassed these sources of wisdom as well as their intellectual offspring, the European philosophers: "We know nobody else to have thus mourned for himself, in other words because of *the circumstances* under which he was dying and not *because* he was dying or because *a person such as himself* was dying" (1877: 145; Valvis' emphasis). The hero of Greek liberation thus succeeds not only to the martial glory of Leonidas, whose finest hour came in similar fashion at nearby Thermopylae, but also—and, for Valvis, more significantly—to the intellectual heritage of the philosophers, tragedians, and Gospel writers. Where Zambelios had sought to demonstrate such spiritual continuity in the persistent relationship between language and concept, Valvis found it in the realm of concept alone.

Valvis' argument brings out more starkly, perhaps, than Zambelios' writings a fundamental problem of the Hellenist thesis. The more extreme Hellenists' claim to an ecumenical vision grew naturally from the transplantation of philhellenism to the intellectual soil of Greece itself. If renascent Greece represented the ultimate vindication and triumph of European culture, who but the Greeks should be best qualified to interpret that larger entity? This, as one might expect, reverses the broadly phenomenological subjectivism of European philosophers by granting the Greeks an intuitive understanding of culture at large. Elsewhere in Europe, the ideas of Hamann (Hammel 1972: 4), Herder (Dorson 1968: 91; Wilson 1976), and Vico (Cocchiara 1952: 278) were being interpreted as defining the distinctiveness and autonomy of each and every people's national character. They were not understood to accord the modern Greeks such intellectual catholicity on the basis of past glories. Not even Vico, with his rapt admiration for Classical culture, mentions the modern Greeks specifically. Hamann actually disliked Classical Greek culture, at least as it was interpreted by his contemporaries; and, while Herder did not absorb this prejudice along with the rest of his mentor's teachings, he opposed the pseudo-Classical posturing of his fellow Europeans as a violation of their inherent national characters (Berlin 1977: 182-192).

What we may call the ecumenical ethnocentrism of Zambelios and Valvis thus came at a time when Europe was little disposed to listen. Other intellectual currents were now abroad in Europe; Max Müller, for example, was in the process of exciting his contemporaries' imagination by reversing Vico's view of the relationship between mythology and language (cf. Cocchiara 1952: 314). The new ethnological fashions quite passed the older Hellenists by, and it was now a new generation of Greek scholars (with Nikolaos Politis at their head) who turned to these developments for their own researches. Yet Zambelios should not be forgotten. His intermediate paper of 1856 (see Spiridakis 1966) spurred the periodical *Pandora* into folklore publication, giving the very youthful Politis one of his first platforms, and it also galvanized the Greek Parliament into providing regular funds for folklore research. While Zambelios' intellectual path led in the direction of such writers as Valvis, his own observations were full of insight as well as ideologically directed exaggeration, and his energy and enthusiasm brought about the earliest official recognition in Greece of the importance of the folk traditions.

Chapter 3
National Character, National Consciousness

". . . the virile habits of the Europeans . . ."

National Character in a European Context

Zambelios' repeated references to "national spirit," to "race" and *ethnos*, and to concepts of national consciousness all reproduce the definitive concerns of nineteenth-century ideological nationalism in Europe. The terminology itself represents a gloss, possibly at more than one remove, on the language of Hamann and Herder; these German philosophers' ideas had been disseminated throughout the European continent, notably in France by Madame de Staël (Cocchiara 1952: 278-303), and had received further application by Fauriel and many others. That this broad tradition should have influenced Zambelios in no way contradicts his apparent adherence to Vico, for Herder himself came to admire Vico greatly and to recognize that the Neapolitan's thinking was at times startlingly similar to his own (Berlin 1977: 91). By the middle of the nineteenth century, the language and concepts of the German romantic nationalists were in general use throughout Europe, often in a more aggressive and explicitly statist frame of reference than Herder, at least, had found palatable.

It is thus difficult to estimate the range of Herder's influence in Greece. Recall, too, that Greek folklore studies began in earnest only after the founding of the state, as a source of a posteriori exegesis. This contrasts radically with the situation in Finland, where, long before the prospect of national redemption had become at all immediate, such leading early students of folklore as Sjögren and Poppius could point to Herder as the wellspring of their ideological formation (Wilson 1976: 3). By the time Herder's thinking came to affect the direction of ethnological thought in Greece, there were several modern intermediaries (including the brothers Grimm) from whose works the Herderian idiom could be absorbed by folklorists and others; by midcentury, moreover, the broad concepts of *Volksgeist* and *Zeitgeist* had been too generally disseminated for their appearance in Greek writings to be attributable to a specifically Herderian source.

What Cocchiara rather contemptuously calls "the myth of *Volksgeist*" (1952: 278) encouraged the development of academic folklore throughout Europe, as scholars scurried to find empirical evidence that such a spirit really existed. To call it a myth, moreover, is to miss its *ordering* potential. The notion of a Greek national consciousness became a kind of cognitive map (cf. Geertz 1973: 220) wherein cultural similarities, common language and religion, and a burgeoning restiveness with Turkish rule were given a certain unity of meaning. While it has been argued (St. Clair 1972) that few rural Greeks were in a position, in 1821, to predict what national politics would do to their values and allegiances, they clearly already recognized the principle of nationhood; such proselytizing agencies as the Odessa-based Filiki Eteria had already done much to bring this about. National consciousness has been defined by a Greek folklorist as "the conscious knowledge of every individual that he is part of a nation, partaking to [*sic*] the strong groupal [*sic*] aspirations that bind him to the other individuals around him, creating thus the common will of all to belong to this and not to any other nation" (Kiriakidis 1955: 11). Whatever the mystical possibilities of the *Volksgeist* concept, it emerges in this admirably specific definition as a form of collective self-identification.

The definition is useful, too, in that it stresses the aspect of individual self-knowledge in relation to the larger entity of the nation. As an abstraction, however, it is very much a product of learned rather than folk discourse. The Greek term for "consciousness" in this context, *syneidēsis*,[1] is the New Testament and ecclesiastical term for "conscience" or "self-knowledge" (cf. Latin *con* and *scientia*). When this word appears in village usage, it tends to be conflated with the phonetically similar but etymologically noncognate word for "custom" (*synētheia*; see Herzfeld 1980a: 346–347).

Such a lack of fit between scholarly terminology and village usage is an indication of the pedigree of "national consciousness." *Syneidēsis* seems to be a convenient gloss on the French *conscience*, which conflates the ideas of "conscience" (German *Gewissen*) and "consciousness" (*Bewusstsein*). Representative of the Europeans' "very great debt" to Greek culture, this particular repayment, indeed, probably owes something to Koraes' own writings. It is a Western European notion, dressed up in the language of early Christianity and put to work in the service of the European nation-state ideal. Not only was the *concept* of national consciousness a European conceit, but that consciousness itself was increasingly perceived as a definitively European possession. In consequence, moreover, the various distinctive nationalities of Europe derived from this shared proclivity a sense of transcendent unity, and the increasingly comparativist perspective of folklore studies fostered that perception of unity in diversity. "Folklore, indeed, pressed the learned into thinking in German, in English, in French, in Russian, or in something else, but it also simultaneously pressed them, to use an expression of Madame de Staël's, into 'thinking in European'" (Cocchiara 1952: 303). Given this background, and given also the pattern of reversal which stemmed from its origins in philhellenism, the Hellenist thesis could only benefit from the development of folklore. If Greece had been the *fons et origo* of all Europe, then Greek folklore would enshrine the quintessence of the European spirit.

D'Istria and the Premise of European Character

Although Dora d'Istria was not of Greek origin, it was she who launched this methodological perspective on Greek folklore into a wider, European perspective. Zambelios and other Greek writers had already developed it in their own researches, but d'Istria expounded it to a more international audience, and it is instructive to see how much her views converge with those of the indigenous Hellenists.

A brief review of her life may help explain her intense involvement in the description and defense of the Greek national character. She was born in 1828 in Bucharest as Helen Ghikas, a Romanian princess of Albanian extraction. Her father, Prince Michael Ghikas, was a provincial governor who had been among the first of his circle to adopt western dress and who, throughout his life, took a deep interest in the study of archaeology; from him, presumably, the young princess first absorbed the idiom of European antiquarianism. Her mother was the first Wallachian woman to write in the Romanian language, thereby setting her an example combining female emancipation and linguistic nationalism. D'Istria was educated according to principles of supposedly Classical Greek derivation. These included admitting a respected place in the curriculum for physical training—which proved fortunate one dark Moscow night in 1854 when her younger sister's governess, who could not swim, fell into a pond! In 1849, she married a Russian prince but soon left him for an independent life of travel, adventure, and the wars of the pen.

Despite her enthusiasm for the various forms of Balkan nationalism, d'Istria chose to reside in Italy. She wrote principally in French, the language of diplomacy. For her vocal endorsement of Greek aspirations, especially of the ill-fated Cretan insurrection of 1866, she was granted Hellenic nationality by a special decree of Parliament. In expressing her gratitude for the honor, which was unprecedented for a woman, she remarked that she had "always considered Greece as a second fatherland"—a reference to that superior education, perhaps, which made many Balkan aristocrats of the period refer to themselves as Hellenes.

Such affectations of Hellenic identity were neither literal nor absolute. They certainly did not prevent d'Istria from exploiting her Albanian ancestry when, in 1860, she wrote to Prime Minister Dimitrios Voulgaris (Boulgares)[2] to solicit support for her plans to conduct research in Greece. She told him, among other things, that she had been deeply moved on a visit to the island of Hydra by the memory of the Hydriote sea captains' heroic participation in the War of Independence (cf. Dakin 1973: 122–123), recalling that the Hydriotes, *like Voulgaris as well as herself*, were of Albanian origin.

Her interests spanned the entire Balkan area and beyond. Her published work, which draws extensively on folksong as a repository of national character, deals with the Greeks, Albanians, Bulgarians, Magyars, eastern Turks, Romanians, and Serbs. She died in 1888, a revered and internationally recognized authority on Balkan nationalism as well as on the position of women in Balkan and other societies (see Anon. 1860–61; Cecchetti 1868, 1873; Pommier 1863; Mandouvalou 1969).

Dora d'Istria's instatement as an honorary Greek citizen coincided with the broader sense in which she chose to regard herself as a Hellene. Her conception of modern Greek nationality was primarily antiquarian and so did not conflict with her more literal claims to Albanian and Romanian identity. Some allowance must be made, in considering her letter to Voulgaris with its references to their shared Albanian origins, for the polite rhetoric of diplomacy; but the same provision applies equally to her letter of thanks to the Greek Parliament, in which her Hellenic feelings, of course, take center stage. Yet her multiple sense of nationality was much more than a diplomatic conceit, to be manipulated according to circumstances. Her extensive writings show that she fully subscribed to the philhellenic view of Greece as in every sense the continuation of its ancient predecessor. Her gracious acceptance of Greek citizenship was above all a confirmation, in personal terms, of a consistent ideology.

D'Istria subscribed wholeheartedly to the twin concepts of national character and national consciousness, although it is in terms of the first of these that her ethnographic studies are principally organized. She portrayed individuals as capable of behaving only in accordance with the social values, the character, of the cultures to which they belonged. The cultures themselves were subsumed under the larger opposition between European and Asiatic peoples; and, adopting a convention widely accepted by her contemporaries, she attributed to the former the prize of absolute superiority. For the Albanians, she maintained, the sight of the Greek flag fluttering over Corfu after that island's cession to Greece "appeared to the sons of Skanderbeg as the symbol of Europe's definitive triumph over Asia" (1866: 417).[3]

In like manner, too, d'Istria was able to "explain" the failure of the Serbs to achieve rapid independence:

> Had the Turks been the sole adversaries of the Serbs, the latter might have had grounds for hoping that the Asiatic mores, enervating influ-

ences that they are, would have delivered them sooner or later; but the Moslem Serbs and Albanians [who fought for the Turks] , having conserved the virile habits of the Europeans, are far more redoubtable enemies for them than is the entire Ottoman army.   (1865: 360)

Striking a somewhat backhanded blow for her fellow Albanians, she anticipates prejudices still far from uncommon in Greece, to the effect that the Turks, as Asiatics, are worthless in battle against Christians and Europeans.

Within the generality of European peoples, d'Istria sought to make finer discriminations. She discerned, as it were, different grades of European character, different degrees of adherence to the absolute ideal. Her comment on the folksongs lamenting the Fall of Constantinople in 1453 is extremely revealing:

> Whereas the ruin of the Serbian Empire at Kossovo inspired the popular poets of Serbia to their best works, the collapse of Constantine's empire did not provoke from the mouths of the people a single cry worthy of retention for posterity. The fact is that great poets are not always born, in each country, at the moment of great disasters. On the other hand, it is also true that the Serbian Empire was struck down in its prime, that of the Greeks when in full decline. There is perhaps a further reason for the difference: *the Serbs have the somehow communistic influence of the Slavs* and are interested above all in those conflicts where the nation as a whole is itself the hero; by contrast, the Greeks, *whose genius is entirely European*, seek in the multitude for an Ajax, a Ulysses, an Agamemnon, for great figures who vigorously stand out from the confused, misty masses and strikingly describe, to some extent, their character and passions.   (1867: 590; my emphasis)

These lines were written before the Greek folklorists had come to make the popular laments for the Fall of Constantinople an object of their especial interest and veneration (see chap. 6). D'Istria was herself evidently unacquainted with them, to judge by her view of the Greek folk poet's style, for, when the emperor appears in those laments at all, he does little to earn a hero's distinctive lineaments.

In d'Istria's scheme, the Serbs—even when Moslem by religion—are more European than the Turks, but the Greeks are the most European of all. Their distinguishing mark is that penchant for individualistic character drawing, that seeking "in the multitude . . . for great figures," which links the Greeks of today both with their ancient forebears (especially as represented by the Homeric heroes) and with contemporary Europeans. That national characteristic, moreover, had survived the vicissitudes of foreign domination. Like Zambelios, d'Istria regarded the Byzantine imperium as a foreign growth on true Hellenism (1867: 592), but, perhaps because she felt no need to "justify" Christianity, she dismissed the church as a destructive foreign influence too. Only the heroes of the folksongs entirely escape these effete sources of corruption, for they "are new men, in many respects more like the rude companions of Achilles than they are like the timid subjects of the last [Byzantine emperor] Constantine." The heroes of the songs to which d'Istria refers here are the so-called klefts (*kleftes*), or brigand-guerrillas. It may seem oddly contradictory to use these klefts as symbols of spiritual continuity with the heroes of Homer while fixing the earliest date of their activities in the eighteenth century (d'Istria 1867: 592), but in fact this pair of apparently incompatible propositions is also contained in the work of indigenous folklorists, where we shall shortly examine them more critically.

D'Istria's attribution of "communistic influence" to the Slavs, some eight decades before they officially adopted Marxist constitutions, curiously foreshadows the modern Greek convention of condemning political communism as an imported Slavic doctrine (cf. Kofos 1964). Certain events, notably the hostile relations between Greece and the neighboring countries during the Greek Civil War, have reinforced that attitude. For d'Istria, as for her contemporaries in general, continuity between Classical and modern Greek culture was the best proof that there was indeed such a thing as a Greek national character, which contrasted so strongly with the national characters of neighboring peoples. Thus, while praising Fauriel for having "taught an astonished Europe that bards still existed in the land of Homer" (1867: 587), she did not so much as mention his useful work on Slav folk poetry (cf. Ibrovac 1966). It was not until many decades later that Parry and Lord introduced to the scholarly world the possibility that the techniques of the Yugoslav *guslari* could help penetrate the complexities of Homeric composition and style (see Lord 1960; Finnegan 1977).

Pagan Heroism

The premise of national character enabled the early nationalist writers to extract a measure of continuity from what could otherwise be presented as an exceptionally radical break in the cultural history of Greece. This was the religious change from the worship of local deities and the Olympian pantheon in Classical times to the centralized unity and doctrinal monotheism of the Greek Orthodox church.

Dora d'Istria had only contempt for the influence of the church and its leadership:

> The reaction is such that the kleftic poems were soon to seek inspiration in the vague recollections of a free, pagan Greece, rather than in

the craven teachings of a theology fashioned over the centuries to suit
the tastes of autocratic rulers. Outlaws and fugitives gathered in the
mountains: Olympus was once more to open its miraculous flanks to its
old children . . .   (1867: 591)

But this scornful formulation was not a happy one for those resident in
Greece itself who, unlike the peripatetic princess, had to achieve a balance between their religious affiliations and their pagan ancestry. Zambelios, as we
saw, viewed the Orthodox church as the very means whereby democracy survived in the Greek spirit. This argument was better suited to the needs of the
new nation than d'Istria's, since the priesthood and the monastic tradition
had maintained necessarily close social connections with the rural population;
the lower clergy, unlike the senior hierarchy, had supported the revolutionary
movement actively.

But, if the relationship between Classical paganism and Orthodox Christianity was a dangerous subject, d'Istria concentrated her analysis on aspects
of the Greek *Volksgeist* over which the Hellenists could comfortably agree
with her. Stressing the ethnic purity of the Greeks, she argued that this was
revealed in a unique combination of heroism and, as the quoted passages
show, individualism. That the Greeks had indeed fought hard for their independence was indisputable. That the Greek guerrillas thought it generally
more prudent to abandon hopeless confrontations and could not understand
the last-ditch heroism of their philhellenic supporters (St. Clair 1972: 35-40)
is no reflection on their commitment to the cause as such but conforms to a
code of combined bravura and prudence which still has some currency in
rural areas. A Cretan or Sarakatsan shepherd may, for example, be forced on
moral grounds to defend his reputation with his fists or a knife but prefers to
confront his enemies in the presence of others who will intervene—being
killed over an insult is foolish, since it leaves one's family exposed to poverty
and ridicule (Campbell 1964: 196). The Greek revolutionary guerrillas fought
hard when there was reason to hope for a successful outcome or when there
was no alternative, but they did not see any reason to throw their lives away
for no obvious practical end. Some of the philhellenes who came to fight with
them were dismayed at what, to European gentlemen, looked like cowardice;
but cowardice, like collaboration (cf. Petropulos 1976a), is a term which does
little justice to the indigenous values and circumstances against which the
guerrillas' performance should be interpreted.

One recognized component of the guerrillas' behavior was an aggressive
idiom of self-assertion. Such self-assertion is not individualism in a psychological sense. On the contrary, the indigenous terms for it (*eghoïsmos, pallikaris-
mos*) denote conformity to an ideal.[4] The conventional stance of the guerrilla, which was dismissed as mere swashbuckling in the *post*-revolutionary

brigand, was a socially validated norm. When d'Istria compared this to the "communistic influence of the Slavs," she seems to have read institutional values as psychological attitudes on both sides; Slavic "communism" probably refers to the structure of the *zadruga*, which, significantly, has been treated as discouraging "individualism" by some Yugoslav writers (cf. Winner 1977)! Whether individualism and heroism are discovered is a function less of what is really there than of the principles of descriptive selection involved, and we find the dispute over the respective national characters of Greeks and Bulgarians expressed in strikingly similar terms (cf. Colocotronis 1918; Jireček 1891; Kiriakidis 1955; Kofos 1964; Megas 1946). By refusing the Bulgarians their claim to having originated heroic songs and a national epic of their own, the Greek folklorists were able to deny them the trait of heroic individualism which they had accorded themselves on the strength of their own, Greek folklore.

Heroes or Brigands?

The Greeks' claim to that trait was thus an important argument in support of the overall Hellenist thesis. It combined in a single formula the recent struggle and the ancient glories. That the trait was especially evident among the heroes of the struggle in the countryside, that it was celebrated in rural songs, meant that the incorporation of the *laos*, the folk, into the historical *ethnos* could be placed on a solid scholarly basis. The essays of Zambelios, Valvis, and d'Istria, while substantially different from each other in style and content, are all elaborations of this seminal idea.

D'Istria, in particular, dwelt on the activities of the Greek guerrillas as the embodiment of Hellenic valor. Her views were widely shared, both in Greece and elsewhere. Yet this enthusiasm for the category of fighters who called themselves *kleftes*, and who made such a signal contribution to the cause of Greek independence, did not extend to those of their compatriots who continued to bear arms once that independence had been achieved, for by this time their activity was mostly directed not against the Turkish enemy but against the representatives of the Greek State. Those guerrillas who might have challenged the politicians' authority but had died too soon could be apotheosized, since they no longer constituted a threat; even that archenemy of the political establishment, Odhisseas Androutsos, appears on schoolroom posters to this day, resplendent in his Classical helmet. Others, however, many of them only minor figures in the recorded history of the war, lived on to continue their more parochial battles, performing acts of brigandage whenever opportunity arose. They posed a serious problem not only for the representatives of law and order but, more generally, for the proponents of ideological Hellenism: they undermined the image of the valiant Hellene who fights only to defend hearth and homeland.

At this point, it will be necessary to move away from our examination of individual folklorists' work, in order to explore the more general issues posed by these fighters and their traditions. For they were not of interest only to those scholars, like Zambelios and d'Istria, who attempted to construct a generalized picture of the Greek national character. On the contrary, the very widespread concern with them among Greek folklorists of the period is only part of the commotion which they caused among the intellectual and political leadership of the nation. We shall see that they were retrospectively coopted into the national mythology wherever possible and that this necessitated the development of a formal taxonomic category suitable for such a task. Furthermore, the definitively Hellenic character that was attributed to them gave them a special interest for folklorists who wanted to make a case for the cultural supremacy of a particular region. For all these reasons, the following discussion of the phenomenon will provide a bridge between the *Volksgeist* models we have been considering so far and the development of a more empirical kind of culture history which we will consider as we return in the remaining chapters to the work of particular scholars.

Kleftism and the Constitution of History

The category of kleftic songs appears early in the writings of foreign observers. Fauriel found it useful, while Kind (1827: v, x, 1), following Fauriel's lead, explained that since the klefts were not mere brigands (*Räuber*) the songs about them deserved special consideration. By the time the German philologist Arnold Passow assembled his critical compendium of Greek folksongs in 1860, the kleftic category had become a vital part of the classification of Greek folklore. D'Istria's airy reference to "kleftic poems" shows how familiar the category had become even outside the immediate world of Greek philology. Nor was any challenge mounted to the historical and chronological status of "the klefts." While their patriotic motives were later questioned to some extent, or at least substantially reinterpreted (Kordatos 1972; Lambrinos 1947; Katsoulis 1975), and while the concept of nationalism in the Greek context has been considerably refined (see Petropulos 1976a; Vasdravellis 1975), only occasionally do we find "the klefts" replaced by the more careful "kleftism" (e.g., Petropulos 1968: 31-34).

That very definite phrase, "the klefts," suggests a historical movement with clear chronological boundaries. The duration of the kleftic period, apparently accepted by even so iconoclastic a writer as Lambrinos (1947: 78-79), is given as the century immediately preceding the Revolution. In this determination, the dearth of documentary evidence has resulted in great prominence being given to certain personal names which recur in the folk-songs; these names, interpreted with varying degrees of credibility as belonging to particular klefts whose activities are suggested by the thin documentary sources, do not carry us back to before about 1720.

The literalist interpretation of these names, the assumption that they referred to specific personalities, is symptomatic of the archaeological view of oral transmission. This view assumes that historical names will provide chronological markers for the whole text of a given song, much as a coin or a potsherd can perform the same service for an archaeological stratum. The stemmatic approach to textual comparison, whereby a series of copyists' manuscripts is located on a philological *Stammbaum*, was thus applied to oral texts despite the fact that these materials can go on changing right up to the moment they are recorded. When Evlambios attacked Fauriel's use of invented song titles, he very accurately pinpointed one of the major sources of the problem: such titles as "The Siege of Rhodes, 1522" (cf. Herzfeld 1969, 1973) or "The Death of Zidros" imply that the songs to which they are attached are literally *historical* texts to which dates can be attached with great precision. "Kleftic songs" seemed particularly amenable to such treatment because of their frequent mention of personal names.

Names, to the more literalistic among the folklorists, meant dates. In extreme cases, the evidence might even be fabricated, perhaps on the usual reasoning that the folklorists and the folk shared a common culture; this seems to apply to some of the references to the major guerrilla leader Theodhoros Kolokotronis (e.g., Lelekos 1868: 21–25). Of course, not all named references to Kolokotronis are necessarily forgeries. On the contrary, his name was without doubt a familiar one in the Greek countryside: he lived on after the war until 1843, and his memoirs are an important contribution to the historical literature of the period. His family name, at least, does appear in songs of apparently genuine rural provenance. The addition of Classical motifs in the forged texts is another matter—an extreme consequence, it would appear, of treating folksongs as "historical" and "national."

Often, moreover, Kolokotronis appears in song texts under his baptismal name of Theodhoros, sometimes in the affectionately diminutive form Thodhorakis. It was common practice to extol a guerrilla by his baptismal name in this way; occasionally, too, a widely used hypocoristic (*paratsoukli*) might be employed instead.[5] This use of common names instead of distinctive surnames, however, had the effect of eroding rather than preserving a man's posterity as an identifiable individual.

This erosion of identity in folksongs is not, of course, confined to personalities. Places, dates, even the course of particular events are all liable to the same process. Thus, the more distant in time that historical events are, the less factually specific do popular verse accounts of them tend to be. The

1822 fall of Nauplion to the Greeks is recounted in far more graphic detail
(presumably by Greek-speaking *Moslem* singers again!) than the Turkish capture of that city in 1715, and with still more circumstantial and factual elaboration than the 1522 siege of Rhodes by the Turks, even though all three
verse accounts share a common pool of motifs and expressive devices. Probably no nineteenth-century villager could have recounted the exact details of
the sixteenth-century siege; what was of interest, to judge from the extant
corpus of such songs, was the *generic* image of a Christian island falling to the
infidel Turks. Once the events in question were outside living memory, they
were gradually absorbed into a set of generalities. There is no reason to suppose that the same would not have happened to songs celebrating the minor
adventures of local brigands.

On the contrary, a recurrent feature of Greek naming symbolism suggests
that these songs are likely to have undergone the same process. Greek baptismal names are usually bestowed, especially on firstborn sons and daughters,
in commemoration (or "resurrection," as it is called) of the parents' own
parents or other close (especially prematurely deceased) kin. Only the order
of preference varies regionally. In all geographical areas, on the other hand,
this ostensibly commemorative act really results in a progressive forgetting of
the commemorated individuals' distinctive personalities. So many individuals
of the same name lie in a person's more distant ancestry that they have inevitably lost their distinct identities; only those who lie within a genealogical
distance of at most four or five generations from the present are remembered
as specific members of the community. When all this is borne in mind, it is
only to be expected that the brigands who operated at a genealogical distance
of more than five generations from the outbreak of war in 1821 should lack
identifiable, personal dimensions in the oral sources. After 1821, the situation changed radically; as literacy began to spread throughout the countryside, the last generation of prestatehood heroes was caught like insects in the
amber of official history.

This emergence from anonymity also coincides with the accelerated
growth of a national consciousness. Yet for us to treat the klefts as a discrete
analytical category, and thereby separate them both from their predecessors
and from the later brigands who defied the authority of Athens, is to violate
the indigenous usage of the term *kleftis* itself. Petropulos rightly observes
(1976a: 23) that the palpable existence of a national consciousness differ-
entiates the Greek uprising from any general model of "social banditry"
(Hobsbawm 1959), but he is careful not to claim that patriotic kleftism was
the only form that had ever existed; Vryonis, too, suggests that the acknowledged klefts who fought the Ottoman administration represent *social* continuity with the earlier, Byzantine phase (1976: 56). Once we thus escape the
narrow chronological limits which were formerly placed on the klefts' histori-

cal role, kleftism as a social institution—rather than the single, patriotically motivated form of kleftism which the earlier writers selected for study—becomes more amenable to the treatment suggested by Hobsbawm's essay. While "social banditry" is perhaps still too general, the more local model of "kleftism" suggests a similar flexibility, a sense of a coherent value system stretched across a fairly wide spectrum of specific kinds of historical situation but seen within the peculiar context of Greek society.

Such a usage would correspond more closely to what can still be gleaned of the rural use of the term *kleftis*. The island of Crete, particularly the mountainous areas in the west, is one suggestive source of information.[6] Although the Cretans valiantly resisted the Turks, as they had resisted their predecessors the Venetians, one does not find many references to the activities of "the klefts" on Crete. Yet the style of guerrilla warfare was not very different from what was happening on the mainland. What is more, *kleftes* are still found in western Crete; today they are, quite specifically, animal thieves. Yet one aspect of this usage is extremely germane to the present inquiry. Those who are described as *kleftes* are not professionals, and they are not described in general terms as *kleftes*, any more than they would usually be described as habitual liars: both imputations constitute grave insults which may lead to bloodshed among these frequently armed men. On the other hand, just as one may lie in a particular context (such as the defense of family interests) and be thought worthy for doing so, one may also steal sheep or goats from neighboring villages under conventionally prescribed circumstances and in conformity with a set of procedural rules. Virtually all the active shepherds of certain villages are *kleftes*, and *kala kleftes* ("good at stealing")[7] at that, at certain times and in appropriate conditions. But, when they are not out on a raid, they are not *kleftes*.

Conversely, moreover, the approach of sheep thieves may still bring the warning cry, "The *kleftes* have come!" The definite article in this expression does not, of course, mean that the entire category of named, professional brigands has suddenly appeared; so, even if the historical conception of "the klefts" has some basis in vernacular usage, it is still not necessary to argue that the usage itself refers to an absolute, discrete category of people. *Kleftis* is, rather, a category of *performative role*. It may be objected that one cannot interpret a widespread historical phenomenon on the basis of so geographically restricted a datum. The objective here, however, is somewhat more modest. First, we need only show that interpretations other than the conventional historicist one are possible; the Cretan usage, which seems to have been classified out of the laographic record as "un-Greek," points in one possible direction, albeit a highly suggestive one.

Second, even standard Greek terminological usage raises doubts about the literalist view of "the klefts." The Greek definite article is ambiguous in such a context, since it can introduce both a finite category ("the klefts") and a generic description ("people of the type described as 'klefts'"); historical circumstances, especially the formation of the Hellenist ideology, favored the finite over the generic usage because, as will become apparent below, the independent Greek State could thereby dissociate itself conceptually from the successors of those men who had played so vital a role in its foundation. Something very similar happened in Sicily: as Blok (1974) has amply demonstrated, "the *mafia*" describes a range of social behaviors and values rather than a specific, bounded criminal organization. Even more apposite, perhaps, is the United States usage of "rebel," a term that "served as a touchstone to show the sympathies of the speaker" during and after the Civil War as well as during the earlier struggle for independence (Read 1978).[8]

The geographical, social, and historical limitations of the usual definition of "the klefts" are replicated in the folkloric category of "kleftic songs." Here, for example, is a song which would qualify as kleftic in any collection were it not Cretan:

> *At dawn I'll leave the foothills of the mountain*
> *and run to see the dawn, mountain mine, at your summit.*
> *I'll find a solid boulder and there sit down*
> *to fire off gunshots to gather some* kleftes *nigh:*
> *I'll put a* kleftis *in as a judge, and a* kleftis *as prosecutor,*
> *so that I won't hand out life sentences!*
>
> (Papagrigorakis 1956-57: 280, no. 493)

Kleftism is a broad behavioral continuum, and this song would sit well with several variants of the brigand's life. A burst of gunfire is still the (illegal) summons to a wedding procession in western Crete.

The chronological limits on the "kleftic song" category seem to be as selective as the social. There is in fact some evidence that guerrillas were commemorated in song long before the arrival of the Turks (cf. Morgan 1960: 26; Lambrinos 1947: 76). That such songs have disappeared or shed such personal references as they may have possessed does not mean that the guerrillas themselves never existed, and the evidence that encroaching anonymity is a common feature of oral transmission makes this particular *argumentum ex silentio* especially weak.

Another limitation of the category of "the klefts" is its restriction of a particular range of social behaviors to Greece. This is simplistic—Greek historians have recently discovered important evidence that Albanians and other non-Greek brigands participated in kleftic activities during the prerevolutionary phase (e.g., Vasdravellis 1975). The circumstances of the Greek Revolution were certainly very different from those of the subsequent uprisings in the neighboring countries, but this does not mean that treating kleftism as an exclusively Greek phenomenon does not impose an artificial sense of cultural demarcation. This, too, is reflected in the treatment of "kleftic songs," in which the conventional conception of the kleft as an individualist—the image which d'Istria had so assiduously fostered—could be contrasted with the Bulgarians' failure to make personalities of *their* guerrillas. This device is logically dependent on the literalist assumption that the names in the Greek songs represent specific, individuated klefts:

> . . . Bulgarian popular poetry cannot offer us a single historical or heroic poem: it can only take in certain Bacchic or amorous poems; or, indeed, *in the absence of any other sort of hero*, it exalts the *haidouts*, otherwise known as brigands, who have *absolutely no connection* with the Serbian *hajduks* or the Greek klefts. The latter are national heroes, *after a historical model*; the Bulgarian *haidouts* are common-law criminals, devoid of personality and lacking even the virile audacity of ordinary brigands.
>
> (Colocotronis 1918: 129; my emphasis)

Here is the legacy of d'Istria, transformed only in that the events of the First World War had ranged Greece and Serbia against Bulgaria, with the result that the Serbs, though Slavs, are now conceptually as well as politically closer to the Greeks. In comparison to the hated Bulgarians, even "ordinary brigands" display that "virile" character which d'Istria had declared to be the innate possession of the European peoples in general. Ideological boundaries are now erected across the existing linguistic ones (*haidout* and *hajduk* vs. *kleftis*, but cf. also Cretan *haïnis*). New cultural discontinuities are perceived where new political alignments have arisen. But the presumption of a Greek national character, exemplified by the behavior of "the klefts" and described in "their" songs, survives such ephemeral transformations.[9]

The Denial of Banditry

The ideal image of the Greek kleft was supported by the content of the published "kleftic songs." There was a certain amount of evidence in these songs, it is true, that the klefts had sometimes been indiscriminate brigands who raided Moslem and Christian alike (e.g., Baggally 1936: 73). Zambelios' suppression of the ransom story nevertheless suggests a pattern of bowdlerization which undoubtedly contributed to the usual picture of uniform patriotism which most of the folklore collections suggest. Songs in which *kleftes* behaved reprehensibly were classified into other categories; thus, a famous song in which a young merchant is ambushed and killed by a brigand (*kleftis*) who turns out to be his own brother is classified as a "ballad" (*paraloyi*; see Ioannou 1975: 97-99). Doubtless this could be justified on the grounds that other, thematically and stylistically similar songs describing fatal family conflicts do not mention klefts at all, so that it is the narrative theme which should determine the taxonomic placement. This, however, means that the entire classification is contingent upon the accident of which songs have been preserved in a sufficient number of variants for such resemblances to be evident. The terms in which the "kleftic" category has been constituted, moreover, are patriotic, historical, and descriptive. This song, however, narrates a sorry tale of fratricide in which social warfare (by the brigands against the wealthy) rather than defense of the homeland provides the setting and even, to some extent, the theme. The category of "kleftic songs" supports a different view of history.

Brigandage against fellow Greeks was thus not subsumed under the Hellenist concept of *kleftouria*. The distinction between the patriot-klefts and the latter-day brigands soon became a feature of the official vocabulary. *Kleptis*, in Classical Greek, had meant "thief," and the Hellenists clearly hoped that the ancient form would reappear in the language with that meaning and that the obviously demotic *kleftis* might retain its newly patriotic sense (see Politis 1871: xxxvi). The latter form was given a set of *katharevousa* inflections, so that a "new" word was actually added in this way to the neo-Classical language—but one which was still recognizably Greek. At the same time, a Classical term, *listis*, was reintroduced to denote "brigand"; all the *post*-revolutionary brigands are so named in official writings. After a while, indeed, the distinction between klefts and brigands became so widely accepted that the negative term, *listis*, acquired a set of alternative demotic inflections; this is the corollary of what happened to *kleftis* in the official tongue.

In 1870 there occurred an event which sharpened the definitional discrimination which had been created in the following manner. Four foreign travelers were murdered by a party of brigands whose extravagant demands for ransom and amnesty had been turned down. Public opinion, both in Greece and abroad, was outraged (see Jenkins 1961). The Hellenists, ever concerned about the external image of Greece, were forced to confront a small epidemic of anti-Greek feeling:

> If, however, one were carefully to go through the ancient and modern history of Greece, he would not find it difficult, if not to induce the West to alter its opinion entirely, then at least to persuade it that by using the word "brigandage" (*listia*) it frequently confuses the Greeks' inherent honor and patriotism—the so-called *pallikarismos*—with it.
>
> But, however eager the Hellene may be to become a kleft in order to exercise his *pallikarismos* at complete liberty in the mountains, to the same degree it is in his nature to reject brigandage (*listia*) . . .
>
> (Goudas n.d.: 1-2)

This is a much more precise statement of the distinction than one encounters in references of only ten or even five years earlier (e.g., Xenos 1865); after the Dilessi incident, kleftism and brigandage were irrevocably exclusive of each other. The more neutral Classical term *kleptis* has, in the course of these semantic shifts, been relegated to the meaning of "petty thief," while the form *kleftis* is generally used for the patriot-brigand of the national redemption (cf. Politis 1973: xii–xviii).

As a major consequence of this development, brigandage has now been defined as foreign to the Greek national character. In the aftermath of the Dilessi incident, this was of great concern to the naturally much embarrassed Greek élite. It has been described as the creation of an "ethnic truth" (Jenkins 1961: 99-117); this is a useful label provided that it is taken not as a concocted falsehood (e.g., Howarth 1976: 122) but as an internally consistent ideological statement. The Greeks did not try to pretend that there were no brigands in Greece at all, despite subsequent foreign claims to the contrary. Their concern was instead to demonstrate that brigandage was extrinsic to the pure Hellenic character, to that collective will which was still in the process of recovering from the foreign yoke. Within the set of definitions which such a perspective entailed, the klefts had been true Greeks; the surviving brigands were either of foreign blood (Albanians, Koutsovlachs) or the relics of Turkish oppression.

This argument had a Classical analogue, in that at least one ancient writer had similarly treated brigandage as something foreign to true Greek culture. Such a parallel lent redoubled force to the nineteenth-century Greek position:

> We are not unaware, moreover, of Thucydides' observation that "the Greeks in OLDEN times *were prone to brigandage*," but Thucydides himself, in the very same book, attributes this hateful deed to the Kares, whom Minos drove out (of Greece), setting up his own sons as leaders. . . . Besides, on the subject of the brigandage (*listia*) done by the Greeks, this same Thucydides says, "They are not ashamed of this deed (i.e., brigandage), but, rather, treat it as something glorious . . . and, until now, most of it, in Greece, is to be found according to the OLD style among the Locrians, the Ozolae, the Aetolians and the Acarnanians, and in Epirus" [I, iv-viii] . Here we must observe, first of all, that Thucydides does not attribute brigandage in Greece to the Hellenes but to the Kares, whom Minos drove out of Greece; and, second, that Thucydides is not writing about his own era but about OLDEN times . . . in his day, only the Locrians, the Ozolae, the Aetolians and the Acarnanians lived in an *old-style* polity, that, in other words, which obtained before the Kares were driven out of Greece.
>
> (Goudas n.d.: 4)

In Crete, villagers still attribute the incidence of animal rustling to the privations and bad moral conditions of the Turkocracy. The point of such a defense is obviously not to claim that banditry literally never occurs. While its endemic nature may not be so freely conceded, as British officials who tried to force the Greek authorities into giving satisfaction discovered, its persistence has to be explained in terms of existing ideological assumptions rather than unrealistically denied out of hand.[10]

Bandits to Nationalists: The Process of Transformation

The progressive canonization of the klefts is manifest in the treatment of songs which mention their activities. As the distinction between klefts and brigands hardened, its effects spread beyond the immediate confines of the "kleftic song" category to other texts in which klefts were mentioned. Since the view prevailed that, for every set of variant texts, one was most "correct" or closest to a putative *Urtext*, one criterion for preferring a particular variant was its apparent endorsement of the prevailing kleftic image.

An example is provided by this song:

> *Mount Olympus and Mount Kissavos are quarreling, the two of them . . .*
> *"Don't cross me, Kissavos, you Turk-trodden mountain . . .*
> *I'm old Olympus, famed throughout the world!"*

And Olympus goes on to boast that on him perches an eagle, holding a kleft's head in its talons. The eagle asks the kleft how he came to die, and the head responds with a tale of his exploits.

To Zambelios (1852: 605) and his followers (e.g., Ellinismos 1896: 92), the song conveyed (and was consequently entitled by them) "Hellenic freedom." Fauriel commented at an early date that the opening theme of the quarreling mountains had apparently been "borrowed" from other folk theme patterns in order to give dramatic emphasis to the heroic portrayal of the kleft (1824: 38-39; cf. Apostolakis 1950: 80). It is known as an independent theme in its own right, as in a similarly disputatious exchange between the three mighty mountains of Crete, although the progressive shortening of Cretan folksongs, which is well documented (cf. Morgan 1960: 50-51), may have deprived it of some comparable narrative conclusion. The theme belongs, however, to a pattern of songs in which the protagonists, who use similar formulaic expressions, may be birds (Kriaris 1920: 243) or flowers (Politis 1914: 235, no. 232); again, there is no attached kleftic tale. The common feature of all these texts is a motif of dissension rather than of specifically national unity.

Such national unity can be read into the text only if the epithet "Turk-trodden" is retained. Without suggesting that the line is in any way spurious,

however, we may legitimately question its historical priority. A version recorded by the German philhellene Theodor Kind has "kleft-trodden" addressed *by* Kissavos *to* Olympus (1833: 1-2). If it was sometimes insulting to
be called "kleft-trodden" before 1833, this is further evidence for a change in
the significance of *kleftis*. The sequence of textual changes, however, is less
easy to interpret, especially as Haxthausen records a still earlier rendering
with a form of "Turk-trampled" (1935: 48, no. 9).

But, what is perhaps most revealing of all, in the third edition of his collection Kind replaced his own original text with a "Turk-trodden" (*koniaropati-
mene*)[11] version taken from an anonymous Athenian disquisition, *On the
State* (Kind 1861: 24-27, 225). Again, this is not, in all probability, a case of
deliberate distortion; Kind does cite the source for his new rendering. But
what must have recommended the 1861 text to him was the fact that it made
far better sense than the 1833 variant in terms of the philhellenic-Hellenist
ideology. It represented the klefts as an unambiguously positive category, in
explicit opposition to a named, *national* enemy.

Regional Claims on National Character

The quarrel between Olympus and Kissavos, while perhaps sometimes interpreted as an expression of nationwide values, also reveals the intense localism
that often characterized relations among the various guerrilla groups and village communities involved in the fight for freedom. Such localism was likewise not uncommon among scholars and writers and became noticeably
stronger as amateur folklorists began to emerge from the ranks of the schoolteachers and other educated members of local communities. Even among the
professional scholars, the same phenomenon can be observed. It did not
necessarily conflict directly with the nationalist ideal, however, as local allegiances often took the form of claiming that the home region was the finest
repository of that ideal. Nor should the work of local folklorists be under-
estimated in assessing their contribution to the growth of national consciousness. Especially in Asia Minor (see Bryer 1976: 186-189), these enthusiasts
discovered and published the evidence of persistent and flourishing Greek
culture.

The province of Epirus remained under Turkish rule until the Greek in-
vasion of 1913. Many of the klefts who had aided in the liberation of the rest
of Greece were from Epirus, and sustained efforts were made to show that
these men and their exploits, the continued occupation of the province not-
withstanding, exemplified the heroic tradition of the Hellenes. In particular,
Epirote folklore proved a rich source of "kleftic songs," so much so that this
genre was soon said to be of Epirote origin in its entirety. Indeed, the extreme view was sometimes taken that *all* Greek folksong had originated in

Epirus (see especially Khristovasilis 1902). But the "kleftic songs" proved to be a particularly popular focus with local folklorists; the large number of texts actually recorded in Epirus itself is evidence of the collectors' enthusiasm as well as of, perhaps, the late demise of "legitimate" kleftism in the province. The quantity of accredited Epirote texts also benefited from the local folklorists' methodological assumptions:

> And if on the one hand it is true that amongst the above [texts] reckoned [by us as Epirote] there are some which are common in other rural districts of Greece, and thus not to be classified as purely Epirote, yet—since it is difficult to establish their homeland (*patris*), and they are to be encountered in general use in Epirus—we are justified in accounting them as such.   (Aravandinos 1880: ix)

Such reasoning is not always restricted to the single category of "kleftic songs":

> But, if Epirus is the homeland (*patridha*) of the kleftic songs, it is no less the home of the songs of exile. Naturally, other regions also have their songs of exile, but Epirus stands in the front rank. [This is] because the poverty-stricken populace of Epirus was given to emigration as far back as prehistoric times.... Out of the numbers of the expatriate Epirotes came the Great Benefactors of the nation (*ethnos*), making Epirus the intellectual center of Hellenism during the years of servitude.... Again, the funeral dirges (*miroloyia*), a pure product of the Epirote women's creativity, are among the most moving in the world *and may compete with the famous Maniat laments*: both sets originate in the ancient laments of the Hellenes.
>   (Yangas n.d.: 25; my emphasis)

Note the explicit statement of competitive relations within the larger, national unity. Since the loyalties concerned are essentially concentric, rather than opposed to each other, the smaller allegiance could be justified in terms of the larger.

This balance between the two loyalties is especially well illustrated by the Epirote folklorists' treatment of the "kleftic songs." It was assumed that these songs would be found in their pristine form only in places where the klefts had been active; their presence was thus indicative of a region's devotion to the national cause. But they could also be used to point out the regional exemplification of true Hellenism in another way. Since these "kleftic songs" were commonly taken as the prototypical Greek folksongs par excellence, it was by attributing their origin to Epirus that local folklorists could argue that the province was the fount of all Greek folksong without exception (Aravandinos 1880: vii–ix; Yangas n.d.: 23-25). The success of their claim may be gauged from the alacrity with which the proponents of other localisms (e.g., Lanitis 1946 for Cyprus) accepted it, even while hymning the aesthetic qualities of their own local songs.

The Epirotes' argument depended on the successful blending of taxonomies. On the one hand, the historical and folkloristic "kleftic" categories were already immune to effective challenge within Greece. On the other hand, the classification of Greece by geographical regions had not yet settled down to its present exact disposition. The Epirus to which Aravandinos referred was larger than the modern province of the same name (Yangas n.d.: 23). Even aside from "Northern Epirus," which is today part of Albania, sections of the old Turkish Epirus are today incorporated into two other provinces of the Greek State. In short, there was some confusion over precisely what Epirus was. It was consequently possible to propound different cultural configurations on the basis of these differing definitions of the provincial borders, and Aravandinos' defense of the Epirote contribution to Hellenism was helped by his inclusion of a larger area and, therefore, of a greater demographic and cultural reservoir.

Aravandinos restricted his argument, however, to the comparatively modest claim that, if a song were known to Epirote singers, it could then be considered Epirote *in that sense* (1880: ix). His position was then extended to a more contentious view by Yangas. After first apparently endorsing Aravandinos' position, he showed that his conception of cultural origins was of a far more literal order: he complained of "hearing kleftic songs described on the radio as Peloponnesian, when they are nothing other than kleftic songs" (n.d.: 24). Since for Yangas kleftic songs were by definition Epirote, his position may be paraphrased: when songs are sung in Epirus they are Epirote; but, when they are sung in the Peloponnese, they are merely variants of Epirote songs.

Language and National Character: The Koutsovlach Case

The richness of the ethnographic record in Epirus thus served to illustrate the Hellenic heritage of the region. That same record, however, differently interpreted, could have posed a serious liability because of the province's several minority groups, which could and sometimes did offer neighboring countries the pretext for making territorial claims. The most consistently sensitive group of this kind was that of the Koutsovlachs; their language is closely akin to Romanian, and this has led Romanian scholars (e.g., Capidan n.d.) to advance ethnological arguments in support of their country's territorial interests. The Greek response has been largely philological, ranging from the "political philology" which derived *Koutsovlakhos* from Turkish roots to mean "only slightly Wallachian"[12] (Wace and Thompson 1914: 3) to a recent word count of the Koutsovlach language in which "the Turkish [words] have been counted among the modern Greek ones" (Papazisis 1976: 8), presumably on the assumption that they must have been channeled to Koutsovlach via Greek.

Such academic contortion was not an immediate political necessity, although it was doubtless intensified under the incessant pressures of Balkan realpolitik. To understand the Greeks' response in context, it is necessary to stress two fundamental points. First, they were not alone in using scholarly arguments for such purposes. Capidan's ethnological arguments for the Romanian case were matched by Bulgarian and Yugoslav attempts to claim parts of Greek Macedonia as their own. Second, while the Greeks might have rested their case with the simple argument that the Koutsovlachs were a numerical minority within a political nation-state, their own original claims to nationhood had been based on the concept of cultural resurgence; this imposed a certain pattern on their subsequent dealings with other newly formed Balkan states, at least in terms of scholarly and political rhetoric.

Folksongs, as linguistic evidence as well as the expression of *Volksgeist*, naturally fed these disputatious fires. The songs of the Koutsovlachs were of special interest to the Greek apologists, because some were in Greek rather than the Koutsovlachs' own language; of these, furthermore, many were "kleftic." Koutsovlachs, too, had made a signal contribution to the cause of Greek independence (see Papazisis 1976). Thus, although it is the Koutsovlachs' language which marks them as a distinctive group to this day (cf. Schein 1975), their performance of "kleftic" songs in Epirote Greek provides a potential basis for demonstrating their espousal of the Greek national consciousness. Local folklorists soon seized on this point.

Once again, the perception of ethnological relationships depends on the processes by which evidence is selected as relevant. It is true that the Koutsovlachs sing many songs in Greek, and the Koutsovlach community of Metsovo is bilingual. On the other hand, there are also many songs in the Koutsovlach language. These are often excluded from the published folklore, since few non-Koutsovlachs would be able to read them; in effect, then, they are excluded from "Hellenic laography" at large. The Greek-language songs, by contrast, are given primary significance. The Koutsovlachs, writes Aravandinos,

> though they do not use the Greek language at home, nevertheless compose [*sic*!] their songs in it. The reader will find many such songs in the present collection, mostly gathered in Metsovo, Grevena, and Malakasi— Vlach districts in part, certainly, but where one almost never hears a Vlach song. In their dances, at weddings, saint's day festivities, or at home when their women sing lullabies to their babies or keen dirges

> over the dead, they always sing in Greek, even though occasionally some of them, *in their ignorance of the Greek language,* do not precisely understand the meaning of what they sing. Let this therefore stand as *yet one more proof of the almost complete assimilation of this race with that of the Hellenes.*   (1880: vii; my emphasis)

The author of these words, though undoubtedly eager to claim a special role for his much loved Epirus, was certainly no secessionist.[13] On the contrary, localism of this sort was but a more minutely focused expression of ideological Hellenism. The literature is full of essays in which a particular region is held up as the fullest realization of Greek culture.[14] Like the essays of more obviously national scope, moreover, these localist works looked to European models of propriety. Aravandinos, for example, cleaned up his klefts; "that dog" became "the bad man" (Apostolakis 1950: 77, n. 2). For, if the klefts embodied Greek heroism, they must also participate in "the virile habits of the Europeans." So, too, must all those members of minority groups whose destiny it is to enter the national consciousness of the Hellenes.

Such was the Hellenists' perspective. It is the perspective which we encounter when a Greek refers to "Europe" (*Evropi*) as including Greece. Yet there is an alternative usage, whereby "Europe" and "Greece" are treated as terms in a complementary opposition; and here the view expressed is the Romeic one, with its readier acceptance of Greece's more recent past. European observers in the nineteenth century were mostly inclined to favor the former interpretation. There was, however, one exponent, not so much of a "Romeic" as of a virulently anti-Greek culture theory. This was the *bête noire* already mentioned earlier, Jakob Philipp Fallmerayer. Now it is time to step back to the earliest years of Greek independence, to examine Fallmerayer's ideas in brief review, and to trace their galvanizing effect on the development of Greek folklore research.

Chapter 4
Attack and Reaction

". . . no Greek but a Slav . . ."

Fallmerayer against Hellas

The constitution of "the klefts" as a chronologically and ethnically bounded entity served three closely interconnected aims of the Hellenist ideology. It presented the modern Greeks as worthy descendants of the ancient heroes; it validated their claim, as true individualists, to a Hellenic and therefore also to a European cultural identity; and it provided a theme which would permit the conceptual assimilation of Christian ethnic minorities to that identity. These three goals were essential components of the philhellenic and nationalist search for a Greek "national consciousness." The kleftic theme has provided us with a specific context in which to examine in some detail how these goals were pursued. The creation of a kleftic history and folklore serves as a paradigm for the emergent methods of national culture history in mid nineteenth-century Greece.

We now return to the broader canvas. For the importance which Greek nationalists attributed to kleftism was by no means an isolated phenomenon, as must already be evident. More generally, indeed, the concern to establish a national history might never have generated such impressive results had it not been for the provocation offered by those foreigners who, unlike the more numerous philhellenes, had scant liking for the Greek cause. Chief among these was Jakob Philipp Fallmerayer (1790-1861), a pamphleteer, historian, and liberal pan-German nationalist of Tyrolean origin. The very name of Fallmerayer has been execrated in Greece from 1830 until our own time as the symbol and epitome of anti-Greek sentiment. That execration, however, was extraordinarily productive, for Fallmerayer flung down a challenge which the Greeks could ill afford to ignore; and they met it magnificently.[1]

Fallmerayer's crime consisted in denying the Greeks their claim to descent from the ancient Hellenes. Enough has already been said about that claim to show that he was, in effect, denying them their national raison d'être. In explicitly treating modern Greece as conceptually outside "Europe," moreover,

Fallmerayer (1845, II: 259-260) expressed a perspective which conflicted terminologically, ideologically, and politically with the Greeks' national aspirations. Unlike Kind (1861: xxii-xxiii), who proposed a pan-European folklore concordance that would include all the Greek material, Fallmerayer rejected the very notion of the Greeks as Europeans. He not only regarded them as mere chattels of an oriental dominion but argued that their claims to Hellenic identity had completely misled the gullible intelligentsia of "true" Europe (1845, II: 261). He thus made political capital of the ambiguity of the term "Europe" in the Greek context. The Greeks, not to be outdone, contemptuously informed him that he was "no Greek but a Slav" (Fallmerayer 1845, II: 462). In this debate, nationality and ideology were fully conflated.

Fallmerayer was not the first foreigner to sneer at the claims of Greek nationalism, but his use of supposedly ethnographic evidence for that purpose was certainly something new. Other observers who felt that the Greeks were not yet ready for self-government nevertheless conceded their essential Greekness. The British aristocrat F. S. N. Douglas, a notable exponent of this more moderate attitude, was convinced that the Greeks of his day still spoke a language akin to Classical Greek, although he "called the present Greek language Romaic, the term by which the modern Greeks distinguish themselves on account of their titular character of Romans, in distinction to Hellenic, by which they designate their ancestors" (1813: 30). He listed numerous parallels between ancient and modern custom in ritual, marriage practices, feasting, symbolism, and religious attitudes. None of this prevented him from opposing Greek independence; any threat to Turkish power was an encouragement to Russian ambitions in the area, and these ran directly counter to British interests (e.g., 1813: 187-195). In particular, Douglas feared the possible consequences for British trade should Russia ever gain control of Constantinople. "These may be considered as only national and British arguments: but while the weight of ignorance and superstition continues to oppress the Greeks, in vain may you confer upon them nominal freedom [*sic*!]: they cannot feel the value of the gift you bestow." The logic is that of the purest nineteenth-century colonialism: "An infant may be more safely entrusted with a sword, than the ignorant and the bigotted with the sacred weapon of liberty and dominion" (1813: 197). In the end, however, "if the wild fancies of politicians and enthusiasts do not hurry them out of the course in which they are advancing with cautious but accelerated steps, another age may witness the glorious period when the torch of knowledge shall conduct the Greeks to the enjoyment of happiness and freedom" (1813: 198). Events did not await the pleasure of this British apologist, but they did not bring the Russians to Constantinople either. Nevertheless, the fear that this might happen was a very real one at the time.

It is in his fear of Russia, moreover, that Douglas anticipates Fallmerayer. He shared with the German writer the conviction that the modern Greeks were largely descended from Hellenized *barbaroi* (1813: 40), attributing to this the features which to his mind bespoke decadence and superstition. Unlike Fallmerayer, however, Douglas also accepted a substantial element of true Hellenism in the modern Greeks; thus, he argued, when they showed that they once again measured up to the standards of their illustrious ancestors—standards which only a true "European" could judge!—they might then be allowed to have their independence.

Fallmerayer, similarly motivated by the fear of Russian expansionism, nevertheless developed a far more sweeping attack on Greek national identity. He denied the very basis of that identity as conceived by philhellenes and Greek nationalists alike, arguing that the Classical Greeks' heritage could not possibly have survived successive Slav and Albanian invasions during the Byzantine era; as a result, he maintained, the present population of the country must be of entirely non-Greek "racial" origin. His evidence for these claims was historical and cultural rather than genetic. Like his detractors (and, indeed, most of his contemporaries), he made no distinction between these two aspects of the problem, the cultural and the "racial," using the evidence of the one in order to support claims related to the other; it was not until later (Wachsmuth 1864; Lawson 1910: 25-28) that this crucial refinement was brought to the debate. Both Fallmerayer and the Greek nationalists saw the modern Greeks' "racial" origins as the key issue and ethnographic and historical evidence as the means of resolving it. They differed, however, both in their conclusions and in the political principles which guided their researches. It was the political aspect, furthermore, which determined those principles of selection and ordering by which we may explain so radical a divergence in their respective conclusions.

Fallmerayer's political stance offers a study in internal contradiction. Although aggressively liberal in domestic matters, he was "an ardent supporter of the Ottoman Empire" (Hussey 1978: 83). This was not merely a case of double political standards, although the Ottoman sultans were regarded in European intellectual circles as the very incarnation of despotism. Rather, it should be seen in the context of Fallmerayer's commitment to German unification. A liberal, united Germany would not be able, he thought, to resist the territorial ambitions of a strong Russia; therefore, any obstacle to Russian power was welcome. The older Fallmerayer grew, the more he protested against what was seen as the increasingly probable dissolution of the Ottoman Empire. His view of the importance of Turkey, which was shared by some of his German contemporaries, was to become a key motivation in postunification German policy in the Balkans (see Couloumbis, Petropulos, and Psomiades 1976: 30-32; Taillandier 1862: 129-130). Fallmerayer's fierce convictions in this respect certainly explain his implacable opposition to Greek nationalism and, perhaps, help show why he was apparently more extreme in his published views on Greek racial origins than he was in private conversation (Hussey 1978: 83).

Fallmerayer was thus not merely an academic commentator; his views held enormous political significance both for himself and for the Greeks. Abroad, his theories threatened to erode support for the Greek cause, or so his opponents feared. Within Greece, dominated as it was by a foreign monarchy and bureaucracy, he represented a potentially serious danger. Even King Otto came increasingly to endorse his views and to refer to them in his dealings with diplomats and administrators (Hussey 1978: 80). The view expressed by a fellow German, K. B. Hase, that Fallmerayer's theories could be endorsed without danger to the nation-state was thus hardly a plausible one. Even Fallmerayer himself did not trouble to dissociate his ethnology from his anti-Russian feelings. It may even be that he was aware that some of the earliest collectors of Greek folklore, notably Mustoxidi and Papadopoulos-Vrettos, had been ardently pro-Russian.

The truth of the matter is, of course, that virtually any position on the question of Greek ethnicity would have been invested with political significance: given the circumstances under which Greece became a nation-state, there was quite simply no such thing as a neutral stance. Fallmerayer, bluffly insensitive to such matters, seems to have been genuinely amazed at the hostile reception he received on the occasion of his first visit to Greece in 1840 (cf. also Politis 1871: ii). Undoubtedly, there was some irritation at his having performed his armchair ethnology *before* visiting the land itself. An instructive contrast is provided by the Frenchman Edgar Quinet, who initially shared some of Fallmerayer's interest in the Slavic and Albanian heritage of the modern Greeks; but Quinet expressed his views *after* visiting the country and subsequently modified them in deference to the young nation's quest for recognition (Karatza 1970: 48). However one approached it, the problem of Hellenic authenticity could not be separated from ideology, and Fallmerayer's attitude represented a threatening extreme.

It was in 1830 that Fallmerayer first achieved notoriety in the annals of Greek cultural studies, with the publication of volume 1 of his ethnologically oriented history of the Peloponnese (Morea). In this work, Fallmerayer first expounded in detail the theory that so enraged the Greeks and their supporters: the original Hellenic population had been completely destroyed and replaced in the course of successive invasions during the Byzantine period. Although he had already begun to establish his academic standing with his historical work on Trebizond, his Peloponnesian history gave his views on modern Greek ethnicity their first wide exposure. The reaction, which was further exacerbated by his subsequent writings (1845, 1860), was furious and sustained. Not only Greeks but foreign scholars also leaped into the fray; prominent among the foreigners were two other Germans, Kurt Wachsmuth and Bernhard Schmidt. Greek ethnology was suddenly well on its way.

Whether judged by contemporary or present-day standards, Fallmerayer's scholarship is uneven at best and makes extensive use of special pleading and blank assertion. For example, he attributed the absence of an aspirate (/h/) in modern Greek to Slavic influence, on the grounds that the Cyrillic alphabet used a *g* for the aspirate of foreign words (e.g., "Gamburg"; see Fallmerayer 1830: 236). Such confusion of the phonetic with the alphabetic makes for a weak philological argument, especially since the closeness of modern to ancient Greek in general was already well established by Fallmerayer's time. In another attempt to demonstrate the Slavicization of the Greek language, Fallmerayer contended that the loss of the infinitive verb forms in Greek was similarly the result of foreign models. This view did not stand up to close inspection for very long; it was soon established that the dropping of the infinitive forms occurred earlier in Greek than in neighboring languages (Hesseling 1892: 43–44; Sandfeld 1930: 178; Joseph 1978).[2] As for Fallmerayer's complaint that the modern Athenians spoke Albanian, this impressed few observers as having any real significance since (as he himself recognized) the Athenians also spoke Greek. One of his earliest Greek critics, Anastasios Lefkias, offered the sensible rejoinder that, since bilingualism and trilingualism in Northern Europe were not always taken as indicating separate nationality, it was scarcely reasonable to insist on so interpreting them in Greece (1843: 52). Much the same kind of objection may be raised against Fallmerayer's use of toponyms. Slavic place-names have little more bearing on the inhabitants' ethnicity or ancestry than do their present-day Hellenized replacements. They are an indication, certainly, of some sort of political or cultural event, but they do not justify claims of massive demographic change.

While some of these objections are more easily made with the help of concepts and materials that were not available to Fallmerayer's contemporaries, there is no doubt that they were uncomfortable with his polemical mode of argument. Many of them were nevertheless tempted into much the same intemperate style when responding to him, often at the expense of scholarship in those early years (but cf. Politis 1871). Even Lefkias, for all his perceptiveness on the subject of bilingualism, was not above hyperbole, as the title of his crusading treatise against Fallmerayerism shows: *Overthrow of What Has Been Claimed* . . . The fact of the matter is that the entire scholarly establishment of Greece was both dismayed and profoundly offended by Fallmerayer's activities.

The most remarkable outcome of the Greek reaction was the sudden flowering of folklore studies. While it would be absurd to suggest that folklore would never have attracted scholarly interest without the stimulus pro-

vided by Fallmerayer, it is certainly true that much of the best work done by
the first Greek folklorists represents a conscious response to the German
scholar's theories—and the political implications of these theories insured
folklore a role in Greek national life that was much more than purely academic. Most, if not all, of the volumes of "national folklore" which appeared
in the years between Fallmerayer's *Geschichte* and the beginning of the twentieth century were directly inspired by the goal of proving "the German"
wrong. Not all the folklorists explicitly said that this was their intention;
Zambelios, for example, does not, although a reviewer praised his essay on
the word *traghoudho* as "demolishing the rotten edifice of the crazy historian
from Germany" (Anon. 1859-60: 495). The reviewer made it abundantly
clear, moreover, that the "patriotic or archaeological" import of Zambelios'
work was appreciated:

> . . . words signify objects, and objects have history. As the discovery of
> a stone bearing some phrase engraved upon it, a name or a date, often
> clarifies an obscure aspect of antiquity, so too the philosophical in-
> vestigation of the origins, rise, decline, and degeneration of a word
> sometimes suffices not only to correct or refute erroneous opinions
> about history but also, by Zeus! to bear witness to the identity of an
> entire nation (*ethnos*).

The national significance of Zambelios' argument was so unambiguous that
neither he nor his reviewer had to mention Fallmerayer by name. Papadopoulos-Vrettos had already noted of Zambelios' 1852 historical work that "the
study of the history of one's forefathers is rarely a purely theoretical study.
But for us this history has come to acquire a more practical significance than
is usual, since the time that this historical doctrine took hold and began to
spread, that the great turmoil of medieval times totally uprooted the hoary
tree of ancient Hellenism" (1852-53: 397). Readers of such words did not
need to be reminded that this was the critical issue for their national identity
or that Fallmerayer was the target.

In describing the effects of Fallmerayer's writings upon the growth of
Greek folklore studies generally, we shall depart somewhat from strict chronological order. The development of a nationalist discipline of folklore in
Greece was not a simple chain of cause and effect or a straightforwardly unilineal sequence of books and articles. The development of a taxonomic system which adequately reflected the concerns of the Greek folklorists and
historians was uneven, a process of trial and error involving a wide range of
personalities and interests. In order to discern what presuppositions guided
Fallmerayer's critics, we may begin not necessarily with the earliest but with
some of the most vitriolic and uncompromising of their responses. If some of

these seem absurd today, that is partly because time and place no longer give
them meaning. In the context of the newly emergent Greek nation-state,
however, what might otherwise pass for mere invective cries out instead as the
voice of a passionate, threatened commitment. Some of the apparent absurdity, moreover, simply reflects the very different state of anthropological and
linguistic method at that time, not only in Greece but throughout all of
Europe.

We should also remember that, at a less overt level, the reaction was not
directed at Fallmerayer alone, although he was no mere figurehead. In the
early years of the Greek kingdom, anti-German sentiment was provoked by
the high-handedness of King Otto and his advisers. Even after major popular
unrest led, in 1844, to the nominal curtailment of the king's powers, the
work of his earliest ministers in fashioning a "European" administration remained to plague their successors. The entire legal code, for example, was
drawn up by the Bavarian Georg von Maurer. In 1853, when an ostensibly
more "nativist" government commissioned L. Khrisanthopoulos to conduct
a survey of traditional family and inheritance law in the provinces, the questions which this agent sent the local authorities were all predetermined by the
"European" categories of von Maurer's code. The strains were never fully al-
leviated. Popular unrest flared repeatedly; Otto himself was finally deposed in
1862, only to be replaced the following year by yet another foreigner, a
Danish prince who became King George I.

Up to that point, then, Greece was ruled by an unpopular foreign monarch
who fell increasingly under Fallmerayer's influence and who was served by
ministers who largely shared with him a set of values alien to the populace.
The Greek intelligentsia, while sharing their commitment to the nation-state
ideal at the most general level, did not necessarily join in their enthusiasm for
the institution of monarchy. The Greeks also saw both that their national
self-respect demanded their firm resistance to Fallmerayer's influence and
that the justification for a Greek State would ultimately stand or fall on the
ethnological question. At one level, the rest of this book is an account of the
way in which they fought that battle.

Lelekos: A Poetic Response

One prominent participant was Michael Lelekos, who published works on
folklore in 1852 (second edition, 1868) and 1888. Sure that his own elab-
orately doctored "folk" texts had furnished proof incontrovertible of the
Greeks' Hellenic identity, he concluded his first essay with a triumphant
ode in an extreme form of neo-Classical Greek addressed "to the German,
Fallmerayer":

Croak now as thou wouldst, O raven,
  Now behold in thy covetous sight,
Thou black villain in armor black-bronzèd—
  Fallmerayer! O bitter, cruel wight!

Tho' antiently gripp'd in midwinter,
  Of the Hellenes that Olympiad—
After centuries, centuries fighting—
  Sings high odes as she formerly had.

Hail! airy daughter of Tantalus,
  Hail! bashful Muse, who singst fair.
The voices of envy's brave offspring
  Hast thou utterly silenced fore'er . . .

(1868: 224)

The collector-poet apparently saw no irony in this proud claim. The "high odes" to which he refers were nevertheless extensively rewritten (and sometimes entirely concocted) by Lelekos himself (see especially Vlakhoyannis 1935: 228-232), in order to supply Classical parallels whenever none could be wrung from the untouched originals of the folksong texts.

Some of his texts seem to be outright forgeries. Direct references to Sophocles (1868: 31) and to "the Persian dogs" (1868: 21; this refers to the Turks—a metaphorical association of the ancient and the recent) are surprising in any folk text at so early a date, before widespread education had wrought extensive changes in the language and imagery of folk poetry. Likewise, the characterization of the Albanian ruler of Yannina, Ali Pasha, as a *tyrannos* ("tyrant") sounds like a suspiciously Classical gloss for any of a whole range of equally trenchant demotic terms (1868: 52).[3] Sometimes, Lelekos gives what may perhaps be adjusted forms in mid text (e.g., *ton* for *tous* in 1868: 126, 1. 30). On occasion, the purpose of all this classicizing virtually declares itself:

Leonidas' sword—
Kolokotronis wears it;
as soon as a Turk sees it he falls wounded
and his blood runs ice-cold. . . .

(1868: 25, no. 5)

Such texts are clearly "offered to national philology," and the "protests which the mountain-dwelling priests of liberty sang in the mountains and caves at times of national adventure and tyrannical proscriptions of Hellenism" have in many instances been amplified or composed with that purpose in mind (Lelekos 1852: iii, v; cf. also Apostolakis 1929: 115, n. 1).

Many of Lelekos' footnoted parallels with the great Attic dramatists and other ancient authors seem especially contrived. When no obvious parallel with antiquity could be found, he supplied weighty paraphrases of the songs themselves in neo-Classical doggerel. As an exercise in projecting the "European" image, the latter device was entirely characteristic: although the words and grammatical forms were largely simplified Classical Greek, he also used rhyme—which was not Classical but had a long and respectable ancestry in more recent Western European poetry as well as in vernacular Greek. Unlike the forged folksong texts, all these neo-Classical renditions as well as a few specially composed celebratory verses (including the ode to Fallmerayer) bear Lelekos' own name or initials. In this way, he "foregrounded" his own assumed role as the interpreter of vernacular poetry to an educated posterity.

That the forgeries escaped attention for many decades is not as surprising as it may seem. For one thing, textual accuracy had not yet become quite as much of a fundamental doctrine as it is in modern folklore scholarship. Insofar as he thought about it consciously, Lelekos may even have felt entitled, as a Greek, to participate actively in both the vernacular and the scholarly traditions. Furthermore, it was well understood by his Greek contemporaries that the value of Lelekos' work lay not only in the preservation of a steadily disappearing heritage (the same reason that had prompted the periodical *Pandora* to publish folksongs sporadically from 1854 on) but also in the presentation of that heritage to the West. Lelekos himself seems to have formed a highly personal view of the latter goal, showing at every juncture that he hoped to convince even Fallmerayer that Greek folksongs preserved "both the language and poetry and the manners and customs of their [i.e., the Greeks'] fathers, pure and genuine" (1868: 224). Other Greek commentators, while praising Lelekos' efforts, took a broader view of their significance. A group of professors and headmasters, in recommending that the Ministry of Church Affairs and Public Education reward Lelekos' dedication financially, remarked—in a manner strikingly reminiscent of Zambelios—that "our nation's popular songs are so much admired by the Europeans that Mendelssohn, that historian of modern Greece, was not slow to say that no art poetry possesses such internal power or deep feeling"; the group went on to list the names of Fauriel, Kind, and Passow as other worthy saviors of this precious heritage (Lelekos 1888: 5). Even had they been aware of Lelekos' textual interventions, it is unlikely that these enthusiasts would have felt terribly put out.

On the contrary, Lelekos' additions and alterations were a means of strengthening the case for cultural continuity. Not only was textual accuracy still a relatively minor issue, but, in a manner of speaking, the reverse principle held sway: the *folk* had corrupted their heritage, so that it was the task of scholars to purify it anew. In Lelekos' later collection, his supporters declared, "one could recognize as in a crystal-clear mirror the physiognomy of the Hellenic nation as it was in the years when, living in servitude, it could demonstrate only the very slightest trace of its character in political and public life. For this reason we judge these [songs] , *given careful cleaning and accurate classification*, most worthy of publication as a national treasure, and the labors of Mr. Lelekos in collecting them both impeccable [*sic*] and deserving of reward by the honorable Government" (Lelekos 1888: 7-8; my emphasis). Finally, the committee members point out, Lelekos deserved praise from *both Greeks and foreigners* for his work.

Three interrelated aspects of this statement are central to our theme. First, there is the reiterated appeal to foreign observers, as well as the concern that Lelekos' work should reflect glory on his country in their eyes. This reproduces Lelekos' own earlier affirmation of pride in the interest which Greek folksongs had already elicited from "German, French, and Italian neo-Hellenists" (1852: v). Second, for such an international appeal to be properly effective, the historical and spiritual purity of the texts themselves had to be restored before they could be published. Lelekos was especially well qualified for this task, thought his admirers, because he had devoted many years to the necessary research and had already (1852) published a book on it. In any case, there is no sign of doubt as to the necessity or propriety of textual emendation. The attitude which lies behind this state of affairs both reinforced and was fed by the presupposition of cultural continuity: since folk poets were the heirs of the Classical tradition, that tradition would provide the appropriate criteria for textual criticism by appropriately qualified scholars.

The third aspect of the committee's statement, though not heavily stressed in the official letter, is crucially important. It concerns the question of "accurate classification." Explicit interest in taxonomy was relatively slow to appear in the writings of the Greek folklorists, although the presuppositions on which it came to be based are present from the beginning. The various references to a category of "kleftic songs" are the first signs of its emergence as a central issue. Even before these became systematic, however, something of the same concern can be seen in the titles which the earliest collectors gave their folksongs. Lelekos himself actually did little to advance classificatory principles, but his supporters' enthusiasm for this aspect of his work is all the more revealing for that reason: it shows that they, at least, sensed the implications of the song titles and even of the order in which the texts were ranged. These implications still awaited a scholar who would articulate them into a comprehensive scheme of classification. Nonetheless, they were gradually taking on a more palpable form.

One factor which contributed to this process was the sheer volume of the material collected. Clearly, as the collections grew in number and size, some sort of order would have to be introduced, and for this purpose selectional criteria had to be formulated. While the earlier writers like Zambelios and Lelekos do not seem, from a present-day perspective, to have achieved a great deal of taxonomic sophistication, their attempts to equip texts with titles indicate an emergent awareness of the problem. In heading a "kleftic song" with its hero's name, for example, they indicated their sense that the song had something in common with those of the "historical" category.

But there is another guiding principle in Lelekos' work which is no less taxonomic for rarely being recognized as such. This is the process of selection whereby texts either were accepted as suitably "Hellenic" or were Hellenized to a sufficient degree. Implicit in this operation is a set of assumptions, not merely about folksongs but about vernacular culture in general: certain things were *Greek*, others were not, and the validating criterion was a demonstrable link with antiquity. In other words, the ethnological division between Greek and non-Greek was translatable into a historical theory of origins. This was the encompassing principle of the entire emergent system of classification of Greek folklore.

Lelekos' espousal of this principle may seem exceptionally immoderate today. It is nevertheless of great interest, in that it highlights the selectional principle involved. That his work was acceptable to his academic peers is evident in their support for his venture and in his hopes—realized in the form of funding for his later book—of government recognition. It is easy today to see Lelekos as an insufferable pedant and a poor scholar, to criticize the rambling format of his writings. But in his own day what he did exemplified an entire tradition of nationalistic scholarship and, as such, is still of prime significance in understanding that tradition.

For Lelekos' writings established folk poetry as recognizably *Greek*. He was not the first to do this, of course, but his uncompromising commitment to the task he set himself put him in the front line of the anti-Fallmerayer crusade. As he wrote:

> The poetic spirit which characterizes these popular epics does not reflect adulation or imitation of foreign models, nor does the arrogant pomposity of braggartism and noise sully their excellence; but sometimes the phrasing of the epic pours down in a rushing, living stream, to refresh the aesthetic judgment of the reader, sometimes the striving of the kleftic soldier-poet against tyranny and subjugation crashes thunderously out, sometimes again ecstatic love beholds its very own language and gracefully phrased, delicate expression in the expressiveness [*sic*] of a single love couplet. (1852: iii)

In this passage, the connections with Classical literature are spelled out with explicit clarity, so that we can see how the methods of Classical philology established a virtual template for the study of the modern oral traditions of Greece. In particular, the peculiar taxonomic idiom of that scholarly tradition has taken firm hold. Songs of perhaps fifteen lines of verbal text are described as "epics," a term which recalls the ancient glories of a very different genre (cf. Bynum 1969). The poetic virtues are those not of a foreign elegance but of a homespun honesty and expressiveness. The message is the same as the one which we have already encountered in the writings of d'Istria and Zambelios: there is something untarnishably, uniquely Greek both in the material itself and in the deeds which it celebrates. To such material, only the methods of Classical scholarship can do sufficient honor.

Vivilakis: A Scholarly Response

Lelekos' works, although largely devoted to songs, contain a limited amount of other material, such as dialect forms, descriptions of customs, and proverbial phrases—a somewhat uneven miscellany. Here, too, a major classificatory problem lurked, as yet unformulated: how could the rapidly increasing laographic corpus be organized so that materials of different kinds might be separately recorded but efficiently cross-referenced? The scope of Lelekos' interests did not extend to tackling this issue. Others, however, had already begun to deal with it, on the basis of selectional criteria that had once again largely originated in the antiquarian scholarship of Western Europe.

The title of Douglas' *Essay on Certain Points of Resemblance between the Ancient and Modern Greeks* spells out the main organizing focus of this endeavor. His account, however, was not a systematic collection; it represents a rather haphazard search for ethnographic evidence, although the search for identifiable parallels certainly acted as a filter through which the experiences of Douglas and other travel-minded authors could be sifted.

In Germany, however, more thorough ethnological research soon began, notably the remarkable work of a Greek scholar. In 1840 in Berlin, Emmanuel Vivilakis (Bybilakis), a Cretan who had lived through the War of Independence in Greece, published a short but significant treatise on parallels between ancient and modern Greek life. His aim was explicit:

> . . . to make an accurate comparison of the manners and customs of ancient with those of modern Greece, and therein to provide irrefutable proof not only that ancient Hellas is as yet far from defunct but that, just as these customs dwelt in her millennia ago, so today they live on in her children's children; that the preservation of the same manners and customs would have been impossible had there taken place at any one time a complete interruption in the existence of this people (*Volk*); finally, that the assertions of certain individuals (their number is for-

tunately quite negligible) are quite as far from the truth as heaven from earth, when they publish its very opposite *hōs ek tripodos* ("as from the [oracular] tripod [of the ancients] "), "in order," as they say, "to rescue educated Europe from the erroneous views it has held heretofore concerning the descent of today's Hellenes from the ancient Greeks."

(1840: viii–ix)

This first real salvo from the Greek side both anticipates Lelekos' works chronologically and surpasses them in scholarly sophistication. The reference to Fallmerayer is quite unambiguous, and the irritation over his attempt to divide "Greece" from "Europe" stands out sharply.

Vivilakis' argument, clearly and simply described in a brief introductory passage, is worth quoting in full:

> The material for comparing the modern Greeks with those ancestors who inhabited the same places three millennia ago, in relation to their manners and customs, religious festivals, etc., offers itself to us in such rich abundance that it almost causes us embarrassment, not as to how but as to what material we shall begin to solve our task with.
>
> It would seem expedient to us to begin our descriptions with the birth of children and to continue in like vein, through all the stages of life, taking all the different circumstances of life into consideration, finally accompanying today's Greek in his withered old age right to the grave, and from there following him even beyond the grave to darkest Orcus [Hades]. One should therefore not meanwhile expect, in this brief treatise of ours, that we shall also depict life in all the aspects of its physical and moral development; that would take us away from our proper purpose. We thus consider it only insofar as it allows us to make a comparison with ancient Greece, for this alone is the task which we have set ourselves.   (1840: 1–2)

This statement is remarkable both for what it proposes to do and for the care which its author takes to exclude unnecessary side issues. We are promised a description of the entire series of life-cycle rites. This is a very early instance of systematic interest in the subject, and, although it may have served as a model for some of the later Greek folklorists' work (e.g., Politis 1871, 1874; see chap. 5), the obscurity which has since enveloped it does scant justice to its sophisticated conception and careful scholarship. Its descriptive detail is outstanding for the time at which it was written. For example, its analysis of wedding feasts and dances goes far beyond Douglas' vague generalizations on the same subject; while Lefkias (1843: 20, 80) simply contented himself with citing Vivilakis rather than attempt an analysis of his own.

Throughout his book, Vivilakis describes modern customs and practices in considerable detail; ancient parallels are discussed in each section, with appropriate references to Classical sources. The greater thoroughness of his work may not lie solely in some difference of ability or training between him and Lelekos. Subject matter must also have had some effect; Lelekos' heavy emphasis on folk *poetry* constrained him to look for literary parallels, rather than for similarities in life-style or ritual practice. Unlike Lelekos, Vivilakis was concerned to avoid dealing with anything as nebulous as *spiritual* continuity and says so. By excluding the kind of speculations about "national character" to which Lelekos, Zambelios, Valvis, and many others were so prone, he kept his field to manageable proportions.

Like any artificial grid on a body of data, however, Vivilakis' schema did result in some curious omissions and distortions. Thus, for example, evil-eye beliefs and practices are discussed in the section on childhood, as is a range of amuletic practices and associated concepts. The logic of this is clear: these matters are primarily concerned with the protection of children. But Vivilakis does briefly describe the alleged effects of the evil eye on animals (and implicitly also on adult humans) in the same passage. One gets the impression that this material has had to be forced into the unilineal format of the book, although it probably does represent a preponderance of childhood-linked beliefs in the data at Vivilakis' disposal.

Such difficulties are minor. A work written so early should not be faulted for occasional distortions which arise from the very sophistication of its overall design. Vivilakis' response to Fallmerayer was both timely and scholarly. Its subsequent lapse into obscurity may have been caused partly by the importance of the work soon to be done by Nikolaos Politis, who was not ashamed to acknowledge his debt to Vivilakis in appropriate citations.

Scholarly Reaction Abroad

Vivilakis set a high scholarly standard which was not surpassed for over two decades. Several specialized collections of a single genre appeared (e.g., Venizelos 1846 for proverbs; von Hahn 1864 for folktales; and Passow 1860 for songs), and these provided a sound basis for detailed research of a philological nature. A few general attempts at synthesis appeared abroad (notably Voutier 1826; Quinet 1830; Sanders 1844), and both in Germany (see Spiridakis 1966: 482-484) and in Greece Fallmerayerism remained the focus of heated discussion. Relatively little of this work, however, was to have a deep influence on the future development of Greek folklore studies in an epistemological sense.[4]

In 1864, however, the German philologist Kurt Wachsmuth (1837-1905) published *Das alte Griechenland im neuen*, a work not unlike Vivilakis' in scope and purpose but with considerably more ethnographic detail and less

passionate rhetoric in defense of the Greeks' national origins. The book opens
with a plea for calm and reason and with the complete rejection of one-sided
polemics of the kind that Fallmerayer had both issued and provoked. Wachsmuth clarifies his own position immediately, however: he is going to show
that there is indeed considerable evidence for continuity from ancient times.
It would actually be unreasonable to expect anything else, he argues, since
the historical evidence alone does not bear out the notion of a complete
demographic change. Of course, he conceded, the sheer numbers of Albanians
who passed into Greece in the fourteenth and fifteenth centuries would have
resulted in some admixture through intermarriage; and one does indeed see,
"here and there, clear traces of the Slavic type" (1864: 9)—presumably left
over from those earlier invasions of which Fallmerayer had made such capital.
On the other hand, wherever "the ancient blood has demonstrably kept its
purity, in the Mani, the Cyclades, and especially in Asia Minor and among the
Phanariots, there one encounters everywhere the finest ancient figures and
heads of the true Classical pattern" (1864: 10).

This does not sound like a promising approach. Here are the familiar
pseudogenetic attributions, the same apparent inability to distinguish between physical type and cultural pattern. But at this very point the picture
changes, and we are suddenly transported into a different epistemology:

> Finally, moreover, the nationality of a people (*die Nationalität eines
> Volkes*) is never completely displaced by foreign elements. Or were we
> therefore not really German anymore, just because we have absorbed a
> goodly quantity of Slavic and Wendish blood? A nation's essence and
> character lie, I think, quite incomparably more in its language, its
> thought and sensibility, its whole style and civilization . . . (1864:10)

This is a substantive change from the "racial" style of argument.

The argument continues in the same reasonable, moderate tone. Wachsmuth argues that loanwords in modern Greek do not hold great significance
for the issue of origins. One can easily counter such evidence with the fact
that some outlying dialects preserve highly archaic morphological features.
This is a useful addition to Lefkias' comments about the limited significance
of bilingualism for establishing national identity.

Here, then, Wachsmuth has rejected the simplistic equation of "blood"
with "nationality" and, with it, the notion of "purity" in any sense. What is
important in his scheme is not physical descent (though even on this score
Fallmerayer's argument can be shown to have been unsound), not what
people call themselves (a concern of later scholarship), but, quite simply, the
observable facts of their culture. If these people continue traditions which we
can recognize in the ancient sources, then they do indeed exemplify "the
ancient Greece in the new." The positivistic character of this approach be-

trays its origins in an archaeological, or artifactual, view of culture; we shall return to this point shortly. Whatever its merits or weaknesses, this represents a commonsense view of the continuity issue, deliberately phrased in a cool and detached manner so as to contrast with what Hussey has called Fallmerayer's "hasty, often sarcastic, temperament" (1978: 83).

Wachsmuth dealt with many of the culture traits that were soon to become crucial to the arguments of Greek commentators also. His treatment of concepts of death and fate, while more thorough, recalled the similar work of Vivilakis and also certainly provided some points of reference for the work on these topics which the young Politis was shortly to undertake. He gave us the first really detailed analysis of the "swallow song" (1864: 35-37), again anticipating Politis (1871, 1876). Lefkias had already attempted a brief analysis but claimed—almost certainly without any basis in ethnographic fact—that the terminology of the "swallow song" remained in popular use even in modern times (1843: 24-25). Wachsmuth adopted the same assumption (*schwalbelt*, p. 36; cf. Herzfeld 1974) and also continued the practice of conjoining the ancient text, which was from Rhodes, with a modern one from quite somewhere else—in his case, Epirus or Macedonia. Despite these difficulties, however, his analysis was the most careful and detailed to date. In general, his work represents a considerable advance in the level of documentation brought to the study of parallel traits.

The work of yet another German scholar, Bernhard Schmidt (1837-1917), surpassed even Wachsmuth's study in its attention to fine detail, though his aim—similarly expressed with unambiguous clarity in the title of his 1871 study, *Das Volksleben der Neugriechen und das hellenische Alterthum*—was much the same. But, if the study of Classical survivals was now well launched in Germany, it was also beginning to accelerate in Greece itself. A distinctively Greek laography was on the point of emergence, fusing the techniques of Western European scholarship with the special interests and firsthand knowledge that went with being a Greek oneself.

Christianity and Paganism in Greek Identity

In the next chapter, we shall look at the full flowering of Greek survivalism in the work of Nikolaos Politis. Before doing so, however, we must consider the development of a related issue—one which has already been encountered in the work of Zambelios, d'Istria, and Valvis and which was about to become critical. The Greeks claimed descent from the ancient Hellenes, who were (as it were by definition) "pagan"; yet they officially espoused Orthodox Christianity. With the growth of a more scholarly discussion of the continuity question, the contrast between these two religious traditions posed increasingly serious difficulties.

For foreign scholars, especially for those—and they were numerous—who had little patience with the Orthodox church, the problem was of course less acute. Pashley, for example, devoted a lengthy chapter to the Classical and pan-European parallels of modern Greek vampirism and nereid stories, and he did not hesitate to discuss the involvement of the local clergy in these decidedly un-Christian belief systems. As an antiquarian traveler, moreover, he positively delighted in the evidence for pagan cosmology and ritual among the Cretans of his own time:

> It is quite certain that the observance of the great celestial luminary [the sun], adopted by the Christians, has at times degenerated into something little better than the Persian worship, of which Herodotus and other ancient authors speak. I myself once met an ignorant Greek, who told me that the great difference between Christianity and Mohammedanism consisted in this, that the Christian worships the sun, and the Mohammedan the moon: and we learn from the mouth of one of the successors of St. Peter, that this adoration of the bright orb of day was practised by many Christians of his time. They even turned their backs on the altar, in the most splendid temple which Christian piety has ever erected, that they might bow down in their pagan adoration of the rising sun. (1837, II: 36-37)

Presumably Pashley had encountered in his "ignorant Greek" the usual attempt to describe Christian and Moslem as polar opposites (cf. "as the cat and the dog": Herzfeld 1980b), perhaps reinforced by the Islamic crescent symbol. His account displays all the ingenuous glee of the archaeologist, untrammeled by any commitment to local dogmas, upon discovering the survival of relics of the pagan past.

Wachsmuth, as usual, demonstrates both greater caution and an extremely good grasp of the data (1864: 19-23). He carefully discusses the location of chapels dedicated to the prophet Elijah and located on mountaintops in relation to the ancient worship of the sun, notes the similarity of names (*Ilias*, "Elijah"; *ilios*, "sun"), and then (and only then) comments: "Thus, underneath the change of names, the basic significance of the greatly adored Being remains largely the same, and for a considerable time the people may, half unconsciously, have worshiped their old deities under their new names"—a modest claim, indeed, which was to remain relatively unchallenged and unaltered in subsequent folklore scholarship right up to the present.

Wachsmuth describes a fair range of similar evidence for the survival of the pagan belief system. In his discussion of concepts of death, astronomical mythology, and the mythology of fertility and rebirth, he laid a sure foundation on which later authors were able to build. Linguistic survivals are especially useful if they are accompanied by thematic links. Thus, for example, he notes the transformation of Charon, the infernal boatman of the ancients, into the modern Charos, the personification of death; then, citing a song text which describes Charos' wily seizure of all earthly souls, he remarks: "Thus does Charon accompany the souls [of the dead] to Hades. For the modern Greeks, too, this is still a dark, cold, and waterless dwelling beneath the earth; it is a completely comfortless resting-place, since water and light are for the Greeks the two things which are precious and indispensable to life. A stairway leads down into this Hades; a gate closes it in; here sits the implacable watchman Charos, who lets no soul go back toward the light for which it yearns" (1864: 21). This account is a conflation of materials, possibly recorded at different times, from different parts of Greece; the assumption that Greece was historically a single, homogeneous culture left little room for considering regional variation in the overall system of belief. Wachsmuth also allows himself the antiquarian luxury of using the Classical form Charon to denote the *modern* death figure. On the whole, however, his argument for the survival of pagan ideas about the afterlife is well taken and restrained.

Wachsmuth is consistently cautious about asserting such continuity between pagan and folk Christian cosmology. He is especially careful to distinguish between the material proper and its ulterior implications. After a (disappointingly brief) discussion of "astronomical myths," he remarks: "Plainly, then, in these accounts there certainly lies no great abundance of the tradition of the ancient mythology today, but, under the covering of Christianity, only lightly veiled, numerous traces of paganism reveal themselves" (1864: 22). In other words, we should not look for the literally unaltered mythology of yesteryear. Instead, we should try to tear away the Christian veil in order to reveal the essential elements of that same mythology. To some extent, this is what Pashley and others had already been doing, though less systematically. It should be distinguished from the characterology of d'Istria and Valvis, on the other hand, since Wachsmuth was concerned strictly with observable culture traits. Like Vivilakis before him, he avoided discussing "spiritual" survivals save in the most general sense possible.

This more ethnographic focus, while relatively unproblematical for non-Greeks, created a painful dilemma for local scholars, who had to integrate cultural survivalism with at least a nominal profession of Christian faith. For the earlier writers concerned with "national character," the dilemma was not brought into particularly sharp focus, since general attitudes and "spirit" do not necessarily require the detailed explication of underlying cosmological beliefs. To describe the klefts as heirs to the glorious heroic tradition of yore did not entail an elaborate analysis of their beliefs or ritual practices; and, since they had been categorically separated from the present, their supposedly pagan attitudes to life—which could, anyway, be blamed on the exigencies of outlawry and subjugation under the Turks—caused little offense. The new style of antiquarian ethnography was much more dangerous. It brought the pagan past, detail by detail, into the Christian present and claimed to represent the true national heritage by so doing. To such an endeavor, needless to say, the religiously minded—especially the ecclesiastical establishment—were far from friendly. Although the Greek church had been made independent of the Patriarchate of Constantinople as early as 1837, primarily to free it from domination by an authority which was itself answerable to the Turkish government, the higher clergy remained suspicious of the Hellenizing notions of the secular nationalists; this strain is still occasionally felt. The antiquarian folklorists therefore had to work under the disapproving eye of a church which had scant tolerance for their ideas or their activities and which was itself a powerful force in the political and social life of the nation.

The folklorists seem to have been quite undaunted. While they did not particularly reiterate the anticlericalism of Zambelios and d'Istria, they openly pointed to the many pagan elements which had survived in the very forms of worship to which the folk still clung—even, not uncommonly, in rituals of the church itself. They had a powerful argument on their side, that of national interest, since a primary aim continued to be the refutation of Fallmerayer. Since political life in nineteenth-century Greece was always dominated by one form of irredentism or another, these antiquarian folklorists—the doyens of the Hellenist ideology—were able, and indeed encouraged, to pursue their investigations.

Before we turn to the work of the greatest Hellenist folklorist of all, Nikolaos Politis, we might usefully consider the contribution of a far less well known and geographically more restricted scholar, one who was nevertheless in the forefront of the same methodological development. In 1874, Georgios Loukas published a work with the self-explanatory title, *Philological Visits to the Monuments of the Ancients in the Life of the Modern Cypriots.* While Politis' partly contemporaneous *Modern Greek Mythology* has remained a classic of Greek folklore, Loukas' book has fallen into obscurity. The reasons for this are not entirely clear. It cannot be simply a matter of the comparatively limited geographical scope of Loukas' work—Sakellarios' monumental two-volume compendium of Cypriot lore and language, published from 1855 to 1868 and revised in 1890 and 1891, has kept its place far more successfully; the original edition was even reprinted as recently as 1955. Perhaps Sakellarios' work has eclipsed that of Loukas simply because of its more massive format and coverage. On the other hand, the striking resemblances between Loukas' and Politis' works suggest that Loukas' deserves more recognition, if only on historiographic grounds, than it has in fact received.

Loukas' preface is both a vision and a scientific statement of purpose:

On a visit to my homeland, Cyprus, in 1869, and resting in her
bosom for a short while, one day I suddenly found myself in a tempest
of various roiling emotions. . . . The entire recollection of my studies in
Athens stood clearly before me at that moment, and all the cares of my
life were thrust away like a cloud; fortunately, I was concealed in a
lonely house, so that nobody chanced to interrupt these initial stirrings
of my thoughts or break the chain of my ideas. There lay before me
some manuscript pages which I had written at intervals years before and
had completed shortly after my return. In these pages were some accounts of the language and life of the Cypriots, of which the detailed
comparison with the language and life of our ancestors reminded one in
lively fashion of the names of the blessed Teachers of the modern
Greeks—especially those of Koraes and Mavrophrydes, men who warm-
ly recommended the study of the modern language and life of Greeks
everywhere. While I lay thus motionless, my body relaxed, occupying
my mind with lively thoughts, there strangely struck my hearing certain
squeaks and thuds, such as occur when a vehicle is thrown on its side
and into a ditch by suddenly startled horses. And behold, suddenly
there before me, the very Teachers who were the subject of my reminis-
cences, dragging along with them a certain German heretic. . . . "Come
along," said both Teachers to him with [feigned] anxiety, "and show
us these Slavs dwelling in the heartlands of Asia!" At the conclusion of
those words the problem of the modern Greeks' authenticity leaped
agitatedly into my memory, I recognized the face of the German Fallmerayer, and I understood that the superficially anxious irony of
this invitation of the Teachers boded well for a significant national
discussion.   (1874: v-vi)

The political implications of this passage are thinly disguised. Cyprus, then
still under Turkish rule (until 1878, when it was ceded to Britain), might
superficially resemble an oriental land, even as Fallmerayer had insultingly
treated the Greek mainland as part of "the Orient." In this fanciful passage,
Fallmerayer even speaks of Cyprus as "Syria," a poetic synonym for the
lands of Islam. Yet if that were true, for the sake of argument, how then
could the inhabitants of Cyprus also be Slavs? Is not the solution that even
outlying Cyprus must in fact be considered wholly Greek?

In Loukas' vision, Fallmerayer is taught a lesson, although his skepticism is
initially hard to overcome. He is shown Cypriot boys playing ball games, the
names of which are known from antiquity. Fallmerayer is suspicious: perhaps
these boys were taught the names of their ball games by overly patriotic
schoolteachers? The reply was a proud one:

"Yes!" responded our grand old Koraes, "and indeed by the famous Lycurgus himself, the lawgiver of Sparta, as well as by other men of antiquity." "How is it," replied the German ironically, "that after so many centuries Lycurgus could be resurrected, and in this corner of Syria at that?" "Continue with your visit," replied the old man, "and you shall see him before you at every step." (1874: vii)

Eventually, indeed, Fallmerayer is forced to admit to the Greekness of Cyprus. He is a grudging loser, however: what about the Greek mainland, where his own researches started the whole trouble? "'Just so,' Mavrophrydes took up the point. 'Those places also keep up Hellenic customs and to this very day live the life of their ancient forefathers. This doubt of yours ought to be subjected to another visit to those parts.'"

Fallmerayer finally gives in entirely:

> Visiting the town and villages of the island with the Teachers . . . he found in them the purest customs and most Hellenic life-style in humble huts and in the ravines inhabited by shepherds and farmers. . . . From time to time, he would express to the Teachers his wonder at the fact that so many centuries had not managed to obliterate Greek customs from the lives of the Cypriots; for they are recognizably preserved, to the shame of the enemies of Hellenism and especially to the shame of that pseudocivilization which at that time had begun to rise up fanatically against these most holy relics of antiquity! (1874: ix)

The vision thus ends in triumph: the participants all make for a village at the foot of (the Cypriot) Mount Olympus, where a wise priest makes them welcome—and Loukas suddenly finds himself alone again in his recluse's study by the Limassol seashore, the manuscript which had originally fired his imagination still in his hands, "while unhappily this philological vision had dissolved."

So wishful a dream speaks eloquently both of the ardor with which the Greeks longed to disprove Fallmerayer's views and of the personal idiom in which they responded to his challenge. Loukas surpasses even Evlambios and Zambelios in what he expects folklore to prove; Greece should not be *resurrected*, he declares in marked contrast to those authors' favorite metaphor, but *rediscovered*. "Yes! unaltered, the Hellas of Perikles lives!" (1874: xii). For Loukas, the academic issue of "survivalism" took second place to the question of national "survival": an uncompromising response to Fallmerayer's no less uncompromising provocation, one couched in not altogether dissimilar terms.

Loukas' treatment of his material makes no concession to ecclesiastical sensibilities over the question of latent paganism. Like Wachsmuth (and Politis), he presented the assimilation of pagan concepts to Christian iconography as a common and easily understood phenomenon:

> In general, whenever they mention or invoke Charon, they also have the Angel in mind, and whenever they shout and revile the Angel, they are reviling Charon too. What is the cause of the assimilation of these two characters? Is there any doubt that the cause is Christianity [itself]?
> (1874: 38)

And a little later we are told:

> The Cypriots, strict adherents (as I have said) to the Hellenic customs . . . , both discharged their ideas about Charon into [the figure of] the Angel and dressed this Hellenic idea in the cloak of Christianity, but as we observe, *faithful to Hellenism,* they once again demonstrate to this day in many ways the texture and brilliance of these hallowed relics, preserving both the concepts *and their national character.*
> (1874: 44-45; my emphasis)

Clearly there were more kinds of faith than simply that demanded by the church.

A major part of Loukas' book is devoted to "mythology." That word, which he (again like Politis) preferred to the demotic cognate *paramithia* ("folktales"), gives some idea of his firm conviction that he was dealing with living antiquity. The ancients had myths, rather than tales, and their descendants were logically assumed to follow suit. Mythology, moreover, was associated with the doings of supernatural beings. Viewed in such terms, the "cloak of Christianity" seemed a superficial disguise indeed.

Loukas was completely overshadowed by his fellow philologist and folklorist, Nikolaos Politis. Politis' *Modern Greek Mythology* appeared in two sections—one in the year of Schmidt's *Volksleben* (1871), the other in that of Loukas' *Philological Visits* (1874).[5] Politis, too, conjoined the notion of a modern "mythology" with penetrating insights into the character of folk religion. He conducted his researches on an inestimably vaster scale than Loukas, however, and brought to them a more international breadth of scholarship, a keenly inquisitive and analytical attitude, and a fund of sheer energy that was itself almost of mythological dimensions. He was the inventor of the Greek term for folklore (*laografia*), the founder of the highly respected scholarly journal of the same name, an active participant in several scholarly institutions, a taxonomist extraordinary, and perhaps the most scholarly protagonist of the Greeks' claim to the name of Hellenes. In his work, we reach the climactic point, historically and epistemologically, of Greek folklore studies.

Chapter 5
The Creation of a Discipline

"... a discipline whose object is the study of the people ... "

Politis and the Constitution of Folklore

Since it was Nikolaos Politis' particular achievement to organize the whole ground plan of laography and give the subject its name, a chapter devoted to his work should start with a review of the state of the art at the beginning of his long and productive career. Politis did not so much revolutionize as *constitute* the discipline by organizing his predecessors' ideas and goals into a comprehensive taxonomic system. In consequence, his work can be read semiotically as a "text" (Winner and Winner 1976) of the Hellenists' view of Greek culture much more efficiently, and with more coherent results, than can the scattered efforts of earlier scholars. Yet Politis undoubtedly leaned quite heavily on the achievements of his predecessors—he freely and honestly acknowledged his material debt to them for a rich fund of data, drawn from all over the Greek-speaking world and consequently ideal for the purposes of comparative study. His ideological debt is hardly less important, however; and, although it was above all his talent for synthesis that finally translated the Hellenists' perspective into a unified study of Greek culture, many key concepts came into his hands already half-formed.

The fundamental notion of cultural continuity was already well established by Politis' day, of course, but there was as yet little interest in cross-cultural comparisons of a sort that would place Greek cultural history in a more international perspective. The earlier Hellenists did not even consider that to be a topic of interest; they knew perfectly well that Greece was the *fons et origo* of European civilization. A few attempts at comparative studies by foreigners, notably Pashley's ethnological disquisition on vampirism (1837, II: 195-234), received little attention among Greek scholars before Politis' time. Although the Greeks saw themselves as the quintessential Europeans, it was not the culture of non-Greek *peasants* that interested them; rather, as in the admittedly extreme case of Valvis, their interest in the peasantry was directed toward showing that their own country folk might equal even educated Western Europeans in wit and sensitivity. Politis was to change all that.

Politis was also to give a definitive answer to the problem of whether the study of vernacular culture should have an autonomous status, thereby distinguishing it from history, archaeology, and philology—all disciplines which had contributed a great deal to it. The data basis of ethnological studies was uncertain; no consensus had been achieved as to what it might legitimately include, so that a separate branch of scholarship had not yet come into being to deal with folk culture. Those who wrote extensively about such things did so under other titles—Zambelios as a historian, Manousos as an editor, Vivilakis and Lelekos as philologists, Valvis in his capacity as a doctor of law. Although terms like "folklore" and "ethnology" were now coming into use abroad, their initial impact on Greek scholarship was minimal. Nor was the development of an autonomous discipline encouraged by the midcentury foreign scholars who wrote about Greece. Among the German scholars, for example, Schmidt—who disliked the English word "folklore"—rejected the very notion of comparative mythology in favor of a strictly antiquarian approach (1877: 5). Politis rebelled passionately against this narrow and exclusive focus (Kiriakidis 1937: 20-21), even though he made good use of its results and undertook a great deal of "patriotic or archaeological" research himself. For him, the real challenge did not lie in choosing which of the sundry disciplines already in existence would furnish the ideal methodology. It lay instead in abstracting from each those principles which could most usefully contribute to a unified discipline of folklore. The laography of Politis and his followers retains the textual analysis of classical philology, the goal of historical reconstruction which it derived from archaeological and archival research, and a set of concepts partially derived from the emergent anthropology of Tylor and others. To all this, a continuing concern to rebut Fallmerayerism gave a certain circumstantial unity. To some extent, we can say that Politis inherited a methodological ragbag and made a quilt, but it was a quilt of remarkably harmonious design.

The choice of methods and concepts was far from fortuitous. Folklore studies in Greece were in large measure a response to Fallmerayer's assault, which was primarily a historical one. All the various epistemological elements which Politis now brought together consequently shared one dominant characteristic: a highly literalist sense of historical fact. We have already witnessed this trend in the steady hypostatization of "the klefts" as a discrete historical phenomenon. To this we should add the growing acceptance (e.g., Zambelios 1852; Passow 1860; Kind 1861) of certain song texts as "historical" as well as the attendant subjection of these texts to criteria of factual "accuracy." Here was a real danger of circularity: if a text did not fully justify being so labeled, it was assumed to be the text rather than the classification that was at fault.

Politis both inherited and in turn elaborated this brand of historical literalism, not only in the study of "obviously" historical song texts but, more generally, in the interpretation of all ethnological data.

While he never seems to have questioned this basic premise, he was constantly aware of the difficulties of interpretation into which it led him. In attempting to deal with these, he progressively elaborated his classificatory system, apparently thinking that the fault lay in the underdeveloped state of that system rather than in its articulating principles. In so doing, however, he also created a much stronger sense of epistemological cohesion than had hitherto existed. The result was the creation of a distinctive branch of folklore studies to which Politis, in 1884, finally gave the name of *laografia*, by which it has been known in Greece ever since.

Politis and the Mythology of the Modern Greeks

Nikolaos Politis was born in 1852, the year in which Zambelios published his monumental history and folksong collection. The son of a lawyer of rural origins, the young Politis seems to have shown academic inclinations at an early age. Indeed, he published his first articles in learned journals at the age of thirteen. A year later, he was publishing brief notes on linguistics and folklore in *Pandora*; from 1868 on he also published articles in *Efimeris ton Filomathon*, a journal whose involvement with philological folklore studies had originally been prompted by Zambelios' call to all Greek scholars to engage in active ethnological research. There can be no doubt that Politis knew, even as a child, of the intense debate which Fallmerayer had provoked (cf. Kiriakidis 1923: ix-xi) and that this was a major influence in his precocious attraction to the subject that was to dominate his entire career.

In 1867, *Pandora* announced a philological prize competition, sponsored by the wealthy Odessa philanthropist Th. P. Rhodokanakis. The second such contest, in 1871, had as its theme "the collection from as many Greek locations as possible of the Greek manners, customs, and practices and their comparison with what is recorded in the surviving [ancient] authors, so that their [respective] similarities and differences [with regard to the latter] may be made known" (quoted by Politis 1871: iii). The youthful Politis, then a university student, responded enthusiastically. He was the only candidate. Yet the work which he produced for the Rhodokanakis competition, the first major essay from his pen, represents a landmark in the development of Greek folklore scholarship.[1]

This is his *Modern Greek Mythology*, a compendium of cosmological tales and related materials with detailed notes on possible contemporary non-Greek as well as Classical Greek parallels. A primary motive is, as one would expect, to refute Fallmerayer—but, says Politis, this must be done scientifically, not in the confused and polemical way that had prevailed up to that point. Textual materials are not sufficient for the purpose by themselves; customs provide the most telling evidence, since they "are not taught by others, nor are they transplanted from external sources among foreign races, but are transmitted only by word of mouth from parent to child, from old to young" (1871: ix). The materials of folklore must therefore be taken from real-life situations in order to establish the true continuity of the Greek people.

Modern Greek Mythology introduces a systematic crosscultural perspective for the first time. The competition judges criticized this as going too far beyond the contest's antiquarian objectives. But in fact, as Politis retorted, the discussion of non-Greek parallels certainly did no harm to the basic aim of establishing historical continuity within Greece and added greatly to our understanding of the Greek material itself. This stance is in marked contrast to Schmidt's explicit rejection of comparativism. When Kiriakidis, a pupil of Politis, remarked in 1923 that his teacher had moved away from a strictly "archaeological" view of folklore, this in no way diminished the "patriotic" intentions of *Modern Greek Mythology*, nor did it prevent Politis in 1909 from defining "monuments of the word"—verbal archaeology, as it were—as one of the two principal concerns of folklore research. Politis' approach was virtually a form of "ethnoarchaeology": he never ceased to seek out the ancient derivations of present-day culture traits, but he simultaneously looked for parallel (and sometimes historically related) phenomena in other lands. Kiriakidis points out that although Politis did not go to Germany until 1876 (i.e., after the Rhodokanakis competition), and although the German ethnologist and Politis' teacher-to-be Albrecht Dieterich did not publish his exposition of comparative folklore until 1902, *Modern Greek Mythology* anticipates some of the methodological aspects of Dieterich's treatise. More to the point, however, Politis had already thoroughly familiarized himself with the work of the brothers Grimm, who were the real founders of German comparative ethnology. The Grimms were also unsympathetic to Christianity, and their determination to find pre-Christian ideologies beneath the veneer of Christian symbolism undoubtedly spoke directly to the antiquarian Hellenist in Politis.

One of the most astonishing features of *Modern Greek Mythology* is its almost fanatical concern with accurate, detailed scholarship. Politis, well aware that many of his predecessors had proved scholastically deficient by the standards of their own time, frankly says so (1871: i). Although still only a student at Athens University, he was not afraid to criticize established figures of the scholarly world, at least in general terms. He also responded in print, point by point, to the criticisms which the Rhodokanakis competition judges had addressed to his manuscript, "not," he said, "being motivated by an attitude of contrariness, since in any case we respect the opinion of such established teachers, but because, as we think, the judgments made on scholarly writings are not like those appropriate to the products of light literature—which are dependent for the most part on the peculiar tastes of the judges—but, in order to carry weight, should be accepted on the basis of discussion" (1871: iv).

One of the highlights of Politis' defense is his discussion of the term *kleftis* ("kleft"). The judges had objected to his use of this form (as opposed to the Classical *kleptis*) as a violation of good *katharevousa* style. Not at all, replied the undaunted scholar; the form *kleftis* and its derivatives, "hallowed by the brave bulwarks of Hellenic freedom, are no longer equivalent to *kleptis*, etc." (1871: xv–xxxvi). Writing as he was in the immediate aftermath of the Dilessi affair, Politis had spotted the semantic shift which we have already noted, although he failed to see its historical implications; his concern was to use the "right form," rather than to probe the reasons why usage had developed in this particular way. Indeed, it was Politis who, perhaps more than any other scholar, accorded the "kleftic songs" their autonomous status in the classification of Greek folklore. The care with which he tried to rebut the judges' criticism on this seemingly minor stylistic point was thus a patriotic gesture; he wanted to guarantee "the klefts" their place in history.

In general, as the opening remarks about Fallmerayer disclose, *Modern Greek Mythology* is truly a patriotic enterprise. Its aim is explicitly stated as being "to seek the kinship between our own manners and customs and those of the ancient Hellenes" and "our continuity with our ancestors" (1871: xxii, xxix). Continuity, however, does not necessarily mean identity, and (as Politis realized) it certainly does not preclude similarities to other cultures. Even kleftism can be assimilated to this new, comparativist perspective. The klefts' name was a fact of *modern* Greek culture which could nevertheless be brought into line with the neo-Classical language; the etymological root and the patriotic and heroic virtues with which it was associated were the relevant elements of continuity here. Again, in 1885 Politis explicitly accepts the Serbian *hajduk* and Bulgarian *haidout* as "klefts," although the Bulgarians' "kleftic" poetry "lacks that ineffable charm which the folk poetry of every nation breathes, even that of those mountain-dwelling brigands (*listai*) of the Taurus, the wild Kurds." His prejudices occasionally got the better of his detachment, as in this passage, but he still thought it worthwhile to compare the "klefts" of different Balkan lands, even if only to demonstrate the poverty of the Bulgarians' kleftic tradition. He would probably have rejected the extreme view that the Bulgarians had never had klefts at all (e.g., Colocotronis 1918). For Politis, it was sufficient that the traditions of modern Greece could be both intimately related to those of the ancient past and scientifically compared with those of the contemporary cultures of Europe and the Orient.

A Greek Version of Survivalism

In 1865, six years before the compilation of *Modern Greek Mythology*, Edward Burnett Tylor's *Researches into the Early History of Mankind and the Development of Civilization* had introduced the "doctrine of survivals" to the scholarly world, and the theme was taken up again in his two-volume *Primitive Culture* in 1871. By 1880 at the latest, Politis (who read Tylor's works in French translations) had tried to engage the British anthropologist's interest by sending him a signed reprint, dedicated with "Hommage respectueux de l'auteur à M. Edw. Tylor" and currently preserved in the Tylor Anthropological Library at Oxford; two more signed pamphlets followed in 1882. Of course, these tell us nothing about Tylor's attitude, if he had one, toward Politis, but they do suggest that the Greek folklorist was interested in establishing some kind of communication with him.

What exactly was the influence of the British founder of "anthropology" upon the Greek founder of "laography," and how faithful a reflection of Tylor's is Politis' "survivalism"? Again, there is no evidence that Tylor ever actively encouraged Politis; more probably, Politis developed his own ideas independently and then drew on Tylor's for elaboration. Thus, for example, the short passage on sun worship in *Modern Greek Mythology* (1871: 17-24), which is strictly a survey of Greek materials, makes no acknowledged use of Tylorean theory; by contrast, its successor, the essay "The Sun in Popular Myths," is much broader in its comparativism and also admits to some explicit knowledge of the British anthropologist's writings (e.g., 1882a: 12, n. 4).

Kiriakidis (1923: xxii; 1937: 23) describes Politis' early work as "purely archaeological" and suggests that the influence of Tylor and Dieterich really appears in his later *Proverbs* (1899-1902) and *Traditions* (1904). But the Tylor Library reprints, while later than *Modern Greek Mythology*, at least show that Politis was exposed to Tylor's influence at a relatively early date. Not all forms of survivalism necessarily originated with Tylor himself, however, and it is apparent that Politis' intellectual path was already set in this general direction well before he began citing Tylor in his own works. In consequence, Politis was able not only to quote Tylor in support of his Hellenist version of survivalism but to exclude those aspects of the Tylorean thesis which conflicted with Greek nationalism—especially the conception of survivals as essentially relics of a *primitive* past, which would not have suited the Hellenist argument at all.

We have already noted Politis' debt to the German tradition of philological antiquarianism. Certainly, too, there are traces in his early work of the "national character" rhetoric of Zambelios, especially where Politis borrows Zambelios' own material in order to demonstrate the tragic sensibilities of the Greeks in a cheerful song which nevertheless represents death—"a dancing song, full (so to speak) of cheerful melancholy, and withal a faithful portrait of the Hellenic character" (1874: 242). But, amidst all these borrowings from more familiar scholarly traditions, Politis also displays a more "anthropologically" oriented kind of survivalism.

First of all, there is the general title, *Study of the Life (vios) of the Modern Greeks*. Politis retained the notion of studying "life" in the general title of the series which encompassed the later *Proverbs* and *Traditions*; *epiviosis* ("survival") is cognate with this term. From the outset, it seems, he regarded his task as being to establish connections between modern and ancient *ways of life* (1871: viii). If he acknowledges his debt to Tylor more generously in later years, this is not necessarily because Tylor's influence on him was as great as he himself seems to have been disposed to believe; indeed, as Kiriakidis has noted, Politis never really accepted the doctrine of survivals in its entirety. We might go further still and suggest that Politis' increasing acknowledgment of Tylor may not represent much more than an ex post facto attempt to connect his work with international scholarship. More even than that, it seems likely that Politis either misunderstood or misrepresented the full import of Tylorean survivalism. (Since Tylor does not seem to have reciprocated Politis' interest at any time, the discrepancies were probably never directly confronted by the two scholars.) Politis appears to have done much the same as many of Tylor's admiring contemporaries: reading "survivalism" not as a theory of societal progression which encompassed the fossils of a primitive stage but as a static doctrine of cultural continuity.

This has to be put in a wider context. In her authoritative study of the doctrine of survivals, Margaret Hodgen (1936: 48, n. 1) has shown that many of Tylor's imitators made no effort "in the Tylorean tradition to arrive at origins or to uphold the presuppositions of developmentalism." Notable among the offenders is John Cuthbert Lawson, whose *Modern Greek Folklore and Ancient Greek Religion* (1910) drew heavily on Politis' publications—and may indeed have absorbed more of Politis' than of Tylor's presuppositional framework. Hodgen presents the concern in such writings with the persistence of paganism as a continuation of the Renaissance antiquarians' search for "the indications of pagan or popish past" in folk practices. Now while in England this essentially negative emphasis may have transferred easily from antipapist rhetoric in the seventeenth century to colonialist ideology and ethnocentrism in the nineteenth, there are two reasons why the same process could not have occurred in Greece. First, no serious folklore studies were done by Greeks before the Revolution of 1821; as we have seen, the growth of folklore studies there was a *retrospective* response to the acquisition of statehood.

The second reason follows from the first: since the ideological basis of the Greeks' antiquarian philology was the alleged *superiority* of the ancient Hellenes, the developmentalist thesis that survivals were the relics of a primitive past made no sense. The Greek version of survivalism could only be a static model. Furthermore, a strictly developmentalist model would have allowed "the Europeans" to claim cultural superiority over the ancient Greeks and perhaps also over their descendants. Indeed, even those European scholars who adopted the philhellenic position, while using Tylor's terminology, preferred to treat the Classical world as an unsurpassed exemplar. An extreme exponent of this school of thought was the Celtic scholar J. S. Stuart-Glennie, who used folklore materials to demonstrate the *lack* of change in Greek speech and culture and went on to argue that the Greeks represented a "race" which had been superior in both ancient and recent times; thus, Tylor's advocacy of the essential homogeneity of humankind could not be allowed to pass (cf. Garnett and Stuart-Glennie 1896: 3).

While Politis was not usually concerned with these wider issues (see Kiriakidou-Nestoros 1978: 151), he seems to have been comfortable with the assumption that Classical Greek culture represented a superior form of civilization and that the doctrine of survivals could be brought into line with this view. As he explained:

> [Tylor] includes among the survivals absolutely all remains of past civilizations, but we think it would be better to single out for inclusion in another category all those [traits] which are in no way unseemly but preserve their original rationale and meaning, and which can be regarded as the partial but unbroken continuation of an earlier life (*vios*).
>
> (1909a: 6)

In this way, Politis sought to bypass the contradictions inherent in using Tylorean survivalism for a culture whose antecedents supposedly marked the very antithesis of the primitive. His method was frankly selective: he preferred to establish a "partial" continuity which at least had the virtue of being "unbroken." The selectional basis of Greek folklore classification begins to emerge very clearly here, especially if we keep in mind that the notion of cultural continuity was itself a taxonomic device for defining the extent of Hellenism.

Politis' ability to so transform Tylorean survivalism was hardly unique at the time. The problem lay in the ambiguities of Tylor's own expository style—in particular, in his use of archaeological metaphors for nonmaterial culture. Tylor's critics, indeed, "deprecated an explanation of the persistence of nonmaterial culture elements which endowed them figuratively with the physical endurance of the material" (Hodgen 1936: 146). It seems, moreover, that

Tylor himself was reluctant to face the implications of this criticism. Of course, neither Tylor nor his imitators (including Politis) assumed that ancient cultural forms would be preserved completely intact, any more than were archaeological artifacts under normal conditions. In this sense, Politis' survivalism is no less "archaeological" than Tylor's. The difference is only that, whereas Tylor makes his archaeological appeal to the anonymous reaches of prehistory, Politis makes his to the very starting point of historical time in the European tradition—to ancient Hellas. Yet the implications of this difference are radical enough.[2]

The Hypothesis of Original Texts

In using Classical Greece as his point of reference, Politis was treading the same path as his predecessors in Greece. Yet, far more aware than they had been of the unplumbed time depth of prehistory, he often asserted that the Classical traditions rested in turn on still older strata of myth and custom. His acquaintance with the development of Indo-European scholarship manifests itself as early as *Modern Greek Mythology*. Some of the themes in that book seem to offer glimpses into the mysterious older traditions of pre-Classical times and were given more detailed treatment from this angle in subsequent articles. Two of the reprints which Politis sent Tylor are of this type: "Popular Meteorological Myths" and "The Sun in Popular Myths." Indeed, in the sun mythology essay, Politis mentions Tylor's view that the Perseus myth may represent the survival of pre-Classical elements.

In this piece, moreover, Politis demonstrated a striking breadth of scholarship. His ability to see the relevance of Sanskrit materials is especially novel in local Greek scholarship. The interpretive restraint which this piece reveals is all the more extraordinary given the ideological and methodological background to Politis' work. The introductory passage deserves to be quoted in full:

> When we look at the host of myths which are demonstrably based on the observation of solar phenomena, we will find it hard to explain why the sun holds a secondary place in the Greek pantheon. But expert study and analysis of solar myths convince us that these myths, the first seeds of which are an inheritance from the prehistoric Aryans, rapidly became identified and fused with the myths about other gods, especially those about Herakles and Apollo, and that later certain of the attributes of the Sun were shaped into mythological matrices of their own, such as those of Hyperion-Sun, Phoebus-Sun, Phaëthon-Sun. We observe something analogous in Roman mythology, too, where Apollo, Liber, Hercules, and Mercury took on many of the characteristics of the

Sun god (Sol), and in Vedic mythology (which in addition to Sûryâ, the principal personification of the sun, mentions others such as the gods Savitri, Mitra, Vishnu, Pûshan, Aditya). Because of this sharing out of the solar myths, the importance of the Sun as a self-contained deity was radically lessened; not only in Greek mythology but even in the Vedas themselves, the sun is relegated to an inferior position.

In Classical times, to put it generally, the worship of the Sun was not a habitual practice and was indeed extremely rare. The *hēlieia* ("sun shrines") and the altars and statues of Helios (the Sun) which existed in some places should perhaps be regarded as the relics of a more ancient cult which had held sway before the Sun became identified with other gods. Most of the extremely ancient myths which derived from this cult were attributed to Herakles and other solar heroes, as well as to Apollo. Those which referred to Apollo are the most concerned with ideals, since they gradually took on moral significance and a thoroughly proper character; those which referred to Herakles more faithfully retained their old uncouth, artless style—this doubtless being reinforced by comedy and satyrical drama and the art of humor, pleasantly intermingled with such subjects; but above all the preservation of those archetypical myths is due to the fact that they were easily understood by the masses, whose intellectual level they did not exceed. For this reason, it is easy to understand why most of the myths have survived the passage of many centuries among our people, having undergone a negligible amount of insignificant change.

The aim of the present essay is to assemble these myths of our people and, in general, all mythological representations and images of the sun. Of these, some must be considered the remnants of extremely ancient myths, of which not the slightest mention is made by the ancient authors; others may be explained or completed by reference to Hellenic mythology or to the mythology of related peoples. They are to be found scattered in traditions, especially in folksongs and tales (*paramithia*), but nevertheless in altered and obscure form. Some traces of them, moreover, are to be clearly discerned in popular speech but unconsciously preserved, since they have long ago lost their mythological meaning.   (1882a: 3-5)

This passage is characteristic. It not only demonstrates Politis' concern to establish ancient links with modern folklore but shows how far he was prepared to push that search beyond the chronological and geographical limits of Hellenism. He was the first Greek scholar to draw systematically on Sanskritic research in order to illuminate both ancient and modern traditions of his own country. Much of this Sanskrit material came from the publications of Max

Müller, but there is nothing to suggest that Politis absorbed with it all the theoretical trappings of Müller's "solarism." Politis never became embroiled in the debate over this theory of the solar origins of mythology; his interests, although more international in scope, were ultimately directed toward the elucidation of the Greek materials rather than toward the broader ethnological questions of the day. He studied solar and meteorological myths for their own intrinsic interest, instead of trying to prove that they were ancestral to *all* mythology.[3] Moreover, he was not seriously affected by Müller's admonition to Tylor that all ethnological comparativism should be kept within linguistic boundaries, since his principal focus never strayed, in the final analysis, from the linguistically homogeneous area of the Greek-speaking world. Tylor was in any case far from being a severe critic of Müller's theories (cf. Dorson 1968: 169, 187), and there is no reason to suppose that Politis felt very differently. In one important respect, however, Politis' essay on solar mythology reverses the flow of a classic Müller argument: rather than treating myth as a "disease of language," Politis chose to view metaphorical usage as the scattered and degenerate relics of myth (see especially 1882a: 28-42). This, again, is a logical outcome of a form of survivalism which takes the Classical period as its sole point of departure. It is also consistent with the literalism which was so characteristic of Politis' thinking but which was antithetical to Müller's view of language (cf. Crick 1976: 15-35).

Recourse to a *pre*-Classical past was new in Greek folklore studies at this time, despite obscure hints of its possible relevance in Zambelios' reference to the eastern origins of some Classical culture traits. In the long passage just quoted, Politis mentions myths "of which not the slightest mention is made by the ancient authors." This approach involves bringing in non-Hellenic materials, of course, but it also permits an *argumentum ex silentio* whereby continuity can be posited even in the total absence of evidence from ancient literature. The device became popular; it could also be convincing, as in Lawson's attempt to show that the figure of Charos represents a true survival even though not in its literary guise as the ferryman of the Styx (1910: 106).

The fragmentation of this extremely ancient mythological stratum is traced through successive stages. It begins with the personification of the sun and the distribution of the sun's attributes among various heroes and gods— this being perhaps a pale refraction of Müller's "disease of language" theory, in that it represents the progressive fragmentation of a single, unified, and named concept (cf. also Dorson 1968: 162). Later, the specialized myths themselves became fragmented. Some became songs, others tales; note that Politis treats folktales, *paramithia*, as incomplete mythological segments rather than as full-fledged myths in their own right. Modern Greece has its mythology, but this takes a variety of forms which, when examined singly, lack complete historical autonomy.

At a more microscopic level, too, the search for original forms deeply interested Politis. Throughout his career, he exhibited a conviction that all legends and songs began as specific, if hypothetical, *Urtext* forms. In this, he differed from Zambelios in two significant respects. First, he explicitly rejected the notion—Vician or otherwise—of collective composition; it conflicted too deeply with his literalist perspective. "On a priori grounds, however, we may proclaim as a dogma which admits of no doubt that the people (*laos*), qua people, as a collectivity (*sinolon*), is incapable of composing a poem. Collective poetry is an impossibility" (Politis 1916: 8). This flat rejection of collective composition does not preclude the existence of processes of textual change; on the contrary, these are extensively discussed in many of Politis' publications. But the point is that variant texts are precisely what they are supposed to be: departures in each case from an individually composed *Urtext*.

This was the approach which Politis brought even to songs of a patently social nature. A notable example is provided by the so-called swallow song (*khelidhonisma*). The very name of this textual type illustrates the use of the Classical period as the one reliable, fixed reference point: it was concocted from a verb (*khelidonizein*) which the Greco-Egyptian writer Athenaeus (2d-3d century A.D.) associated with an apparently complete song text (Ath. *Deipn.* viii, 360b-d = Page 1962: 450-451). The noun form is thus a nineteenth-century scholastic neologism which Politis, building on an initial review of the subject by Wachsmuth, used to bring the ancient text together with thirteen modern "variants" from scattered locations (Politis 1872). The term "swallow song" appears to be unknown in present-day rural Greece, and it is not clear whether all of Politis' "variants" came from analogous performative contexts (cf. Herzfeld 1974, 1977). Yet his classification, rooted as it is in the search for continuity, remains popular among folklorists of essentially Hellenist outlook despite the vast increase in the volume of the material that has to be dealt with (e.g., Spiridakis 1969, with 164 texts). The appeal of the *Urtext* hypothesis is still considerable, and its ideological implications were already present in such early studies of Politis as his paper on the "swallow song."

But Politis, whose acquaintance with Indo-European scholarship seems to have made him properly wary of reconstructed forms, never went so far as to attempt a critical edition of a folksong *Urtext*. Such an extreme of philological antiquarianism, which was attempted by at least one later scholar (Romaios 1966, 1966-67; but cf. Kiriakidou-Nestoros 1975: 178-190), could not be reconciled with Politis' characteristically restrained conclusion that, "if we except the historical songs, the chronological point of origin of folksongs is generally unstable and uncertain, so that the examination of this substantial fragment of Greek poetry by historical periods is not feasible, at least for the present" (1916: 4). That the historical songs constituted an exception in this respect was possible only through Politis' literalist assumption that each song was "composed for" the event which it celebrated. More generally, the concept of an *Urtext* meant that he could treat local variants as sources on which to base textual criticism, albeit with due care: "The choice of a variant of each [song text] was not sufficient, because even the most perfect variant presents lacunae, which may nonetheless be corrected with ease on the basis of other variants. . . . My work is like that of the editor of a literary text, who treats it on the basis of the manuscript versions, limiting himself exclusively to restoration (*recensio*) and not daring to attempt correction (*emendatio*)" (1914: 7). This was not a hypocritical position, even though Politis attacked other scholars' (e.g., Khristovasilis') textual alterations. What he disliked was *invented* textual material, rather than careful philological reconstructions; indeed, the latter were, in his view, a legitimate means of purifying an *Urtext* of its later accretions, both folk and learned.

The second major difference between Zambelios and Politis modifies this picture somewhat. For, whereas Zambelios treated the whole Classical period as, one might say, a grand *Urtext* for the general national regeneration that was to follow, Politis treated Classical antiquity as but one stage in the panoramic progression of Greek history. Zambelios had conceded the influence of eastern art and religious thought on the formation of Greek culture, but his view of Greece as the "cause" of all true civilization meant that he could still treat Classical Greece as the real point of origin. Not so Politis, who realized that a good deal of what was preserved in modern folklore might have bypassed the Classical literati entirely. For Politis, then, an *Urtext* was not necessarily the origin of the *ideas* which it contained, although he generally assumed that it was contemporaneous with any *facts* which it might convey. Rather, an *Urtext* fixed the ideas in a particular *form*, and to this—in theory, at least—a date might be attached. The ideas themselves were virtually timeless, but they were also distinctively and unarguably Greek in the way in which they were expressed.

Thus, from the very beginning of his scholarly career, Politis avoided equating the form of texts with their intellectual content. On the other hand, he never rejected the key assumption that textual forms were fixed in historical time and that their relevance was above all historical. He began *Modern Greek Mythology* with a version of this theme:

> The history of a nation (*ethnos*) does not consist solely in the narration of those events which have had some influence on its destiny; rather, the accurate and detailed knowledge of this nation's character and spirit (*pnevma*) is also needed in order to supplement that history and put it together more perfectly. [This is] because such knowledge, apart

from the fact that it contributes to the easier discovery and understanding of the causes and consequences of such events, not infrequent-
ly aids in the elucidation of obscure and problematical historical
questions.   (1871: i)

The concern with "national character" is mainly rhetorical here. The approach which Politis suggests might more justly be described as a compound
of ethnohistorical aims and philological methods. Although the passage just
quoted sounds like something Zambelios might have written, the intention
behind it is substantially different. Politis does not seek historical "laws" *in*
the material itself so much as explanations of the material which will *also*
serve as explanations of events in national history. That perspective remained
with him to the end and was to bear bittersweet fruit when he turned to the
folklore associated with the main irredentist objective, the recapture of Constantinople (see chap. 6). It is perhaps best explained by saying that, for
Politis, the "survivals" of culture meant in a very real sense the physical survival of the nation itself. If the nation did not remember its identity, it was
no nation. Thus, the *vios* ("life") of the nation depended on the recognition
and maintenance of its *epiviosis* ("survivals"). Conversely, the past and present "survival" of national identity could be understood only by studying the
nation's "life."

Laography: Definition and Organization

In 1884, Politis publicly coined the word *laografia* for the first time (Kiriakidis 1931: 12). For some time, he had been moving toward a unified theoretical perspective. A founding member of the Historical and Ethnological Society of Greece (1882), in whose journal he now introduced the new term,
he distrusted the wide coverage of terms like "ethnography" and "anthropology"; as he later remarked in the first issue of another major journal,
Laografia:

The term "demography" was concocted in 1855 by the Frenchman
Guillard; this was the name given to the statistically based study of
human life. Older still is the term "ethnography," which denotes the
science that examines man as a political animal, constituting groups or
nations, being distinct from "anthropology," which examines humankind as an animal genus, as an isolated individual, without regard to
social or national grouping.   (1909a: 2)

This is a somewhat curious statement to come from an admirer of Tylor. It
represents a simplification of Tylor's view that "stages of culture may be
compared without taking into account how far tribes who use the same

implement, follow the same custom, or believe the same myth, may differ in their bodily configuration and the colour of their skin and hair" (1924: 7).

It was in 1909 that laography finally gained official status with the foundation, under Politis' direction, of the Hellenic Folklore Society (Elliniki Laografiki Eteria). This institution published a journal, *Laografia*, the first issue of which contained Politis' now classic definition of the discipline (see also app. A). It opens with a historical survey of the antecedents and equivalents of the term *laografia* itself:

> The word *laografia*, which we have been using for the last twenty-five years to denote studies of folk traditions, beliefs, customs, the unwritten literature of the folk, and every possible contribution to a more accurate knowledge of the people (*laos*), is found in ancient Greek from the last years of the Alexandrian period but used in an entirely different, special sense. *Laographia* was the name of the poll tax paid by a large proportion of the inhabitants of Egypt from fourteen to fifty years of age. It was the "per capita contribution," as Josephus calls it, or the "head tax," as it is named in some papyri. The imposition of this tax, from which the Jews had been exempt, is mentioned in the passage of the apocryphal book of the Maccabees in which are recorded the edicts of the Egyptian king Ptolemy Philopator which were so crushing to the Jews (208 B.C.) [*sic*: now usually dated ca. 217 B.C. but historically dubious]. Those who paid the head tax were called *laographoumenoi* to distinguish them from those who were exempted from this tax (*epikekrimenoi*); the latter, however, were required to serve in the army. *Laographoi* were village headmen responsible for organizing the *laographia*.
>
> Despite the different meaning which it had in Egypt, this word is most suitable as the name of a discipline whose object is the study of the people (*laos*). Otherwise, similar words have been introduced and taken by us into scholarly usage; they are compounds of synonyms for the words *laos* ("people") and *grafo* ("write") and are used to denote sciences not wholly unconnected with laography, such as "demography" and "ethnography."
>
> In many European languages, the word "folklore" is used; it means *laografia*. This term was invented by the Englishman William John Thoms, who, writing under a pseudonym, published an article in the London literary journal *Athenaeum* of 27 August 1846 (pp. 842-843), in which he suggested that a special term was needed for those studies which already then were certainly widespread but were not regarded as constituting a special and distinctive discipline. The term, which was composed of the English "folk" (*laos*) and "lore" (knowledge, teach-

ing) on the model of the German compounds *Volkslied, Volksepos, Volksfest*, etc., was in many cases more suitable than the circumlocutions then current in English usage, "popular antiquities" and "popular literature" [as Thoms had in fact pointed out; see Dorson 1968: 1]. From that point on, the term kept its place in English and was also introduced into other European languages. The Danes, who were acquainted with the English word and cirtually "misetymologized" it, called laography *"Folkeminder"* ("folk recollections").

But certain folklorists, even though the English term has been introduced into their languages, have preferred some other term taken from their own tongue, in the interests of easier comprehension. The Italians call *tradizioni popolari* and the French likewise *traditions populaires* virtually all the subject matter of folklore, thereby investing a one-sided term with more general meaning. From here, some proceeded to add the word *traditionnisme*. This, as the French folklorist Gaidoz observes, is not only vague but necessarily confusing, since it means two different things: first, a love of tradition and an inclination to preserve it, and second the study of tradition, which is not the same thing at all—it is possible for one who loves tradition not to study it, and for one who studies it not to love it.

Thus, the French will be compelled to have recourse to the English term, using [for it] the French *traditions populaires* when and if they want to be understood by ordinary people. Gaston Paris concocted the term *mythographie*, but in the narrower sense of the "study of tales" for which the English use "storiology."

The Germans, again, having accepted the English term, now seem to prefer another which has been concocted out of their own language, the term *Volkskunde* ("acquaintance with the folk, knowledge of the people"). But that term has the following disadvantage: taken in its principal meaning, it extends the field of laographic studies more widely than it ought.   (1909a: 1-3)

This lengthy passage has been quoted in full here because it looks both forward to the creation of a new discipline and backward to that discipline's antecedents. In fact, Politis' formulation exhibits a presuppositional framework which is fully consistent with the previous history of Greek folklore studies, even if it does go much further in explicating a systematic basis for the organization of those studies. First, the search for an "ancient" (actually Hellenistic) term is presented as essential to the success of the enterprise. Then, that term is defined more precisely in relation to Western European concepts and labels. Politis seems to imply that the English word "folklore" is the most exact equivalent to *laografia*. He nevertheless adds in a footnote that Bernhard Schmidt had written this to him: "The term *laografia*, which you first introduced, seems most aptly chosen to me and very suitable for naturalization in other languages too. I never approved of the entry of the English word 'folklore' into our usage but always avoided that word, as did my late friend Reinhold Köhler. But the term *Volkskunde*, the use of which is now predominant in Germany, also seems apt to me" (1909a: 3, n. 3). Thus, Politis was able to hint that, in the absence of any real consensus among European scholars on this question, they might like to consider the Greek *laografia*, with its clarity and appropriateness; indeed, he also mentions an Italian proposal to do just that (1909a: 2, n. 3). But the idea never took hold. The reasons lay less in the term itself—though certainly other languages had their homespun equivalents to Thoms' "good Saxon compound"—than in the parochial nature of Greek laography as a discipline. Greek folklorists rarely tried to answer questions that were not of direct relevance to specifically Greek concerns, and Politis was no exception. *Laografia* remained locked into its ideological commitment to a derivative neo-Classicism. Politis himself, as he grew increasingly liberal in his political convictions (Kiriakidou-Nestoros 1978: 154-157), directed his magnificent scorn against the excesses of the earlier and more polemical anti-Fallmerayerists; yet still the newly defined discipline could not escape its inherited, one-sided dependence upon "European" models and "European" approval. This was, after all, a fair reflection of the continuing political condition of the Greek State, and Politis—who had spent part of his student career in Germany—was thoroughly familiar with western scholarship.

Taxonomy and Ideology

Politis gave *laografia* its name. In addition, he undertook to give it its first really systematic taxonomy and thus also the pattern for its future development. The materials which he listed as appropriate to the discipline (see app. A) constitute an almost exhaustive list of what were then considered to be recognizable cultural artifacts. These are divided between two main headings, "monuments of the word" and "traditional activities or practices." His bipartite division reflects the special status which the Greek folklorists always accorded vernacular literature; this is further borne out by the rather miscellaneous character of the second group, which seems to lack a clear, central organizing principle. It is the literary material, too, which receives "monumental" status; the archaeological allusion is no accident. Again, the second category seems to cover the "ordinary" aspects of folklife, although there are some items which suggest "art" (e.g., sculpture). Whatever its peculiarities and biases, however, Politis' organization of the materials of folklore into this general schema was to exert a massive influence on all subsequent scholar-

ship. Most later classifications (e.g., Mazarakis 1964; Spiridakis 1962) are
little more than elaborations of his system (cf. chap. 1, n. 1).

Like any classificatory system, Politis' schema set an artificial grid on the
material and so partly predetermined what would be collected. In that sense,
it became something of a self-fulfilling prophecy—the process which we have
already noted in the very earliest stages of Greek folklore research. At least,
however, the clarity with which he set up his grand schema is such that its
operative principles are relatively easy, from a present-day standpoint, to
identify.

Taking the "monuments of the word" first, we find a remarkable range of
degrees of elaboration in the various categories. Songs, which significantly
head this list, are divided into numerous subcategories; this indicates the
central position which they had held since the very beginning. The lists en-
closed in parentheses represent a still finer order of classification: "e.g.,
carols, songs of Lazarus, Holy Week laments, swallow songs, songs performed
in the course of certain games, songs of the *perperouna* and *klidhonas*, swing
songs, wedding songs, funeral dirges."[4] Politis indicates that this particular
sublisting is not exhaustive, but it suffices to define the next most inclusive
level of the taxonomy. Order and selection are dictated by academic rather
than folk principles—for example, in the dissociation of personal laments
from those sung for the dead Christ during Holy Week. The "swallow song"
appears as an autonomous subcategory, without further elaboration. Yet
Politis' classification of songs does in fact move laography substantially away
from its earlier obsession to present only "seemly" material: "Apart from the
lyrical, epic, religious," and other forms of song already well represented in
the published collections, certain less "literary" genres are now also to be included—a great advance on Evlambios, for example. Obscene songs, which
would formally have come under the "satirical" heading, are absent, however,
and do not appear in Politis' 1914 collection of folksongs either—whether because of his own self-censorship, for fear of possible trouble with the authorities, or because of lack of available material, we can only guess.

Politis' handling of narrative categories is eloquent witness to his special
preoccupations. The belief that narratives of one sort are true (item no. 9)
sets them apart from "myths" (no. 6), "humorous stories" (no. 7), and
"legends or tales" (no. 8); they are essentially cosmological narratives of the
kind which form so important a part of *Modern Greek Mythology*. What,
then, are myths and legends, and how do they really differ from each other?
Here the classification seems to have become somewhat entangled in its commitment to doing two things simultaneously: establishing cultural continuity
between ancient myths and modern fables but, at the same time, keeping
them conceptually separate so as to preserve the inviolability of myth as a

category of Classical discourse. Politis' British contemporaries seem, for all their disagreements, to have accepted a unitary category of "myth" as the proper object of both folklore and anthropology (e.g., Lang 1885: 22-23). While they tended to use the word "tales" to denote the less exotic and more recent forms of mythology, they did not attempt to create a clear analytical distinction between the two categories *for the purpose of studying their own culture by itself*. Again, *foreign* observers in Greece tended to use "myth" for the ancient and "legend" or "tale" for the modern stories, even when an intrinsic connection between them was recognized (e.g., Lenormant 1864: 524). Politis, by contrast, was trapped between a static model of cultural continuity, on the one hand, and the desire to demonstrate the "European" character of Greek culture on the other. These two motivations, tugging in opposed directions, are represented by "myths" (no. 6) and "tales" (nos. 7-9) respectively. The distinction was never worked out in detail in the actual classification of material, and indeed it is difficult to see, in practical terms, how it could have been.

In his treatment of proverbs (no. 5), by contrast, Politis demonstrates a sense of the interpretive importance of context that is quite new in Greek folklore studies. Once again, there is a slight clash with other categories, this time through his insistence on recording "the myths in which [the proverbs] are sometimes mentioned." But in this case the slight inconvenience is potentially far outweighed by the gain. In fact, we see Politis' sense of the intrinsic connection between proverb and tale as early as *Modern Greek Mythology*, where he cites numerous examples. A more surprising omission is the lack of any reference to the *social* context of proverb use as a necessary datum—surprising if only because Politis does in fact often cite the real-life situations to which particular proverbs are appropriate. It may be that the literary nature of his interests here deflected his attention away from this aspect of paroemiology.

Sociological considerations really appear only in the second, more heterogeneous division of Politis' laography. "Customs" (nos. 6, 7), "social organization" (no. 4), "justice" (no. 9), and "worship" (no. 10) are scattered throughout this list. The categories of this incipient sociology are still governed by the old principles. Particularly noteworthy in this respect is the perpetuation of the "kleft-brigand" opposition (in no. 4). Politis was too careful an observer to overlook the fact that "brigands" had their own concepts and means of applying justice, but he still could not bring himself to *equate* them with "klefts" or to catalog their forms of law under the more formal (and implicitly statist) notion of "justice" in general. The items listed under "justice," moreover, all correspond directly to the categories of state law in some obvious way; they are principally concerned with property ownership and transfer, and the reader is further directed to the works of Khrisanthopoulos and von Maurer. The ideology of the nation-state thus directs the organization of Politis' classification of such phenomena.

A rare exception to this domination of the methodology by the forms of state law is seen in the search for traces of patrilineal organization in village society (in no. 4). This, however, is easily explained, despite the fact that the state kinship ideology follows the usual "European" format of the bilateral kindred. The point is that the patrilineal *genos* of Classical times might legitimately be sought as a survival, and it is in fact recognized minimally under state law through the requirement that a bride-to-be announce her mother's *genos* (i.e., maiden name).

In matters religious, Politis is somewhat more adventurous, perhaps because his first loyalty was to the Hellenist ideal rather than to the Orthodox church. Under "worship," he distinguishes between ecclesiastical and nonecclesiastical cult practices. Among the latter, he recognizes a category of "orgiastic" cults, though this is an instance of neo-Classical hyperbole: both of the cults listed under this heading are in some degree ecstatic, but their Dionysiac origins—if such they be (Kakouri 1965; but cf. Danforth 1979)— are at best muted in present-day performance. In general, Politis seems to have had no hesitation in listing ostensibly Christian cults as pagan survivals. Influenced by the Grimms and Wachsmuth in particular, he recognized the syncretic character of many saints' cults; and, while he was not the first to do this, he dealt with the material more thoroughly than any of his predecessors. In his early discussion of the cult of Saint Nicholas, for example, he acknowledged the insights of d'Istria (1863) and Wachsmuth (1864) into its origins in the worship of the maritime god Poseidon, but he proposes "to examine the connection between the sea god of the ancients with this saint, because the above-mentioned writers confined themselves to merely hinting at the similarity between Poseidon and Saint Nicholas" (1871: 58). His discussion indicates some knowledge of the medieval literature as well as of the more usual Classical and modern folk sources.

At the most general level, Politis' laographic taxonomy may be seen as an amalgam of Classical and modern categories. The choice of each term seems to have been largely contingent on whether the material in question already formed part of the existing corpus of folklore or whether its existence in modern Greek culture was simply presumed on the basis of Classical or ethnographic parallels. Such speculative projection undoubtedly did take place during the construction of the taxonomy. Politis lists divination by sieving, for example, yet Lawson soon afterward reported that he had not in fact encountered any present-day instances of this Classical practice (1910: 331). In numerous such ways the taxonomy was predisposed to register possible survivals, whether or not there was much evidence for their widespread existence, whereas other traits might not be catered for in advance by this schema. This is yet another instance of the way in which the Hellenist model could be characterized as largely self-perpetuating.

Politis' grand taxonomy remained essentially unmodified throughout his subsequent writings. It captures for us many of the strains inherent in the Greek folklorists' peculiar form of survivalism. Possibly Politis himself viewed it as little more than a first approximation, although all the operative principles were well in place. Later work, such as his immensely popular *Selections from the Songs of the Greek People* (1914), elaborates the original schema without substantially affecting its overall orientation. Most of the secondary trimming and adding, moreover, arose from a steady increase in the availability of historical and ethnographic data, much of it a direct outcome of Politis' own efforts to organize the discipline into an efficient operation. The new material which this process generated was thus selected and ordered to confirm, not to challenge, the tenets of ideological Hellenism. That ideology was now openly and actively irredentist.

A Verbal Archaeology

Greek irredentism was an explicitly historical movement: past glories would be restored in the none too distant future. In this context, Politis' focus on the "monumental" aspects of verbal folklore is not simply an abstruse archaeological metaphor. He regarded songs and folktales both as relics and commemorations of the past and as prophecies of future redemption. His extreme historical literalism is particularly well exemplified by his espousal of the "*Urtext* hypothesis," that essentially stemmatic arrangement of oral texts on a philological *Stammbaum*; but it was also buttressed by the growing record of folk texts which mentioned significant places and personalities of history. The desire to commemorate individual deeds, the peculiarly Hellenic characteristic of which d'Istria had made so much, was equally necessary to Politis' view of culture history as a series of fixed points to guide the voyage of national self-discovery.

It is thus no accident that Politis begins his *Selections from the Songs of the Greek People* with the category of "historical" songs. These are verses which commemorate events known from documentary sources, starting with the sack of Adrianople (1361) and, significantly (as we shall shortly see), the Fall of Constantinople and the ravishing of its famed Hagia Sophia cathedral (1453). The latest event to be commemorated in the songs of this section, Greece's failure to wrest the major portion of Epirus from Turkey under the terms of the Treaty of Berlin, occurred in 1881. Note that, although "anti-establishment" and factional songs have commemorated *internal* political events (e.g., see Katsoulis 1975: 225 on the politico-military upheavals of

1897), these found no place in Politis' collection—least of all in the "historical" section, which was concerned with events of a strictly territorial and international nature.

The next section of the *Selections* consists of "kleftic songs." Given the
elaborate critical notes in which Politis addresses the historical background to
some of these texts, it may seem surprising that they have not been included
in the preceding category. It should be remembered, however, that the notion
of a distinctive genre of kleftic song was already established in the ethnological literature by the time he entered the scene. The songs in this section,
moreover, do not deal with single events which—and this is the significant
point—can be given specific dates. In addition, the activities of the klefts, although conventionally interpreted by Politis as contributions to the patriotic
cause, are both *sui generis* and comparatively small in scale; they do not take
the form of pitched battles or the capture of cities, alien ways of fighting to
the mountain guerrillas and brigands, but celebrate the klefts' rugged life-
style. For all these reasons, Politis found no cause to challenge the viability of
the "kleftic" category of folksongs.

The "historical" songs deal with events which occurred before the places
which they celebrate became parts of a free and independent Greece, and the
"kleftic songs" commemorate a historical phase within the same time con-
straint. After the "kleftic" category, however, comes another group which
seems suddenly to take us further *back* in time to the Byzantine period. This
consists of the so-called Akritic songs.

It had been recognized for some time that certain narrative songs apparently recalled names and events of an identifiably Byzantine character (e.g.,
Zambelios 1852; Büdinger 1866). In 1875, however, the philological world
was given details of the discovery, some five years earlier, of the first known
manuscript of the "Akritic epic"—a long poem dealing with those same personalities and events (Sathas and Legrand 1875; Ioannidis 1887; cf. Kalonaros
1970). The thematic resemblances were striking in the extreme, and the
philologist-historian K. Sathas immediately proclaimed the folksong texts to
be the constituents of an "Akritic cycle." On January 14, 1907, on the occasion of his installation as rector of the University of Athens, Nikolaos Politis proclaimed that the entire textual corpus represented "the national epic of
the modern Greeks"; he followed this two years later with the publication of
a set of "Akritic" folksong texts in the first volume of *Laografia* (Politis
1909a).

The scholars' excitement was understandable. Quite apart from the possible literary merit of these materials, the manuscript epic—of which other versions soon came to light—seemed to confirm Zambelios' confident assertion
that Byzantium had provided the link in the popular culture between ancient

and modern times; indeed, he had based that opinion in part on a folksong text, "Andronikos' Sons," which was now classified as "Akritic."

To Politis, the songs no less than the manuscript texts supported both the territorial and the historical claims of ideological Hellenism:

> From the edges of Cappadocia to the Ionian Islands, and from Macedonia and the western regions of the Black Sea down as far as Crete and Cyprus, songs are sung to this day that relate the feats and adventures of Digenes and his struggles against the Apelates and Saracens; and traditions are recounted by word of mouth which recall the places and objects which are associated with Digenes' name. In these, the imagination of the people embroidered myths [*sic*], most of which it took over and renewed out of the rich mythical [*sic*] heritage of antiquity, and constructed the ideal type of the hero—as youthful as Achilles, as strong as Herakles, and as glorious as Alexander. To put the matter in its appropriately proud context, in Digenes Akrites the desires and ideals of the Hellenic nation reach their peak, because in this man the long centuries of ceaseless struggle by the Hellenic against the Islamic world are symbolized. (1907: 11)

The antiquity of the heroic ideals is combined with the presumed historicity of the actual text to present an epic that is truly "national." The argument is entirely characteristic of Politis. The territorial extent of Hellenism is claimed, as it were, by the songs themselves, and the border is clearly marked as that which separates Hellenism (rather than Christianity) from Islam. This is the philological embodiment of the Great Idea (*Megali Idhea*), the doctrine of Greek irredentism whereby all the lands of Classical and Byzantine Hellenism should be reclaimed for the reborn nation.

Politis' political involvement in the irredentist movement had always been intense. Even as a schoolboy, he had attempted to enlist as a volunteer to fight in the 1866 uprising in Crete. He later ran undercover courier missions for nationalist groups in Constantinople; although he himself escaped detection, his brother was accidentally arrested in his place by the Turkish police. Now he had a means at his disposal for pursuing the national goal in an arena more suited to his academic talents. The Akritic songs, while found virtually everywhere in the Greek-speaking world, were reported in particularly large numbers from Asia Minor (especially Cappadocia), Crete, and Cyprus—all lands which were still under foreign rule. Since these songs seemed to combine a form of mythology with medieval prosopography, the latter reinforced by the discovery of the manuscript poems, they rapidly assumed great importance in the scholarly dimensions of the Great Idea.

The label "Akritic," however, created something of a paradox. It was taken to refer to the borders (*akrai*) of the Byzantine Empire, which the Akritai were expected to defend against the depredations of both brigandlike Apelates and Arab marauders. But, in practice, the status of these border regions seems to have been unstable. As border barons, the Akritai evidently attended to their own interests at least as assiduously as they did to those of their imperial masters. This emerges quite clearly in the epic and the folksongs, as well as from independent documentary sources.[5]

A related difficulty concerns the name Digenes. Conventionally translated as "twy-born" (e.g., Mavrogordato 1956: xxvii), it has been taken as a reference to the hero's mixed ancestry. The epics have him as the son of an Arab emir and a Greek woman; the songs, while preserving the basic element of dual ancestry, vary the actual "ethnicities" involved. Politis nevertheless presented Digenes as the very epitome of the Hellenic virtues; after all, as more recent scholars have pointed out (notably Veloudis 1968), Alexander the Great was also of mixed parentage. But a small minority of Politis' contemporaries were uncomfortable with his conception of the Akritic hero. Karolidis (1906) was the first to point out that one might just as easily take the name as symbolizing the "twy-born culture (*politismos*)" of the border regions and, thus, as something very far removed from a cultural exemplar for Hellenism. While it is evident that Digenes' dual ancestry represents some sort of social conflict, as it does in the songs, there is no reason to suppose that this conflict was necessarily concerned with anything that we might call ethnicity (cf. Lambrinos 1947; Herzfeld 1980b).

Politis, who had studied in Germany under the great Byzantinologist Karl Krumbacher, nevertheless chose to interpret the "Akritic cycle" in the literalist terms of his ideology, according to which everything "Byzantine" was also "Greek." He was of course aware that parallels could be found in other periods and places. Nor did he ignore the similarity of some of the texts that he classified as Akritic to songs placed in other categories (mainly "kleftic songs" and "ballads"), as his detailed commentaries show. But Politis had never been deaf to the possibility of non-Greek parallels in any area of Greek folklore; for him, these did not detract in the least from the Greekness of the local materials. To explain the relationship between Akritic and other songs, he applied the concept of *simfirmos*—literally, "conflation," but carrying a strong sense of "contamination" that fits well with his concern and that of his successors to maintain clear-cut distinctions between "pure" types of cultural artifact. As a result, the integrity of the "Akritic cycle" has never been seriously challenged by Greek scholars; even those who have disagreed with the irredentist interpretation of the songs (e.g., Apostolakis 1929; Lambrinos 1947) have accepted the basic premise of the classification itself. The Hellenists stuck to their view that the Akritic manuscripts represented a "national epic," while their critics objected to the "ethnic" implications of that title. But that the Akritic texts represent a discrete phase in Greek culture-history, somewhat analogous to that of the klefts, has never been the object of a sustained critique in Greece.

Politis' technique for dealing with cross-categorial similarities, especially his use of "conflation" as an explanatory device, shows how and why the taxonomy was able to remain a self-fulfilling prophecy for so long. The notion of formulaic variation had not yet been developed in the context of Greek folklore, and Politis evidently thought that texts moved around the country as massive unities. Not only single texts but even the entire categories of "kleftic" and "Akritic" texts were presented as invariant arrangements of ideas and motifs. Thus, for example, in discussing the "Song of Mavrianos and His Sister," Politis, unable to detect clear thematic links with the Akritic poems or identifiable episodes from Byzantine history, wrote: "The song has a certain similarity with the Akritic songs: the names of the characters, where names are mentioned, are the well-known ones of the Akritic songs; in some variants, indeed, Digenes is mentioned by name" (1914: 112).

It is indicative of the thinking which this passage illustrates that *sinafia*, the word here translated as "similarity," can also mean "contact." There is thus a strong hint of the kind of textual miscegenation conveyed by that other Greek term, *simfirmos*. Formally, the line between the category of "ballads" (which includes the song in question) and that of "Akritic songs" is sharp and clear, even if the texts themselves do sometimes inconveniently straddle it. The taxonomy, moreover, is a strictly academic one and does not reflect ordinary vernacular usage. Although the term for "ballads," *paraloyes*, may just conceivably have been taken from the folk idiom (Economides 1969), its folk use covers many of the texts classified by Politis as "Akritic" (which is *not* a folk term). Given the premises on which the taxonomy was initially constructed, one can easily understand how the folk category of *paraloyes* could be artificially emasculated to allow the "Akritic songs" a discrete (and sufficiently numerous) existence in the corpus.

The self-fulfilling character of the taxonomy should be evident by now. The Greek folklorists' attempt to build up a sound classification of the national folklore, their static view of history, and the effect of the taxonomy itself upon the kinds of data that were collected—all jointly contributed to a rapid reinforcement of the most important among the original articles of faith, those of cultural continuity with ancient Greece, the European character of the entire Greek people, and the territorial and chronological boundaries of Hellenism. There is no point in trying to prove that any of these tenets was factually wrong. Rather, as we have stressed throughout this book, they all represented a particular selection of cultural phenomena as significant. The size and sophistication of Politis' schema simply amplified the effects of the original selectional criteria. The self-reinforcement of the folklore taxonomy became, in his hands, an affirmation of the eventual triumph of Hellenic culture. The prophecy was thus a political one. When it failed, in what the Greeks still call *the* Catastrophe of their defeat in Asia Minor in 1922, the active political role of irredentist folklore also effectively came to an end. Politis presided over the achievement of a unified discipline, and it was only shortly after his death in 1921 that events pushed that discipline away from the center of the ideological stage. It is to be hoped that what has been said thus far will now lend some meaning to the final burgeoning of hope and its total, destructive collapse, as we examine these developments in the next chapter.

Chapter 6
Expansion and Collapse

". . . ours once more . . ."

Seeds of Contradiction: Defining Hellenism

Although the irredentists based their goals on the premise of continuity with the Classical era, it was the Byzantine capital, Constantinople (İstanbul), that they hoped to turn into the capital of a totally liberated Greek nation-state. The historians and folklorists did much, as we have seen, to reinstate the Byzantine period as the essential link between high antiquity and the present. The ironic result was to make Constantinople, the New Rome, the *Hellenists'* goal rather than that of more "Romeic" thinkers and politicians. Of course, we should not insist on drawing a rigid line between the two ideological trends insofar as their attitudes to irredentism were concerned. But it is fair to say that it was the Hellenists who showed particular alacrity in the pursuit of the Great Idea.

The Greeks' claim to be the modern representatives of Hellas did sometimes raise complex questions about the exact nature of their collective identity. That there were many different forms of the Greek language was the least of the difficulties: some of the most outlying or (to an urban Greek) incomprehensible dialects could be shown to preserve particularly archaic forms (cf. Browning 1969), and there was no doubt about the closeness of their relationship to each other and to ancient Greek. Even the non-Greek languages spoken on Greek territory revealed extensive traces of Greek influence, though claims of "Homeric" derivation for lexical items in Koutsovlach (Papazisis 1976: 8) and Cypriot Greek (Kiprianou 1967: 51) should be treated with great circumspection.[1] Politically, the geographical extent of the Greek language and its widespread etymological connections with minority languages provided a powerful argument for those who insisted that political boundaries should recognize the full expanse of Hellenism. The presence of songs and narratives that could be linked to Classical or Byzantine themes further strengthened such language-based claims, especially when the folk traditions could be interpreted as themselves giving voice to some irredentist sentiment. This, as we shall shortly see, was not thought to be at all improbable.

One nagging question has never been satisfactorily resolved. It concerns the use of the word "Hellenes" as a term of collective self-designation. The ancient Greeks at least as far back as Homer, as Zambelios had proudly noted, shared some awareness of their common cultural traditions; this was hardly diminished by their failure to translate it into political unity or by their bitter recognition of that failure. Their categorical distinction between "Hellenes" and "barbarians" became part of the latter-day nationalist vocabulary. Indeed, the literary antiquarian Eustathius, bishop of Thessaloniki, had roundly declared as early as the twelfth century that humanity could be divided into the opposed categories of "Hellene" and "barbarian" (Migne *PG* 135: 708; Politis 1901: 11). Such self-conscious archaism was not uncommon among Byzantine writers. On the other hand, some ecclesiastical writers used "Hellenes" as a term of *exclusion*, to describe all those who clung to their ancestral religion and refused to become Christians. From there, it was not a difficult step to using the term for any religious outsiders at all; Theodoret of Cyrrhus even described the Old Testament priests of Baal as "priests of the Hellenes" (Politis 1901: 7)!

The literary sources make their terms of reference reasonably clear. What is not at all certain is the degree to which their usages correspond to those of the populace at large. Knowledge of the "idolatrous" implications of "Hellenes" prevailed among the ecclesiastically minded until (and beyond) the 1821 Revolution. Some evidence from the folklore suggests that the name itself was preserved in popular usage (see especially Kakridis 1967), though whether rural Greeks commonly used it of themselves before the nineteenth century is far from clear. It is also uncertain how uninterruptedly the term had remained in vernacular speech or whether it had enjoyed equal currency in all parts of the Greek-speaking world.

Defining Greeks: Hellenic or Romeic?

The alternative term was *Romii*. Of its popularity there can be no doubt whatsoever, and its cognate *romeika* was no less unquestionably the usual label for the spoken language. Thus it was entirely logical for the protagonists of linguistic demoticism to prefer the term to "Hellenes" (although this was not a rigid association) and to make an ideological issue out of its use. It is this terminological opposition which has given us the labels used in this study for the two main ideological currents in Greek culture history; "Hellenist" and "Romeicist" are more suitable for our present purposes than *katharevousianos* (or "purist") and "demoticist," since the cultural issue is much broader in scope than the latter pair of terms, with their linguistic referents, would imply.

Politis, predictably, declared himself in favor of the name "Hellenes." Just a year before the language question (*ghlossiko zitima*) erupted in serious rioting in Athens, he published a defense of the Hellenic name against the views of the more extreme demoticists. The poet Palamas had criticized another writer, Eftaliotis, for publishing a *History of the Hellenic Nation* rather than of *Romiossini*. Politis, ever mindful of the need to deal with both sides of an argument, responded that "there never was any need whatsoever for evidence to prove that the Hellenes called themselves *Romii* also; nobody ever doubted that. But [Palamas] . . . ought to have demonstrated, first, that the foundation of the Byzantine state cut every link connecting the Hellene of the old world with the subject of the Byzantine emperors and, then, that from the years of Justinian's rule until the 1821 Revolution the name of 'Hellene' had disappeared from the national consciousness" (1901: 4).

Politis' essay on this subject is of interest for two reasons. In the first place, it gives a good picture of his careful scholarship, especially of his conscientious avoidance of purely *ad hominem* vituperation, even when he was discussing a matter about which he held passionate convictions. The other reason is more general and is also more closely related to the articulating theme of this book: the essay illustrates how a scholar, fully in possession of the evidence for both points of view, could still decide unequivocally in favor of one over the other. In the end, of course, as Politis himself saw, the issue was not one of deciding who was factually right. Rather, it was a question of which term was more *appropriate*. Where, in other words, was the most significant (rather than the "real") starting point of Greek history, in Classical Greece or in Christian Byzantium? The entire history of laography is that of attempts to derive significance from the riotous variety of Greek culture.

Hellenes or *Romii*? In posing and then attempting to answer that question, Politis was acting principally as a philologist, not a sociologist. He was not investigating ethnicity as a view of the collective self. Instead, he tried to establish that the term "Hellenes" had been *in use* among the Greeks since ancient times. His goal was thus to establish a link that was above all artifactual, or archaeological, in accordance with the wider principles of his methodology.

Politis was fully aware of the reasons why "Hellenes" gave way to *Romii* in popular favor: ecclesiastical disapproval of "Hellenism," the maintenance of "Roman" law in the Byzantine Empire, and the post-1453 continuation of the patriarch's temporal power as head of the "Romans" (*Rum*) (Politis 1901: 6). He also had detailed knowledge of the mythical character of the "Hellenes" who appear in folktales. Yet his unwillingness to examine such usages in context seems to have prevented him from exploring the sense of exclusion, quite apparent in some of his own ethnographic materials, which the term conveyed.

A single example will illustrate the problem. At least as early as 1871, Politis had read Robert Pashley's colorful *Travels in Crete*, for he makes several references to that work in *Modern Greek Mythology*—even, in the 1874 section on "Hellenes" itself, to Pashley's discussion of the related phenomenon of "the forty-cubit giant's tomb" (*tou sarandapikhou to mnima*). But he does *not* discuss Pashley's fully explicit reference to the term "Hellenes." When we look at the relevant passage in Pashley, the reason for such a curious omission becomes a little clearer:

> I find the belief in the ancient site said to exist above Samaría, and to have been the last refuge of the ancient Hellenes, is entertained by the Samarióte peasant who undertakes to shew me the way to them, and by most of his fellow-villagers. . . .
>
> As to the Hellenic remains my ascent ended in disappointment. . . . On my throwing out some slight doubts about the vestiges which I saw being *very* ancient, and suggesting that they could hardly belong to the celebrated "Hellenes," my Samarióte guide exclaimed, in the tone of one half offended at my ignorance or incredulity: *"Here* was the end of them my good Sir!" as if the matter had been one in which his local information entitled him to pronounce with authority.
>
> (1837, II: 267–269)

We need not necessarily suppose that Politis intentionally suppressed this passage. Given his assumption that the memory of the name "Hellenes" alone was sufficient evidence of continuity, he may simply have dismissed the local guide's comment (*"Here* was the end of them . . .") as simpleminded nonsense; in Politis' view, the man was a Hellene himself! Pashley's own rather dubious remarks about this informant can hardly have inspired much confidence.

Yet what Pashley records is an unequivocal statement by a local person to the effect that he did not regard himself as a "Hellene" or think of the "Hellenes" as still in existence. This does not mean that, as a Cretan still living under Turkish rule, he would necessarily not have called his mainland compatriots "Hellenes" in the contemporary political sense of the word; such variable usage is characteristic of rural Greek "ethnic" terminology to this day. In this context, however, Pashley's Samariote guide was clearly not using "Hellene" as a term of self-designation.

Politis never denied that folk tradition had the Hellenes as a race of mythical giants; those stories were his main source of evidence for the continued use of the term. It is thus hardly likely that he deliberately suppressed such evidence as Pashley's in favor of "chauvinistic follies" (Kordatos 1972: 22,

n. 1). His interest, quite simply, was directed elsewhere. He is very forthright
about the archaeological style of his arguments:

> As to [the Hellenes'] strength, there exist many traditions, one of
> which we present here. In it, *the recollections of ancient Hellas are ap-*
> *parently linked to those of Byzantium, since the scene is set in Con-*
> *stantinople.* Heuzey heard this tradition among the inhabitants of the
> village of Khrisovitsi in Acarnania. "This happened," they recount, "in
> the time of our grandfathers' grandfathers. Certain people from our
> village went to Constantinople. There, learning that there was a cer-
> tain old woman of the race of the Hellenes, they went to see her. She
> was of supernatural height but was blind with advanced age. She asked
> them about the place whence they came and, turning to one of them,
> said to him, 'Give me your hand.' He was frightened and did not dare
> do so, but snatched up a fire iron, one end of which was broadened out
> (as is usual in the East), and offered it to the old woman. She squeezed
> it between her fingers and crushed it! 'You're strong,' she said, 'but not
> as strong as we are.' She thought she was holding his hand."
> (1874: 503-504; my emphasis)

The very name "Hellenes" alone was an artifact that, for Politis, claimed all
the territories in which it was found for the Greek nation.

Politis concludes this particular passage by citing a Danish parallel, and we
may be tempted to wonder why this, at least, did not deter him from so literal an interpretation. Given his frame of reference, however, there is no reason
why it should have done so. Artifactual parallels between different cultures
no more dissolved the conceptual boundaries between them than cross-
categorial textual similarities between songs undermined the taxonomy which
had been set up to accommodate them.

Some of the fluctuations in the fortunes of the Hellenic name were a matter of historical record. As Politis observed, its relative popularity was somewhat contingent upon political events during the Byzantine era; after the
Latin sack of Constantinople in 1204, for example, "Hellenes" seems to have
become more popular for a while, since any "Roman" term carried unplea-
sant associations. Folksongs which mention the last Byzantine ruler as "the
Hellene Constantine" apparently mirror late Byzantine literary usage, even
that of ecclesiastical authors, and references to "Hellene dragons" as the de-
fenders of the last Byzantine outposts may reflect popular usage (Politis
1901: 15; cf. Vacalopoulos 1970: 183-186, 230-232, 356, nn. 93-95). But it
is difficult to be sure: given the reputation of the mythical Hellenes of the
folk narratives for superhuman strength and size, some of these usages may be
metaphorical in origin. Politis, naturally, thought not, if indeed the idea ever
suggested itself to him. It may be significant that these "historical" references

come from the eastern parts of the Greek-speaking world, especially Cappadocia—relatively near to the source, that is—and may indeed represent the
survival of a true self-designation.

Even among the eastern Greeks, however, the generic *Romania* remained
in common use as a term for the Greek-speaking regions. Again, this did not
really affect Politis' argument, since he never tried (or needed) to establish
that the Greeks had never used the term of themselves. In fact, his argument
went in the opposite direction at this point, revealing his assumption that the
Greeks had prior rights to the choice of nomenclature (1901: 18). Pointing
out that the Wallachians and Moldavians called their combined territories
Romania and themselves *Romani*, he argued that, had the Greeks wanted to
use these names officially of themselves, they would have had to force the
"real" Romanians to choose something else! Even allowing for rhetorical exaggeration, we see here the ethnocentrism of the true irredentist, the assertion
of prior rights to ethnic self-determination over an expanding geographical
space.

Unity, Homogeneity, and the Irredentist Ideal

From the foregoing, we can see something of the historicist logic whereby
New Rome was to become the capital of the new Hellas. The exponents of
the Great Idea, the *meghaloïdheates*, were determined to restore Greek hege-
mony over the widest territorial expanse that Greek culture had ever experienced. That dream never died completely; even the last king of Greece,
Constantine II, preferred to count his name in the line of Byzantine emperors
as Constantine XIII. But far and away the greatest flowering of the Great Idea
came in the first two decades of the present century, and the folklorists, led
by Politis, were active in its scholarly defense.

That the recapture of Constantinople remained a constant theme in both
learned and popular discourse ever since the destruction of the Byzantine
Empire is beyond doubt. But it was not a theme which held identical appeal
for all. The higher clergy, especially, discovered that their temporal power
over the Christian subjects of the sultan was actually greater in some respects
than it had been under the Byzantine emperors. Many of them consequently
opposed the rise of nationalistic activity during the years immediately before
independence (see, e.g., Dakin 1973: 46, 58, 238-239, n. 1; Kordatos 1972:
71-72; Katsoulis 1975: 17-49; Anthimos of Jerusalem in Clogg 1976: 56-
66). They argued that it was the will of God that Christendom should suffer
for its sins through subjugation to the Turks. This explanation of an otherwise (to the religiously minded) inexplicable event is reproduced also in the
folksongs, according to which "it is the will of God (*thelima Theu*) that the

City [i.e., Constantinople] should turn Turk [i.e., Moslem]." The crucial question here is thus to what extent the recognition of divine intervention constitutes a form of fatalism, a resignation to disaster.

The Fall of the City had been predicted in numerous popular prophecies, although the inhabitants of Constantinople had continued to hope for the last-minute intervention of God on their side. When the City finally fell, "the last glimmer of hope disappeared" (Vacalopoulos 1970: 203). At first, the despondency of the Christians must have been enormous. Some of the prophecies of the City's recapture—notably the story of the fish which leaped from the frying pan only half-cooked when the Turks arrived and would jump back into the pan to finish frying when the City reverted to Christendom— sound almost like allegories of the impossible.[2] Others, drawing on the mysterious circumstances of the disappearance of the last emperor's body, offered more hope: the emperor—having meanwhile been temporarily transformed into marble—would return one day with sword in hand and chase the Turks all the way back to their legendary ancestral home, the "Red Apple-Tree."[3] Some of the prophecies, again, were more contrived. The so-called *Prophecies of Agathangelos* "were reputedly written in Sicily in 1279 and printed in Milan in 1555. In fact they were forgeries compiled by the archimandrite Theoklitos Polyeidis, a native of Edirne [Adrianople], towards the middle of the eighteenth century" (Clogg 1973: 21; cf. Politis 1918: 165-169). Whatever their origins, most such prophecies seem to have exercised a considerable influence upon the popular imagination, especially as the new national consciousness began to take hold. That they were interpreted as signs of hope and imminent redemption is not at issue. It is less clear whether they represent a continuous desire to achieve that redemption on the part of the masses ever since 1453.

Politis thought that they did. Not only did he consider them evidence of widespread national aspirations, but he saw their extensive distribution throughout the Greek-speaking world as proof of the Greeks' cultural homogeneity and shared sense of destiny. In an important article on popular beliefs concerning the reestablishment of the Hellenic nation, he explained his position:

> One of the most solid foundations of national consciousness resides in a community of manners and customs, of beliefs and traditions; in a uniform perception of the outside world; and, above all, in an identical display of feelings, of aspirations, and of hopes. These are the *homo-tropic* customs which, in their admirable definition of the idea of fatherland and national solidarity, consumed the Athenians (according to Herodotus) when on the eve of the Battle of Plataea they rejected Mardonius' tempting and advantageous blandishments and showed the

Lacedaemonians [i.e., Spartans] that they had a very explicit sense of
the bonds which united them to the rest of the Hellenes.

(1918: 151-152)[4]

Heterotropic customs are those which one finds among ethnically mixed pop-
ulations. Such people, when they form a nation-state, are simply committing
an act of political invention; their collective identity is a wholly artificial construct. The Greeks, by contrast, aimed at a political union which by its very
nature would be indissoluble; for Politis, there was nothing "constructed" or
"constituted" about Greek national identity. The Greeks' aspirations, the
product of a "homotropic" culture, were said to be summed up in the Great
Idea, which above all else called for the recapture of Constantinople and the
resumption of the liturgy in the great church of Hagia Sophia: "voilà le cou-
ronnement de l'idéal grec."

Politis realized that, in the immediate aftermath of the Fall, the Greeks
virtually abandoned hope (1918: 154). This state of affairs did not, however,
last for a long while. The Greeks were not "oriental fatalists," he argued, and
they soon began to look forward to the future with renewed optimism. Politis' observation is not without some ethnographic support; whether "fatalism" as such exists anywhere in the world is a moot point, but it is certainly
true that Greek villagers disapprove of those who simply refuse to struggle
against the odds (Sanders 1962; Herzfeld 1981b). More relevant to our present concerns, however, is Politis' view of the more optimistic attitude as characteristic of Greek culture, not merely in general terms but also in the form
of specific beliefs about national redemption. Here, the verbal artifacts in
question combine the quality of archaeological culture traits with that of
ideological statements in their own right.

Of these texts, the most famous is probably the so-called "Song of Hagia
Sophia." Its last line became a rallying cry, not merely for scholars and politicians but for all Greeks who looked forward to the new golden age of Hellenism. For all of them, the song was a text which signified the ultimate goal.
I use the words "text" and "signify" advisedly: the semiotic dimension of
laography, its construction as a political and cultural text, is nowhere more
palpable than in the prominence accorded this one song, with what was interpreted as a stirring promise that all would be "ours once more."

Redeeming the Fall of the City

Here follows the text in full, preceded by Politis' explanatory comment:

Among the numerous laments for the sack of Constantinople which
were composed right after that disaster, the folksongs have pride of
place because, with profound simplicity, they express a feeling of per-

severance throughout the great national travails and the enslaved people's certain hope of being restored to its freedom and to its rightful position. It is indeed a matter for wonder that these were generated at a time when the nation seemed to have lost all, with the Fall of Constantinople [just past] and not a glimmer of hope anywhere in sight. But the nation's great disaster comes exactly midway between fear and hope, desperation and encouragement. For before this disaster the prophecies of the future were pessimistic and predicted calamities and disasters, whereas after the sack [of Constantinople] they spread a completely different message, one which indicated a change in the national attitude. For a long time before the sack of the state capital, oracles predicted the imminent disaster, but immediately after the sack positive hopes for the nation's future destiny were born, and the conviction took root among the Greek people that it would inevitably regain by the sword the paternal heritage which the enemy had [likewise] seized by the sword:

God sounds forth, the earth sounds forth, the heavens too sound forth,
and the great church (monastiri) of Hagia Sophia sounds forth also,
with its four hundred sounding boards (simandra), sixty-two bells,
where for every bell there's a priest, for every priest a deacon.
The king sings to the left, to the right the patriarch,
and the very columns shook from the sound of so much psalmody.
As they began the mass and the king came out
a voice came to them from heaven, from the mouth of an archangel:
"cease the mass, bring down the saints' [icons],
priests—take the holy objects; you, O candles, snuff out your light,
for it is the will of God that the City should turn Turk.
Only send word to the West that three ships should come—
one to take the crucifix, the next to take the Gospel,
and the third and last to take our holy altar
that these dogs may not seize them from us and desecrate them."
The Holy Virgin was seized with trembling, and the icons wept tears.
"Be silent, Lady and Mistress, do not weep so much:
again in years and times to come, all will be yours again."

(1914: 12-13)[5]

The text given by Politis has been challenged in copious detail (Apostolakis 1939; Kordatos 1972: 55-56; cf. also Dimaras 1972: 55; Romaios 1959: 119-138). Here, however, we shall simply focus on the last line, which differs in one minute but enormously significant detail from the version quoted in Politis' 1918 'Popular Beliefs': the possessive pronoun "yours" is used instead of "ours." "Yours" is what Politis' sources mostly give, and "yours" is

what every responsible reprinting of the complete text (including Politis'
own) provides, but "*ours*" is commonly substituted whenever the two lines
(or just the second one) appear on their own, out of context. While it is unlikely that this habit originated with Politis, it did find in him an early propa-
gator.

We should not underestimate this seemingly minor alteration. Its importance does not lie merely in the extent to which it enables us to see how far
Politis could tolerate contradiction between his accurate scholarship and the
interpretation that he sought; that contradiction lies more in our own retrospective view than in his schema of interpretation. The import of the pronoun
shift is of a vastly more general kind. In it lies a whole conception of the
Hellenes' place in the world, of their identity as a people, and of the territorial implications of the Great Idea. It calls for a detailed analysis and provides a
fitting climax to this account of the development of laography as an ideological text.

A Text for a New Age?

The final line of the "ours" version fits with Politis' view that the Greeks,
after the initial shock in 1453, had soon come to regard the future with renewed optimism. This view directs his interpretation of oracles about the
restoration of Constantinople generally, as an example will illustrate. Referring to a Trapezuntine song in which the Fall of the City is blamed on a trai-
tor who had handed the keys to the Turks, he observes that "the key of Hagia
Sophia will fall from heaven and, in order to open the basilica, a mason from
heaven and a workman from the earth will be needed, which clearly means
that Hagia Sophia will not be restored to its first masters except by the help
of God and with the assistance of a hero" (1918: 155). Here is that individualistic Greek hero once again. For Politis, the prophecy seemed to be a
genuine folk expression of what later became the Great Idea. The senior
clergy were often far less convinced that such predictions were divine calls to
action. They preferred a more passive interpretation, for what evidence was
there that God intended to help the Greek nation at that particular time? Or,
in the words of Anthimos of Jerusalem: "Who cannot take as an example in
the present life this same God [i.e., Jesus] , seeing him hunger and thirst, suffering tribulation, distress, persecution? This truly is the present existence,
the life of the true Christian, if he wishes to be worthy of the heavenly kingdom" (Clogg 1976: 58). Prophecies of divine intervention are especially ambiguous symbols, liable to diverse interpretations according to the ideological
convictions of the interpreter.

Politis saw the promise of redemption as addressed to the Greek *ethnos*,
rather than to Christendom (1918: 154). Such was the assumption which he

brought to the "Song of Hagia Sophia"—found, he asserted with (in this case) more enthusiasm than accuracy, wherever Greek was spoken, "and even among the Vlach-speaking people of Macedonia," who are thereby brought within the sway of the Greek national consciousness. The song, he remarks, "explains the endurance of the race"—a synonym for the Greek *ethnos*—"in the face of national calamities and the ineradicable optimism with which the enslaved nation envisages its liberation and reorganization" (1918: 155-156).

Politis' interpretation of the song as national rather than religious in its frame of reference hinges to some extent on that errant pronoun. A recent commentator, Kostas Romaios, thought Politis' version improbable, but on the strictly literalist grounds that "*ours* once more" makes no sense in the mouth of an archangel (1968: 169). Yet this will not do either: apart from the fact that it is far from clear that the famous final line is meant to be spoken by the archangel, it is impossible to be sure what criteria of "sense" are applicable to a song wrested from its social context and displayed in a verbal museum. Besides, the familiar version obviously made, and makes, perfectly good sense to all those many Greeks who still quote it as the quintessential motto of national sentiment. There are nevertheless good—but quite different—grounds for doubting that the final line promises "us," the people, the realization of our national hopes. At least two comparatively reliable texts from early collections (Fauriel 1824: 340; Manousos 1850: 179) have the form "yours" instead. The "you" of these earlier texts is clearly the Virgin Mary, possibly (when the plural form is given) accompanied by the saints whose icons had to be taken down along with hers.[6]

Why did Politis go along with the popular rewording? That he did so from dishonest motives is extremely unlikely, since he elsewhere cited and published versions with "yours." Ironically, he shares the "ours" version with Khristovasilis (1902: 15), a folksong collector whom he castigated for irresponsibly altering texts because "he wanted to present the popular songs, not as they are, but as they should have been—in *his* judgment, be it understood" (1903: 275). Drastic textual emendation was no part of Politis' methodology. We can therefore conclude only that his acceptance of the "ours" version for the purpose of quotation was an act of carelessness prompted, no doubt, by patriotic enthusiasm. It is a rare lapse. As an exception to Politis' long record of painstaking scholarship, it illustrates in an extreme form how the most conscientious scholar's perception may be affected by preconceived assumptions—in this case, that the "Song of Hagia Sophia" was both "national" and "historical."

In fact, its "historical" is scarcely less problematical than its "national" significance. That the known variants do lament the actual sacking of Constantinople in 1453 seems beyond question. But the purportedly prophetic conclusion—"it *will be* yours/ours *once more*"—is also usually presented in historicist terms; if such a prophecy is tautologous, this is because it projects past events into future time, promising that what *was* ours *will again* be ours. It is not at all certain, however, that the phrase which (following the spirit of the nationalist writers) we have translated here as "will be yours/ours once more" really meant anything of the sort.

The future verb "will be" (*tha 'ne*) is found only in later renderings of the text, again not including Politis' *Selections* version. The usual early rendering has the present tense; and, while this may not be conclusive, since a good deal of semantically insignificant tense switching does take place in many of the songs, it does at least suggest that we should not accept the historicist "translation" unquestioningly. There is, furthermore, no guarantee that *pali* must mean "again" in a temporal sense. It also commonly has the meaning of "still," in the sense of "whatever the case may be." If we regloss the line to remove the intimation of future, historically conceived time, it acquires a radically different cast: "And still, whatever the times may bring, it is *still* yours!" Under a church committed to Ottoman rule for the foreseeable future, and for a populace convinced that even under the most adverse circumstances Christianity represented the eternal verities, such an interpretation might make better sense than the conventional one. Of course we cannot be sure about this. The line may be capable of carrying a wide variety of meanings, among which the nationalist interpretation has certainly enjoyed extraordinarily wide currency in our own time. But here lies the rub. Today, following Politis' lead, scholars and politicians present it as *the* interpretation, the only one suitable for the united nation-state whose symbol of collective regeneration it has become. It is only by assuming that the folklorists were totally divorced from their society that we could argue that they were "right" or "wrong" in their interpretation. In the political context to which they had contributed so much themselves, their reading of the line is neither right nor wrong but ideologically appropriate.

It is also an organic part of that cultural and ideological text whose development we have now followed through nearly a century of scholarship. The historicist assumptions involved in giving the song its title ("of Hagia Sophia"), its date, and its position in the *Selections* are self-evident. Politis also seems to have assumed, in accordance with his methodology, that the song was derived from an *Urtext*, albeit probably an irrecoverable one. Such an *Urtext* would have been a strictly historical account of the tragic end of Constantinople: the number of priests (sixty-two), for example, is upheld as a possibly accurate figure (1914: 12, n.). In such a presuppositional context, it was both logical and consistent for Politis to represent that final, ambiguous line as a temporal prophecy rather than simply as an undying truth. It was this same framework, moreover, that enabled him to suggest how the apparent volte-face from pre-Fall fatalism to post-Fall optimism had come about. For him, it was not a reversal at all. The truly Hellenic character thrived on adversity without the slightest disrespect to the "will of God."

Expanding Horizons

Exactly when the "ours" version originated is a matter for conjecture. It certainly appeared early in the century in quotation form (e.g., Khristovasilis 1902: 18, where it is described as "our national lament"). Even the "yours" versions were susceptible of interpretation in nationalist terms, however, as became evident in a memorial speech in 1906. The speaker declared that no Greek

> forgets that the popular muse . . . turned the aftermath of the sack of Constantinople into an unshakable conviction that divine Providence would return the captured city to the Hellenes . . . as, falling in battle on its ramparts, and intoning his swan song, the immortal emperor of the Greeks thundered unto the generations to come:
> *Our Lady was seized with trembling, and the icons wept tears.*
> *"Be silent, Lady and Mistress; and you, icons, weep not.*
> *Again in years and times to come it will be yours once more."*
>
> (Filaretos 1906: 60)

Whether spoken by emperor or archangel, whether claiming the City as "yours" or "ours," the song serves well as an anthem for resurgent Hellenism. And in fact, perhaps because it was easier to identify with, the "ours" version has remained the one which everybody quotes to this day.

The theme of "ours once more" has enjoyed a considerable vogue in patriotic works of literature also (e.g., Viziinos 1949), not to mention some of the more popularizing pronouncements of scholars (e.g., Megas 1953; Zoras 1953: 116; Sperantsas 1949). As early as the 1860s, Aristotle Valaoritis has the revolutionary hero Athanasios (Thanassis) Diakos—the object of Valvis' especial praise—contemplate the eventual realization of the Great Idea, even as he was still fighting in the original War of Independence:

> *—Bow before the throne*
> *of the first king, the monument of our last one . . .*
> *What's this? You tremble, Diakos? Why do you weep?*
> *Thanassi . . . it is ours!*

This passage (Fourth Song, quoted in Apostolakis 1950: 64, n. 1) shows how well entrenched that final phrase had become long before Politis' scholarly endorsement of it.

It was also taken up by at least one non-Greek writer. The English philhellene Ronald Burrows was moved to compose a paean to the Hellenic

"race" of Europe, on the occasion of the Greeks' capture of Thessaloniki
from Turkey in 1912:

> *We too of the younger North*
> *Claim that Hellas brought us forth,*
> *Made us all we boast to be,*
> *In our islands of the free,*
> *We who are of Byron's kin,*
> *We who fought at Navarin.*
> *Saloníka! Saloníka!*
> *We do seek her! We do seek her!*
> *After centuries of wrong*
> *Cometh true the ancient song.*
> *Lady! Stay thee from thy moan!*
> *Once again she is our own!*
>
> (1913: 92)[7]

Burrows, who enthusiastically dedicated a copy of this poem to the Greek
scholar-diplomat John Gennadius,[8] evidently thought that the "ancient song"
referred to the fall of Thessaloniki around 1430. It mattered little; Burrows
believed that *all* the Greek-speaking territories still under foreign control
should be handed over to the Greek State forthwith. Arguing for the cession
of Cyprus (which the British had in fact offered Greece, vainly, in return for
a promise of neutrality during the First World War), he contended:

> The Greek race is not decadent, not on the down grade, but on the up
> grade—fertile, progressive, constantly expanding. It has at its head one
> of the great men of the century [Prime Minister Eleftherios Venizelos],
> a man who fulfills in his own person the ideals and aspirations of the
> race.   (1919: 158)

Venizelos had already demonstrated his sympathy for the Allied cause by the
time Burrows penned these words. Forced to resign by the pro-German King
Constantine in March 1915, in October of the following year he assumed the
leadership of an alternative government in Thessaloniki. In 1917, a series of
events forced the king to abdicate in favor of his second son, Alexander, and
Venizelos once again headed a united government in Athens. To a British
philhellene such as Burrows, Venizelos embodied all the appropriate qualities—
patriotism, leadership, military initiative, and strongly pro-Allies sentiments.
Burrows had already apostrophized Venizelos in his 1913 poem:

> *Strength thou hast to rule our [sic] race:*
> *Great in war and great in peace,*
> *Thou, our second Pericles!*

Venizelos, a Cretan who had first led the government of Greece as recently as 1910, seemed set fair to achieve the goals of the *meghaloïdheates*. The Balkan Wars of 1912 to 1913 gave Greece Macedonia and Epirus; the Treaty of London (1913) placed Venizelos' own homeland under full Greek suzerainty; and the Treaty of Bucharest (1913) placed much of western Thrace in Greek hands also. Several of the eastern Aegean Islands were likewise incorporated into the Greek State during this period. On Venizelos' return to full power in 1917, Greek sympathy for the Allies seemed to promise further territorial gains as a reward.

Thus we see, in Burrows' enthusiasm for Venizelos' leadership, a classic instance of the overlap between political ideology and philhellenic sentiment. The assumption that Hellas embodied the virtues of "the race" (i.e., of the Europeans) is conflated with—rather than made explicitly contingent upon— the identification of Greek with Allied or "European" political goals; this foreshadows the similar rejection of the "un-European" or "anti-Hellenic" traits later attributed to the "foreign dogmas" and "Slavic" ideals of communism.

Indeed, that identification of communism with Slavic culture was developing its own internal logic. D'Istria had written about the "somehow communistic influence" of the Slavs half a century earlier, and we have followed the growth of the contrasted "individualism" of the Hellenes in subsequent ethnological writings. Now, too, with Bulgaria on the side of Germany along with Turkey, a case could be made for dismissing Bulgarian culture as essentially antithetical to everything that the Greeks held most dear. In an article which carries Politis' 1885 critical review of Bulgarian "kleftic songs" to an extreme of sorts, Vassilis Colocotronis remarked:

> The most suggestive antithesis between the Greek soul and the Bulgarian soul rings out in the popular poetry developed in Greece and Bulgaria during the Turkish occupation. During this dark age, the popular muse of the Greeks, as that of the Serbs also, sang of the ancient glories and the exalted deeds of heroes who frequently turned against the Turkish tyrant; by contrast, Bulgarian popular poetry cannot offer us a single historical or heroic poem . . .   (1918: 129)

And, as we have already noted in another context, Colocotronis portrayed the Bulgarian *haidouts* as characterless "common-law criminals" in contrast to their Greek and Serbian counterparts. Here is ideological folklore at its most explicit, defending the northern flanks of Hellenism even as others are guarding the east. Note, however, that the Serbs, who had been allied with Venizelist Greece and harbored analogous suspicions of Bulgarian expansionism, are presented in a kindly light. While the Greeks' songs even express "chivalrous feelings" (Colocotronis 1918: 140-141), surely the most "European" of attitudes, even the songs of the Serbs are relatively "historical" and "individualized." Such favored treatment is a clear reflection of international relations in the Venizelist age.

The main quarrel continued to be with Turkey; indeed, Bulgaria had even been allied with Greece and Serbia against their former overlords during the Balkan Wars. The Greeks looked toward Constantinople with ever increasing fervor. There, in Politis' phrase, lay the goal whose successful achievement would "crown the Greek ideal."

Catastrophe

But that success never came. Politis himself died just before the Great Idea collapsed in total ruin. On January 12, 1921, he suffered a fatal heart attack, "intensified," as his friend, student, and academic successor Stilpon Kiriakidis has written, "by the labor which continued uninterrupted up to the last moment of his life" (1923: xxvi). By that time, Greece seemed to be on the verge of entering that promised land which Politis would not live to enjoy. The Treaty of Sèvres (1920) gave Greece most of Thrace, including Adrianople, the eastern Aegean Islands, and administrative control over Smyrna. With this territorial expansion, the population of the Greek State had by now more than doubled its 1912 figure of below three million. Constantinople was still in Turkish hands, but the border seemed to be moving inexorably closer as Greek forces continued to skirmish with the Turks in Asia Minor. Venizelos was internationally respected, while many Greeks saw him as the national savior who would make the City "theirs once more."

At the critical point, with the Treaty of Sèvres still unratified, King Alexander died suddenly of a bite from his pet monkey. There followed a major constitutional crisis which led, in November of 1920, to Venizelos' electoral defeat. He went into voluntary exile, and his old enemy Constantine returned to the throne. Greece rapidly lost the support of the Allies; in particular, the representatives of Britain, France, and Italy set to work on a revision of the Treaty of Sèvres that would be more favorable to Turkey. Far worse was yet to come. During the course of 1922, the Greek army suffered humiliating setbacks at the hands of the Turks, and in September the Turkish army occupied Smyrna. The burning of that city spelled the end of Greek political and military operations in Asia Minor. The sadly battered Greek forces were immediately demobilized, while hordes of refugees fled to the state which many of them had never seen but which called them its own. Instead of total redemption, Greece now faced total *Katastrofi*; the martial call of the Great Idea had become an ironic echo in a wasteland.

Thus, too, the scholars who had dedicated their lives to providing a firm factual foundation for the irredentist movement found themselves suddenly thrust outside the main current of events and ideas. Their own prophet and doyen, Nikolaos Politis, was already dead, and the discipline to which he had given a name and a system only a few years before now became a truly academic concern, largely removed from the exigencies that confronted the shocked, humiliated nation. That the researches of folklorists had contributed so greatly to the national sense of identity was now a matter of past history. Despite the excellence of much of the laographic research done after 1922, the further development of that sense of identity passed mostly into other hands.

Epilogue

It would not be true to say that the discipline itself never recovered. The institutions which Politis had done so much to set in motion continued their scholarly labors; the collection of folklore materials went on apace; and the refugees of the *Katastrofi*, uprooted from their homelands, made every effort to record and preserve their precious local heritage for posterity. In the general reaction against the more extreme manifestations of the Great Idea, moreover, those who espoused a "Romeic" view of the national culture began to be heard more extensively; and they were able to produce some fairly trenchant criticisms of such founding fathers as Zambelios and Politis himself (see especially Apostolakis 1929). New circumstances spawned new interpretations and perspectives and undermined the sanctity of the old.[1]

But folklore studies never quite regained their erstwhile political importance. That they continued to rest on ideological tenets of one sort or another is obvious; given the origins of the discipline, it is hard to see how *any* statement about folklore in Greece could be ideologically neutral. Most folklorists, though in varying degrees of conformity, continued to work within the broad framework established by Politis; some of this work was tempered by the influence of other methodologies, notably the German *Kulturkreis* theories (see especially Kiriakidis 1937; Kiriakidou-Nestoros 1975: 74-77). For those, however, who regarded an efficient taxonomy as the crowning achievement of *laografia*, all that Politis' work left them to do consisted of tactical refinements (especially Mazarakis 1964; Spiridakis 1962, 1969) and the collection of more and more material within the established categories: from Politis' original 13 "swallow songs" in 1872, for example, we move to Spiridakis' 164 in 1969, without any substantive change in method or result. Ideological conservatism, linguistic purism, and a reluctance to countenance radical innovation in scholarship—these were the marks of a school of thought which had been rudely thrust aside from the mainstream of practical politics. The extreme chauvinism of the military junta of 1967 to 1974 did little to rejuvenate Hellenist laography; the basic work had been done long ago, and the prophecies were too well known.

Nationalist laography did nevertheless enjoy one brief period of real resurgence. This was the time of and around the Civil War (1944-1949), when communism had taken over the role of pan-Slavism as the epitome of treacherous "foreign dogma." Old enmities with neighboring lands to the north flared anew, fueled now by ideological strife of worldwide implications. Some of the old hatreds were thinly disguised: *Greek* communists, for example, might be called "Bulgarians" (e.g., Llewellyn Smith 1965: 164), on the old principle—recall the taunting of Fallmerayer as a Slav—of equating nationality with ideology. Within the same internal logic, there emerged a clear symbolic opposition between "Hellenes" and "communists" as mutually exclusive categories. The old antipathy between Orthodoxy and Hellenism was conveniently resolved in the emergent concept, whose origins go back at least to Zambelios, of *ellinokhristianikos politismos*—"Hellenic-Christian civilization" (e.g., Alivisatos 1949). Perhaps its most sinister embodiment, and certainly one of its most recent, is seen in the credo of George Papadopoulos, a leading member of the military junta of 1967 to 1974: "Hellas of the Hellene-Christians!"[2] In the heyday of his power, this slogan met the eye all over the Greek countryside.

Partly as a reaction to this ideological pattern, the Romeic interpretation of folklore gained some ground. Already, Yannis Apostolakis' attacks on the Hellenists' "national self-regard" (*ethnikos eghoïsmos*) had provided a focus, while the Marxist historian Yanis Kordatos made considerable use of folklore materials in order to establish the social conditions under which the modern Greeks had emerged into nationhood. In the course of the Civil War, a Marxist (and sharply antiirredentist) treatise on Greek folklore was composed by "George Lambrinos" (1947; the name is a pseudonym). This work addressed the nationalists' use of folklore classification; it severely criticized the "national epic" interpretation of the Akritic materials and treated both the Akritic and the kleftic songs as manifestations of class conflict instead.

None of these writers, however, seriously attacked the organizing principles on which the classification itself rested (but cf. Kiriakidou-Nestoros 1975: 50). They continued to write about *the* Akritic songs and *the* klefts, thereby perpetuating categories that had been designed to carry rather different ideological messages. Meanwhile, the Hellenists strengthened the conventional uses of the classification by collecting and publishing vast amounts of material organized in its inflexible structure. Even Stilpon Kiriakidis, whose sense of ethnography was far more holistic than Politis', maintained the basic format and the assumptions on which it depended. Despite his shift away from Politis' concern with historical origins to a greater concern with

the synchronic and social dimensions of folklore, he preserved Politis' bipartite division of the corpus and transmitted it to other scholars in turn
(see Kiriakidou-Nestoros 1975: 63-85). His commitment to a fundamentally
Hellenist perspective seems never to have wavered, despite his growing liberal-
ism in other spheres (Kiriakidou-Nestoros 1978: 154); the international development of more rigorous approaches to the study of culture traits—a development of which he made extensive use—served to amplify rather than
challenge the intrinsic assumptions this entailed.

The Civil War gave new life to the Hellenist approach. Folklorists of this
persuasion once again saw their task as the scholarly defense of Greece's
borders, this time against an international menace. The communist movement
in Greece failed to achieve lasting power, and, when Tito closed off the Yugoslav border as a result of his quarrel with Stalin, it collapsed rapidly. Some
years after the Civil War, in an essay appropriately entitled *The Northern
Ethnological Boundaries of Hellenism*, Kiriakidis felt able to claim:

> . . . after the happy and victorious end of this long and cruel war, which
> was fought in the name of freedom against the powers of darkness, the
> Greek people is justified to ask for the rearrangement of his [*sic*] fron-
> tiers on the basis of the historical and of the present-day facts. This re-
> arrangement . . . will help the Greek nation not only to survive but also
> to continue its life of progress and civilization which meant so much to
> the history of the world.   (1955: 60)

Although the "powers of darkness" are the communists, their identification
with the Slav nations gives the desire to preserve and expand the northern
borders considerable historical depth; the use to which ethnology has been
put here does not represent much of a change from similar, earlier arguments.

Other weapons likewise appear to come from the same armory as before.
Megas, to cite another example, claimed:

> . . . the causes that induced the Bulgarian klefts, the *haidouts* as they
> are called in their language, to spurn social life and turn to the moun-
> tains [for refuge] were not (as in Greece and Serbia) the desire for free-
> dom or any noble sentiment of patriotism but the fear of punishment
> for crimes already committed—the same fear that makes brigands
> (*listai*), too, become enemies of society.   (1946: 3)

As a further contrast between Greek and Bulgarian klefts, we are told that the
Bulgarians (and, by implication, only the Bulgarians) made no distinction in
their pillaging between Turks and Christians "if the latter were well-to-do"
(1946: 4). Interestingly, even here the Serbs are treated with relative friendli-
ness; the ranking of national enemies and allies which had grown up over
decades of complex politics died hard.

Megas also maintained that the Bulgarians had no "national epic" of their own but only a poor, fragmentary imitation of the Greeks' Akritic poems (1946, 1950: 21-29). This position, which seems to be mainly derived from the related arguments of Politis and perhaps also of Colocotronis (1918), was part of a larger attempt by Megas to show that the entire "so-called Balkan civilization" was in fact the product of cultural diffusion from Greece. This would in turn entail denying the possibility that other Balkan cultures could independently give birth to genres, such as "epic," comparable to those of Greece. Even the ground plans of houses from various parts of the Balkan Peninsula were agglutinated to the overall scheme (Megas 1951).

The Civil War ended, as we have noted, with the defeat of the Communists and the repression of most overt forms of communist political activity until 1974.[3] Marxist interpretations of folklore received little currency within Greek academic circles, although there were some stirrings of interest among Greek scholars abroad (e.g., Zakhos 1966). The more conventional folklorists, on the other hand, continued much as before, their major archive being the one which Politis had been instrumental in creating, under the aegis of the Academy of Athens. A few adventurous scholars have broached hitherto un-tried (and potentially offensive) fields, such as the *rebetika* songs of the un-derworld and the urban slums (Damianakos 1976; Petropoulos 1968) or the adaptation of traditional lore to such things as football, election campaigns, advertising, and traffic signals (Loukatos 1963). Damianakos and Zakhos, again, have brought sociological perspectives to bear on the various traditions of song, rural and urban, so that the arbitrary banishment of "the folk" to the countryside begins to weaken. Others have adapted new models from social anthropology, textual structuralism, and the semiotics of ritual and social interaction (e.g., Kakouri 1965; Gizelis 1974, 1976; Kiriakidou-Nes-toros 1975, 1978; Kapsomenos 1978, 1979; Skouteri-Didaskalou 1980) to the special problems of Greek folklore, while the growth of a more reflexive historiography (Politis 1973; Kiriakidou-Nestoros 1978; see also Kondogiorgis 1979) puts folklore research itself in a new light. These writers, in their quite different ways, represent a strong urge to escape the isolating effects of an existing intellectual tradition: the critical research of Kiriakidou-Nestoros, in particular, brings a welcome (and hitherto largely absent) perspective on the historical and global context of Greek folklore epistemology.[4] Yet change is often difficult to achieve. Some, at least, of the old battles are still being fought. Thus, for example, Kiriakidou-Nestoros' pithy critique of Romaios' "critical editions" of folksongs, both recalls and—to a striking degree—actually reproduces Apostolakis' similar criticisms of Zambelios, Lelekos, and Politis.

A consistent set of ideological concerns has thus dominated Greek laogra-phy from its inception right up to the 1922 disaster and, to some extent, for the next half century after that. The study of the national culture was simultaneously itself part of that culture, in which it has indeed played a critical role. What are at one level collections and discussions of folklore are thus, at another level, a textual record of that dialectic. It is fashionable among anthropologists and others who have worked in Greece to scoff at the local scholarly traditions in folklore, on the grounds that they are geared to narrow ideological interests. In this study, it has been my primary aim to show that such concerns are precisely what make the history of laography worthy of serious attention and that indeed—since in a real sense laography helped *define* the national culture—no student of Greek society can afford not to take some account of it. The development of an indigenous folklore discipline was not a boastful mixture of cynical forgery and political opportunism. On the contrary, it was a sustained, often painful attempt to discern order in chaos, on the part of a people whose national identity was often threatened by the very nations which had appointed themselves as its guardians. It gave the Greeks a chance of applying one of their most celebrated ancient proverbs— "know thyself"—by providing a framework for discovery. In this sense, Greek folklore studies were an organic part of the making of modern Greece.

Appendix A
Politis' Folklore Taxonomy

The following is excerpted from Politis' classic statement on the definition and organization of laografia *(1909a: 6-10). Representing the first comprehensive attempt to list the materials appropriate to folkloric research in Greece, it remained the primary model for most later attempts at systematic classification. It is translated here in full; only a small number of Greek terms, mostly alternative or local forms, are omitted as being irrelevant in an English-language version, and this is indicated by ellipses. I have added brief explanatory notes where these seemed potentially helpful.*

From the foregoing it may be inferred that, since the psychic and social life of the people is manifested in two ways—viz., by word and by acts or deeds—the folklorists' task is double-stranded: it consists of *transcription* and *description*. For it both transcribes oral tradition, the monuments of the word, and describes traditional acts or deeds.

In the following synoptic diagram, we list the principal themes with which the Greek folklorist has to be concerned.

Monuments of the Word

1. Songs. Apart from the lyrical, epic, religious, satirical, and humorous or disrespectful songs, as well as those which are sung on prescribed days or occasions (e.g., carols, songs of Lazarus,[1] Holy Week laments, swallow songs, songs performed in the course of certain games, songs of the *perperouna* [a rain-making ritual] and *klidhonas* [a fortune-telling rite associated with Saint John's Day],[2] swing songs, wedding songs, funeral dirges), this category includes dramatic games, children's songs (sung or spoken by or to children), and work songs (such as those which accompany rowing, milling, etc.); these last serve the purpose of rhythmically regulating the worker's movements or simply of enabling him to relax through song as he works.

2. Refrains (exorcisms, spells . . .).

3. Riddles (. . .) and word games. Riddlelike stories. Playful or echolike responses. Tongue twisters (. . .).

4. Wishes, greetings, drinking toasts, curses, oaths, blasphemies, with a description of the acts or movements with which they are sometimes performed. (In this category also come religious curses [anathemas] and the heaping up of stones [i.e., in verbal magic] .)

5. Proverbs, with their interpretation and the transcription of the myths in which they are sometimes mentioned.

6. Myths (*mithi*).

7. Humorous stories (in which we include those that mock [particular] villages).

8. Legends or tales (*paramithia*).

9. Traditions, or mythical stories, believed to be true, which mention places or persons, heavenly bodies, meteorological phenomena, Christ and the saints, demons, and other imaginary beings.

10. From the treasury of language, those words and phrases through which are revealed customs, beliefs, popular superstitions, and jobs and occupations of the people, or those words which recall historical events or certain situations derived from them. Examples: names (baptismal, family), nicknames, toponyms, names of seasons of the year, months, days; personal names of cats, dogs, horses, oxen, and other domestic animals; generalized nicknames for animals (e.g., Nikos or Mendios for the donkey, Sir Nikolos for the wolf, Madam Maria for the fox); personal names given to weapons, utensils, dwellings, ships, boats; euphemisms (circumlocutions or metonyms or name substitutes or phrases used in response to [the mention of] feared names); names of animals and plants which betray traditions or beliefs or superstitions. Names of instruments and tools and the special names for the parts of each. Professional terms appropriate to each craft or occupation. *Korakistika*—a secret code language, which uses newly fashioned words or changes the meanings of words or inserts meaningless syllables into the words. Names of costumes and of the parts of each separately. Exclamatory expressions (shepherds', plowmen's, muleteers' sounds used to direct animals). Imitations of animal sounds. Words connected with some particular situation (e.g., *moskhomangas*, "urchin, blackguard"; *tramboukos*, "taker of petty bribes"). Metaphors and other tropes demonstrating a mythopoeic perception of the external world, such as the personification of natural phenomena and generally of the inanimate.

Traditional Activities or Practices

1. The house. Parts of the house, mode of existence therein, utensils, and furnishings. Special kinds of habitation (shepherds' huts, stone huts,[3] lake dwellings).

2. Food. Common and special victuals of the Greeks. Prescribed foods for certain days (e.g., Christmas loaves, Easter cookies, red eggs [for Easter] , foods specially associated with particular festivals). Abstention from particular eatables, whether absolute or imposed for fixed periods (other than

religious fasts) or for certain people (as in the prohibition which debars those with only one brother from eating the eye of an animal, etc.). Beliefs about the effects of foods on the eater (e.g., that the eating of certain parts of animals strengthens the corresponding parts of the eater—such as the notion that eating the tongue makes one eloquent or that [according to legendary accounts] the liver of a bird shows the one who tasted it to be a mind reader). Foods eaten to ward off evil.

3. Costumes, hairstyles, personal ornament.

4. Social organization. Customs related to the administration of the community or to the management of communal property. Customs indicating the former division of the village by patrilineages. Social relations (participation of outsiders in family festivals, visiting, social etiquette, feasts, guest-host reciprocity [*ksenia*]).[4] Life away from home. Women's position in the home. Special communities. Blood brotherhood. Klefts. Brigands' laws. Employer-laborer relations, servant-master relations.

5. The child. Customs, beliefs, and superstitions regarding pregnancy, birth, and the postnatal phase. Care and treatment of the newly born. Foundlings. Matters related to baptism. Matters concerning children's upbringing. School customs. Apprenticeship (apprentice masons, shipboys, etc.). Children's language—as an appendix, the reading of popular books could also be added here.

6. Wedding customs.

7. Customs concerned with death. Funeral, tomb, mourning, memorial services.

8. Life-styles (*vii*).[5] Farmer's life (customs during sowing, reaping, grape harvesting, etc.). Herding life (special customs of animal herders, especially nomads).[6] Life-styles of soldiers, sailors, fishermen, hunters. Industrial professions. Miners. Female tasks and professions.

9. Justice. Ideas of the people regarding justice and jural relations. Popular customs concerned with family and inheritance law. (Especially worthy of study are certain entirely specialized customs such as, for example, the occasional, localized rights of only sons [sing. *kanakaris*] and only daughters [sing. *kanakarissa*].) Adoption. Disinheriting. Customary ways of concluding and drawing up contractual agreements, archaic customs concerned with confirming a legal situation such as bankruptcy. Signs of ownership (e.g., incisions in herd animals' ears, tattooing of horses' buttocks [like the brands or seals of the ancients], color codes, etc.). Written certifications of contracts; marriage contracts (*prikosimfona*). Penalties (public shaming, shaving of the head, school punishments, *falangas* [sitting in a variety of stocks while the soles of the feet are whipped]). Popular courts (e.g., in Olympia or Chios, during carnival).

10. Worship. Popular beliefs about God and the saints and their intervention in human affairs. Invocations to them by the use of special names. Miraculous aid and cures. Icons. Incubation.[7] Blessing with holy water. Sacrifices and offerings (occasional offerings of flowers and fruits in church, on prescribed days). Firstfruits. Blessings and curses (*tamata* [ex-votos]). Pro-

cessions. Feast days. Saints' days (special saint's day customs, especially during the twelve days between Christmas and Epiphany, carnival, Easter). Feast days not appointed by the church (such as May Day) and customs appropriate to them. Festival of the summer solstice (Saint John *Liotropios*),[8] bonfires during these. Bonfires to celebrate other days (Epiphany, Easter [(the burning of) Judas (in effigy)], Cheese-eating Week,[9] Saint Elijah, the first days of August). "Unsleeping lamps" [left burning for forty days in the room where someone has died], renewal of flames. Orgiastic cults (*Anastenaria*, Thracian *Kaloyiri*). Purificatory rites.

11. Popular philosophy. Beliefs about the soul and the afterlife. Beliefs about nature. Practices consistent with such beliefs.

12. Popular medicine. Medical learning. Doctors and doctors' wives. Community doctors. The use of curative herbs and their modes of collection. Curative properties of animals' limbs, skin, hair, nails. Curative power of metals and rocks. Preparations of medicines. Therapy. Curing by the use of similarity or analogy. Curing according to the principle that "he who wounded shall also cure." Cure of nonexistent illnesses and injuries (wandering navel, rising kidneys, etc.). Dietetics. Surgery. Veterinary medicine.

13. Fortune-telling. Various forms of fortune-telling. Diagnosis of facial features. Palmistry. *Klidhonas*. Fortune-telling by the use of various aids: oracle bones (shoulder blades [of sheep or goats]), fire, lead, eggs, keys, sieves, etc. Fortune-telling on special days or occasions (New Year, Saint John's [*klidhonas*], carnival, Saint Andrew's, first day of Lent).

14. Astrology. The influence of heavenly bodies on human life. Unlucky days. Days of the month. *Dhrimes* [first days of March and August, associated with homonymous evil spirits]. Numerological beliefs. Meteorological beliefs.

15. Magic. Magicians male and female. Magical books, utensils, and instruments. Magical acts. Angels and demons in charge of days and of hours of the day and night. Exorcisms. Fortune-telling using a basin of water, the [palm of the] hand, cards. Philters, binding spells. Haunting of houses.

16. Magical and superstitious customs to ward off evil or obtain good fortune. Magical customs in time of drought (*perperouna*, rain litanies, etc.). Amulets. Kinds of protection against witchcraft. Symbolic burial and expulsion of sickness, patient's abandonment of sickness in a prescribed place. Superstitions of curing by analogy, or similarity, or difference, or opposition.

17. Children's games and athletic contests.

18. Dances and their music. Mimicry, gestures of head and hands, their meaning.

19. Music and musical instruments. The precise transcription of the melodies of folksongs—if possible, in regular sol-fa notation, otherwise in ecclesiastical—is of maximum value.

20. Fine arts. Sculpture (wood); graphics. Ornament (especially ornamentation of clothing, sculpted or inscribed decoration of furniture, instruments, dwellings). Aesthetics of color and form.

Appendix B
Basic Chronology

This table is intended to provide a handy means of situating the development of Greek folklore studies in a general chronological framework. To that end, it is divided into three columns: Greek political history, Greek folklore studies, and general European and related history (including folklore studies). There is necessarily some overlap between these three categories, and the choice of key events can never be anything but arbitrary. The chart is thus meant simply as a reference for the reader's convenience.

Greek Political History	Greek Folklore Studies	General European and Related History (Including Folklore Studies)
B.C.	**B.C.**	
461–429: Perikles in power in Athens	**6th century:** Probable date of earliest attempt to transcribe "swallow song"	
447–438: Parthenon built	**484?–424?:** Herodotus, "father of anthropology and history"	
338: Battle of Chaeronea brings Athens under Macedonian rule		
A.D.	**A.D.**	**A.D.**
	2d–3d centuries: Athenaeus compiles *Deipnosophistae*; includes "swallow song" and other folk texts	**Ca. 100:** *Germania* of Tacitus (ca. 55 to ca. 117) introduces rich ethnographic description
285: Diocletian divides Roman Empire in two		
313: Edict of Milan formally proscribes persecution of Christians		
330: Byzantium dedicated as New Rome, capital of Eastern Roman Empire		
391: Theodosius I declares Christianity official religion by formally abolishing paganism	**407:** Death of St. John Chrysostom, who had campaigned actively against pagan folk practices	
		7th century: Foundation of kingdom by Turkic-speaking Bulgars; through assimilation, become Slav-speaking by mid ninth century
		622: *Hejirah* (Mohammed's flight from Mecca)

746: Widespread plague reduces Greek population; followed by massive Slavic incursions and massacres. These continue intermittently and with varying intensity

961: Nicephoros Phocas captures Crete from Saracens, massacres population, and introduces "twelve noble families" (*Arkhontopouloi*) to repopulate island

Late 11th century: Eustathius of Thessaloniki's commentaries on Homer include much folklore

12th century?: Vallicellian manuscript F-73 contains early example of "swallow song"

1204: Venetians, probably for mercantile reasons, incite Fourth Crusade soldiers to conduct (Latin) sack of Constantinople; kingdom established at Trebizond by Alexios Comnenos

1205 on: Doges of Venice style themselves "Lord of one-fourth and one-eighth of the Empire of Romania"—i.e., of the "Roman" world

1332–1406: Ibn-Khaldūn, historian-ethnologist of Arab society

1361: Sack of Adrianople

Ca. 1380: Turks occupy Macedonia

1393: Turks occupy Thessaly

1453: Sack of Constantinople

1461: Turks take Trebizond

1470: Ottoman Turks divide Greece proper into six *sanjak* (administrative districts)

1492: Discovery of New World; expulsion of Jews from Spain—many move to Thessaloniki

1520: Joannes Boemus, *Omnium Gentium Mores, Leges et Ritus* (ethnological medley)

1522: After unsuccessful first attempt (1480), Turks take Dodecanese (including Rhodes) from Knights of St. John of Jerusalem, who move to Malta

1571: Cyprus taken by Turks from Venice

1645-69: Crete, in Venetian hands since 1204, falls to Turks. Many refugees go to the Ionian Islands, carrying with them a lively literary tradition

1770: Unsuccessful revolts in Crete (under Daskaloyannis) and the Peloponnese, incited by Russia in connection with war against Turkey

1814: Foundation of Filikí Etería ("Friendly Society")—a secret group of Greek nationalists actively engaged in propaganda, etc., in Odessa

1821: Outbreak of Greek War of Independence

1822: Constitution of Epidaurus declares Greece a nation-state under presidency of Alexander Mavrokordatos

1590-1645: Flowering of Cretan vernacular literature; incorporates many folk influences

17th century: In Iviron Monastery (Mt. Athos), early transcriptions of folksongs (words and music)

18th and 19th centuries: Greek writers begin to build a case for the essentially Hellenic nature of European civilization—especially Katartzis (d. 1807), Moisiodax (d. 1800), Voulgaris (d. 1806). In 1791, Katartzis "translates" own work from demotic to katharevousa. See Henderson 1970: 140

1803: Koraes publishes memoir (in French) on cultural conditions in Greece

1813: Douglas' Essay seeks the resemblances between ancient and modern Greek culture

1534: Sebastian Franck's Weltbuch oder Cosmographey includes much German folklore

1619-20: Richard James records Russian historical songs

Ca. 1660-70: Samuel Collins records Russian folktales

1679: J.-B. Thiers, Superstitions anciennes et modernes—an attack on nonecclesiastical religious practices; cf. contemporary antipapist works in England

1725: Giambattista Vico (1668-1744), Scienza nuova

1730-88: J. G. Hamann, teacher of Herder

1744-1803: J. G. von Herder (1778-79: Volkslieder)

1750: Carmeli's Storia di veri costumi . . .

1776-78: H. G. Porthan, Poësi Fennica

1789: Outbreak of French Revolution

1802-74: Niccolò Tommaseo

1807: G. W. F. Hegel (1770-1831), Phänomenologie des Geistes

1812-15: Grimms' Kinder- und Hausmärchen

1814: Inspired by Herder, Sjögren and Poppius solemnly swear to collect the folklore of their native Finland

1816-18: Grimms' Deutsche Sagen

1824–25: Fauriel's *Chants*		
1825: Papadopoulos-Vrettos publishes memoir (second edition) on "some ancient Greek customs still existing in the island of Lefkas"	**1827:** At Battle of Navarino, a French-British-Russian fleet defeats Turks and Egyptians	
1830: Fallmerayer's *Geschichte*	**1833:** Otto crowned in Nauplion; sets up government with mainly German senior officials, including von Maurer (jurist)	**1835:** Jacob Grimm's *Deutsche Mythologie* shows links between ancient and modern German lore
1835: Kind's anthology of Greek folksongs, first edition		**1835–36:** Elias Lönnrot's first edition of *Kalevala*, acclaimed as Finns' national epic
1840: Fallmerayer, visiting Greece for first time, coldly received	**1837:** Athens becomes national capital; Athens University founded; Greek church becomes independent of Patriarchate of Constantinople	**1841–1916:** Giuseppe Pitrè, major Sicilian folklorist with whose work Politis later became acquainted
1842: Tommaseo's Greek volume		**1846:** Thoms coins term "folklore"
1843: Evlambios' collection published in St. Petersburg; Lefkias refutes Fallmerayer	**1844:** Greece becomes a constitutional monarchy; French party achieves dominance	**1848:** *Communist Manifesto*; liberal revolutions throughout Europe
1850: Manousos publishes clearly Romeicist volume of folksongs		
1852: Zambelios publishes folksong collection to reinforce his claim that Byzantine period is essential link between ancient and modern Greece	**1854–57:** Anglo-French military force occupies Piraeus in order to discourage irredentist Greeks from taking advantage of Crimean War to gain more territory	**1855:** Guillard coins term *ethnologie*

1862: Otto deposed in coup d'état

1863: George I, second son of king of Denmark, ascends Greek throne

1864: Britain cedes Ionian Islands to Greece

1866: Uprising in Crete provokes violent Turkish response

1870: Dilessi affair

1870: Under Russian pressure, Turkey constitutes Bulgarian exarchate (ecclesiastical authority) independent of Patriarchate of Constantinople; its cultural proselytism becomes source of conflict with Greeks

1896: Renewed troubles in Crete

1897: Disastrous thirty-day war with Turkey follows border skirmishes in Thessaly; Greece loses some territory in Thessaly, but Crete is now given autonomy within the Ottoman Empire

1859: Zambelios advances theory of history-in-language to demonstrate continuity between Classical Greek tragedy and modern folksongs

1860: Polilas replies to Zambelios' essay in defense of Solomos

1867: D'Istria explores Greek folksongs for evidence of "nationality"

1871: Politis wins the Rhodokanakis competition with *Modern Greek Mythology*

1875: First publication of a manuscript of the "Akritic epic"

1896: Garnett and Stuart-Glennie, *Greek Folk Poesy*. This includes discussion of "survival of paganism" which was to influence Lawson (1910). Explicitly rejected Tylorean view of essential equality of humankind, claiming Greeks as superior in ancient *and* modern times

1855–63: Afanas'ev publishes major collection of Russian folktales

1859: Bulgarian nationalist Rakovski claims that Bulgarians were of Sanskritic origin and that Delphic oracle and ancient Greek place-names were of Bulgarian origin

1865: Tylor's *Researches into the Early History of Mankind*

1871: Tylor's *Primitive Culture*

1871: Germany unified and proclaimed an empire under Wilhelm I

1875: Dozon publishes major collection of Bulgarian folksongs

1908: Young Turk revolution

1909: Van Gennep, *Les Rites de passage*, a major work on the structure of ritual, influential in folklore and anthropology

1913: Bulgarian General Kirkoff claims Alexander the Great as "the most glorious of our countrymen"—i.e., this was a Bulgarian claim to Macedonia

1914: Outbreak of First World War

1917: Revolution in Russia; establishment of Soviet State

1918: Conclusion of First World War

1909: Volume 1 of *Laografia*

1910: Lawson, *Modern Greek Folklore and Ancient Greek Religion*

1914: First publication of Politis' *Selections from the Songs of the Greek People*

1918: Colocotronis publishes disquisition on Bulgarian and Greek "souls" as mirrored in folk poetry

1921: Death of Politis

1910: Venizelos becomes prime minister of Greece for first time

1912–13: Balkan Wars

1913: George I assassinated in Thessaloniki; Constantine I succeeds to throne; Crete finally incorporated into Greece

1915: Venizelos invites Anglo-French landing at Thessaloniki in response to Bulgarian alliance with Germany

1916: Venizelos, in opposition to the king, sets up alternative government in Thessaloniki

1917: Entente Powers force Constantine to abdicate in favor of his son Alexander

1920: Treaty of Sèvres

1922: *Katastrofi* in Asia Minor

Notes

1. Past Glories, Present Politics

1. Cf. Geertz' observation that nationalist revolutions are commonly epistemological as well as political (1973: 239). He also rightly criticizes the negative valuation of "ideology" as counterproductive (1973: 199), although, as he clearly recognizes, it is necessary for analysis to take the selectivity of ideological "truth" into account (e.g., Mannheim 1936: 20; cf. also Jenkins 1961: 99–117 for his formulation of Greek "ethnic truth"). On the tendency of the scholars' arguments to become cumulatively self-reinforcing, a theme repeatedly sounded throughout this book, cf. Burke's observation that "the instruments of precision and thought by which we made our examinations were themselves shaped by the same point of view" (1954: 258).

The selectional basis of ideological codes is treated analytically by Eco (1976: 139–142, 289–290), whose definition of ideology is extremely pertinent here: ". . . a message which starts with a factual description, and then tries to justify it theoretically, gradually being accepted through a process of overcoding" (1976: 290). Since I am here discussing culture historians as ideologically motivated, I also lean heavily on Goldstein's (1976) lucid treatment of the "construction" of history by its practitioners. Crick's critique of anthropological literalism is also germane (1976: 154–159).

Henderson raises the related possibility of alternative interpretations as to whether or not there was continuity in Greek thought after the Fall of Constantinople in 1453 (1970: 1–2). It should also be noted that the admiration of Classical culture abroad had ideological and political implications that did not necessarily have anything to do with the modern Greek cause at all; see especially Jenkyns 1980: 4, 84.

2. It should be noted, however, that the Old Testament provided an alternative "origin myth" for Christian Europe, perhaps most notably in Ireland; traces of the notion that the Greeks are somehow "descended" from the Old Testament Jews may even be found today among rural Greeks (cf. Herzfeld 1980c). In addition, various northern European scholars attempted to find more localized origins in recorded mythology, especially in Germany and Scandinavia.

3. Cf. Geertz on the problem, often faced by emergent nation-states, of reconciling "epochalism" with "essentialism" (1973: 240-249).

4. This is a paraphrase of the programmatic dimension of Hallowell 1965.

5. To these references we might usefully add the ethnological information contained in the writings of Crusius (1526-1607), a professor of Greek at the University of Tübingen, as well as the subsequent works of such observers as La Guilletière (1676), Stephanopoli (1800), Pouqueville (1805), and Leake (especially 1814); Bondelmonti (fl. 1420; see Sinner 1824) is a useful early source for historical demography. The information provided by these and other outside observers before independence, though generally no more systematic than that of local sources, adds up to a fairly substantial corpus of data. See especially Simopoulos 1972, 1973, and 1975, for an exhaustive account of foreign travelers in Greece, and Spiridakis 1966: 477-481; cf. also Loukatos 1978.

Folklore studies were similarly initiated by foreigners in Russia (the Englishmen James and Collins; see Oinas 1961 and Sokolov 1950: 44). Ecclesiastical fear of a pagan revival clearly motivated some of the early local-level opposition to the study of folklore in various parts of Europe, although this does not seem to have been a major factor in the relatively late development of folklore research in Greece.

6. The term *Altneuland* was coined by Theodor Herzl to denote the projected Jewish national home. Political Hellenism shared with political Zionism a preoccupation with the physical site of the nation's history and cultural evolution, and both faced the paradox (cf. also n. 3, above) which Herzl's phrase so concisely suggests. Note the title of Wachsmuth's 1864 *Das alte Griechenland im neuen* and others like it.

7. The Greeks are sometimes referred to in formal discourse as *i Fili* ("the Race"); cf. demotic *ratsa*, not often used on its own in this way but often combined with a specifying qualifier (possessive pronoun or adjective) to denote a particular "race" (Herzfeld 1980c). In general, the Greek vernacular terminology of "ethnicity" is extremely context-sensitive; even such apparently precise terms as "Vlach" or "Hellene" may refer to more than one level of group inclusiveness. Politicians usually use such terms in more fixed senses to denote a set of absolute demographic or geopolitical entities. The phenomenon, which is widely characteristic of emergent national identities, makes it very difficult to speak confidently of "*the* people of a given ethnic group" (cf. especially Ardener 1972).

8. It is less clear whether they explicitly perceived the semantic shift in the term "politics"—Classical Greek *politikē*, "matters relating to the city-state (*polis*)"; cf. Kitto 1957: 75-79. On the persistence of this model of the Greek role in cultural evolution, and its pervasive effects in educational practice, see Bialor 1973: 476-477 and Frangoudaki 1978. Cf. also Chapman's (1978: 197-198) application of Ardener's concept of an "englobing" self-view, to explain Scottish perceptions of the position of Gaelic culture in Britain as a whole: economic and political subordination is not necessarily reflected in the Scots' view of their *cultural* role, any more than the Greeks

found it absurd to claim intellectual primacy over a politically dominant West.

9. In the "old" (i.e., Julian) calendar, then still in use in Greece. With the introduction of the "new" (Gregorian) calendar, the date of March 25 has been retained for the celebration of Independence Day (and of the Feast of the Annunciation). For convenience, I have retained the dates 1821 to 1833 for the War of Independence, although in practical terms the Greek cause was secure after the Battle of Navarino and the first Treaty of London in 1827.

2. Extroversion and Introspection

1. Tipaldo and Mustoxidi were Heptanesian Greeks, Tommaseo a Dalmatian. Their main language of intellectual discourse was nevertheless Italian.

2. The French collector Marcellus also, from 1816 to 1820, obtained folksongs from the Greek poet Christopoulos. The latter was clearly aware of the political potentialities of "these cries of the national muse, which resound unheard but yet unextinguished from Trebizond to Cyprus" (Christopoulos in Marcellus 1860: vii). An account of Tommaseo's life and work is provided by Ciampini 1945.

3. E.g., *leo* ("I say") can take *traghoudhia* ("songs") as well as *miroloyia* ("dirges, laments") as its object. Zambelios (1859), too, implicitly treats *miroloyia* as a subset of *traghoudhia*, with consequent difficulties for his own argument; cf. Menardos 1921 and the extended treatment in Herzfeld 1981.

3. National Character, National Consciousness

1. Classical Greek *sun* ("syn") and *oida* ("know").

2. This name means "Bulgarian" but has no "ethnic" significance for its bearer, since it may have originated as a *paratsoukli* (hypocoristic name) with one of his ancestors.

3. George Castriota Skanderbeg (1403?–1468) was a national hero of the Albanians; he led a successful revolt against the Turks in 1443. With intermittent help from Venice, Naples, and the papacy, he succeeded in keeping the Turks at bay until his death, after which Albania—with the exception of a few districts controlled by Venice—reverted to the Ottomans.

4. See especially the detailed study by Campbell (1964) of these values as they are found among the transhumant Sarakatsani of northern Greece.

Zannetos (1883: 3) explicitly attempts to demonstrate the continuity of "manliness" (*andria*) from the Homeric heroes to the klefts, using folksongs as a principal source.

5. *Paratsouklia*, sometimes translated as "nicknames," are often handed down in the male line; in highland western Crete, they frequently become the collective names of lineage segments.

6. The data from western Crete are taken from my own fieldwork there, conducted intermittently from 1974 to 1978. See Herzfeld 1980a.

7. *Kala kleftis* will strike the reader with a knowledge of standard demotic Greek as an unusual form (adverb and noun). In western Crete, however, the combination of the adverbial *kala* ("well") with a noun suggesting a
"heroic role" is not uncommon: *kala eghoïstis*, "a man who is good at demonstrating his aggressive self-regard"; *kala 'ndras*, "one whose manliness has
been proved beyond doubt." Cf. also *etsa dhoulies*, "goings-on like that" (lit.,
"thus works").

8. I am extremely grateful to Allen Walker Read for permission to cite
his unpublished paper. Its thorough documentation indicates a wide range of
similarities in the respective ranges of implication of "rebel" and *"kleftis."*

9. Even in the popular press, the "kleftic song" category became widely
used in defense of the Hellenist argument. One recent newspaper article
(Motsias 1977) mined these songs in order to demonstrate that the klefts had
revived the athletic contests which had disappeared with the abolition of the
Olympic games in 393. References to jousting and rock hurling, which recall
medieval at least as much as ancient accounts, are overlooked, and the legendary ability of the kleft leader Tasoulas to leap from one mountain peak to
another is cited without any reference to the similar exploits of the "Byzantine" hero Digenes; thus, the "Akritic songs" (cf. chap. 5) are kept apart from
the "kleftic," confirming the established taxonomy, and the "kleftic songs"
serve to provide a conceptual link with Classical antiquity. While Motsias' is a
popular, journalistic essay, it usefully reminds us of the broad appeal of such
arguments and their capacity for bridging the gap between academic and lay
modes of discourse.

10. For a comparable taxonomy applied to Yugoslav Macedonian materials, cf. Trærup: "There are among the *hajduks* robbers (*hajduk* or *aramija*),
whose deeds are so frightful that even their own mothers on their deathbed
condemn them" (1970: 21); the songs about both types of outlaw are distinguished from "historical" songs. Baggally deals with the problem of an
obviously "brigandlike" kleft by allowing that the term *kleftis* might occur in
a particular song "in the wider sense of a robber" (1936: 28). Cf. further Baggally 1936: 6-8, on the earlier history of the term. Iatridis provides good
early examples of the "translation" of *kleftes* into *listai* in the "titles" of
songs whose heroes were clearly brigands (1859: 22, 42, 57). Quinet treats
klefts as revolutionary soldiers (1859: 258, 290, 541). For a contemporary
account of post-1821 kleftism, see Soteropoulos 1868.

11. Lit., "trampled by [Turks] from Konya." Quinet, on the other hand,
may have been more deliberately serving the Greek position when he changed
"Albanian songs" to "modern folksongs" and "Albanian Corinth" to "Christian Corinth" (Karatza 1970: 57, noting Quinet 1830: 294, 275, 1859: 215,
202).

12. From a confusion of Greek *koutsos* ("lame") with Turkish *küçük*
("small, little"): "Political philology has shown that Koutsovlach means 'little Vlach' and that 'a little Vlach' means one who is mostly a Hellene" (Wace
and Thompson 1914: 9).

13. See also his *Monograph on the Koutsovlachs* (Aravandinos 1905). A

similar view is expressed by an anonymous writer in the journal *Pandora*:
"This race . . . since it has been accustomed for centuries to regard the Hellenes as brothers and has mixed Greek into its own language, in a short time will of course erase from its speech (lit., mouth) the last remnants of foreign ancestry and will speak that pure Greek language which alone has the incomparable right to be heard under such a sky and in the midst of such recollections, i.e., the ancient monuments" (1852-53: 283).

14. This is particularly true of certain outlying areas which were not part of the original Greek State. See especially Lanitis 1946 (Cyprus); Vlastos 1909 and Lambithianaki-Papadaki 1972 (Crete); and the cited works on Epirus.

4. Attack and Reaction

1. Further references to the (nonfolkloric) scholars' reactions to Fallmerayer are given in Xydis 1968: 4, especially nn. 9 and 10. For a current Greek view of the demographic aspects of the problem, see Zakythinos 1975: 4-6.

2. I am indebted to Brian Joseph for directing my attention to pertinent information on this problem.

3. Ali Pasha (1741-1822) was a semiindependent Albanian governor whose rule, based on Yannina, extended over much of Epirus and Thessaly. He entertained ambitions of creating his own independent state, and Sultan Mahmud II had him deposed and assassinated. His opposition to the Porte earned him the retrospective admiration of many Greeks, although he is also commemorated in a much quoted Greek folksong ("Kira Frossini") for having a wealthy Greek merchant's wife and her attendants drowned when she refused to yield to his advances.

4. Marcellus, though a collector of folksongs, seems to have had little interest in the analytical study of cultural continuity. Rather, he sought through his Greek travels the kind of inspiration that would help him understand the Classical authors: "Thus, I am persuaded that, having seen the Naxian girls washing their brothers' *foustanelles* [pleated skirts] at the beautiful springs by the sea, then showing astonishment at my foreign dress and smiling at the imperfection of my [Greek] speech, I am better prepared for [the task of] reproducing the games of Nausicaa's companions as they washed Alcinoous' tunics and fled at the sight of Ulysses" (1861: 2). Earlier, Voutier (1826: 40, 42) had sought reflections of ancient speech and even of historical events in the modern folklore; but this, too, was the scarcely systematic hobby of an observant soldier.

5. And of Schmidt's collection of folksongs and tales.

5. The Creation of a Discipline

1. *Pandora* 22 (1871-72) carried the original report from the judges and a description of the announcement of the result (p. 83), as well as a review

praising Politis' work but criticizing his youthful presumption in attempting to rebut the judges' critical remarks (pp. 471–472).

2. Politis' survivalism is the version which continues to guide Greek folklore research: "Laography as the science of 'survivals' (the English ethnologist Tylor's *survivals in culture*) has been served in but a single manner by the Cypriots. The Cypriot folklorists worked according to the mainland Greek procedural model under the influence of that great figure N. Politis, the father of Greek laography" (Kiprianou 1967: 7). The reprints Politis sent Tylor are filed in the Tylor Library as "Neo-Hellenic, Polites, etc.," cat. ref. O 5/7.

3. In this Politis was a good deal more restrained than some non-Greek commentators (e.g., Geldart 1884: vi, who treated German tales as less solar and therefore as more recent than their Greek counterparts). The connection between Müller's theory of the "disease of language" and the notion of textual "corruption" is much more fully developed in the work of the Russian folklorist A. N. Afanes'ev (see Sokolov 1950: 50–52). On the pre- and post-Classical "borrowing" of cultural traits, within a general Indo-European context, Fauriel (whose interest in Sanskrit was considerable) had already anticipated Politis' approach in terms of historical linguistics (1854: 58–61). Kind (1861: xiv) provides an early instance of comparison between modern Greek and German myths, drawing on Jacob Grimm for the latter.

4. Explanations and further references are given in the notes to appendix A.

5. See Herzfeld 1980b for a discussion of the taxonomic issue.

6. Expansion and Collapse

1. E.g., the attempt to derive *ois* ("sheep") in both languages from a Homeric form, even though a Latin derivation (*ovis*) would seem at least as plausible (particularly for Koutsovlach).

2. For these legends in detail, see Politis 1904: 21-22, 656-674. The *adynaton* (e.g., "when the crow turns white and becomes a dove") is a long-established figure of speech in Greek tradition; see Tuffin 1972-73 and Petropoulos 1954: 96-103.

3. The significance and origin of this image are uncertain.

4. The Battle of Plataea, at which the Persian general Mardonius met defeat at the hands of a combined Greek force, took place in 479 B.C. The Athenians had threatened to fight the Persians unaided, until the Spartans were goaded into cooperating. See Herodotus, *Hist.* viii: 143-144; ix: 6-11.

5. In lines 1 and 2 the verb is *simeno*, "toll," but also "mean, signify"—hence perhaps having connotations, in the present context, of "marking" an especially "significant" event; cf. *simandro*, "sounding board," an instrument used to summon people to church for worship.

6. It is also possible that the plural form is the result of "polite" editing, although this is perhaps less likely.

7. At the Battle of Navarino (October 20, 1827), a British, French, and Russian naval force under the British Admiral Codrington defeated a combined Turkish-Egyptian fleet and thereby effectively confirmed the victory of the Greek cause. Codrington, who had originally been meant not to engage in active battle but merely to make the Turks accept a truce to which the Greeks had already agreed, was apparently goaded into making an attack when a British officer bearing a message from him to the Turkish admiral was killed.

8. The copy is preserved in the Gennadius Library, Athens, which is based on Gennadius' own collection.

Epilogue

1. On Apostolakis' life, see Koukhtsoglou 1947 and, in general, the special issue of *Nea Estia* devoted to him. For a more critical view, see especially Kiriakidou-Nestoros 1978: 155.

2. Clogg (1972) gives an excellent critical account of the colonels' "ethnic" and "religious" ideology.

3. In 1974, with the restoration of democracy, communist parties were legalized. Before the military dictatorship of 1967 to 1974, the only legal party of Marxist ideology had been the United Democratic Left (EDA).

4. Kakouri (1965), however, is still concerned with the problem of establishing cultural continuity. Papadopoullos (1970) provides an account of the development of folklore and anthropology internationally in relation to Greek (including Cypriot) scholarly concerns.

Appendix A. Politis' Folklore Taxonomy

1. A carol performed on Lazarus Saturday, which precedes Holy (i.e., Easter) Week.

2. The *perperouna* is performed by a naked child festooned with leaves, grass, and flowers (Lawson 1910: 23-25). The *klidhonas* (cf. Homeric and Classical *klidōn*) is a form of divination performed on the feast day of Saint John the Baptist at midsummer (see Lawson 1910: 304-305). A boy (preferably the firstborn son of living parents) is sent to fetch the "speechless water," so called because he may not speak to anyone on his way. Unmarried girls throw some object, usually an apple, into the water; as each of these objects is recovered the next morning—by the boy or by the girls themselves in rotation—a verse is recited or improvised, and this is held to indicate the marriage prospects of the girl whose contribution the recovered object is then discovered to be.

3. E.g., the so-called *mitata*, built by Cretan shepherds in their upland summer pasturage.

4. *Xenia* is a Classical term for the reciprocity between those who stood as *xenoi* (reciprocal hosts) to each other. Today, *kseni* are "outsiders" (i.e., to

any reference group); reciprocal host relationships (e.g., between *yarenidhes* on Rhodes) subsisted in some areas at least until recently.

5. *Vios*, "life, way of life"; cf. the titles of Politis 1871, 1874, 1899–1902, and 1904.

6. E.g., the Sarakatsani—who are, strictly speaking, transhumant rather than nomadic; see Campbell 1964.

7. Incubation: sleeping overnight in a church, in order to be cured or to receive guidance through the medium of a dream on the right way to find a cure.

8. From *ilios* ("sun") and *tropi* ("turning").

9. The last week before the Lenten fast.

Bibliography

Note. *Works in Greek are given translated titles and marked with an asterisk.*

Alexiou, Margaret B. 1973. *The Ritual Lament in Greek Tradition*. Cambridge, Eng.: Cambridge University Press.

Alivisatos, Hamilcar S. [1949.] *Marriage and Divorce in Accordance with the Canons of the Orthodox Church*. London: Faith Press.

Anonymous. 1852-53. "Vlach Men and Women." *(Nea) Pandora* 3: 282-283.*

————. 1859-60. Review of Zambelios 1859. *Pandora* 10: 495-499.*

————. 1860-61. "Dora d'Istria." *Pandora* 11: 113-114.*

————. 1871-72. Bibliography. Includes review of Politis 1871. *Pandora* 22: 470-472.*

Apostolakis, Yannis M. 1929. *Folksongs: The Collections*. Pt. 1 (no other published). Athens: Kondomaris.*

————. 1939. *The Song of Hagia Sophia*. Thessaloniki.*

————. 1950. *The Kleftic Song: Its Spirit and Art*. Athens: Estia.*

Aravandinos, P. 1880. *Collection of Folksongs of Epirus*. Athens: Petros Perris.*

————. 1905. *Monograph on the Koutsovlachs*. Athens: S. Kousoulinos.*

Ardener, E. W. 1972. "Language, Ethnicity and Population." *Journal of the Anthropological Society of Oxford* 3: 125-132. Reprinted in J. H. M. Beattie and R. G. Lienhardt, eds., *Studies in Social Anthropology: Essays in Memory of E. E. Evans-Pritchard by His Former Oxford Colleagues*, pp. 343-353. Oxford: Clarendon Press, 1975.

Austin, J. L. 1975. *How to Do Things with Words*. 2d ed. Ed. Marina Sbisà and J. O. Urmson. Cambridge, Mass.: Harvard University Press.

Babiniotis, G. 1979. "A Linguistic Approach to the 'Language Question' in Greece." *Byzantine and Modern Greek Studies* 5: 1-16.

Baggally, John W. 1936. *The Klephtic Ballads in Relation to Greek History (1715-1821)*. Oxford: Basil Blackwell.

Beaton, Roderick. 1980. *Folk Poetry of Modern Greece*. Cambridge, Eng.: Cambridge University Press.

Bees (Veis), Nikos A. 1956. "Claude-Charles Fauriel and Greek Folksongs." Editor's note in Fauriel 1956: i-xiv.*

Berlin, Isaiah. 1977. *Vico and Herder: Two Studies in the History of Ideas*. New York: Vintage. Also London: Hogarth, 1976.

Bialor, Perry A. 1973. "A Century and a Half of Change: Transformations of a Greek Farming Community in the Northwestern Peloponessos, Greece." Ph.D. dissertation, Department of Anthropology, University of Chicago.

Blok, Anton. 1974. *The Mafia of a Sicilian Village, 1860-1960: A Study of Violent Peasant Entrepreneurs*. New York: Harper & Row.

Blum, Richard, and Eva Blum. 1970. *The Dangerous Hour: The Lore of Crisis and Mystery in Rural Greece*. London: Chatto & Windus.

Bouvier, Bertrand. 1960. *Folksongs from a Manuscript in the Iviron Monastery*. Athens: Institut Français d'Athènes.*

Browning, Robert. 1969. *Medieval and Modern Greek*. London: Hutchinson University Library.

Bryer, Anthony A. M. 1976. "The Pontic Revival and the New Greece." In Diamandouros et al. 1976: 171-190.

Büdinger, Max. 1866. *Mittelgriechisches Volksepos: Ein Versuch*. Leipzig: B. G. Teubner.

Burke, Kenneth. 1954. *Permanence and Change*. 2d ed. Palo Alto: Bobbs-Merrill.

Burrows, Ronald. 1913. "Song of the Hellenes to Venizelos, the Cretan." *Manchester University Magazine* 9 (3): 92.

―――. 1919. "The Unity of the Greek Race." *Contemporary Review* 115: 153-164.

Bybilakis, Emmanuel. See Vivilakis, Emmanuel.

Bynum, David E. 1969. "The Generic Nature of Oral Epic Poetry." *Genre* 2 (3): 236-258.

Campbell, J. K. 1964. *Honour, Family, and Patronage: A Study of Institutions and Moral Values in a Greek Mountain Community*. Oxford: Clarendon Press.

―――. 1976. "Regionalism and Local Community." In Muriel Dimen and Ernestine Friedl, eds., *Regional Variation in Modern Greece and Cyprus: Toward a Perspective on the Ethnography of Greece*, pp. 18-27. Annals of the New York Academy of Sciences 268.

Capidan, Théodore. N.d. *Les Macédo-Roumains*. Académie Roumaine: Connaissance de la Terre et de la Pensée Roumaine 5. Paris: Ernest Leroux.

Cecchetti, Bartolomeo. 1868. *Di alcune opere della principessa Dora d'Istria*. Venice.

―――. 1873. *Bibliografia della principessa Dora d'Istria*. 5th ed. Florence: Rivista Europea.

Chapman, John Jay. 1915. *Greek Genius and Other Essays*. New York: Moffat, Tard.

Chapman, Malcolm. 1978. *The Gaelic Vision in Scottish Culture*. London: Croom Helm.

Ciampini, Raffaele. 1945. *Vita di Niccolò Tommaseo*. Florence: G. C. Sansoni.

Clogg, Richard. 1972. "The Ideology of the 'Revolution of 21 April 1967.'" In Richard Clogg and George Yannopoulos, eds., *Greece under Military Rule*, pp. 36–58. London: Secker & Warburg/New York: Basic Books.

————, ed. 1973. *The Struggle for Greek Independence: Essays to Mark the 150th Anniversary of the Greek War of Independence*. Hamden, Conn.: Anchor Press.

————, ed. 1976. *The Movement for Greek Independence, 1770–1821: A Collection of Documents*. New York: Barnes & Noble.

Cocchiara, Giuseppe. 1952. *Storia del folklore in Europa*. Turin: Edizioni Scientifiche Einaudi—Collezione di studi religiosi, etnologici e psicologici 20.

————. N.d. *Storia degli studi delle tradizioni popolari in Italia*. Palermo: G. B. Palumbo.

Colocotronis, Vassilis. 1918. "L'Ame bulgare et l'âme grecque d'après la poésie populaire." *Revue de Grèce* 1 (1): 129–143.

Colquhoun, Archibald. 1954. *Manzoni and His Times*. London: J. M. Dent.

Couloumbis, T. A., John A. Petropulos, and H. J. Psomiades. 1976. *Foreign Interference in Greek Politics: An Historical Perspective*. New York: Pella.

Crick, Malcolm. 1976. *Explorations in Language and Meaning: Towards a Semantic Anthropology*. New York: John Wiley.

Croce, Benedetto, and Fausto Nicolini (editor and additional author). 1947 (vol. 1), 1948 (vol. 2). *Bibliografia Vichiana*. Naples: Ricciardi.

Dakin, Douglas. 1973. *The Greek Struggle for Independence, 1821–1833*. London: Batsford.

Damianakos, Stathis. 1976. *Sociology of the "Rebetiko."* [Athens]: Ermia.*

Danforth, Loring M. 1979. "The Role of Dance in the Ritual Therapy of the Anastenaria." *Byzantine and Modern Greek Studies* 5: 141–163.

Dawkins, R. M. 1916. *Modern Greek in Asia Minor: A Study of the Dialects of Sílli, Cappadocia and Phárasa, with Grammar, Texts, Translations and Commentary*. Cambridge, Eng.: Cambridge University Press.

Diamandouros, Nikiforos P., John P. Anton, John A. Petropulos, and Peter Topping, eds. 1976. *Hellenism and the First Greek War of Liberation (1821–1830): Continuity and Change*. Thessaloniki: Institute for Balkan Studies 156.

Dimaras, C. Th. 1972. *A History of Modern Greek Literature*. Translated by Mary P. Gianos from the fourth Greek edition (Athens: Ikaros, 1948). Albany: State University of New York Press.

Dimou, Nikos. N.d. [1975 or later.] *The Misery of Being Greek*. 5th ed. Athens: Ikaria.*

d'Istria, Dora. 1863. *Excursions en Rumélie et en Morée*. 2 vols. Zurich: Meyer & Zeller.

———. 1865. "La Nationalité serbe d'après les chants populaires." *Revue des Deux Mondes* 55: 315–360.

———. 1866. "La Nationalité albanaise d'après les chants populaires." *Revue des Deux Mondes* 63: 382–418.

———. 1867. "La Nationalité hellénique d'après les chants populaires." *Revue des Deux Mondes* 70: 584–627.

Dorson, Richard M., ed. 1961. *Folklore Research around the World: A North American Point of View*. Indiana University Folklore Series 16. Bloomington: Indiana University Press.

———. 1966. "The Question of Folklore in a New Nation." *Journal of the Folklore Institute* 3: 277–298.

———. 1968. *The British Folklorists: A History*. Chicago: University of Chicago Press.

Douglas, F. S. N. 1813. *An Essay on Certain Points of Resemblance between the Ancient and Modern Greeks*. 3d ed. London: John Murray.

Dozon, Auguste. 1875. *Chansons populaires bulgares*. Paris: Maisonneuve.

Eco, Umberto. 1976. *A Theory of Semiotics*. Bloomington: Indiana University Press.

Economides, Dimitr. V. 1969. "The Folk Terminology of Greek Popular Song." *Epet. Kentr. Erevnis Ellin. Laografias* 20–21 (1967–68, published 1969): 126–150.*

Ellinismos. 1896. *National Songs of Greece, 1453–1821*. Athens.*

Evlambios, George. 1843. *The Amaranth: The Roses of Hellas Reborn: Folk Poems of the Modern Greeks*. In Greek and Russian. St. Petersburg: Academy of Sciences. Reprinted in Greek edition, Athens: Notis Karavias, 1973.*

Fallmerayer, Jakob Philipp. 1827. *Geschichte des Kaiserthums von Trapezunt*. Munich: Weber.

———. 1830 (vol. 1), 1836 (vol. 2). *Geschichte der Halbinsel Morea während des Mittelalters*. Stuttgart & Tübingen: J. G. Cotta.

———. 1845. *Fragmente aus dem Orient*. 2 vols. Stuttgart & Tübingen: J. G. Cotta.

———. 1860. "Das Albanesische Element in Griechenland." *Abhandlungen der Historischen Classe der Koeniglich Bayerischen Akademie* 8: 419–487. Munich: Verlag der K. Akademie.

Fauriel, Claude. 1824 (vol. 1), 1825 (vol. 2). *Chants populaires de la Grèce moderne*. Paris: Dondey-Dupré. Further renditions were published in German (by W. Müller in 1825), English (by C. B. Sheridan in 1825), French (by L. J. N. Lemercier in 1824), and Italian (by P. Aporti in 1881).

———. 1854. *Dante et les origines de la langue et de la littérature italienne*. Vol. 2. Paris: Auguste Durand.

———. 1956. *Greek Folksongs*. Greek edition of Fauriel 1824 and 1825, rendered with an introduction by Nikos A. Bees (Veis). Athens: Nikos D. Nikas.*

Filaretos, George N. 1906. *The 28th May 1453: Speech Delivered during the Civil Memorial for Constantine Palaeologos (on May 28, 1906)*. Athens: To Kratos Press.*

Finnegan, Ruth. 1977. *Oral Poetry: Its Nature, Significance and Social Context*. Cambridge, Eng.: Cambridge University Press.

Frangoudaki, Anna. 1978. *The Reading Books of Grade School: Ideological Coercion and Pedagogical Violence*. Athens: Themelio.*

Garnett, Lucy M. J., and J. S. Stuart-Glennie. 1896. *New Folklore Researches: Greek Folk Poesy: Annotated Translations, from the Whole Cycle of Romaic Folk-verse and Folk-prose*. Includes Stuart-Glennie's essays on "the science of folklore, Greek folkspeech, and the survival of paganism." Guildford, Eng.: privately published (printers Billing & Son).

Geanakoplos, Deno John. 1962. *Greek Scholars in Venice: Studies in the Dissemination of Greek Learning from Byzantium to Western Europe*. Cambridge, Mass.: Harvard University Press.

————. 1966. *Byzantine East and Latin West: Two Worlds of Christendom in Middle Ages and Renaissance*. New York: Barnes & Noble.

Geertz, Clifford. 1973. *The Interpretation of Cultures*. New York: Basic Books.

Geldart, E. M. 1884. *Folk-Lore of Modern Greece: The Tales of the People*. London: W. Swan Sonnenschein.

Gizelis, Gregory Kh. 1974. *Narrative Rhetorical Devices of Persuasion: Folklore Communication in a Greek-American Community*. Athens: National Center of Social Research.

————. 1976. "Modern Analytical Approaches to Artistic Narrative Communication: A Case Study." *Spira*: 408–429.*

Goldstein, K. 1967. "Bowdlerization and Expurgation: Academic and Folk." *Journal of American Folklore* 80: 374–386.

Goldstein, Leon J. 1976. *Historical Knowing*. Austin: University of Texas Press.

Goodfield, June, and Stephen Edelston Toulmin. 1965. *The Discovery of Time*. New York: Harper & Row.

[Goudas, A.] N.d. [1870?] *Fourth Memorandum: On the Nature of Brigandage in Greece, on the Causes of Its Genesis and Existence, and on the Means of Its Extirpation*. [Athens?]*

Hahn, Johann Georg von. 1864. *Griechische und Albanesische Märchen*. 2 vols. Leipzig: W. Engelmann.

Hallowell, A. I. 1965. "The History of Anthropology as an Anthropological Problem." *Journal of the History of the Behavioral Sciences* 1: 24–38.

Hammel, Eugene A. 1972. *The Myth of Structural Analysis: Lévi-Strauss and the Three Bears*. Modules in Anthropology 25, pp. 1–29. Reading, Mass.: Addison-Wesley.

Haxthausen, Werner von. 1935. *Neugriechische Volkslieder*. Ed. Karl Schulte Kemminghausen and Gustav Sonter. Münster i.W.: Aschendorffsche Verlagsbuchhandlung, Veröffentlichungen der Annette von Droste-Gesellschaft, no. 4.

Henderson, G. P. 1970. *The Revival of Greek Thought, 1620-1830*. Albany: State University of New York Press.

Herzfeld, Michael. 1969. "The Song of the Siege of Rhodes and Its Variants." *Kritika Khronika* 21: 494-498.*

――――. 1973. "'The Siege of Rhodes' and the Ethnography of Greek Oral Tradition." *Kritika Khronika* 25: 413-440.

――――. 1974. "Oral Tradition and Cultural Continuity in the Spring Rituals of Southern Rhodian Villages." *Dodekanisiaka Khronika* 2: 270-289.*

――――. 1977. "Ritual and Textual Structures: The Advent of Spring in Rural Greece." In Ravindra K. Jain, ed. *Text and Context: The Social Anthropology of Tradition*, pp. 29-50. A.S.A. Essays 2. Philadelphia: Institute for the Study of Human Issues.

――――. 1979. "Exploring a Metaphor of Exposure." *Journal of American Folklore* 92: 285-301.

――――. 1980a. "Honour and Shame: Problems in the Comparative Analysis of Moral Systems." *Man*, n.s. 15: 339-351.

――――. 1980b. "Social Borderers: Themes of Ambiguity and Conflict in Greek Folk-Song." *Byzantine and Modern Greek Studies* 6: 61-80.

――――. 1980c. "On the Ethnography of 'Prejudice' in an Exclusive Community." *Ethnic Groups* 2: 283-305.

――――. 1981a. "Performative Categories and Symbols of Passage in Rural Greece." *Journal of American Folklore* 94: 44-57.

――――. 1981b. "Meaning and Morality: A Semiotic Approach to Evil Eye Accusations in a Greek Village." *American Ethnologist* 8: 560-574.

――――. 1981c. "An Indigenous Theory of Meaning and Its Elicitation in Performative Context." *Semiotica* 34.

Hesseling, D. 1892. "Essai historique sur l'Infinitif Grec." In J. Psichari, ed., *Etudes de philologie néo-grecque*, pp. 1-44. Paris: Emile Bouillon, Ecole Pratique des Hautes Etudes: Bibliothèque: Sciences Historiques et Philologiques 92.

Hobsbawm, Eric. 1959. *Primitive Rebels: Studies in Archaic Forms of Social Movement in the 19th and 20th Centuries*. Manchester: Manchester University Press.

Hodgen, Margaret T. 1936. *The Doctrine of Survivals: A Chapter in the History of Scientific Method in the Study of Man*. London: Allenson.

Holden, David. 1972. *Greece without Columns: The Making of the Modern Greeks*. London: Faber & Faber.

Howarth, David. 1976. *The Greek Adventure: Lord Byron and Other Eccentrics in the War of Independence*. New York: Atheneum.

Hussey, J. M. 1978. "Jakob Philipp Fallmerayer and George Finlay." *Byzantine and Modern Greek Studies* 4: 78-87.

Iatridis, A. 1859. *Collection of Old and New Folksongs, with Various Illustrations.* Athens: D. Ath. Mavrommatis.*

Ibrovac, Miodrag. 1966. *Claude Fauriel et la fortune européenne des poésies populaires grecques et serbes: Etude d'histoire romantique, suivie du cours de Fauriel professé en Sorbonne (1831-1832).* Paris: Marcel Didier.

Ioannidis, S. 1887. *A Medieval Epic from the Trebizond Manuscript: Basil Digenes Akrites the Cappadocian.* Constantinople.*

Ioannou, G. 1975. *Folksong: Ballads.* Athens: Ermis New Greek Library.*

Jenkins, Romilly. 1940. *Dionysios Solomos.* Cambridge, Eng.: Cambridge University Press.

―――. 1961. *The Dilessi Murders.* London: Longmans.

Jenkyns, Richard. 1980. *The Victorians and Ancient Greece.* Cambridge, Mass.: Harvard University Press.

Jireček, C. 1891. *Das Fürstentum Bulgarien: Seine Bodengestaltung, Natur, Bevölkerung, Wirtschaftlische Zustände, Geistige Cultur, Staatsverfassung, Staatsverwaltung, und neueste Geschichte.* Wien: F. Tempsky.

Jones, Maldwyn Allen. 1960. *American Immigration.* Chicago: University of Chicago Press.

Joseph, Brian Daniel. 1978. *Morphology and Universals in Syntactic Change: Evidence from Medieval and Modern Greek.* Bloomington: Indiana University Linguistics Club.

Kakouri, Katerina. 1965. *Dionysiaka: Aspects of the Popular Thracian Religion of To-day.* Athens: G. C. Eleftheroudakis. Greek edition, 1963, same publisher and location.*

Kakridis, Johannes Theoph. 1967. *Die alten Hellenen im Neugriechischen Volksglauben.* Munich: Heimeran.

Kalonaros, Petros P. 1970. *Basil Digenes Akritas: The Verse Texts.* Athens: Papadimas.* Reprint of the 1941 edition.

Kambanis, Aristos. 1920. *Kalligas and Zambelios: Lectures on Greek Narrative Writers.* Lectures of the Parnassos Philological Society 4. Athens: Michael S. Zimakis.*

Kapsomenos, Eratosthenis G. 1978. *Greek Folk Song: Its Aesthetics, Myth, and Ideology.* Rethinno: privately published.*

―――. 1979. *The Modern Cretan Historical Song: Its Structure and Ideology.* Athens: Themelio.*

Karatza, Eleni. 1970. *Edgar Quinet and Modern Greece.* Athens.*

Karolidis, P. 1906. "Critical, Historical, and Topographical Notes on the Medieval Greek Epic *Akritas.*" *Epistimoniki Epetiris* of the National University of Athens for 1905-1906: 188-246.*

Katsoulis, George D. 1975. *The Establishment in Modern Greek History.* Athens: Nea Sinora.*

Kemminghausen, Karl Schulte, and Gustav Sonter. 1935. "Einleitung." In Haxthausen 1935.

Khrisanthopoulos, L. 1853. *Collection of the Local Customs of Greece, from Official Responses of the Local Authorities to the Greek Government.* Athens: K. Garpolas.*

Khristovasilis, Kh. 1902. *National Songs, 1453-1821.* 2d ed. Athens: Ellinismos.*

Kind, Theodor. 1827. *Eunomia.* Vol. 3. Grimma: Carl Friedrich Göschen Beyer.

———. 1833. *Neugriechische Poesien.* Vol. 1. Leipzig: in der Deutschen Buchhandlung.

———. 1838. *Geschichte der Griechischen Revolution vom Jahre 1821 bis zur Thronbesteigung des Koenigs Otto I.* Leipzig: Literarisches Museum (Schiller und Robitzsch).

———. 1861. *Anthologie neugriechischer Volkslieder.* 3d ed. of King 1827; 2d ed., 1849. Leipzig: Veit.

Kiprianou, Khrisanthos S. 1967. *The Pan-Cypriot Gymnasium and Folklore.* Vol. 1. Nicosia.*

Kiriakidis, Stilpon P. 1923. "N. G. Politis." *Laografia* 7: ix–li.*

———. 1931. "Gli studi folkloristici in Grecia." *Lares* 2 (2): 11-15.

———. 1934. *The Historical Beginnings of Modern Greek Popular Poetry.* Rector's speech. Thessaloniki: University of Thessaloniki.*

———. 1937. *What Is Laography and What Ends Can the Study of It Serve?* Thessaloniki.*

———. 1955. *The Northern Ethnological Boundaries of Hellenism.* Thessaloniki: Institute for Balkan Studies 5.

Kiriakidou-Nestoros, Alki. 1975. *Folklore Studies.* Athens: Olkos.*

———. 1978. *The Theory of Greek Folklore.* Athens: Moraitis School.*

Kitto, H. D. F. 1957. *The Greeks.* Harmondsworth, Eng.: Penguin.

Kofos, Evangelos. 1964. *Nationalism and Communism in Macedonia.* Thessaloniki: Institute for Balkan Studies 70.

Kondogiorgis, George D. 1979. *Helladic Folk Ideology.* Athens: Nea Sinora.*

Koraes, Adamantios. [1803.] *Mémoire de l'état actuel de la civilisation dans la Grèce, lu à la Société des Observateurs de l'Homme le 16 nivôse, en XI (6 janvier 1803).*

———. 1805. Letter, February 2. In A. Koraes, *Correspondence,* 2 (1799-1809): 230-234. Athens: Estia/Society for the Study of the Hellenic Enlightenment.*

———. 1972. *The Social Significance of the 1821 Revolution.* 5th ed. Athens: Ekdosis Diethnous Epikairotitos.*

Kordatos, Yanis. 1972. *The Social Significance of the Greek Revolution of 1821.* Athens: Ekd. Diethnous Epikerotitos.* 5th ed. Edited with an introduction by Than. Kh. Papadopoulos.

Koukhtsoglou, Yannis. 1947. "The Man Apostolakis." *Nea Estia* 42 (491): 204-209.*

Koukoules, Phaidon I. 1950. *The Folkloristic Materials of Eustathius of Thessaloniki.* 2 vols. Athens: Society for Macedonian Studies, Scientific Treatises, Philological and Theological Series 5-6.*

Kriaris, Aristidis. 1920. *Complete Collection of Cretan Folksongs.* 2d ed. Athens: Frantzeskakis & Kaitatzis.*

La Guilletière, Sieur de [Guillet, André Georges]. 1676. *Lacédémone ancienne et nouvelle, où l'on voit les mœurs et les coutûmes des grecs modernes, des mahométans, & des juifs du pays.* Paris: Jean Ribou.

Lambithianaki-Papadaki, Evangelia. 1972. *The Passion of the Young Brave: Marriage Brokerage, Engagement, and the Wedding in a Village of Crete.* Iraklion.*

Lambrinos, George. 1947. *Folksong.* Historical Library 8. Athens: Ta Nea Vivlia.*

Lang, Andrew. 1885. *Custom and Myth.* 2d ed. London: Longmans, Green. Reprinted 1970 by Oosterhout N. B., Anthropological Publications.

Lanitis, Nik. Kl. 1946. *The Soul of Cyprus.* Athens: Aetos.*

Lascaris, M. 1934. "N. Tommaseo ed A. Mustoxidi." *Società Dalmata di Storia Patria, Atti e Memorie* 3: 5–39.

Lawson, John Cuthbert. 1910. *Modern Greek Folklore and Ancient Greek Religion: A Study in Survivals.* Cambridge, Eng.: Cambridge University Press. Reprinted 1964, with a foreword by Al. N. Oikonomides, New Hyde Park, N.Y.: University Books.

Leake, William Martin. 1814. *Researches in Greece.* London: Booth.

———. 1835. *Travels in Northern Greece.* Vol. 1. London: Rodwell.

Lee, Dorothy. 1953. "Greece." Anon. article in Margaret Mead, ed., *Cultural Patterns and Technical Change.* Paris: UNESCO. Reprinted in Dorothy Lee, *Freedom and Culture*, Englewood Cliffs, N.J.: Prentice-Hall/Spectrum, 1959.

Lefkias, Anastasios Georgiadis. 1843. *Overthrow of What Has Been Claimed, Written, and Broadcast in the Press, That None of Those Now Living in Greece Is a Descendant of the Ancient Greeks.* Athens.* With Latin translation.

Legrand, Emile. 1870. *Collection de monuments pour servir à l'étude de la langue néo-hellénique.* Vol. 12. Paris: Maisonneuve.

———. 1876. *Chansons populaires grecques.* Paris: Maisonneuve.

Leigh Fermor, Patrick. 1966. *Roumeli: Travels in Northern Greece.* New York: Harper & Row.

Lelekos, Michael S. 1852. *Demotic Anthology.* Athens: P. Angelidis.*

———. 1868 (vol. 1), 1869 (vol. 2). *Demotic Anthology.* Athens: Nikolaos Rousopoulos.*

———. 1888. *Dessert.* 2 vols. Athens: A. Papageorgiou.*

Lenormant, François. 1864. *Monographie de la voie sacrée éleusinienne, de ses monuments et de ses souvenirs.* Vol. 1 (no other published). Paris: L. Hachette.

Lipset, Seymour Martin. 1963. *The First New Nation: The United States in Historical and Comparative Perspective.* New York: Basic Books. Republished 1967, Garden City, N.Y.: Doubleday.

Llewellyn Smith, Michael. 1965. *The Great Island: A Study of Crete.* London: Longmans.

Loomis, Louise Ropes. 1906. *Medieval Hellenism.* Lancaster, Pa.: Wickersham Press.

Lord, Albert B. 1960. *The Singer of Tales*. Harvard Studies in Comparative
    Literature 24. Cambridge, Mass.: Harvard University Press.
Loukas, Georgios. 1874. *Philological Visits to the Monuments of the Ancients
    in the Life of the Modern Cypriots*. Vol. 1 (no other published).
    Athens: Nikolaos Rousopoulos.*
Loukatos, Dim. S. 1963. *Folklorica contemporanea*. Athens.*
————. 1978. *Introduction to Greek Folklore*. Athens: National Bank of
    Greece.* 2d ed.
Luciani, Vincent. 1967. *A Brief History of Italian Literature*. New York:
    S. F. Vanni.
Mandouvalou, Maria. 1969. *Unknown Correspondence between Dora d'Istria
    and D. Voulgaris*. Athens: Texts and Studies in Modern Greek Philology
    61.*
Manesis, N. V. 1860-61. "Andrea Mustoxidi." *Pandora* 11: 249-252.*
Mannheim, Karl. 1936. *Ideology and Utopia: An Introduction to the Soci-
    ology of Knowledge*. New York (1966 reedition): Harcourt, Brace &
    World.
Manousos, Andonios. 1850. *National Songs*. Vol. 1 (no other published).
    Corfu: Ermis.*
Marcellus, M. L. J. A. C. D. du T., Comte de. 1851. *Chants du peuple en
    Grèce*. Paris: J. Lecoffre.
————. 1860. *Chants populaires de la Grèce moderne*. Paris: Michel Lévy
    frères.
————. 1861. *Les Grecs anciens et les Grecs modernes*. Paris: Michel Lévy
    frères.
Marinoni, Ernesto, ed. 1926. *Prose e poesie di Ugo Foscolo*. 2d ed. Milan:
    Ulrico Hoepli.
Martellotti, Guido. See Tommaseo 1943.
Mavrogordato, John. 1956. *Digenes Akrites*. Oxford: Clarendon Press.
Mazarakis, E. D. 1964. *Folklore Research and Its Systematic Organization*.
    Athens.*
Megas, George A. 1946. *Do the Bulgarians Have a National Epic?* Athens:
    Society for the Propagation of Hellenic Letters.*
————. 1950. "La Civilisation dite balkanique: La Poésie populaire des
    pays des Balkans." *L'Hellénisme Contemporain*: 8-30.
————. 1951. *The Greek House: Its Evolution and Its Relation to the
    Houses of the Other Balkan Peoples*. Athens: Ministry of Reconstruc-
    tion 37. Greek edition, 1949.*
————. 1953. "The Sack of Constantinople in the Songs and Traditions of
    the People." In *1453-1953: The Quinquecentenary of the Sack of
    Constantinople: Commemorative Volume*. Athens: *L'Hellénisme Con-
    temporain*, May 29, pp. 244-255.*
Menardos, Simos. 1921. "History of the Words *Tragōdō* and *Tragōdia*."
    Pamphlet. [Athens?] *
Migne, Jacques Paul. *Patrologiæ cursus completus. Series græca*.

Morgan, Gareth. 1960. *Cretan Poetry: Sources and Inspiration.* Iraklion: A.
   Kalokerinos. Originally published in *Kritika Khronika* 14 (1960): 7–68,
   203–270, 379–434.
Motsias, Khristos. 1977. "In the Kleftic Refuges Athletics Flourished Anew."
   Ta Nea, April 7, p. 7.*
Mure, G. R. G. 1965. *The Philosophy of Hegel.* London: Oxford University
   Press.
Mustoxidi, Andrea. 1821. *Prose varie del Cavaliere Andrea Mustoxidi Cor-
   cirese, con aggiunta di alcuni versi.* Milan: Bettoni.
————. 1860. See Tripaldo 1860.
Nea Estia. 1947. Special issue devoted to Yannis Apostolakis. 42 (491): 188–
   212.*
Nisbet, Robert A. 1969. *Social Change and History: Aspects of the Western
   Theory of Development.* London & New York: Oxford University
   Press.
Oinas, Felix J. 1961. "Folklore Activities in Russia." In Dorson 1961: 76–84.
Orlandos, Anast. 1969. "The Work of the Greek Folklore Research Center in
   the Fifty Years since Its Foundation (1918–1968)." *Epet. Kentr.
   Erevnis Ellin. Laografias* 20–21: 5–14.*
Page, D. L., ed. 1962. *Poetae Melici Graeci.* Oxford: Clarendon Press.
Paleologos, P. 1977. *"That's* What Greece Is All About." *To Vima*, March 23,
   p. 1.*
Papadopoullos, Theodhoros. 1970. "The Field and Content of Folklore Ac-
   cording to Its Definition." *Epet. Kentr. Epist. Erevnon* 3: 1–62.*
Papadopoulos-Vrettos, Andreas. 1825. *Memoria su di alcuni costumi degli
   antichi Greci tuttora esistenti nell'Isola di Leucade.* 2d ed. Naples.
————. 1837. *Mémoires biographiques-historiques sur le président de la
   Grèce, le Comte Jean Capodistrias.* Paris: Firmin Didot.
————. 1852–53. Bibliography. Review of Zambelios 1852. *Pandora* 3:
   397–406.*
————. 1860. See Tipaldo 1860.
Papagrigorakis, Idomenefs I. 1956–57. *The Cretan "Rizitiká" Songs.* Vol. 1
   (no other published): *For the Feast and the Road.* Chania.*
Papazisis, Dimitrios Tr. 1976. *Vlachs (Koutsovlachs).* Athens.*
Pashley, Robert. 1837. *Travels in Crete.* 2 vols. London: John Murray.
Passow, Arnold. 1860. *Carmina popularia Graeciae recentioris.* Leipzig: B. G.
   Teubner.
Petropoulos, D. 1954. *La Comparaison dans la chanson populaire grecque.*
   Athens: Institut Français d'Athènes (coll. 86).
Petropoulos, Ilias. 1968. *"Rebetika" Songs.* Athens.*
Petropulos, John. 1968. *Politics and Statecraft in the Kingdom of Greece,
   1833–1843.* Princeton, N.J.: Princeton University Press.
————. 1976a. Introduction. In Diamandouros et al. 1976: 19–41.
————. 1976b. "Forms of Collaboration with the Enemy during the First
   Greek War of Liberation." In Diamandouros et al. 1976: 131–143.
Polilas, Iakovos. See Valetas 1950.

Politis, Alexis. 1973. *Folksong: Kleftic.* Athens: Ermis New Greek Library.*

Politis, Nikolaos G. 1871 (pt. 1, to p. 204), 1874 (pt. 2). *Study of the Life of the Modern Greeks.* Vol. 1 (no other issued in this series): *Modern Greek Mythology.* Athens: Karl Wilberg & N. A. Nakis.*

————. 1872. "Swallow Song [*Khelidhonisma*]." *Neoellinika Analekta* 1: 354-368.*

————. 1876. "The First of March." *Estia* 1: 142-143.*

————. 1880. "Popular Meteorological Myths." Athens: Parnassos. Originally published in *Parnassos* 4.*

————. 1882a. "The Sun in Popular Myths." Athens: Enosis.*

————. 1882b. "Introductory Lecture for the Class in Hellenic Mythology." Athens: Aion. Originally published in *Aion*, December 7-9.*

————. 1885. "Bulgarian Klefts According to Popular Bulgarian Songs." *Estia* 19: 754-758.*

————. 1899-1902. *Studies of the Life and Language of the Greek People: Proverbs.* Vol. 1. Athens: Marasli.*

————. 1901. "Hellenes or *Romii*?" Athens: Agon Press.*

————. 1903. "The Mistranscription of the National Songs." Athens: *Athinai* (June 10, 11, 12, 16) and *Agon* (August 1, 8, 15).*

————. 1904. *Studies of the Life and Language of the Greek People: Traditions.* Athens: Marasli.*

————. 1907. *On the National Epic of the Modern Greeks.* Rector's speech, delivered in 1906. Athens: University of Athens.*

————. 1909a. "Laography." *Laografia* 1: 3-18.* See appendix A.

————. 1909b. "Akritic Songs: The Death of Digenes." *Laografia* 1: 169-272.*

————. 1914. *Selections from the Songs of the Greek People.* Athens: Estia.*

————. 1916. *Known Poets of Folksongs.* Athens: Lectures of the Parnassos Philological Society 1.*

————. 1918. "Croyances populaires sur le rétablissement de la nation hellénique." *Revue de Grèce* 1 (1): 151-170.

Pommier, Armand. 1863. *Mme. La Comtesse Dora d'Istria.* In the series Profils contemporains. Paris: Lecrivain & Tonbon.

Pouqueville, F. C. H. L. 1805. *Voyage en Morée, à Constantinople, en Albanie, et dans plusieurs autres parties de l'Empire Othoman . . .* Paris: Gabon.

Quinet, Edgar. 1830. *De la Grèce moderne et des rapports avec l'antiquité.* Paris & Strasbourg: F. G. Levrault.

————. 1859. *Oeuvres complètes.* Vol. 5, pp. 173-598. Paris: Pagnerre.

Read, Allen Walker. 1978. "The Persistence of Verbal Symbols of Emotion in Charged Contexts." Paper delivered at the annual meeting of the Semiotic Society of America in Providence, R.I., cited by kind permission of the author.

Romaios, Kostas A. 1959. *Close to the Roots: Research on the Psychic World of the Greek People.* Athens.*

————. 1966. "*Ksandinon the Far-Famed*: A New Methodological Beginning for a Critical Edition of the Texts of Folksongs." *Arkhion Pondou* 27: 150-206.*

————. 1966-67. "The Poet and the Betrayed Fortress." *Arkhion Pondou* 28: 197-212.*

————. 1968. *The Poetry of a People*. Athens: Folklore Institute of the Greek Travelers' Club 1.*

St. Clair, William. 1972. *That Greece Might Still Be Free: The Philhellenes in the War of Independence*. London: Oxford University Press.

Sainte-Beuve, C.-A. 1870, *Portraits contemporains*. Vol. 4. Paris: Michel Lévy frères. Fauriel is presented on pp. 125-268.

Sakellarios, Athanasios A. 1891. *Kypriaka*. Vol. 2: *Language in Cyprus*. Athens: P. D. Sakellarios.*

Sanders, D. 1844. *Das Volksleben der Neugriechen, dargestellt und erklärt aus Liedern, Sprichworten, Kunstgedichten, nebst einem Anhange von Musikbeilagen und zwei kritischen Abhandlungen*. Mannheim: F. Bassermann.

Sanders, Irwin T. 1962. *Rainbow in the Rock: The People of Rural Greece*. Cambridge, Mass.: Harvard University Press.

Sandfeld, K. 1930. *Linguistique balkanique: Problèmes et résultats*. Collection de la Société Linguistique de Paris 31. Paris: H. Champion.

Sathas, K., and Emile Legrand. 1875. *Les Exploits de Basile Digénis Acritas: Epopée byzantine du dixième siècle* . . . Paris: Maisonneuve/Athens: Coromilas.

Schein, Muriel Dimen. 1975. "When Is an Ethnic Group? Ecology and Class Structure in Northern Greece." *Ethnology* 14: 83-97.

Schmidt, Bernhard. 1871. *Das Volksleben der Neugriechen und das hellenische Alterthum*, Leipzig: B. G. Teubner.

————. 1877. *Griechische Märchen, Sagen und Volkslieder*. Leipzig: B. G. Teubner.

Simopoulos, Kiriakos. 1972 (vol. 1, 2d ed.: 333-1700), 1973 (vol. 2: 1700-1800), 1975 (vol. 3, pt. 1: 1800-1810; pt. 2: 1810-1821). *Foreign Travelers in Greece*. Athens.*

Sinner, G. R. L. de. 1824. *Christoph. Bondelmonti, Florentini, Librum Archipelagi*. Leipzig & Berlin: G. Reimer.

Skouteri-Didaskalou, N. 1980. "For an Ideological Reproduction of Inter-Sexual Discriminations: The Sign-Providing Function of the 'Ritual of Marriage.'" In Karin Boklund-Lagopoulou, ed., *Semiotics and Society*. Athens: Odhisseas.

Sokolov, Y. M. 1950. *Russian Folklore*. Trans. Catherine Ruth Smith. New York: Macmillan.

Soteropoulos, S. 1868. *The Brigands of the Morea: A Narrative of the Captivity of Mr. S. Soteropoulos*. 2 vols. Tran. J. O. Bagdon. London: Saunders, Otley.

Sotiropoulos, Dimitri. 1977. "Diglossia and the National Language Question in Modern Greece." *Linguistics* 197: 5-31.

Spectator, The. Review of G. F. Abbott, *Songs of Modern Greece.* November 3, 1900.

Sperantsas, Stelios. 1949. "'Ours Once More . . .'" *Elliniki Dhimiouryia* 3 (32): 884–886.*

Spiridakis, George K. 1962. *Directions for the Collection of Folklore Material.* Athens: Academy of Athens.*

———. 1966. "The Scientific Foundation of Folklore Studies in Greece." Reprinted from *Epet. Filosofikis Skholis,* Athens University, 1965–66.*

———. 1969. "The Song of the Swallow (*Khelidhonisma*) on the First of March." *Epet. Kentr. Erevnis Ellin. Laografias* 20–21: 15–54.*

Stephanopoli, Dimo. 1800. *Voyage de Dimo et Nicolo Stephanopoli en Grèce pendant les années 1797 et 1798, d'après deux missions . . .* London.

Stuart-Glennie, J. S. See Garnett and Stuart-Glennie 1896.

Taillandier, Saint-René (R. G. E.). 1862. "Publicistes modernes de l'Allemagne: Jacques Philippe Fallmerayer." *Revue des Deux Mondes* 42: 119–154.

Tipaldo, Emilio de. 1860. *Biografia del Cavaliere Andrea Mustoxidi.* Ed. A. Mustoxidi and (subsequently) A. Papadopoulos-Vrettos. Athens: P. A. Sakellarios.

Tommaseo, Niccolò. 1841 (vols. 1, 2), 1842 (vols. 3, 4). *Canti Popolari Toscani, Corsi, Illirici, Greci.* Venice: Girolamo Tasso.

———. 1904. *Il Primo esilio di Nicolò [sic] Tommaseo, 1834–1839: Lettere da lui a Cesare Cantù.* Ed. Ettore Verga. Milan: L. F. Cogliati.

———. 1929. *Colloqui col Manzoni.* Ed. Teresa Lodi. Florence: G. C. Sansoni.

———. 1943. *Canti del popolo Greco.* Ed. Guido Martellotti. Turin: Giulio Einaudi.

———. 1953. *Lettere inedite a Emilio de Tipaldo.* Ed. Raffaele Ciampini. Brescia: Morcelliana.

Trærup, Birthe. 1970. *East Macedonian Folk Songs: Contemporary Traditional Material from Maleševo, Pijanec and the Razlog District Collected and Transcribed by the Author.* Dansk Folkemindesamling, Skrifter 2, Acta Ethnomusicologica Danica 2. Copenhagen: Akademisk Forlag.

Traves, Piero. N.d. *Lo Studio dell'Antichità Classica nell'Ottocento.* La Letteratura Italiana, Storia e Testi, vol. 72. Milan & Naples: Ricciardi.

Tuffin, Paul. 1972–73. "The Whitening Crow: Some *Adynata* in the Greek Tradition." *Epet. Kentr. Episrimonikon Erevnon* 6: 79–92.

Tylor, Edward Burnett. 1865. *Researches into the Early History of Mankind and the Development of Civilization.* London: John Murray.

———. 1871. *Primitive Culture: Researches into the Development of Mythology, Philosophy, Religion, Art, and Custom.* London: John Murray.

———. 1924. 7th edition of Tylor 1871. New York: Brentano's.

Vacalopoulos, Apostolos E. 1970. *Origins of the Greek Nation: The Byzantine Period, 1204–1461.* Rev. ed. Tran. Ian Marks. New Brunswick, N.J.: Rutgers University Press.

Valetas, G., ed. 1950. *Iak. Polilas, Collected Literary and Critical Works*. Includes introductory essay by the editor: "The Life and Work of Polilas." Athens: Piyi.*

Valvis, Stamatios. 1877. "On the Distich of the Hero Athanasios Diakos." *Athinaion* 6 (3): 129-151.*

Vasdravellis, John K. 1975. *Klephts, Armatoles and Pirates in Macedonia during the Rule of the Turks, 1627-1821*. Thessaloniki: Society for Macedonian Studies, Scientific Treatises, Philological and Theological Series 43.

Veloudis, Georg. 1968. *Der neugriechische Alexander-Tradition in Bewahrung und Wandel*. Munich: Institut für byzantinistik and neugriechische Philologie der Universität München.

Venizelos, J. 1846. *Popular Proverbs*. Athens: Vlassaridis.* 2d ed., Ermoupolis: Patris, 1867.

Vico, Giambattista. 1744. *Principi di scienza nuova.* 3d ed. Naples: Stamperia Muziana.

Vivilakis (Bybilakis), Emmanuel. 1840. *Neugriechisches Leben, verglichen mit dem Altgriechischen: Zur Erlauterung beider*. Berlin: Wilhelm Besser.

Viziinos, George, 1949. "The Last Palaeologos." Poem published in *Elliniki Dhimiouryia* 4: 545-547.*

Vlakhoyannis, Yannis. 1935. *Klefts of the Morea: Historical Study Drawn from New Sources* . . . Athens: privately published "through the patriotic grant of Mr. Alex. Pallis."*

Vlastos, Pavlos G. 1909. *Digenes: Ancient Giant and Great Hero of Crete*. Fascicle of *The Cretan People*. Iraklion.*

Voutier, Olivier. 1826. *Lettres sur la Grèce et chants populaires: Extraits du portefeuille du colonel Voutier*. Paris: Firmin Didot.

Vryonis, Speros, Jr. 1976. "The Greeks under Turkish Rule." In Diamandouros et al. 1976: 45-58.

Wace, A. J. B., and M. S. Thompson. 1914. *The Nomads of the Balkans: An Account of Life and Customs among the Vlachs of Northern Pindus*. London: Methuen/New York: E. P. Dutton. Reprint 1972, London: Methuen/New York: Biblo & Tannen.

Wachsmuth, Kurt. 1864. *Das alte Griechenland im neuen*. Bonn: Max Cohen.

Wills, Garry. 1979. *Inventing America: Jefferson's Declaration of Independence*. New York: Random House/Vintage. Originally published in 1978.

Wilson, William A. 1976. *Folklore and Nationalism in Modern Finland*. Bloomington: Indiana University Press.

Winner, Irene Portis. 1977. "The Question of the Zadruga in Slovenia: Myth and Reality in Žerovnica." *Anthropological Quarterly* 50 (3): 125-134.
———, and Thomas G. Winner. 1976. "The Semiotics of Cultural Texts." *Semiotica* 18 (2): 101-156.

Xenos, Stefanos. 1865. *East and West: A Diplomatic History of the Ionian Islands to the Kingdom of Greece*. London: Trübner.

Xydis, Stephen G. 1968. "Medieval Origins of Modern Green Nationalism." *Balkan Studies* 9: 1–20.

Yangas, Athanasios Kh. N.d. [1953.] *Epirote Folksongs, 1000–1958.* Athens: Pirros, for Institute of Epirote Studies.*

Zakhos, Emmanuel. 1966. *Poésie populaire des grecs.* Paris: Maspéro.

Zakythinos, Denis A. 1975. *Le Despotat grec de Morée: Vie et institutions.* French-language edition of the original (Athens 1953), revised and supplemented by Chryssa Maltezou. London: Variorum.

Zambelios, I. 1902. "Autobiography." Ed. D. Kambouroglou. *Armonia* 3: 225–237.*

Zambelios, Spyridon. 1852. *Folksongs of Greece, published with a Study of Medieval Hellenism.* Corfu: Ermis (A. Terzakis & Th. Romaios).*

—————. 1856. "Some Philological Researches on the Modern Greek Language." *Pandora* 7: 369–380, 484–494.*

—————. 1859. *Whence the Vulgar Word* Traghoudho*? Thoughts Concerning Hellenic Poetry.* Athens: P. Soutsas & A. Ktenas.*

—————. 1880. *Parlers grecs et romans: Leur point de contact préhistorique.* Vol. 1 (no other published). Paris: Maisonneuve.

Zannetos, George. 1883. *The Homeric Phrase in Our Folk Poetry.* Athens.*

Zoras, George Th. 1953. "Ideological and Political Directions Formulated before the Fall." In *1453–1953: The Quinquecentenary of the Sack of Constantinople: Commemorative Volume.* Athens: *L'Hellénisme Contemporain.**

Index

No Limits

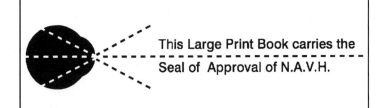

This Large Print Book carries the
Seal of Approval of N.A.V.H.

NO LIMITS

THE WILL TO SUCCEED

MICHAEL PHELPS

WITH ALAN ABRAHAMSON

THORNDIKE PRESS
A part of Gale, Cengage Learning

Detroit • New York • San Francisco • New Haven, Conn • Waterville, Maine • London

GALE
CENGAGE Learning

LIBRARY OF CONGRESS CATALOGING-IN-PUBLICATION DATA

Phelps, Michael, 1985–
  No limits : the will to succeed / by Michael Phelps
    p. cm. — (Thorndike Press large print nonfiction)
  ISBN-13: 978-1-4104-1278-2 (hardcover : alk. paper)
  ISBN-10: 1-4104-1278-4 (hardcover : alk. paper)
    1. Phelps, Michael, 1985– 2. Swimmers — 3. United States —
4. Biography — 4. Large type books. I Title.
  GV838. P54P47 2009
  813'.54—dc22
                                        2008047212

Published in 2008 in arrangement with Free Press, a division of Simon & Schuster, Inc.

Printed in the United States of America
1 2 3 4 5 6 7 12 11 10 09 08

To the power of dreams

Special thanks to my family,
coach, teammates,
and numerous others who helped
me reach my goals
— Michael

To Kayla, Bobby, and Rachel
— Alan

CONTENTS

PROLOGUE

I screamed. You bet I did. I mean, I totally let loose. I clenched my fist and arched my back and screamed and howled and yelled.

And it felt so good. So very good.

No, it felt great.

Better, maybe. It was primal. It was as good as it gets.

I let it all out: joy, relief, excitement, passion, and pride, especially pride in being an American.

It's like that at the Olympic Games. Years of training, of hard work, of desire and discipline — all of it compressed into minutes, sometimes just seconds, and time seems to stand still as history plays itself out.

There's nothing sweeter than winning.

And we had just won. We had set a world record, too, obliterated the old record, really. The Stars and Stripes. The American men. Us.

I had just been part of, had also just been

witness to, the most amazing, thrilling, exciting, supercharged swimming race ever, an instant classic if ever there was one, one of the greatest moments in Olympic history.

Even before the start of the race that morning, the atmosphere inside the Water Cube in Beijing, the swimming and diving venue at the 2008 Summer Games, was electric, the noise ferocious.

This was the 400-meter freestyle relay. Four guys on each team. Each swims two laps of the pool.

Eight lanes in the pool, eight teams, but really only three that were likely to win: the Americans, the French, the Australians.

I went first. Garrett Weber-Gale followed. Cullen Jones followed him. And then came Jason Lezak, our anchor.

When Jason dove in, the French were slightly, ever so slightly, ahead.

Halfway through his leg, Jason, who has for years been one of the truly outstanding sprinters in the entire world, one of the best freestyle relay swimmers ever, had fallen farther behind the French racer, Alain Bernard, who had come into the relay as the world-record holder in the 100.

With 30 meters to go, Jason was behind.
With 20 to go, he was still behind.
But he was charging.

Now Jason was gaining.

On the deck, we were going crazy, Garrett and I. Not that anyone could hear us. It was so loud inside the Water Cube that you couldn't hear yourself think. Not that anyone was thinking. We were wishing, hoping, praying, urging. Shouting, screaming, yelling. Come on, Jason! Get that guy! Get him! Get that guy! Get him!

At the wall, Jason reached out his hand. We turned to look at the big board across the pool and — yes!

Jason had done it! He had, somehow, done it!

Jason had thrown down the fastest relay leg of all time. We needed every bit of that. We had won, the scoreboard said, by eight-hundredths of a second. The French were second, the Australians third.

I had no words. I had only screams.

Because this was not about me.

It was epic.

Of course I had won a gold medal, and that was the goal. But this was about something way bigger than any personal accomplishment. We swam together, competed together, four as one, together, as a team and as Americans.

But that only begins to explain why I had no words.

Of course the relay gold kept alive my quest to chase eight gold medals at a single Olympics. I understood that then even as I understand it now, as I will understand it always.

But that was not why I had no words. The notion of eight golds was always a means to an end. It was never about chasing fame or fortune or celebrity.

Never.

If I could win eight, could go one better than the great Mark Spitz and the seven golds he won at the Munich Olympics in 1972, those eight medals might do what nothing else could. They could help to make real my biggest dream, to elevate swimming's place in the American sports landscape, and to make it an every-year sport instead of a once-every-four-years sport.

I never set out to be the second Mark Spitz.

I only wanted to be the first Michael Phelps.

I wanted to do something no one had ever done before.

Baseball is great, basketball so cool, football so fine; I love the NFL, especially my Baltimore Ravens. But in other countries, particularly Australia, swimming has the same cachet that baseball, basketball, and football have in the United States, with packed houses and passionate fans. Why can't it be like that in the United States?

It can.

That's why, when Jason touched first, I had no words.

A few days later, I found myself again without words, after I swam my last race at the 2008 Summer Games, the 400-meter medley relay. Aaron Peirsol went first, swimming the backstroke; Brendan Hansen swam the breaststroke; I swam the third leg, the butterfly; and then, just as he had done in the 400 free relay, Jason brought us home in first, this time ahead of the Australians.

We had done it, another gold.

I had won eight gold medals.

I let out another scream. I thanked my teammates, and a jumble of emotions washed over and around me. I felt gratitude and relief and joy, just sheer joy at the moment, at the culmination of a journey filled with twists and turns and ups and downs. I felt humbled, too. I felt profound humility at learning how I had become a source of inspiration for so many back home, everyone who said I offered renewed proof that America and Americans could still take on the world with courage and grit, who declared that the virtues so many Americans hold so dear —

hard work, character, commitment to family, team, and country — could still triumph.

No matter where Americans were in the world, I'd been told, they were watching and cheering; that was special. Back home, I'd heard, bars were erupting in cheers when I'd won. I'd heard that my races had been shown on jumbo video screens at Major League Baseball and NFL games, on one of those big screens in Times Square. I understood that the drama and anticipation and excitement of some of my races had kept people glued to their television sets into the night. That very first relay. The 200-meter butterfly, when my goggles filled with water and I couldn't see, literally couldn't see, and still won. And then the 100-meter butterfly, which I had won by one-hundredth of a second.

I looked into the stands, for my mom, Debbie, and my sisters, Whitney and Hilary. When I found them, I walked through a horde of photographers and climbed into the stands to give each of them a kiss, with the memories of where we'd been and what we'd overcome flooding over me. Mom put her arm around my neck and gave me an extra hug.

When I was in grade school, I was diagnosed with attention deficit/hyperactivity disorder, or ADHD. I had overcome that. When I was in school, a teacher said I'd never be successful. Things like that stick with you and motivate you; I flashed back to that with my family there in the stands. I started crying. My mom started crying. My sisters started crying.

I started swimming when I was a little boy. Both Hilary and Whitney were champion swimmers, and when I was very much the baby brother, it looked like Whitney was the one from our family who was going to make it to the Olympics. That didn't happen. And here I was.

I felt lucky for the talent that I have, the drive that I have, the want, the excitement about the sport, felt lucky for every quality I have, and have worked so hard to have. In some sports, you can excel if you have natural talent. Not in swimming. You can have all the talent in the world, be built just the right way, but you can't be good or get good without hard work. In swimming, there's a direct connection between what you put into it and what you get out of it.

I knew I would find my coach and long-time mentor, Bob Bowman, around the pool deck. Bob, the only coach I've ever had. He had trained me, punished me, motivated me, inspired me, and proven to me the connection between hard work and success. Bob has long been one of the very few people in my life to tell me the unadulterated truth, even when I didn't want to listen. Perhaps most important, especially when I didn't want to hear it.

Bob's philosophy is rather simple: We do the things other people can't, or won't, do. Bob's expectations are simple, too. It's like the quote he had up on the whiteboard one day at practice a few months before the Games. It comes from a business book but in sports it's the same: "In business, words are words, explanations are explanations, promises are promises, but only performance is reality."

Bob is exquisitely demanding. But it is with him that I learned this essential truth: Nothing is impossible.

And this: Because nothing is impossible, you have to dream big dreams; the bigger, the better.

So many people along the way, whatever it is you aspire to do, will tell you it can't be done. But all it takes is imagination.

You dream. You plan. You reach.

There will be obstacles. There will be doubters. There will be mistakes.

But with hard work, with belief, with confidence and trust in yourself and those

16

around you, there are no limits. Perseverance, determination, commitment, and
courage — those things are real. The desire
for redemption drives you. And the will to
succeed — it's everything. That's why, on the
pool deck in Beijing in the summer of 2008,
there were sometimes no words, only
screams.

Because, believe it, dreams really can come
true.

1
PERSEVERANCE: THE 400 INDIVIDUAL MEDLEY

Leading up to and through the 2008 U.S. Olympic Trials for swimming, which were held in Omaha, Nebraska, in late June and early July, I kept having a most particular dream.

It involved the number 3:07.

The 2008 Summer Games in Beijing would get under way on August 8. I had no idea what 3:07 meant, or why, or why I kept dreaming about it.

But, there it was: 3:07.

Logically, naturally, it seemed like a time.

But a time for what?

3:07 in the afternoon? In the morning?

I am a fanatic for training and for hard work and discipline. Even so, I wasn't getting up at 3:07 in the morning to go to the pool, that was for sure.

I couldn't figure it out.

It was especially perplexing because swimming, like baseball or football, is a sport with its own history and lore that lends itself elegantly to numbers and statistics.

Everyone who follows baseball knows that Babe Ruth hit 714 home runs during his career, for instance, or that Ted Williams hit .406 in 1941, or that Bob Gibson pitched so magnificently in 1968 that he ended the year with an ERA of 1.12.

Everyone who knows a thing or two about football knows that the Miami Dolphins went 17–0 in 1972, or that Tom Brady threw fifty touchdown passes during the 2007 NFL season.

Even people who don't know much about swimming almost surely know that Mark Spitz won seven gold medals in 1972 at the Olympic Games in Munich. And that I could win eight in Beijing in 2008. Eight is an auspicious number in Chinese culture. The Games were going to start on 8/8/08, at precisely 8:00 p.m. local time; the date and time were picked because the Chinese word for eight, *ba,* sounds like the word for prosperity, *fa.*

The problem I was having, though, was simple. There is nothing in swimming in which 3:07 made any sense whatsoever, which was totally weird, because there are vast columns of numbers in swimming to crunch. The sport is measured mostly in meters but sometimes in yards. There are world records, Olympic records, American records, even what are called U.S. Open records, meaning a mark that is set on American soil, whether by an American or someone from somewhere else.

The swim calendar in recent years has kept to a fairly consistent routine, too, at least for American swimmers, which makes it all the easier to track the numbers: meets early in the year in places as different as Long Beach, California, and Columbia, Missouri; in May or June in Santa Clara, California; and one or two major meets, such as the U.S. Nationals, the Pan Pacific Championships, the swimming world championships, and, every fourth summer, the Olympics.

Moreover, I can, at a given moment, pretty much rattle off times for the events I swim, in either yards or meters.

In none of those columns of records did 3:07 compute.

Still, the dream kept coming.

3:07.

When I'm in training, as I was before the 2008 Olympics in Ann Arbor, Michigan, where I had moved after growing up near Baltimore, we typically practice early in the morning, then again in the late afternoon at the University of Michigan's Canham Natatorium. In between, I usually take a nap.

We would swim miles in the morning, then more miles in the afternoon.

Eat. Swim. Do other workouts, like weightlifting. Sleep. That was the routine. Believe me, working out that hard in the morning and then again in the afternoon made a nap no luxury. It was an essential.

One of the things about my naps is this: If I'm sitting there right before I doze off or immediately after I get up, I can visualize how I want the perfect race to go. I can see the start, the strokes, the walls, the turns, the finish, the strategy, all of it. It's so vivid that I can vividly see incredible detail, down even to the wake behind me.

It's my imagination at work, and I have a big imagination. Visualizing like this is like programming a race in my head, and that programming sometimes seems to make it happen just as I had imagined it.

I can also visualize the worst race, the worst circumstances. That's what I do to prepare myself for what might happen. It's a good thing to visualize the bad stuff. It prepares you. Maybe you dive in and your goggles fill with water. What do you do? How do you respond? What is important right now? You have to have a plan.

I'm not really sure, precisely, why I'm able

to visualize like this. I have always been able to do it, ever since I was little. It's also true that I got lots of practice growing up; since I've been swimming it's been very much a part of the rhythm and routine of my life and of the house in which I grew up.

I grew up the baby brother in a house rumbling with girl power. My sister Whitney is five years older than I am, Hilary seven. When she was little, Hilary wanted to be the next Janet Evans, the record-setting American swimmer who was perhaps the best female distance swimmer of all time; Janet won five Olympic medals, four gold, between the 1988 and 1992 Games. Hilary grew up to be an excellent distance swimmer and set records at the University of Richmond. Whitney, as a teenager, was one of the best butterfly swimmers in the United States; she competed at the 1996 Olympic Trials.

So I was always, always around the pool. When I was a baby, my mom used to pick me up out of my crib, my pajamas still on, and drive me and the girls to the North Baltimore Aquatic Club (NBAC) at the Meadowbrook Aquatic and Fitness Center. She would change me in the car and, while the girls were swimming laps, I would stay there and play.

The North Baltimore club has a tradition of excellence, including female gold medalists at the 1984, 1992, and 1996 Olympics, and training there included sessions during which kids were taught how to visualize, as part of the process of setting goals. Whitney remembers it like it was yesterday. Sit quietly in a room, lights down, see a race from start to finish: diving in, how and when to breathe, what it would feel like to turn hard off the wall, to power to the finish, even how to get out of the pool.

Mom and I used to go through relaxation and programming techniques at home. My coach, Bob Bowman, had my mom buy a book that set out drills and exercises, including one in which I would tighten my right hand into a fist and relax it, then do the same with my left hand, as a way of learning to deal with tension. At night, before falling asleep, I would lie on my bed and she would read to me from that book, and I would practice.

When I was thirteen or fourteen, Bob started asking me to play a race in my head as though it were a video. When we were in training, we'd get to the last repetition of a set, particularly a really hard set, and Bob would want me to do that last repeat close to race speed. He'd say, okay, put in the tape and see yourself, for instance, swimming the 400 individual medley at the nationals.

To this day, if Bob says, okay, put in the videotape, that's what he means.

They say that the mental aspect of sports is just as important as the physical part. There can be no doubt about that: Being mentally tough is critical. At an Olympic final, you know everybody has physical talent. So, who's going to win? The mentally toughest. Bob is a big believer in that. I am, too. Bob also believes that my visualization skills carry over to my training, and to my racing, and that it's part of what makes me different.

Bob and I have been together for so long — we started together when I was eleven, and I turned twenty-three during the 2008 Trials, in Omaha — that he doesn't even have to say much to me now to make sure I'm preparing mentally as well as physically.

He doesn't have to nag. Not like that would work.

He just says something like, how's the visualizing going?

Fine, I'll say.

Or, he'll say, have you started yet?

Yes, I'll say. Or, not yet. Whatever. Bob just wants to make sure it's happening.

It always happens. Always.

But nothing was leading me to the answer

of what my dream meant.

3:07. I kept trying to figure out the mystery.

An Olympic-sized pool is 50 meters long.

I don't swim the 50-meter freestyle sprint in competition. But I knew, of course, that whoever was going to win the sprint at the Beijing Olympics would do so, given advancements in pool technology and in swimsuits, in particular the Speedo LZR Racer, in well under 22 seconds.

The 100-meter freestyle winner would go in about 47 seconds. The 200 free would end in about 1 minute, 43 seconds, the 400 free in about 3:42, maybe slightly under.

There are three other strokes on the Olympic program: the backstroke, the breaststroke, and the butterfly. But races in those two strokes are only at 100 and 200 meters, not anywhere near long enough to be in the water for 3:07.

There are three relays on the Olympic program, too. Two of them are freestyle relays, the 400 and the 800. Four swimmers take turns swimming laps, 100 meters apiece in the 400, 200 apiece in the 800. In neither of those could 3:07 mean anything.

The other relay is what's called the 400 medley relay. Again, four swimmers take turns swimming laps. In the medley each swims a different stroke: in order, the back-stroke, breaststroke, butterfly, freestyle. The winning time in the medley tends to be about three and a half minutes.

I was completely stumped.

Finally, I went to Bob to ask him what he thought it might be. Bob usually has the answers. It can be frustrating but it's true: Bob usually has the answers.

Bob's interests out of the pool range across a wide variety of subjects. He can tell you about thoroughbred horses. About the architecture of Frank Lloyd Wright. About the genius of Beethoven's Ninth Symphony. Bob played violin and went to Florida State because it was an excellent music school; he studied music composition very seriously. He then switched to child psychology. Bob gets asked all the time if I see a sports psychologist. He answers: every day.

The dynamic of our relationship over the years has been this: Bob pushed. I pushed right back. Bob can be gruff. He can be demanding. Sometimes he yells at me; as I've gotten older, I've shouted right back. The venting we do at each other just shows that I'm not scared of him, and he is for sure not scared of me. And the vast majority of the time, as in any partnership that works, and ours works, totally, we get along great. Because, bottom line, Bob is not only coach and mentor but so much more.

When I was younger, he had taught me how to tie a tie. For my first school dance, when I was thirteen, he let me leave practice fifteen minutes early; when I showed up with the tie and went to put it on, he noticed that my shirt was buttoned one button off. So we fixed that together. When I was a teenager, he taught me how to drive. His car was a stick shift, and that's how I learned. I always had trouble: I remember going to school one day, on a hill at a busy intersection, and of course I stalled the car in the middle of the hill. There were tons of people behind me. We fixed that together, too. I remember getting out of a workout and going to the prom — regular black tux, stretch white Hummer limo — and Bob was there to watch me head off.

All the little things like that: Bob has always been there for me.

At the Trials, I told Bob, I'm trying to make sense of this 3:07. What do you think it could be?

At first, he said he didn't know.

The only thing he could think of, he finally said, was that 3:07 somehow related to the 400 individual medley, a race that like the medley relay combines all four strokes. The difference, of course, is that it's just one person doing all the swimming, not four. Also, the order is different from the medley relay. In the IM, it goes: fly, back, breast, free.

I had held the world record in the 400 IM since 2002. When I first set the record, at the summer nationals in Fort Lauderdale, Florida, I touched in 4:11.09. Over the years, I had lowered the record a number of other times. At the 2007 world championships in Melbourne, Australia, I had lowered the 400 IM record to 4:06.22.

3:07, Bob said, had to be a split time, meaning an intermediate time in a given race, in this instance after the breaststroke leg, or three-quarters of the 400 IM, with only the up-and-back freestyle portion to go.

If you do that, he said, you're going to finish in 4:03-something.

That would be at least seven, nearing eight, seconds better than I had gone in first setting the record just six years before.

More than two seconds better than I had gone in Melbourne.

4:03? Obviously, some strong part of me believed I could go 4:03.

If you put a limit on anything, you put a limit on how far you can go. I don't think anything is too high. The more you use your imagination, the faster you go. If you think about doing the unthinkable, you can. The sky is the limit. That's one thing I definitely have learned from Bob: Anything is possible. I deliberately set very high goals for myself; I work very hard to get there.

4:03?

Then again, why not? No limits.

Every year since I have been swimming competitively, I have set goals for myself. In writing.

The goal sheet was mandatory. I got used to it and it became a habit. When I was younger, I used to scribble my goals out by hand and show the sheet to Bob. Now, I might type them on my laptop and e-mail him a copy. Each year, he would take a look at what I'd given him, or sent him, and that would be that. He wouldn't challenge me, say this one's too fast or that one's not. When I was doing this only on paper, he typically would look at it and give it back to me; now he simply files away the electronic copy I send him.

I usually kept my original paper version by the side of my bed.

The two of us are the only ones who have it, who ever got to see it.

The goal sheet was famously secret for a long time . . . Until now.

I didn't look at the sheet every day. I pretty much memorized it, how fast I wanted to swim and what I had to do to get there. If there was a day when I was down, when I was not swimming well, when I simply felt tired or grouchy, I would look at it. It was definitely a pick-me-up.

Pretty soon after I made my first goal sheet, I hit every one of the times to a tenth of a second. Precisely. Exactly. It's like I have an innate body clock. I don't know how or why I was able to do this. I just could, and often still can. It's another way in which Bob says I'm different, and always have been.

When I was thirteen, Bob felt I needed to have some formal lessons in goal-setting. One day, on a school holiday, he surprised my mom by saying, I'm taking Michael to lunch today. He came and picked me up, and we went to this restaurant that I liked. He pulled out a sheet of paper. He said, okay, what are your goals this summer?

Of course, I replied, I don't know.

He started suggesting some things I ought to do and said, why don't we pick three events. Let's start, he said, with the 1500 meters. The 1500 is almost a mile. A Bowman favorite. We were trying, even when I was that young, to lay down a base of endurance work. Let's do that in 16

31

minutes flat, he said.

Let's also pick the 200 fly, Bob said, and I put down 2:04.68. That time was precisely one-hundredth of a second under the national age-group record. That would be a big drop for you, he said.

Okay.

Bob then said, let's pick the 400 IM. He suggested a time of 4:31.68, which was also near the age-group record.

He said, take this paper home and put it on your refrigerator. You'll see it every day.

That summer, at the 1999 junior nationals in Orlando, I didn't win any events.

In the 1500, I went 16:00.08. I was off by eight-hundredths of a second.

In the 400 IM, I swam 4:31.68. Precisely.

In the 200 fly, I swam 2:04.68. Precisely.

The 200 fly time was nearly 10 seconds better than the best time I had done in practice about six weeks beforehand, when Bob had ordered a set of three 200 flys as a tune-up.

In that 200 fly in Orlando I took third place. Bob congratulated me and said first place might have been bad luck. He said he had never coached anyone who had won juniors and then had gone on to win nationals as a senior.

Later that summer, I went to the senior nationals in Minneapolis. In my first race, I finished 41st. My next race was the 200 fly. I finished dead last in my heat, in 2:07.

This was maybe a lesson for Bob. Maybe I wasn't ready just quite yet. Maybe I was just emotionally overwhelmed. I had touched in 2:04.68 a few weeks before; logic said I should have gone at least that fast in Minneapolis.

That summer I turned fourteen. I can still remember being on the pool deck at nationals, getting ready for my heat, and thinking, there's Tom Dolan. Tom Dolan! He was 6-feet-6 and was supposed to have only 3 percent body fat. He had gone to the University of Michigan and had already won a gold medal in the 400 IM at the 1996 Summer Olympics in Atlanta. He was a legend not only for what he had done but also for how he trained: to the point of exhaustion, maybe beyond.

Another time at the meet in Minneapolis, I remember, I was sitting in the stands and there, across the pool deck, went Tom Malchow. Tom Malchow! He had gone to the University of Michigan, too. And he had won a silver medal in the 200 fly in Atlanta.

I was in awe. Here I was, on the very same pool deck with Olympic swimmers.

The last day of the meet in Minneapolis, I

wasn't due to compete in any races. This meant nothing to Bob. "Get ready, Michael," he said. "You're doing a practice today."

What?

I didn't even have a suit with me. Why would I? I wasn't supposed to race.

I thought to myself, we're already at the pool, are we really going to get in the car, go back to the hotel, drive all the way back here and train?

Yes.

It took us a good 40 minutes to go there and back. I didn't like it, didn't like any of it. Bob didn't care. I went back in the water.

That fall, back in Baltimore, we started training for the 2000 spring nationals in Federal Way, Washington, near Seattle.

With six weeks to go, Bob had an idea at practice. Let's do what we did last year as a trial run: a set of three 200 flys. Into the water I went.

My best time of the three turned out to be 2:09. Bob was obviously disappointed. After the 2:04.68 from the year before, he thought I was going to do 2:05, at least. Maybe, he told me, you could even break two minutes.

In the back of his mind, Bob was holding out the possibility, no matter how remote it seemed, that I could finish in the top two at the Olympic Trials that summer in Indianapolis and make the Olympic team. At that point, I had produced nothing to suggest that the 2000 Olympics were truly possible. This did not deter Bob. He believed in me, completely.

The way swim meets work, the heats are usually in the morning or early afternoon, and the finals at night. When I was a teenager, the heats would pretty much always go off in front of just a few people in the stands, typically parents, brothers and sisters, other coaches. I have come to like a noisy crowd. Early that afternoon in Federal Way, there was almost nobody in the stands.

I went 1:59.6.

That broke the age-group record for fifteen- and sixteen-year-olds. I was still only fourteen.

That night I came back and raced the 200 fly again. I finished in 1:59.02, behind only Stephen Parry of Great Britain and Malchow.

Afterward, I had my first interview. I was asked, did you think you could break two minutes in the 200 fly? Here's what I said: My coach told me I could do it.

It's after that 1:59.6, Bob likes to say, that he knew I would make the Olympic team, maybe sooner than later. I had no idea. I was, after all, fourteen.

The day after that, I set another age-group record in the 400 IM, lowering my time in that race by seven seconds, to 4:24.

The next day, I wasn't swimming in any finals. Sightseeing? No way. Into the pool I went.

We got home from Federal Way on a school day. My mom, who was at work, had put a large banner saying, "Congratulations," on the lawn and had trimmed it in red, white, and blue. Bob, who had brought me back to the house, took down the entire display. When she got home, Mom was furious. Bob was unmoved. It was a matter, Bob said, of tempering expectations. Best to keep everything in perspective. Bob asked my mom, "What are you going to do when he wins nationals? He got third. If he wins, are you going to buy him a car? If he sets a world record, what, a house? You can't get excited about every step. There are so many steps. We're on, like, step 200 of 3,000. How are we going to keep going?"

Bob has, without question, helped refine my intense drive and dedication. He has also, without question, helped me believe that anything is possible. Two seconds faster than the world record? Doesn't matter. Three seconds faster? Doesn't matter. You can swim as fast as you want. You can do anything you want. You just have to dream it, believe it, work at it, go for it.

I wrote the sheet that lay out my goals for 2008 a few weeks after coming back from those 2007 world championships in Melbourne. That meet in Australia had been one of my best ever. I won seven gold medals and set five world records, including that 4:06.22 in the 400 IM.

In the 100 free, I wanted in the Olympic year of 2008 to go 47.50.

200 free: 1:43.5.

100 fly: 49.5.

200 fly: 1:51.1.

200 IM: 1:53.5.

And the 400 IM: 4:05 flat.

There's more on the sheet, other races as well as split times for every single race.

But these were races I was likely to swim at the Olympics.

In writing that I wanted to go 4:05 in 2008, I knew full well that was ambitious. That would be more than a full second better than I had ever done before.

And yet: 3:07.

Which meant 4:03.

I started swimming when I was seven.

Mom put me in a stroke clinic taught by

one of her good friends, Cathy Lears.

"I'm cold," I remember saying.

And, "I have to go to the bathroom."

And, "Can't I just sit here and watch the other kids? I'll stay here by the side."

Mostly, I remember, I simply didn't like putting my face under the water.

Miss Cathy told me I could use the backstroke, if that's what I wanted. But I was going to check off every item on the practice plan. "You're going to learn," she said, "one way or the other."

I complained and whined some more.

Even so, I finished every item on her plan. And soon enough I learned how to flip over onto my tummy and learned to swim the freestyle.

It would be a couple years yet until I would be diagnosed with attention-deficit/hyperactivity disorder, or ADHD. All everyone knew, in particular my mom, my sisters, and my coaches, was that I had all this energy and that I could bleed off a lot of it by playing sports: baseball, soccer, lacrosse, swimming, you name it.

What I discovered soon after starting to swim was that the pool was a safe haven. I certainly couldn't have put that into words then but can look back and see it now. Two walls at either end. Lane lines on either side.

A black stripe on the bottom for direction. I could go fast in the pool, it turned out, in part because being in the pool slowed down my mind.

In the water, I felt, for the first time, in control. Swimmers like to say they can "feel" the water. Even early on, I felt it. I didn't have to fight the water. Instead, I could feel how I moved in it. How to be balanced. What might make me go faster or slower.

It would be ridiculous to say that I was a world-class talent from the very start. If it wasn't for the fact that Hilary and Whitney were swimming, I probably wouldn't even have started swimming.

I was a kid. A kid who was given to whining and — it's true — crying. I was seemingly forever on the verge of tears. My coaches remember a kid who was constantly being picked on. When I was younger, it seemed like almost anything could set me off into an emotional jag or launch me into a full-on tantrum, throwing my goggles and generally carrying on.

All this agitation was probably just my way of seeking attention. Mostly, I wanted to fit in, especially with the older kids. I just wanted to be acknowledged.

And yet, amid all this drama, I already had

a dream: I wanted to win an Olympic gold medal.

One.

Just one. That was it at the start. Just one medal.

I also knew that winning Olympic medals was, truly, possible. It happened to people I knew. When I was seven, Anita Nall, a North Baltimore swimmer, won a gold, a silver, and a bronze at the 1992 Olympics in Barcelona. When I was eleven, Beth Botsford, another North Baltimore swimmer, won two gold medals in Atlanta.

My Olympic ambitions might not have been obvious, granted, especially early on and especially in the mornings, when I'd have to get up for practice. I have never been what you'd call enthusiastic about being up early in the morning.

Mom would come to get me out of bed. It would still be dark out. She would turn on a soft light in my room, a little night-light, and say, "Good morning, Michael. It's time for morning workout."

I would grump and groan.

Mom would go down the steps. I would just lie there in bed, nice and comfy. A few minutes later, she would come back and say, "Pop-Tarts are coming out of the toaster now. I'll be in the car waiting for you. Pick them up on your way out the door, because Bob's expecting you at workout."

My mom would go out to the car and sit, waiting for me. Bob is a morning person. He likes to get up before dawn. It's his favorite part of the day. Always has been.

Later, into middle school and high school, I remember driving in the dark to the pool and there never being any lights on at any house on the way there, and it would just be my mom and me, alone, going to practice. Sometimes my mom would yawn; I still can't believe how loud she sounds when she is yawning.

Once my mom had dropped me off at Meadowbrook, about 15 minutes away from where we lived, in Towson, Maryland, I usually wouldn't make it home again until it was dark again. Bob would take me from practice to school, or to breakfast and then to school, and then in the afternoon we would go back to the pool. Mom would come get me at maybe seven at night.

I would always be the last one out of the pool. She was always working so late; I remember it seemed like I was always the last one to leave. Unless I'd been kicked out of practice early by Bob, for not doing what he wanted the way he wanted it done or when he wanted it done; in that case, I had to sit there and wait for her, anyway.

All of this driving around, the back and forth on the roads around her job, required enormous dedication and sacrifice on my mom's part. At the same time, it was a total reflection of who she is. And that's something I am forever grateful for.

She made it abundantly clear that we — she, my sisters, me — came first, even as she insisted that we have a passion for life itself and for something, or some variety of things.

We had to have goals, drive, and determination. We would work for whatever we were going to get. We were going to strive for excellence, and to reach excellence you have to work at it and for it.

Mom calls this common sense. She grew up in a blue-collar area of western Maryland. Her father was a carpenter. Her mother's father was a miner. Neither of my mom's parents went to college. They had four children — Mom was the second of the four — and all four are college graduates; Mom went on to earn a master's degree.

My dad, Fred, used to take me fishing when I was a little boy. He would take me to Baltimore Orioles games. He taught me to look people in the eye when I was meeting them and to shake hands like I meant it. He was a good athlete himself — a small-college football player — and, unquestionably, I inherited my competitive athletic drive from him. If I was playing sports, no matter what it was, my father's direction was simple: Go hard and, remember, good guys finish second. That didn't mean that you were supposed to be a jerk, but it did mean that you were there to compete as hard as you could. The time to be friends was after the race; during it, the idea was to win.

My mother and father were high-school sweethearts in a mill town in western Maryland. Dad played football at Fairmont (West Virginia) State College; Mom followed him there. After they were married, they moved to the Baltimore area. My father moved out of the house when I was seven. As time went on, we spent less and less time together. Eventually, I stopped trying to include him in my activities and he, in turn, stopped trying to involve himself in mine.

The last time I saw my father was at Whitney's wedding, in October 2005. He and I didn't talk at the wedding; there just hasn't been anything to say for a while. Maybe there will be later.

Having said that, I feel I have everything and everyone that anyone could ever ask for. I have the greatest people in the world around me and supporting me.

My mom is an educator, now a school principal, and her passion in life is changing the lives of children. When she recognized a passion in her children for swimming, she was all in to help each of us.

At the same time, things were going to be done in our house, and done a certain way, because that's the way it was. Homework was going to get done. Clothes were going to get picked up off the floor. Kids were going to get taken to practice. We were all in it together.

Not only that: Our house was always the home where any kid was welcome. If there was a kid who needed to stay over to make swim practice the next morning, we had a sleeping bag and a pillow.

That work ethic, and that sense of teamwork, was always in our home. All of that went to the pool with me, from a very early age.

It's why, when I won my first Olympic gold medal, the first people I wanted to see when I had a quiet moment were my mom and my sisters.

They say that what the decathlon is to track and field, the 400 individual medley is to swimming.

Most swimmers, like the vast majority of

those who compete in track and field, are specialists. They do the backstroke, for instance. Or the breaststroke. That's not to say they don't know how to swim the other strokes. They do. But once they get to a certain age, they usually compete only in the one they're best in.

That's why the IM is tough. You have to do all four strokes, and do them all well.

The 400 IM is tougher still because it's all four strokes and at distance. It requires strength, endurance, technique, and versatility.

This race can make you hurt bad. Your shoulders start to burn. Your legs ache. You can't get a breath. The pain is sometimes dull, throbbing. It's like your body isn't even in the unbelievably great shape it's in. All you want is for the pain to stop.

Who's the mentally toughest? That's what the 400 IM is all about.

I had won the 400 IM at the 2003 championships in Barcelona in what was then a world-record time, 4:09.09.

A year later, as I got ready to get into the pool for the 400 IM Olympic final in Athens, Rowdy Gaines, himself an Olympic champion in 1984, now an NBC analyst, was saying that this was the race that was going introduce America to Michael Phelps.

I knew well the recent Olympic history of the event: Americans had gone 1–2 in the 400 IM in 1996 and in 2000. Dolan had won in Atlanta in 1996; Eric Namesnik, another Michigan man, had gotten silver. In 2000, Dolan repeated as Olympic champion; Erik Vendt, who had grown up in Massachusetts and gone to the University of Southern California, took silver.

Lining up that Saturday evening in Athens, I was in Lane 4, Vendt in Lane 1.

I have since watched the video of this race dozens of times, maybe hundreds. It's the one race that, from the eight days of competition in Athens, still stands out most to me.

After the butterfly leg, I led by more than a second; after the back, more than three, more than two body lengths ahead. The breaststroke had long been the weakest of my strokes. It was imperative on this leg that I not give up ground. I didn't.

100 meters to go. I turned and started doing the free.

50.

The swimmers who swim the fastest in the heats are assigned in the finals to the middle lanes. The advantage of swimming in the middle is that it's easier to keep an eye on what everyone else is doing. Coming off the last wall, I saw that Alessio Boggiatto of Italy

46

in Lane 3 was still approaching his turn; in Lane 5, Hungary's Laszlo Cseh was not yet at the wall, either.

I still had that one lap to go.

But I knew already that I had won.

And so, underwater, I smiled.

Not even a half-minute later, I glided into the wall, and I was still smiling.

I popped up and looked for Mom in the stands. Even before I looked at the scoreboard, I looked for Mom, and, there she was, standing next to Whitney and Hilary, all of them cheering and just going crazy. I turned to look at the clock. It said, "WR," meaning world record, next to my name. 4:08.26. I raised my arm into the air.

I had done it.

I had won the Olympic gold medal I had been dreaming of since I was little.

I had also, in that instant, become the first American gold medalist of the 2004 Athens Games.

I really didn't know what to do, or say, or think.

"Mike! Mike!"

It was Vendt. He was swimming over from Lane 1. Truthfully, in the excitement of the moment, I hadn't noticed yet that he had finished second. We had gone 1–2. Cseh had finished third.

In finishing second, Vendt had carried on one of the quirkiest streaks in Olympic history. Four Games in a row an American named Erik or Eric had finished second in the 400 IM; Namesnik had taken silver in 1992 as well.

"Yeah, Vendt! Yeah!" I shouted. "Yeah! We did it!"

I could not stop smiling.

"So proud of you," Bob said.

"It felt great," I replied.

A little while later the top three finishers were called to the medals stand. An olive wreath went onto my head, the gold medal around my neck. The American flag went up, along with another for Vendt's silver and the Hungarian flag for Cseh's bronze. The "Star-Spangled Banner" began to play. I took the wreath off my head. The right thing to do is to take a hat off your head for the anthem; maybe a wreath was the same.

As I listened to the anthem, playing for me, for my country, my eyes grew moist. Even so, I could not stop smiling.

I had done it.

After warming down, I grabbed my cell phone.

When Mom and my sisters go to meets, Hilary is the keeper of the phone.

"Where are you guys?" I asked her.

"We're over by a fence, behind you. They're going to kick us out."

"Hold on. I want to see you guys. Meet at the gate."

Bob went with me, along with a doping official who was doing his official thing, just keeping an eye on me as he was supposed to do. Nothing untoward, nothing unusual about it. I walked toward the fence, my gold medal around my neck. My mom didn't see Bob or the doping guy. She just saw me. To my mom it looked like I was ten, back at Meadowbrook. I had my gold medal around my neck and, in her mind's eye, a peanut butter and jelly sandwich in my hand.

I put the medal through the fence and said, "Look, Mom. Look what I did."

That 400 IM in Athens was, as I see it, the turning point. I was nineteen. I had my first Olympic gold. My mom and sisters were there to watch — that was, to me, what meant so much.

I did not go on to win eight gold medals in Athens. I won six. Eight overall, six gold, two bronze.

On the one hand, the Athens Olympics were an extraordinary success for me. I had met the original goal and gone well beyond.

On the other, I did not meet all my expectations.

Thus I had ample motivation to keep swimming, keep pushing myself. Beijing was four years away. That's a long time. And yet not.

Because stuff happens.

In the fall of 2004, I had major worries about my back.

A year later, I broke a bone in my hand.

In 2008, two years after that, I broke my wrist.

So many newspaper, magazine, and website stories have been written about me that sometimes it seems almost everything about me has been well documented.

But not everything.

I was so worried about my back in 2004: It turned out I had a small stress fracture, and needed rest. There were times I would be in Bob's office feeling broken down physically and emotionally. Whitney had endured back problems that seriously affected her career. I was scared and worried. Plenty scared, seriously worried.

I can't emphasize enough how, during all this, Bob was there for me. This is the side of him that doesn't get depicted often in all the stories that have been written about us, which tend to focus on how it's his way or the highway; this was the side that reminded me why I would never swim for any other coach. Bob made it plain how much he cared. He stayed positive. He sought, time and again, to reassure me. He would say, you're fine, we're going to get through this, we're going to get your back taken care of, it's all going to work out. Which, ultimately, it did.

Later, in the fall of 2005, the first week of November, I was hanging out in Ann Arbor with a bunch of swimmers. I was not in a very good state of mind. I don't remember why. Boys will be boys, I guess.

In fact, I don't recall very much about the entire thing except that we were at this guy's house and I hit something with my right hand — maybe a post, maybe a wall. I don't even remember why I hit it. I'm not aggressive like that. It was just a weird situation. To this day, I have no idea why I did it. But it happened.

The bone underneath the pinky on my right hand broke in half. It popped, just like that. The bone almost came out of the skin.

I put my left hand over it and tried to hold it in place.

I called Keenan Robinson, a trainer at the University of Michigan I had come to trust and rely upon, and he helped me put it in a temporary splint, then got me to the emergency room.

Keenan called Bob. Bob called me back a bunch of times on my phone. I didn't answer. Bob called a girl I was seeing at the time, trying to get her to answer. It wasn't until the next night that he finally got me on my cell.

It was not a pleasant call. I have bad news, I said. Oh, God, he said. After that he said, we really need to get our act together, "we" meaning me. I know what I did was stupid, I said. I know I made a mistake. I can't change it.

Ultimately, I underwent surgery. Doctors fixed the break with a titanium plate and three screws. Keenan did an amazing job helping me with the therapy; the scar is hardly noticeable.

Bob was amazed at how quickly I was able to come back. I rode the stationary bike hard until I was allowed back in the water; the day after Thanksgiving I was back at it.

Fall and early winter are typically not big months on the swimming calendar and while obviously a certain number of people in Ann Arbor knew about the break, Bob and I didn't advertise it.

My second broken bone is far better known.

Then again, the time pressure the second time around was very different.

In the fall of 2007, after dinner one night at Buffalo Wild Wings in Ann Arbor, one of those restaurants with a sports theme, I was walking to my car. As I neared it, walking on the driver's side, I slipped. I fell down and hit the ground. In reacting — you don't really have time to think in this kind of situation — I put my right hand down to cushion the fall. I caught myself. Nothing hurt. Everything seemed all right.

The next morning, Sunday, I woke up and it looked like there was a golf ball on my right wrist.

I thought, this isn't good.

This can't be good.

This could be really bad.

No way I was calling Bob. At least not first.

I called Keenan and said, "Can you come over and look at something?"

He replied, "What is it?"

This was, after all, Sunday morning. It's not like anyone would have been anxious to roll right over.

"It's like there's this giant golf ball on my wrist. I slipped last night and fell."

A few minutes later, Keenan showed up. As soon as he started touching the wrist, started trying to manipulate it, I felt nauseous. Literally sick to my stomach. It was the same feeling I had when he had touched the hand two years before.

I knew right then the wrist was cracked. Fractured. Broken.

I started doing some quick math in my head.

This was late October. The Games were the next August. Two full months left in 2007 plus seven months in 2008. Would there be time?

Wait. The Trials were at the end of June. Two months in 2007, plus less than six months in 2008 to get ready. Would there be time?

I was not sure. I worried that I might be done, not just for the Olympics, but for my entire swim career. I was a mess. In tears.

Keenan said, we have to call Bob.

Bob had decided that day that he was going to make soup. He had gone to Whole Foods and stocked up on vegetables. He was going to make himself a huge pot of sumptuous vegetable soup.

Keenan called Bob. Bob told Keenan, put Michael on the phone.

I was as upset as I could be. I told Bob, I think I just gave away gold medals. I guess it was a good try, I said. I'd had a good run. I don't know how I'm going to be able to come back from this.

Bob listened quietly.

He said, the meet's not next week. Let's see what you can do. He also said, I was there for you in the beginning; I'm going to be here at the end, and however it ends up is how it ends up.

After we hung up, I found out later, Bob threw out his soup. He suddenly had no appetite.

Keenan took me to the emergency room. X-rays confirmed it was broken. At the hospital, I was asked for my autograph; I'm right-handed and couldn't sign. So I was asked for photos. While hooked up to IV lines.

The next day, Keenan, Bob, and I went to see the surgeon. One of the things about being at the University of Michigan, which after the incident two years before I knew full well, is that they have there some of the greatest doctors and nurses in the world. The surgeon said we had two options:

Let it heal on its own, which would take a while. That's what most people do, the doctor said. Your hand would be in a cast for maybe six weeks, he said.

I said, what's the other choice?

Surgery, he said, the advantage of which would be that the bone would be put back into place then and there with a pin, and you'd simply wait for the stitches to come out. About ten days, he said.

That was a no-brainer.

Surgery it was. "You're talking only one pin?" Bob said, mindful that the prior break had involved three screws and a plate.

I said, "When's the next available date?"

They couldn't schedule the surgery immediately; it would be a few days away.

Meanwhile, Bob heard, "Ten days," and thought, okay, maybe this isn't the end of the world. What my clumsiness had done, he made clear, was eliminate my margins. Before the break, I maybe had some wiggle room in my schedule. Now I would have none.

"You can still do this," Bob told me. "But are you ready to listen?"

"Yes."

"Starting right now," he said, "you're going to have to do every single thing I ask you to do. You're going to have to do it my way."

I thought to myself, this is not going to be fun. But that's not what I said.

"Okay," I said. "I'll do it."

I finally worked up the courage to call Mom and tell her, too. That is, I called during school hours, when I knew she would be working and wouldn't have her cell phone with her, and got voice mail. Mom, I said, I've had this little incident on the curb; it's okay, Keenan's taking care of me; talk to you later.

When Mom heard that, she said later, she thought, Oh, good God.

We had gone to the doctor in the morning. That afternoon, per Bob's instructions, I was on a stationary bike.

For me, riding a stationary bike is one of the most boring activities imaginable. It's horrible. One of the worst things I've ever done. Some people think swimming is boring or monotonous. Not me; swimming is fun. Riding a stationary bike is the least amount of fun possible. The thing was, though, I knew I needed to keep working out. The bike was making my legs stronger. Much as I didn't want to do it, I did it. It was the right thing to do. I had given Bob my word. I was going to do exactly what he wanted, exactly how he wanted it done. I rode that bike every day until I underwent the surgery. Bob gave me a day, maybe two, and then I was back on the bike. A few days after that, I had my hand in a plastic bag, and I was back in the water, kicking.

In a weird way, the broken wrist gave me an urgency that in the long run turned out to be a positive.

Right after Thanksgiving, at the short-course national championships in Atlanta — short course in the United States usually means the races are held in a 25-yard pool — I dove in against Ryan Lochte in the 200-yard individual medley. Ryan set an American record, 1:40.08; I finished second in 1:41.32, Eric Shanteau came in third at 1:44.12. Bob couldn't have been more pleased. Here I had not even had the chance to swim even 50 yards of butterfly since the break and yet I could step it up against Ryan, maybe the best short-course racer in the world.

I remember going to a meet in Long Beach, California, in early January, and being asked there about the broken wrist. The scar on my wrist was still fresh, still purple.

The accident, I said, had made me refocus on 2008, which was going to be the biggest year of my life, and my goals.

I told a pack of reporters who were there, "If I could live in a bubble right now, I probably would, so I couldn't get hurt, I couldn't get in trouble, I couldn't do anything. Just swim, eat, and sleep. That's it."

I also said, "I think I'm more excited now than when that happened." I added, "I plan on not screwing around anymore until after the Olympics. I have pretty hefty goals this year. It's going to take a lot to get there."

To get there meant placing first or second in my individual races at the Olympic Trials.

The Trials are never a formality.

It didn't matter that I had won eight medals in Athens. That was then. The fact that I had won the 400 IM at the 2004 Olympics would have absolutely no bearing on whether I would, for instance, again enjoy the privilege of representing the United States at the 2008 Games in the same event. I had to earn it.

Different countries allocate spots on their Olympic teams in different ways. Some, for instance, do it based on results over the preceding years; some allow coaches to pick; some pick by committee.

That's not the American way, at least in swimming. There are no picks.

In the United States, there's only one way to make the Olympic swim team in the individual events: first or second in that race at the Trials.

Third gets you a four-year wait to try again. If you can.

Hayley McGregory finished third in the 2004 Trials in both the 100 and 200 backstrokes. She would go on at the 2008 Trials to set a world record in the 100 back in the preliminaries; in the finals, she finished third. In the 200 back, she finished third. She did not make the team.

It can be like that. So cruel.

"If I'm third at the Olympics, it means I'm on the medal stand in a few minutes. If I'm third at the Trials, it means I'm on the couch for a month," Gary Hall, Jr., one of the most accomplished American sprinters of the last twenty years, once said. Winner of ten Olympic medals between 1996 and 2004, twice the gold medalist in the 50-meter sprint, Gary would finish fourth in the 50 in Omaha. He did not make the 2008 team.

Our selection process is without question the most difficult in the world, far more nerve-wracking than the Olympics, actually, because the depth in the United States in swimming is unmatched anywhere in the world.

And the 2008 Trials were going to be the deepest in history.

During the same week the swim Trials were going on in Omaha, the U.S. Trials in track and field took place in Eugene, Oregon. All over Eugene — at the airport, on buses, on highway billboards — advertisements declared the U.S. track team the "hardest team to make."

Wrong. It's the swim team.

In track, the top three in each event to go the Games.

In swimming, only two.

It figured that, in the 400 IM, those two would be me and Lochte. But nobody was handing us anything. And Lochte was hardly ready to concede first place to me.

A couple months before the Trials, the U.S. Olympic Committee holds what's called a media summit. It gathers a bunch of athletes it figures are good candidates to make the Olympic team and, for the better part of a week, allows hundreds of reporters to have a crack at asking questions for the features their editors want before the Olympics start. Then the athletes can go back to training without being pestered by reporters for the duration.

The 2008 media summit took place in Chicago, at one of the city's landmark hotels, the Palmer House Hilton. At the summit, Lochte was asked about racing me. "I always feel like I can beat him," he said.

Lochte is a good friend, one of my best friends in swimming. It's one of those deals where we are hardly alike but like a lot of the same stuff. I call him Doggy. No good reason. Doggy is a Florida surfer dude; I grew up near Baltimore. Doggy's idol is the rapper Lil Wayne, who is also one of my favorite musicians. Doggy sometimes wears gold chains around his neck, baggy pants, a diamond-encrusted grill in his mouth. Cool that it's Lochte's style; not mine. I have a bulldog named Herman. Lochte's dog, a Doberman, is named Carter, after Lil Wayne, whose real name is Dwayne Michael Carter, Jr. In May, Lochte sprained his left ankle when Carter the dog ran out the front door of Lochte's house in Gainesville; chasing Carter down the street, Lochte said he turned the ankle. At least that was one version of the story. His dad later said it happened after a skateboarding trick gone bad. Who knows? Doggy is a free spirit.

A free spirit who is a hellacious competitor.

Lochte had won silver in the 200 IM in Athens. He didn't swim the 400 IM in Athens because he had finished fourth at the 2004 Trials, 10 seconds behind me. At the 2006 U.S. nationals, Lochte had narrowed the gap to about a second and a half. At the 2007 Worlds in Melbourne, I had beaten him again, this time by about three seconds.

I had not lost a major-meet final in the 400 IM since I started swimming it at the national level. Even so, I knew what I was up against: maybe the second-best all-around swimmer in the world.

I also knew, though, that I had improved, even since Melbourne, even taking into account the broken wrist. My breaststroke had very quietly gotten way better than it had been. In practice, I had been working on subtle differences: keeping my shoulders closer to my ears, my hands flatter, my fingertips up when I accelerated forward. At that Long Beach meet in January, a short-course event, I raced the 100-yard breaststroke; the field included Mark Gangloff, who had come in fourth in the 100-meter breast final in Athens. Mark won the race that night, in 53.09 seconds and, for most, the reporters and the people in the stands, that seemed to be the news — that I'd lost. To me and Bob, that was not at all the news. Instead, to us, it was that I'd finished just behind Mark, in 53.41. I had almost beaten one of the world's best breaststrokers, only a few weeks after surgery. Bob said later, that was one of the most impressive things he'd ever seen me do.

At the same time, my backstroke, for some reason, had been giving me fits. I didn't have the consistency I wanted. And my 400 IM times through the early months of 2008 had been unremarkable. At a meet in Santa

Clara, California, six weeks before the Trials, I won the 400 IM in a flat 4:13.47. My backstroke felt horrible that night, as it had for the previous few weeks. I had no tempo. My kick wasn't there. Instead of 100 meters, I felt like I was swimming a mile on my back. However, two days later, still in Santa Clara, I beat Aaron Peirsol in the 100-meter backstroke. Aaron had won the 100 back in Athens. This was the first time I had ever beaten him in a backstroke event.

So maybe the backstroke was there, after all. I really couldn't be sure.

At some meets, the 400 IM is last on the agenda; that's the way it was in Barcelona, at the 2003 Worlds.

In Beijing, as in Athens, it would be first.

So, in Omaha, at a temporary pool in the middle of the Qwest Center, the best set-up for a meet in the history of American swimming, it would be first, too, as USA Swimming deliberately set up the program for the Trials to mirror the schedule in Beijing.

My first swim in Omaha, the prelims of the 400 IM, turned out not good. I finished in 4:13.43. Lochte, swimming in a different heat, was timed in 4:13.38, faster by five-hundredths of a second.

Lochte told reporters afterward that his ankle was, in fact, bothering him: "The hardest part was the dive. As soon as I dived in, it was like, ugh."

I told reporters, "I'm not really too happy."

In fact, I had gone to meet Bob and told him, I feel awful.

A few minutes later, I had definitive proof. I did feel awful. My lactate test said so.

When you do anything physical, like swimming, and particularly if you're swimming all-out, that exertion creates lactic acid. In scientific circles, there is controversy over whether lactic acid itself is the thing that drags down athletic performance or whether other stuff within the body, signaled by elevated levels of lactic acid, causes fatigue. It doesn't matter to us swimmers. What matters is that we are constantly tested to see the rate at which we can clear lactate from our systems because that indicates our ability to recover.

That's why, at most top meets, moments after a race you can see a parade of swimmers lining up for individual lactate tests. Someone pricks your ear and collects a few drops of blood; those drops are then placed into a machine, which measures the number of millimoles of lactate per liter of blood. For me, the point is to drop the level as close to 2 as possible. The way to make it drop is to swim easily for a certain number of minutes.

These swims are held in a separate pool just steps away from the competition pool. Ideally, you're taking the lactate test three minutes after leaving the competition pool, and then it's into the warm-down pool. The lactate test tells me how long I then need to swim down; typically, it's between 17 and 22 minutes.

My lactate reading after the prelim 400 IM swim read 12.3.

Superhigh.

Nerves, I guess. I had no other explanation. I remember feeling momentarily flustered. Why was my lactate so high? I had a long swim-down to think about it.

At that point, I just wanted to get onto the team. If I was going to have a loss, I started rationalizing, if only for an instant, better at the Trials than at the Olympics.

As soon as I thought that, though, I also thought this: One thing I am for sure good at is responding. At the risk of being obvious, I have an enormous appetite for competition, and a huge will to win. Always have.

Eddie Reese, who is the swim coach at the University of Texas, and also had the honor of being the U.S. men's swim coach at the 2004 and 2008 Olympics, has a saying: 80 percent of swimmers like to win, 20 percent hate to lose, and 95 percent of the Olympic team comes from the hate-to-lose group. When I'm focused, there is not one single thing, person, anything that can stand in my way of doing something. There is not. If I want something bad enough, I feel I'm gonna get there. That's just how I've always been.

So to make the team — no, to win the 400 IM at these Trials — I had to refocus, and quickly. In the finals that night, I had to get a lead. If I did that, I felt confident my competitive instinct would come out. No matter how tired I was, how painful it was, I would get there first, would hold Lochte off.

But it was going to be a battle.

The prelims took place at eleven that Sunday morning Central time; the finals went off at seven that evening.

Just before the finals, my racing gear already on, I went to my bag and took two salt tablets. Bob looked at me quizzically.

He said nothing.

I said nothing.

If I had told him how I was truly feeling, he would have freaked.

My heart was racing. Like an out-of-control freight train barreling down a set of tracks, that kind of racing.

This had been a problem for me dating back at least eight years, to the first time I'd had one of these episodes. Then it was at a practice. My heart rate elevated and, for what seemed an eternity, wouldn't come down. Ultimately, the pounding subsided and we didn't think anything of it until it happened again. Then we went for a battery of tests, including for Marfan syndrome, a disease that affects connective tissues and can be fatal if there is leaking in the vessels that lead to the heart. Flo Hyman, one of the best volleyball players of all time, a silver medalist at the 1984 Los Angeles Summer Games, who died suddenly during a match, had Marfan, though nobody knew that until an autopsy revealed the disorder.

As it turned out, I did not have Marfan. Instead, the doctors said, I was a salty sweater, meaning, simply, I lost high amounts of salt in my sweat. When I got below a certain sodium level, I got dehydrated easily.

The easy fix to this was to supplement my diet with salt pills.

For all the years since I first went to the doctors about this, Bob's concern — make that his out-and-out fear — had been that I would have one of these incidents at a meet.

And here it was happening in Omaha, just moments before the first race of the Trials was to be broadcast live on NBC.

I knew that if I'd told Bob, it might have

sent him over the edge. Just imagine: Live from Omaha! Here he is, Michael Phelps! And he's clutching his chest!

Which is why I didn't say anything.

I just had to go out there and swim.

Once that first swim is over, if it's good, I have momentum. Then the meet feels as if it's all going downhill. It's just getting past that first swim. Four years of work, dedication, drive, and commitment all distilled into four minutes of racing. This was going to be the gateway, the first race in answering what I was going to be doing in Beijing, and how I was likely to do it.

In track they have a starter's pistol that signals the start of a race. In swimming it's a beep.

Beep!

After the opening butterfly leg, I had a lead of about a body length on Lochte.

In the back, he closed to half a length.

In the breast, he pulled even.

With 50 meters to go, the question was clear: Who had enough left?

As I turned, I glanced over at Lochte. I saw where he was. As Lochte rose to the surface, I was still underwater, surging, dolphin-kicking. When I finally broke the surface — the rules are 15 meters underwater, no more — I had left Lochte behind.

I touched in 4:05.25. A new world record.

Lochte finished in 4:06.08. Both of us had gone under the prior record, my 4:06.22. And he was supposed to have a banged-up ankle that was bothering him?

The two of us were far, far ahead of the rest of the field. Robert Margalis, who finished third, was more than seven seconds behind Ryan, eight behind me.

"Nice job, Doggy," I said to him after it was over.

"That hurt," he said.

"Yeah, tell me about it," I said. Then I told him, "We got this in Beijing. Let's go for it. Let's go get gold and silver in Beijing."

All smiles, I saw Bob a few moments later. That's when I let him in on how my heart had been galloping along beforehand. I didn't tell you because I knew it would turn you catatonic, I said.

Lochte's time that night was three seconds better than he had ever gone before. At this level, that's an incredible amount of time to knock off. If I was planning on me getting gold in the 400 IM in Beijing, Lochte silver — for sure, Lochte obviously had other plans. But the question Lochte would now have swirling around inside his head was: Could he get better still, or had he already maxed out?

"Going into the race, I thought I could beat him. I hate to lose. I don't like it at all," Lochte said afterward.

He also said — and this is why after the Trials, heading toward Beijing, I thought the 400 IM could be the toughest individual race on my schedule — "I know there are a lot of places where I can improve."

Though I respect Lochte immensely, love to race him, understand — I was not afraid of him, concerned about him, worried about him.

Whatever he was doing to get himself ready for the Olympics was out of my control.

I don't worry about other guys when I'm training, not even Lochte. I get myself ready. Of course I'm racing at the Olympics, or anywhere, against other guys. But I'm also racing against the clock. And, maybe mostly, against myself, to see how good I can be.

That said, I want to be clear: I have the utmost respect for my competitors. I love to race them. Those guys help me. The faster they get, the faster I get, because I don't want to lose.

If I could do 4:05 at Trials, I thought, maybe I really could do 4:03. My lactate response after the 4:05 proved perfectly normal. Which made me think: I'd had a racing heartbeat beforehand yet had thrown down a world record, and immediately afterward the blood work showed I was completely back to normal.

Which made me also think that it's all in how you respond to pressure.

I also knew there were things I could fix to get me to 4:03. I knew my breaststroke could be faster. I knew I could go out harder in the fly and still be relaxed. That's one of the biggest things I have in the medley; I can go out so much faster than other guys in the fly, that first leg, yet be more relaxed and comfortable. It's called easy speed. I have it.

3:07.

The dream kept visiting me throughout my week in Omaha, as I went on to qualify to represent the United States at the Beijing Games in five individual events: the 400 IM, 200 free, 200 fly, 200 IM, and 100 fly.

I also swam 47.92 in the preliminaries of the 100 free, the tenth-fastest time ever. The point of that swim was to be in the pool for the 400 free relay, nothing more. I didn't even swim the semifinals or finals of the 100 free.

After the Trials, then, it seemed all but certain I would swim at the Games in three relays: the 400 free, the 800 free, and the 400 medley.

All in, eight chances for gold.

All in, including preliminary and semifinal swims, 17 races in just nine days.

After the Trials, all of us on the U.S. team went off to Palo Alto, California, for a training camp; then to Singapore, for more practice but in the same time zone as Beijing; then, finally, on to Beijing.

In Palo Alto, I was on my game. Bob said it felt like every day in Palo Alto for him, watching me, was like Christmas. However, Lochte was on, too.

Lochte and I don't do a lot of head-to-head sets because, as Bob figures, somebody's likely to learn something about the other guy. One morning, however, we lined up for a complicated set, four of each stroke, that ended with fast 50s of each stroke — fast meaning race pace. On the fly, Lochte was close to me; on the back, dead even; on the breast, he was perhaps a full second ahead, a huge difference; we were dead even again on the free.

I was happy with the set. Bob was happy, too, but you could almost see him thinking, hmmm. I knew he had noticed how fast Lochte had gone during the breast.

If I never once imagined Ryan beating me,

Bob probably thought about it every day. Maybe that's the way we have to go.

The Singapore camp was mostly about resting and recovering, not hard training. I did do one butterfly set that undeniably hinted at what kind of shape I was in: three 100 flys, with easy 200s in between, each 100 faster than the other. I did the last one in 51.6. It was maybe the best practice I had ever done, and just to put it in perspective: A week before the 2007 Worlds in Melbourne, I pushed a 53.8, which Bob and I both thought was terrific.

So, a 51.6. Bob walked over to another one of the American coaches and said with a big smile, well, my work is done, I'm officially on vacation.

Hardly. But we were both feeling good about where I was.

When swimmers are gearing up for a big meet, we go through a cycle that's called "shave and taper." As the meet draws near, the idea is to keep training but include more rest, drawing on the weeks and months of hard training beforehand, the objective being to peak at the meet itself. That's called the taper. The challenge is in getting the timing right, complicated by the fact that what works for one swimmer might not — indeed probably won't — work for another. There's no one-size-fits-all. Bob puts it this way: When you taper swimmers, it's like a haircut. You never know if it's any good until it's too late.

That 51.6 also suggested my taper was dead-on where it needed to be.

As for the shave, swimmers shave their bodies before a major competition on the theory that body hair creates resistance. You have to shave everywhere; well, everywhere that isn't covered by your suit. It makes you feel clean and smooth. Super-clean and super-smooth.

For most of the winter, in Ann Arbor, I had let my beard grow. As the year went on, I showed up at most pre-Olympic events with facial hair, sometimes a goatee, other times an excellent Fu Manchu. I'm just messing around with it a little bit, I told everyone after we got to Beijing, sporting the Fu.

When the facial hair goes away, that's how you know I'm getting serious.

I showed up for my first Olympic swim in Beijing, the prelims of the 400 IM, clean shaven. Even the hair on the back of my neck was neatly trimmed. Courtesy of Lochte.

He didn't have me trim his; he likes to keep his hair long and shaggy. Besides, no one would trust me with clippers. Or at least no one should.

If it seems just a little weird that Lochte would be trimming my hair one day and then we'd be racing each other two days after that for Olympic gold — well, that's both the way swimming is and the way he and I get along. Someone's got to trim the hair on the back of your neck if you want it done, right?

During one of the media scrums before the Olympics started, Lochte had said, "When me and Michael talk, it's strictly anything but swimming. We don't talk about swimming at all. That's — I guess that's good for both of us. We're not always getting wound up in this whole Olympic thing. I mean, we have down time to relax."

The day before the 400 medley prelims, Friday, August 8, was the day of the opening ceremony. Much as I would have loved to have gone to the ceremony, there was just no way; I had to swim the next day and couldn't run the risk of marching and then standing in the heat and humidity.

I didn't want to get up and worry about shaving the morning of the prelims, which were the following night, so I decided to shave down then. In our little suite in the Olympic Village, there was nothing on the floor to keep the water from the shower inside the shower itself; we were forever, it seemed, dealing with a small flood. I was in the shower, with my music on, shaving, and Lochte yelled out, hey, why are you shaving now?

When I explained to him what was up, he decided he would shave then, too.

While we were in the midst of shaving down, I said, referring to the 400 IM, let's finish this. One-two again. Erik and I did it in Athens. Dolan and Erik did it in Sydney. Dolan and Namesnik in Atlanta.

Let's get after it, I said.

Let's get after it, he said.

I knew I had to have a good first race, and that was a very good thing. I can't emphasize it enough: A good first race sets the tone.

Laszlo Cseh, the Hungarian who had won the bronze in Athens, was in the first of the three seeded heats. He went 4:09.26. I watched that and thought, I'm going to have to go faster if I want to be in the middle lane in the final. And I definitely wanted to be in the middle in this race.

Lochte went in the next heat. 4:10.33. At this point, with my heat still to go, five guys had already gone 4:12 or better. I was thinking, okay, get after it.

At 150 meters, my butterfly leg already over, halfway through the backstroke, I realized I was going fast. I was, in fact, under world-record pace. I thought to myself, not so fast, not tonight. The last 200 meters, I put it on cruise control. I hit the wall, took my goggles off, looked at the clock, and saw 4:07.82.

An Olympic record.

I did not expect that at all.

My prelim time was a full 44-hundredths better than my winning time in the finals in Athens.

And honestly, while this prelim race didn't hurt that bad, my strokes didn't feel the way I quite wanted them to. I could do better.

Cseh was asked after the prelims if he could win. "That will be hard," he told the reporter. "I'll try everything but that will be hard. If somebody wants to win this race, they need a 4:05." His personal best, as I knew well, was 4:07.96.

Lochte said, "If I'm right there with him, then there's pressure. We'll see what happens."

I felt no pressure. My plan was to get some sleep and be ready to go in the morning.

Amid dreams of 3:07.

In the summer of 2001, Jacques Rogge, who at that time was the newly elected president of the International Olympic Committee, had a conversation with Dick Ebersol, the chairman of NBC Sports. NBC, as it had since 1988, would be broadcasting the Summer Games. Beijing is twelve hours ahead of New York. The 2000 Olympics from Sydney, fifteen hours ahead of New York, had largely been shown on tape delay. That had rubbed some critics entirely the wrong way. Now, Ebersol wanted to know, was it possible for certain events in Beijing — swimming and gymnastics, mostly — to be moved around, switched so the finals took place in the morning, Beijing time? If so, they could be shown live in prime time on the East Coast on NBC, which was paying the IOC nearly $900 million for the right to broadcast the Beijing Olympics.

Rogge said he'd have to get back to Ebersol. The IOC president would have to check with the heads of the international swimming and gymnastics federations. At an Olympics, even though most people think the IOC is in charge of everything, those federations are actually still in charge of running the sports themselves.

More than three years later, Rogge got back to Ebersol. Yes, he said, swimming and gymnastics would be moved.

Over Thanksgiving weekend in 2004, Dick Ebersol was seriously injured in a plane crash in Telluride, Colorado; his son, Charlie, survived the crash; a younger son, Teddy, was killed. Several months later, on what turned out to be the very first day that Dick returned to work, my mom and I happened to be in New York. We asked if we could drop by his office; we wanted to see how Dick and his family were doing. With us was Drew Johnson, who, working with Peter Carlisle, is part of my team at Octagon, the agency that represents me.

It was a very, very emotional meeting.

Sitting in his office, Dick said at one point, I have something to tell you. I want your reaction, please understand it's going to happen no matter what you say, but I want you to know: the swim finals are going to go off in the morning, the heats at night. Would that be a problem?

No way.

I was thrilled.

For real.

Swimming being on during prime time is everything I want for the sport, I told him. I'm trying to leave the sport bigger and better than it was when I was lucky enough to have first found it.

Dick asked me not to tell anyone about the news until it broke, which it eventually did, of course, after which I was asked repeatedly what I thought about swimming in morning finals.

It's the Olympics, I responded. If you can't get up to swim in the morning, don't go.

Which I believed 100 percent. Swimmers swim in the morning, anyway. To get to the Olympics and represent your country is an enormous privilege. How could anyone seriously think about not being able to perform? To say that you didn't want to give your best because it was ten in the morning instead of eight at night was an excuse.

The Olympics are no place for excuses.

The morning of the 400 IM final, Sunday, August 10, I met Bob at our dorm in the village — he was on the first floor, I was on the third — for a wake-up swim at a pool in the village. I was maybe ten minutes late meeting him. That sort of thing drives Bob crazy, especially on race day. He kept looking at his watch but not saying anything. Just looking at the watch.

We had never done a wake-up swim before. Some coaches swear by them. Not Bob. But we'd never had a morning final before, and Bob didn't want to spend the next thirty years wondering if he should have had me do a wake-up swim. So I did 500 to 800 meters, just enough to get moving.

Lochte had already done his wake-up swim. Katie Hoff, who is from Baltimore, too, and is an old friend, was doing hers. She would go on to win three medals in Beijing.

After that, we walked over to the dining hall for breakfast: oatmeal and fruit. And one of those cultural moments: no brown sugar for the oatmeal. I used white sugar. No excuses.

By now we were only three or four minutes behind Bob's schedule. He kept looking at the watch.

This was his way of saying, I want to get this first race over and done with.

Me, too.

For years, I've had the same routine to get ready for a race. I got to the Cube, per the routine, two hours before the race.

Like I always do, I stretched and loosened up a bit first. Then I got into the water, wearing just a brief; it's not the time for competition-style suits, much less full-body gear, and swam my warm-up: 800 mixer to start, alternating a 50 freestyle with a 50 of something else, anything but free; 600 meters of kicking with a kickboard; 400 meters of pulling a pull buoy; however I want to do it, something to warm up my arms; a 200 medley drill; then some 25s just to get the heart going a little bit. Since I was getting ready for a 400 medley, I also did one or two 25s of each stroke. When I was done with that, I swam down for 75 to 100 meters.

That was that.

Usually, while I'm doing this warm-up, Bob goes and gets himself a Diet Coke or a coffee — straight-up black, of course. Not this day. We were both feeling slightly paranoid. I asked him to stick around at one end of the pool with my water bottle. That way we could make extra certain no one was going to do anything outlandishly stupid like trying to poison me.

Warm-up went by uneventfully. I dried off, got warm, put my headphones on, and sat on the massage table. I always sit; I don't lie down. From that point on, no matter the event, Bob and I don't talk until after the end of the race. I mean, what's there to say?

In Beijing, the headphones were plugged into a black iPod, which I had gotten as a bonus for buying an Apple laptop at a store in Ann Arbor a few months before the Olympics. Here was the deal at the store: iPod or free printer. I never print anything so I grabbed the iPod. What's on my iPod? Lil Wayne and Young Jeezy, to name two, especially Young Jeezy's "Go Getta" and Lil Wayne's "I'm Me." The lyrics to "I'm Me" are definitely not G-rated. But that's not, for me, the point. When I hear Lil Wayne do that song, I hear him saying, I'm my own individual, and that's me.

At the Cube, there was a television in front of the massage table. The choices invariably seemed to be archery, volleyball, or women's basketball.

About forty-five minutes out, I hopped into my suit, the Speedo LZR Racer. Some guys like to wear a brief under the LZR. Not my way. Under the LZR it's me. Some swimmers have said they need help putting on the LZR. Not me. I put a plastic garbage bag on my foot and rolled that leg of the suit over the bag, then up my leg; then I put the bag on the other foot and did it on that side. Easy.

For the individual medley I wore a suit that went from waist to the ankles — essentially swim pants. It can feel too constricting, especially trying to do the butterfly, to wear a full suit, one that wraps over the collarbones.

With thirty minutes to go, I got into the water again to do 600 to 800 meters. I was in the water for ten minutes, max. I got out, dried off, and grabbed my USA parka, put my warm-up pants on, put the headphones back on.

With about ten minutes to go, I grabbed my credential and walked to the ready room. The credential is your ID pass at the Olympics; it's a laminated plastic card that includes a picture and a barcode. For security reasons, you can't go anywhere without it.

When I'm in the ready room, I'm there by myself and to be by myself. Usually, the officials who are in the room try to sit all the guys in the same row if you're in the same race or the same heat. I never do that. I just find a seat where I can sit by myself and block the two seats on either side; my caps and goggles go on one, towel on the other.

Lochte came over and said, good luck. I was, like, thanks, man, let's do it.

I knew, and Lochte knew that I knew, that, unfortunately, he wasn't quite himself. He had been dealing with a pretty significant case of the runs. It appeared McDonald's was his attempted solution. For a few days, he had been eating religiously at the one in the village cafeteria, chowing down each time on what seemed to be more than a dozen Chicken McNuggets, a burger or two, and fries. Lunch and dinner. If Lochte wasn't quite himself that day, well, he'd had an ankle problem at the Trials and went under the world record. He was going to bring it as hard as he could, no question.

They called our race. I put on the goggles and caps.

It was time to go.

As I walked out onto the deck, I looked for

85

President Bush; I'd heard he was in the audience. I found him after a few moments, and it looked like he was pointing at me, waving his flag.

After we walked out to behind the blocks, I did what I always do there. I stretched my legs on the blocks, two different stretches, one a straight-leg stretch, the other with a bent knee, left leg first.

I took the right headphone out.

Once they called my name, I took the left headphone out, the parka off. It's my routine to stand on the left side of the block and get onto it from that side.

I made sure the block itself was dry. This is a lesson learned the hard way. At the 2004 Santa Clara meet, before the 400 IM, I didn't notice the block was wet. Instead of diving in, I more or less fell off the block. Embarrassing. Since then I've always made sure to wipe the block with a towel.

Once up there, like I always do, I swung my arms, flapped them, really, in front and then in back, slapping my back.

Some people have suggested that's a routine I do to psych people out. They think that I'm thinking: Even if you can't see me well behind your goggles, here's the sound that's announcing you're going to get your butt kicked. Nothing of the sort. That would be poor sportsmanship in the extreme. It's just a routine. My routine. It's the routine I've gone through my whole life. I'm not going to change it.

I get asked all the time what I think about when I'm up on the blocks, in the instant before the starter says, take your marks.

Nothing.

There's nothing I can change, nothing I can do to get faster. I've done all the training. All I can do is listen for the beep, dive in the water, and swim.

I had told Bob I intended this 400 IM to be the last one I would ever swim competitively.

It's not that I couldn't swim it again. More, I simply didn't want to. It's that demanding.

If I was going to go out, then I wanted to go out in style.

The idea in the first 50 was to use that easy speed and then turn it on just enough so that at 100 I would have a lead of half a body length, maybe even a full body.

At the first wall, Cseh was in first. I was just behind. Perfect.

The next 50, I gave it a little more juice. As the fly leg ended, I was in first, Cseh second, Lochte third.

I figured I'd be ahead after the next 100 as well, after the backstroke.

Lochte apparently had a different idea.

He went out hard over the first 50 of the back and turned there in first.

At 200, I was back in front but not as far ahead as I had planned when I was visualizing. Lochte was just behind me, Cseh third.

We turned for the breaststroke.

This was where Lochte apparently thought he could school me.

No way.

The breaststroke felt as good as my breaststroke has ever felt.

Coming off that 300 wall, I had no idea where either Lochte or Cseh was. I knew only that I had to give it everything I had in the free.

It wasn't until I turned at 350 that I knew what was what. I was in Lane 4. Cseh was in Lane 5, the one next over to my right; Lochte in 6, one more over. When I came off the 350 wall and took my first breath, turning my head to the right to breathe, which was in their direction, I couldn't see either of them, couldn't see the splash from their hands. I was way ahead, and suddenly I had the same feeling I had in Athens. You take your first freestyle stroke on that last leg, the race is almost over, and you're in the lead. Underwater, just as I'd done four years before, I smiled. I smiled as I churned for home, going strong.

After touching, I whipped around so fast, trying to see my time on the big scoreboard at the other end of the Cube, that I bumped my head into the wall.

The scoreboard said I had hammered home in 4:03.84.

Just as I had dreamed it.

My 300 split time: 3:07.05.

4:03.84. I had smashed my own world record by 1.41 seconds. Even I had to say to myself, *wow*.

A little more deliberately now, I leaned up against the wall, then onto the lane line and raised my arms above my head, touchdown style.

Bob was nodding his head up and down in approval, a big smile on his face.

In the stands across the way, my mom gave Whitney a kiss, then put her hands over her face in relief and almost disbelief. Hilary wiped away tears.

Back the other way again, President Bush and the First Lady, and their daughter Barbara, along with the president's father, President George H. W. Bush, were waving and cheering. President Bush gave me a point and a head nod. Cool. I said thanks with a big smile. Later, he told me, "God, what a thrill to cheer for you!"

Wow.

Looking at the scoreboard, I could see that Cseh had finished second, more than two seconds behind me, in 4:06.16. Lochte had gone out too hard in the first leg of the backstroke and paid for it at the end of the race. He was third, more than four seconds back, in 4:08.09.

"I saw Lochte going (slower) and I tried to do everything to go better than Phelps, but I don't have too much power for that," Cseh said. "Anytime you think you can get close to Michael Phelps, he jumps to another level."

I got out and met Bob. That was awesome, he said. Let's swim down.

Later, looking at the numbers closely, Bob said this might have been my best race.

Not like my best race of the year. He meant the best race I had ever done. Considering the circumstances, taking into account all the pressure and distractions and the buildup and the general noise around me and the Games; it was exceptional, he said.

On two of the four legs, I swam faster on the second length than the first. On the backstroke, for instance: 31.37 going out, 30.2 coming home. On freestyle: 28.94 going out, 27.85 coming back.

There's a term in swimming for going

faster in the back length than the first. It's called "negative splitting," and it's a strategy that certainly doesn't work for most everyone else. Common sense says it ought to be harder to go faster on the back half than the front.

It's just the way I've always done it.

Where I really won the race, what made me happiest, was that I had dominated in breaststroke. All the practice, the focus, the effort on the breast had paid off. Cseh was more than three-tenths of a second slower over that 100 meters; Lochte's breast leg was more than a second behind mine.

I had ripped through the first 50 in the breast in 34.77. That was a lifetime best. I came back in 35.79. Not a negative split but still, it got me to 300 right at 3:07.

Wow.

On and around the pool deck, my world-record time instantaneously generated an enormous buzz. I had become the only man in history to have broken the world record in winning both my Olympic 400 IM golds.

Eddie Reese, our U.S. men's head coach, told reporters, "We just don't know how good that is. If somebody ten or fifteen years ago would have said the 400 IM will be won in 2008 in 4:03.8, I'd have bet everything I had or would ever get that it wouldn't happen."

As soon as Bob finished telling me the swim was awesome, he reverted to coach mode. He actually had visualized himself how he would coach at this exact moment, not getting overly excited over any one race.

Even though, as we talked about later, he was also thinking to himself that it may really be hard for Michael to get beat.

On the medals stand a little while after the race, the American flags, along with the Hungarian one, went up, just like in Athens. But no wreath this time.

As the flags were lifted up into the rafters, as "The Star-Spangled Banner" played, my eyes started watering. For me, this was a rare public show of emotion. I couldn't help it, didn't want to help it. I was thinking of all the ups and downs I had weathered since Athens, how hard I had worked, the sacrifices that had been made by so many to help get me to just this moment.

I so appreciated all of it.

I thought to myself: Sing. Sing out the national anthem there on the podium. But I couldn't stop crying.

Bob got teary-eyed, too, glad there was no camera on him.

Just when it looked like I might start sob-

bing or something, as the anthem reached
". . . the home of the brave," the music accidentally cut off.

All I could do was laugh.

And think: seven more chances, maybe, for
the Chinese to get the American anthem
right.

2
BELIEF:
THE 400 FREE RELAY

Bob is not the most technologically advanced individual. He has, however, discovered a little something on the Internet called Google. This was, for him, a major advance. Now he could read almost anything and everything written about me, and us, and about swimming in general.

I don't bother reading much, if any, of it. It can seem overwhelming.

Bob is not overwhelmed. He loves fishing for stories. And he not only reads but remembers what was said.

I won the 400 IM on Sunday morning, the 10th. Because the schedule was flipped — finals in the morning, prelims and heats often at night — the Sunday night schedule included the heats of the 400 free relay. I didn't swim in those heats; instead, I raced in the prelims of the 200 freestyle.

At major swim meets such as the Olympics, the guys who swim the prelims for the American team are not the same four guys who swim the final. There are good reasons for that. One, the prelim saves the guys in the finals lineup from the exertion of an added race. And, two, the prelims give more guys a chance to make the Olympic team, with the bonus that if the finals guys win a medal, the prelim swimmers get that medal, too. So, for instance, a winning swim in the finals means a gold medal not just for those four guys but for each of the prelim swimmers, too. It works the same way in track and field. The prelim guys get a medal if the finals guys do.

At the U.S. Olympic Trials, the prospect of being on the relays makes the 100 and 200 freestyle races that much more exciting. The top two finishers earn the right to swim in the individual event at the Games as well as the relay; for example, the 100 winner gets to swim in the 100 at the Games and the 400 relay. But the third- through sixth-place guys get to go to the Olympics, too, at the very least for the relay prelims, in some cases, the relay final.

Garrett had won the 100 at the Trials. Jason had come in second.

Cullen finished third.

Then came Nathan Adrian, Matt Grevers, and Ben Wildman-Tobriner.

For the finals, Garrett and Jason were locks, and so was I, because of the 47.92 I had produced at the Trials.

Cullen, Nathan, Matt, and Ben would be swimming the prelims with extra incentive. The one who swam the fastest split in the prelims would get to swim in the finals, too.

Each of them was fully deserving.

Cullen is, in a family sense, somewhat like me. He's very close to his mother. In his case, his dad died of lung cancer when Cullen was sixteen; his mother is invariably at our meets and you can tell that he has a very, very good relationship with her. Cullen was born in New York City and nearly drowned as a child when the inner tube he was riding at a water park flipped over. He didn't know how to swim. It took CPR, oxygen, paramedics, all of it to save his life. After that, his parents put him in swim class. In 2006, at the Pan Pacific Swimming Championships, one of the major meets of that year, he set a meet record in winning the 50 free. Cullen, Jason, Neil Walker, and I won the 400 free relay and set a world record, which made Cullen the first African-American swimmer to hold or share a long-course record. Making the Beijing team meant he was the third African-American to make the U.S. Olympic swim team, after Anthony Ervin and Maritza Correia. Cullen was a big part of a USA Swimming program called "Make a Splash," which is based on chilling statistics: Nearly six of every ten black Americans can't swim and African-American kids ages five to fourteen are nearly three times as likely to die of drowning as their white counterparts. One of the reasons that's cited for the dismal figures on minority swimmers — Hispanic-Americans are also far more likely to drown at a young age — is a lack of role models. His message is obvious, so simple, so common-sense: Hey, black kids can swim, too.

Nathan, who's from Washington state and took off what would have been his sophomore year at Berkeley to train for the Olympics, is one of those guys who's poised to be in the next great wave of top American swimmers. He was nineteen in the summer of 2008. "I think Nathan Adrian is a phenomenal talent and you can expect great things from him," Gary Hall, Jr., with whom Nathan had been training, said at the Trials. Mark Schubert, the USA Swimming head coach, said that Nathan "reminds me of Matt Biondi in 1984," which is high praise, no doubt. Matt, who also went to Cal, won five gold medals at the Olympics in 1988 in Seoul. Nathan's story was great because it's not just that he finished fourth in the 100 at the Trials; it's how he got there. In the semi-finals, he had finished in 48.89. That was good enough only for a tie in ninth place, with Alex Righi. Only the top eight go on to the finals. Then, though, Lochte scratched from the 100 final to concentrate on other events, the 200 back and the 200 IM. So Nathan and Alex had a swim-off. Just the two of them in the pool. Nathan won. That got him to the finals and then, in the finals, swimming in an outside lane, he got that fourth-place finish.

Of all the guys on the American team, Matt is the one Bob had been watching with particular interest. Both of Matt's parents are Dutch; thus, he could have swum for Holland. He said, nope, I'm an American. President Bush liked that story so much he told it, with Matt among those looking on, at a ceremony in the Rose Garden in July, before the Olympics. Matt grew up in Lake Forest, Illinois, north of Chicago, and swam in college for Northwestern, where he was a four-time NCAA champion and earned twenty-seven All-America citations. As good as he was there, he got even better when he moved after graduating in 2007 to Tucson, Arizona, to train with Frank Busch and Rick DeMont.

Ben, like Matt, is a phenomenally smart guy. He was a Rhodes Scholar finalist in the fall of 2007, after graduating from Stanford with a degree in biomechanical engineering, and was bound for medical school after the Olympics. His grandfather was a justice on the California Supreme Court. All this, and Ben had won the 50 free at the 2007 Worlds in Melbourne.

When Nathan, Cullen, Ben, and Matt lined up in that order on the blocks on Sunday night in the first of the two relay heats, the world-record still stood at 3:12.46, the time that Cullen and I had helped set in 2006 at the Pan Pacs.

So much for that. When Matt, swimming the anchor leg, touched, the scoreboard said, 3:12.23.

In that heat, the Australians finished second, in 3:12.41, under the 2006 mark, too.

In the next heat, the French finished in 3:12.36, again under what had been the record time.

Afterward, one of the French swimmers, Frederick Bousquet, said, "I talked to my coach, and he said the ideal position was to finish second behind the United States, and they beat the world record and they come in as favorites tomorrow, and tomorrow morning we take all that they have."

He also said he had looked at the four Americans in the ready room just before the prelims and saw uncertainty. "They didn't look at us, although they usually do," he said. "We could sense that they were a little bit afraid."

These remarks followed those of another French swimmer, Alain Bernard, who at the European championships in March had set a world record in the 100 free: 47.5, same as my goal time for 2008. Amid his arrival in Beijing, he uncorked some trash talking.

"The Americans? We're going to smash them. That's what we came here for.

"I'll start my Games in the 4x100 meters freestyle relay final, confident that my pals will have qualified easily.

"If the relay goes according to plans, then we'll be on a roll."

The next morning, Monday the 11th, Bob and I were at the village dining hall, along with Jason and maybe one or two others. Bob, the Internet sleuth, had found the French comments. He said, hey, guess what I read, then proceeded to describe what he had found.

Bob added, and here came a loaded code phrase that he knew would carry extra zing, it says here they think they're pretty much going to smash you like guitars.

Comments like that just make me more fired up.

I said, that's nice; this is going to be fun.

There's no point in talking smack, absolutely no need to talk beforehand about what you're going to do. It's not worth it, not worth playing the mind games. Just get in the water and swim. People who talk about what they're going to do, nine times out of ten don't back it up. It's always better, and a whole lot smarter, not to say anything, to simply let the swimming do the talking.

There's a saying that goes precisely to the point, of course: Actions speak louder than words.

That saying is 100 percent true.

That saying is one of Bob Bowman's all-time favorites.

I learned that early on.

Every summer, the North Baltimore club holds a long-course meet. It's one of the major events on the NBAC calendar. The night before the meet — this was when I was maybe twelve, not all that long after Bob and I had started working together — he was overseeing what was, for him, a pretty easy practice. At the end of it, he asked our group to swim four 50s. Give me a little effort, he said. Well, of all the kids in the group, there was only one who was not giving Bob that little effort. One of the girls in the group even said, Michael, you'd better get going or we're going to have to do this all over.

Everybody got out of the pool, and Bob said, okay, everybody, that'll be it, except, and now he looked right at me, for you.

I uncorked one of the great twelve-year-old tantrums of all time. I screamed, you can't make me do it! And so on. A huge, horrible, public scene, a direct challenge to Bob's authority in front of everyone.

Bob said to me, you can do what you want, but as of now you're not a member of NBAC, and until you come back and do the set, you never will be.

I went home in tears.

That night, Mom called Bob. He told her, until Michael does the set he can't be in the meet. So what, she said, can we do?

Take a meeting, that's what. At five-thirty the next morning.

The meeting was in the club's aerobics room. Bob had set up a table and four chairs.

Four?

I showed up with a baseball hat on my head. Bob made me take it off. Mom and I sat down on two of the chairs, Bob grabbed a third. And in came my father, a Maryland state trooper, in full uniform. My eyes got wide. At that point, my father was still much more involved in my life; even so, for him to show up like that, at that hour of the morning, meant this was no-doubt-about-it serious.

Bob said, Michael, there's a triangle here. There's your dad. Your mom. Me. Guess who's in the middle?

Me, I said, very softly.

That's right, he said. You've got nowhere to run, nowhere to hide. You have to do what we want you to do.

Bob turned to my parents. Before Michael can swim in the meet, Bob said, he has to do the set.

So I did.

And I had to do it to Bob's satisfaction.

Which I did.

When Bob and I started, he knew of me mostly as Whitney's younger brother. He had been introduced as North Baltimore's new assistant the day after I turned eleven. One day, our team was swimming at Towson State, and two of the kids started throwing towels and soap around the men's bathroom. I walked in; some of the older kids started shouting out my name, as if I'd been the one who started the whole thing. In walked Bob.

"Michael Phelps," he said, "what did you do?"

"I didn't do anything! It was them!"

"Well, then why are they shouting your name?"

"Ask them."

"No, Michael. I'm asking you. What did you do?"

Nothing, at least that day. As I walked out there, I thought, it'll really stink if I ever have to work with that guy. As Bob walked away, he was thinking, thank goodness I will never have to coach that kid.

That's how it all began. I thought he was a such a jerk. I thought, no way I'm ever swimming for him.

He soon realized I was just scared out of my mind.

A few months later, the North Baltimore club executed a staff shake-up. Bob was put in charge of a set of promising swimmers ranging in age from high school to me.

I still remember the first set he gave us: a 400 free, a 400 stroke of any sort, one 400 IM and a 400 free. I did each set three times. I still remember it because it hurt. A lot.

Mostly, Bob wanted to see how we would react.

He watched me finish the final set of four 100 frees with intrigue. I was coming back faster at the end of set — 1:05 for each hundred — than at the beginning. He didn't know then what to make of that.

Another early set went like this: a 200 freestyle to start; then a 200 IM; four 50s of each stroke; four 100 frees with a small break in between each one — what's called an interval, the time between depending on any number of things — ending with a 400 IM. We were asked to do this particular set four times. I was twelve, and I just killed it, had a great set. Maybe, Bob thought, this kid really could be something special.

A few months after Bob had been coaching me, he issued orders for a pretty difficult practice, especially for someone my age. When it was over, all the other kids were dragging. They got out of the pool slowly. They got their towels and clothes slowly. I got out but still had a ton of energy, so much that I kept running to the side of the pool, filling up my cap with water and dumping the water on the other kids' heads. Bob ran over to tell me to knock it off. He told me that if I was still this frisky he could for sure make practices a lot harder.

I said, and Bob has never forgotten this, I will never get tired.

We have since dispelled that rumor.

You have to be mentally tough to go

through it with Bob. If you're not mentally tough, you're not learning what he's teaching you. Growing up, I used to tell Bob when he would order a set that would make my eyes widen, I can't do that. He would say, there's a difference between "can't" and "won't." Maybe you won't do that, he would then say. But you can.

If you say "can't," you're restricting what you can do or ever will do. You can use your imagination to do whatever you want. "Can't," he would say, that's a tough word.

Early on, Bob put me through a butterfly workout that went on for 3,000 meters. That was nearly two miles of only butterfly.

When things started getting much more serious, in my midteens, I was worked through a freestyle set that went on for 12,000 meters. That's about seven miles. It went like this: one 800, two 700s, three 600s, four 500s, five 400s, six 300s, seven 200s, eight 100s.

I would do a set built on this combination: 300 free, 200 fly. Each 500 amounted to one. I did ten.

The worst sets ever would involve long repetitions, say thirty 100s, bad enough, but with a twist. At the 50-meter mark you'd have to climb out of the pool, then start the remaining 50 from the blocks. One of my favorite sets, Bob likes to say, because getting out of the pool and diving back in adds an extra component to the thing that's just brutal. After twenty, you're grabbing the block. You can't see straight. Things are blurry. You feel like you can't move.

But you can. That's what I came to understand. At that point it's pretty much just goals. If you want to meet your goals, this is what it takes.

Bob was born and raised in South Carolina. He was an accomplished musician and artist and president of his high school's National Honor Society. He was also a swimmer. Unlike everything else he did, swimming didn't come quite so easily. Even so, he got to Florida State on a swim scholarship and, training with the distance swimmers, qualified for the 1985 spring nationals in the 100 fly. He should have been training with the sprinters, but figured more work meant better.

Not always.

Finishing up at Florida State, Bob got a job coaching with a local swim club. His boss gave him a stack of stuff to read with the understanding Bob was supposed to get it read in a month. He read it all that night, came back the next morning and asked for more.

Early in his coaching career, Bob was perhaps even more impatient and demanding. In nine years, he coached in seven places in five states.

One of those stops came in Napa Valley, north of San Francisco. There he learned from Paul Bergen. In 2001, Inge de Bruijn of the Netherlands won three individual events at a world championships; Tracy Caulkins had done it before her, in 1978. Paul Bergen coached both of them.

Paul was exacting. So is Bob.

Paul liked to train thoroughbred horses. Bob, too. Plus: Horses don't talk. Swimmers can't, either, at least when swimming. Bob and I would learn to communicate without saying a word.

Bob didn't come to Baltimore with the slightest intention of coaching me. He had been turned down in 1995 for what he thought then was his dream job, head coach of the Dynamo Swim Club in Atlanta. The club offered the job to someone else. Bob thought, that's it. He decided to try for a degree in farm management at Auburn University, thinking he ultimately would run a horse farm. While he was there, he figured, he would take a part-time assistant's job at Auburn.

The 1996 Olympics in Atlanta were coming up. Looking for advice, he spoke with Murray Stephens, the head coach at North Baltimore. Murray had trained Anita Nall and Beth Botsford. Murray had developed a culture that demanded excellence. He respected Bob.

How much, Murray asked, is the Auburn job paying?

Told $10,000, Murray said, we'll pay you $35,000. When can you start?

Bob said, how about next week?

From that very first day, even if he hardly showed it, Bob knew I was, as he likes to say now, made for swimming.

My growth spurt came before I turned fifteen. By that time, I was almost as tall as I am now. Getting that big that fast obviously increased the length of my stroke. That meant I could do more in the water and thus became way more accepting of Bob's ever-increasing demands. In turn, he could tell, as could I, that I kept getting better and better.

Which gave me genuine confidence.

Another slogan Bob likes is one from Bill Parcells, the football coach: You can't dream up confidence. Confidence is born of demonstrated ability.

Even when he saw me at eleven, saw my body, the way I was built, Bob knew I would be an excellent swimmer.

I was blessed with very large hands and feet. My feet are now size fourteen. My hands have been compared to dinner plates. Big hands and feet are one of the things coaches look for; they're tools that give a swimmer an excellent way to hold onto the water while swimming. The very best swimmers carry very few bubbles, very little air, when you look at their hands and feet under water; they're able to slide their hands in, and to position both hands and feet on the water, where they're the most effective. That's what "holding onto the water" means.

I have a long torso in relation to my legs. That helps me plane on top of the water like, well, a boat.

My wingspan is longer than my height. I'm now 6-foot-4. My wingspan is three inches longer, 6-foot-7. A swimmer with long arms who takes longer strokes obviously ought to be able to take fewer strokes in a single lap; that can be a big advantage.

In a way, I'm both perfectly tall and short. My shoulders are wide but my waist is only 32 inches. I have the torso of someone 6-foot-8 but the legs of someone more like 6 feet exactly. In the water, that means lower drag.

I'm very flexible in my shoulders, elbows,

knees, and ankles. That's big in swimming because what you want to be able to do is to exert a lot of force but do so fluidly. Also, flexibility gives you a range of motion by which you can hold the water more effectively. The flexibility in my ankles means I can whip my feet through the water as if they were fins.

Flexibility runs in the family. Whitney, when she was a competitive swimmer, used to be able to lock hands behind her back and bring them up, without unlocking, over her shoulders, all the way in front.

Also, I have a very high endurance capacity. Some of this is because I started swimming at seven and had, by the time Bob arrived at NBAC, put in four years in the pool. That was truly important in developing my heart and lung capacity. They think now that you can really do a lot with a young athlete, before he or she hits puberty, to build endurance for later on; longer swimming sets when you're young, for example. That's exactly what I did.

At ages nine and ten, I was swimming seventy-five minutes per day four times a week, then ninety minutes per day five times a week.

At age eleven and twelve, I moved up to swimming every day of the week, each time for two and one-half hours.

With all of that, what struck Bob the most about me when we first started together was not anything physical.

It was what was in my head.

Then as now, I was intensely competitive. Not just in the pool. In anything.

Who was going to be first into the front seat of the car?

Who was going to pick out the first video at Blockbuster?

Who was going to be first at the dinner table?

In practice, I always tried to lap as many people as I could. But I was never, in my head, training against them because I never, ever trained against other people. I always trained against the clock.

At meets, I always wanted to win. I absolutely hated to lose.

Nothing about that has ever changed.

With Bob's prompting, I discovered something else about myself early on, too. I could be motivated not just by winning. By improving my strokes. Hitting split times. Setting records. Doing my best times. There were any number of things I could do to get better. Winning never gets old, but there was a way to win that showed I was getting better, and could get better still.

Bob used to say to me, let's just see what you've got in you; use all the gas in the tank. I started using his saying. I would say to him before a meet, let's just see what I have in me. I wouldn't say, I want to win. It would be, I want to see what I have in me.

At the same time, Bob emphasized sportsmanship, accountability, responsibility. The program placed an extraordinary premium on attitude. It was said, over and again, that the single most important factor in anything we do, and particularly in this endeavor, was this: What is your attitude?

At NBAC, one of the slogans, and Bob had a million slogans, was, "Attitude, Action, Achievement." That was the order in which you could expect things to happen. You could see every day's practice as an ordeal. Or you could see it as adventure.

To that end, Bob would always tell me when I was younger: We become what we think about most.

Bob also used to give a talk that went something like this: Are you going to wait until after you win your gold medal to have a good attitude? No. You're going to do it beforehand. You have to have the right mental attitude, and go from there. You're going to be an Olympic champion in attitude long before there's a gold medal around your neck.

The thing that got me the most, and still does, was to take swimming away from me. NBAC had a program for perfect attendance at practice; if you made each practice, you got to wear a yellow cap that said, in blue letters, "100% Never Settle For Less." I was always wearing a yellow cap.

Bob is one of the most passionate people I've ever seen at what he does. Ever. He works around the clock. I really feel that he lives for the sport of swimming. He is up and going at it way before the sun peeks into the sky. He gets to the pool two hours before I'm out of bed. I've never seen anybody who does what he does. And he brought me along from a kid who really couldn't swim any strokes the way they're supposed to be done to where I am today.

Bob began to remake my strokes the summer I was twelve. Of course he knew exactly what he was doing; he had come to the NBAC with numerous American Swim Coaches Association awards for teaching stroke technique, and his first job was to reshape my basic two-beat freestyle kick to the more advanced six-beat kick.

He pushed. I pushed right back.

On purpose, I would lapse into the basic kick, what I knew and what I also knew had worked for me until then. Other times I'd just be lazy and do two beats. Either way, Bob would kick me out of practice, yellow cap and all. When I'd call my mom, she would tell me, no, she could not leave work early to come get me. I would have to wait until practice was supposed to be over. That's when she would come get me.

This went on until I started doing what I was supposed to do. The first day I went through an entire day of using a six-beat kick is the day Bob out-and-out dared me. He told me I wasn't old enough or mature enough to do it.

I did it.

If it sounds now like Bob was a trainer breaking the wild horse that was me, well, it is what it is.

It was much the same with morning practices, meaning a move to two practices a day, morning and afternoon. All first-rate swimmers practice both morning and afternoon. For months, I resisted. I relented after some college kids told me, hey, you know you might really get a lot better and a lot faster if you get in the pool in the morning, too. Or maybe Bob simply wore me down.

A few months after I turned twelve, Bob had called for a meeting with my mom and my father. It took place at Meadowbrook, upstairs in the babysitting room.

It was possible, Bob said, that Michael might one day make the Olympics. I'm not saying he will. I'm saying he could.

Come on, Bob, my mom said. She was in education. She saw kids every day. Michael's just a kid, she said. We don't know how he's going to change when the hormones kick in. When he wants to hang with other kids in high school.

That's why we're talking now, Bob said. Michael could be the real deal. I don't know when, he said, but he could if everyone here is willing to make the commitment.

And, he added, if he truly, genuinely loves it.

Bob talked about where they might send me to high school, what the schedule of a typical day might look like, and what sorts of sacrifices I would have to make, that we would all have to make. For one, he said, Michael ought to stop playing other sports. This was big. His concern was not just the time that other sports were taking away from practice in the pool, it was that I'd get hurt playing something else. Because I was so energetic, I would bounce from sport to sport to sport. I was the kid with a stick in his hand, a glove, a ball, whatever. One particular afternoon when I was nine stretched into evening, then into night, all of it around sports: I went first to a lacrosse game, where I told the coach I could only play the first three quarters; then to the baseball field, where I'd been selected for a home-run derby; then to the pool for practice until after it got dark outside.

Bob said, we're going to take this sort of thing and ease back. He also told my parents, this has to be normal. Don't talk about anything that you don't normally talk about. We're just going to enjoy the sport of swimming. And then we're going to see where it takes us.

There were, of course, choices that had to be made.

My academic track in high school had to be designed, with help from teachers and school administrators, to allow me to fulfill the essential Maryland state requirements for a diploma but no more. No honors classes, no advanced placement. Could it be worked out so that I might on some days be allowed to arrive at school later than the other kids? Might it be possible to be let out early?

Homework got done. In my mother's house, homework always got done.

There was, naturally, push-back from some in the school. A teacher once said to my mom, I taught your son very little chemistry. She replied that, during that school year, my son visited five countries because of swimming. Which was going to be more important in his life? Seeing what life was like in those five countries, or knowing how many atoms there are in so many grams of carbon-12?

There were other sorts of sacrifice as well.

My freshman year in high school, I wanted to fit in with my football-playing friends.

Let's talk about this, Michael, my mom said.

How many hours of practice a week would you have to commit to in order to play football? Where is football likely to take your friends? Will they make the varsity team? As high school goes along, will they make the county championships? Area all-star teams? Are any of them likely to be good enough to get a Division I scholarship? Play in the pros?

I doubt any of them are going to play in the NFL, I said.

Okay, she said. Now, what can you do with swimming?

I did not play football.

We went through much the same drill when I made a play to be on the school's golf team; it was a noncontact sport, I pointed out. Another nonstarter.

Mom calls what she did "planting seeds." One winter day when I was in high school, it snowed. I suddenly wanted to go sledding. Mom said, oh, are you going to go to the world championships this summer or are you going to break your arm now?

Maybe, I said after I had a second to think, I shouldn't go sledding.

That's a good idea, she said. Because you're the one who'd be calling Bob to tell him you broke your arm, not me.

This was all about learning to weigh options and make decisions. Mom might have asked leading questions to help me get to the smarter choice. But I had to make the decision myself: Did I love swimming enough to push myself to be the very best I could be?

My goals in swimming were set particularly high because they were not — were never — limited to just one stroke. I wanted to do multiple events. I wanted to try everything. Bob simply reinforced that when he made me redo my strokes.

As we went along, Bob's biggest challenge became keeping a step ahead of me. I quickly picked up a keen understanding of how his program operates and how it is put together. To keep it fresh he had to find ways to change it up. He knew that would not only provide variety; it would keep me focused.

So, for instance, I would be asked to swim with my arms only, or my legs only, or with one arm or one leg.

I would even do butterfly and backstroke legs using only my right or left arm. That would isolate the one arm and make me concentrate on the way it moved through the water.

To improve my freestyle technique, I would do a drill that involved me keeping my elbows high while I pulled through the water with my fingertips. That would make my legs do more of the work.

I would swim in sneakers. While tethered to a pulley. Wearing a scuba vest. With an inner tube around my ankles.

All of these devices worked to increase resistance, the same way a baseball player takes swings in the warm-up circle with a donut on the bat. When the donut comes off, and it's time get in the batter's box for real, that bat feels a whole lot lighter and easier to swing.

A week before Bob and I would leave for Federal Way, Washington, those 2000 spring nationals where I would swim 1:59.02 in the 200 fly, Bob convened another meeting. This time it was with my mom, outside Meadow-brook.

"When we get back from Seattle," Bob said, "we should talk."

"Why, Bob? What's wrong?"

"Nothing is wrong at all. In fact, it's all good. But it's a matter of time before things start to change for Michael and nothing is going to be the same."

"What do you mean?"

"He's way ahead of schedule right now and, at some point, I don't know when, we're going to need to get ready for media attention, hype, expectations. He'll need to prepare for that, and it will be on us sooner than we think."

By then, Bob had for weeks been feverishly trying to assess possibilities for 2000, and the Sydney Olympics. He figured that I was suddenly in the mix for Sydney. Come 2004, I ought to make the team and probably win medals, maybe multiple medals. And in 2008, who knew? There were so many uncertainties, so many unforeseeable twists and turns along any journey. But come 2008 I might do something staggering. Something no one had ever done before.

A few weeks after the swim in Federal Way, I went to a meet at the University of Michigan. There I made the Trials qualifying standard in all of the events I entered. Jon Urbanchek, the Michigan coach, had first seen me swim when I was eleven; his daughter was living in Baltimore and so he had stopped by. Urbanchek had been keeping an eye on me since — the boy might be a promising college swimmer — and said at that meet that I would probably make the 2000 Olympic team even though very few people knew even the first thing about me.

That June, as I turned fifteen, I held the American age-group records for boys ages thirteen to fourteen in both the 200 and 400 individual medleys, the 100 and 200 butterflys, and the 400 and 800 freestyles.

Swim geeks knew about me, maybe.

They also knew that were I to make the Games, I would be the youngest male swimmer to have qualified for a U.S. Olympic team since 1932, when thirteen-year-old Ralph Flanagan had made the team. In its 2000 Trials preview, *Swimming World* magazine said, "Fourteen-year-old Michael Phelps swam a phenomenal 1:59.02 at spring nationals but is probably a year or two from being a factor on the world scene."

The 2000 U.S. Olympic Trials were held in August in Indianapolis. The story that year heading into the meet was Dara Torres. At thirty-three, she was trying to become the first swimmer to win medals in four Olympics. Her first Olympics had been in 1984. That was the year before I was born.

I was hardly Dara Torres. I still had braces on my bottom teeth.

Bob and decided I would swim three races: the 200 fly, 200 IM, and 400 IM.

On the second day, in the 400 IM, I finished eleventh. Shake it off, Bob said. Let's focus on the 200 fly.

Malchow, the 1996 Olympic silver medalist and world record holder in 1:55.18, was the clear favorite. Three or four guys, including me, the third seed, were probably capable of going under 1:58. Up in the stands, the seats my family had gotten were crummy. Mom moved down to stand in a tunnel down by the diving well, an area where no standing was allowed. An usher told her to scoot. She said, "Just give me two minutes. Two minutes, two minutes, two minutes."

Before the race, Bob had told me that I'd probably be able to make up ground over the final 50 meters, per my style. Keep it close through the third turn, he said. Instead, at 150 meters, Mom started preparing an "I still love you" speech. Bob, too.

Over that last 50, I knew I was closing. But I had no idea whether I had closed enough. I touched. With my goggles on, I couldn't see the board right away, but I heard the announcer say my name and something about second place. I took the goggles off. The scoreboard said Malchow had come in first in 1:56.87. I was second, in 1:57.48.

My final 50 split had been nearly two seconds faster than Malchow's. He said on the pool deck, "I may have to retire sooner than I thought. He's exactly me four years ago. He doesn't know how much his life is going to change, but it's going to change real soon."

Not that much. Bob made sure of that.

The morning after making the 2000 Olympic team, I swam in a preliminary heat of the 200 IM at the Trials. The top sixteen made it to the next round; I finished twentieth.

In Sydney, for the first time in Olympic history, the U.S. women's swim team roster was older than the men's. Malchow had been the only teenager on the U.S. team in Atlanta. Now there were eight of us, five of whom would serve as mainstays for the American team for years to come:

Vendt was nineteen.

Ian Crocker and Klete Keller were eighteen.

Aaron Peirsol was seventeen.

And I was fifteen, still months away from even having a driver's license.

In Sydney, at the village, I roomed with Peirsol. He would go on to win silver in the 200 back.

In my first Olympic swim, I won my heat, in 1:57.30. In my semi, I lowered that to 1:57 flat. In both races, I swam with the strings of my suit untied. All I can say is, I was fifteen. The good news is, my suit didn't come off. The bad news is, it was like showing up for a job interview wearing a gray suit only to realize you had a blue sock on your left foot and a brown one on the right. A lack of preparation.

Bob had no access to the Olympic Village. At these Games, he was not formally a U.S. coach. He did have access to the pool deck from the people who ran Australian swimming. The times are okay, Michael, he told me. But these are the Olympic Games. You are going to treat them right. What did we say about preparation?

The next night, the plan was for me to leave the village early so I would get to the pool with, as they say in Australia, no worries. Bob wanted me there two-and-a-half hours before the race.

My cell phone rang.

"Hello."

"Hello, Bob."

"Michael, are you here at the pool?"

"No, I'm going back to the village."

"What? Now? Why?"

"I took the wrong credential. I was heading to the door and I grabbed Aaron's instead."

Bad. Very bad. Of course Bob was upset. To his credit, he did not yell.

"Well, okay," he said finally. "Let's get here and figure out what to do."

I got to the pool with a little bit more than an hour to go. We shortened my warm-up. I was jittery. When we walked out onto the deck, instead of doing my thing behind the block I walked over to Malchow to wish him luck. That's not the way it's done on the deck. I still don't know what I was thinking.

I swam that Olympic final in 1:56.50, a personal best, a time that would have won a medal at every previous Olympic final. It got me fifth. I was 33-hundredths of a second back of third place, and bronze.

Fifth. No medal.

Malchow won, in 1:55.35. He patted me on the back and said, "The best is ahead of you."

Bob sent me to the pool the next day for a

workout. The workout sheet said, "Austin WR." That meant the 2001 spring nationals in Austin, Texas. No medal at the Olympics? New goal. World record in the 200 fly in Austin.

The final day of the swim meet in Sydney was medley relay day. I painted my face half red and half blue and wrote "Team USA" across my chest, and as I sat there, watching the American men and the American women win the medleys, I thought how cool it would be to swim the relays, which, at these Games, I had no chance of doing. At North Baltimore, I loved the feeling of being on a team. In Sydney, I loved it even more.

Maybe, I thought, in Athens.

And, I thought, maybe in Athens we could avenge the two freestyle relays, the 400 and the 800. Both were major American disappointments in Sydney, especially the 400.

Before Sydney, the United States had won the 400 each of the seven times it had been included on the Olympic program. The Australians wanted this one bad. It was in their country. The race was to be held on the first night of racing. They had Ian Thorpe, who at those Games would prove he was among the world's most dominant swimmers, assigned to the anchor leg. They were fired up, and then they got fired up even more because of

Gary Hall, Jr., whose multiple Olympic medals included silver in the 100 free in 1996.

In an online diary published a month before the Olympics, Gary had written how much he respected the Australian swimmers. But he closed the article with a prediction that no one in Australia was soon going to forget: "We're going to smash them like guitars."

Everyone knew Gary would swim the anchor leg for the American team.

The rest was history.

An hour before the relay, Ian won the 400 free. He barely had time to change for the medals ceremony and then back into his bodysuit.

The Australians got out on the first leg. The Americans came back in the second. The Americans grabbed the lead in the first half of the third leg, but the Aussies came back. In the anchor leg, Gary passed Ian in the first length and turned six-tenths of a second ahead. With the home crowd roaring, Ian, who seemed so controlled, so languid almost in the water even as he was driving with ferocity to the wall, caught Gary with about 20 meters to go and edged ahead.

Ian knew when he touched that he had won. He sprang from the pool, and the Australians celebrated, with Michael Klim, who had taken the leadoff leg for the Aussies, memorably performing a mocking air-guitar concert on the deck.

"I doff my swimming cap to the great Ian Thorpe," Gary said later. "He had a better finish than I did."

I took it all in.

Lost in the commotion, at least for most people, was that third leg.

The American who swam that third leg: Jason Lezak.

The United States won thirty-three swimming medals in Sydney. Of the forty-eight swimmers on our team, forty-one came home with at least one medal. I was one of the seven who didn't.

In Austin the next spring, I got my world record. I defeated Malchow and went 1:54.92 in the 200 fly. I had become the youngest male ever to hold a world record. I was fifteen years and nine months old. Thorpe had been the youngest before that, sixteen years and ten months.

Not accomplishing my goal in Sydney had driven me for all the months in between. I had always known how badly it hurt to lose, how much I hated it. Now I had concrete proof of how losing could motivate me to reach my goals at the highest levels of swimming.

The win in Austin earned me a trip to the 2001 world championships, in Fukuoka, Japan. I won the 200 fly — my first world title — and lowered the world record again, to 1:54.58.

That summer, I started to get asked more and more about the 2004 Olympics. If I could make the team, I said, I'd like the chance to medal in more than just one event. I was looking at the two flys, the 100 and 200, and the two medleys, the 200 and 400. This wasn't bragging. This was a reflection of how I had always trained, with an emphasis on versatility.

That summer, too, I signed an endorsement contract with Speedo. The deal was for four years, through 2005. I was barely sixteen, the youngest American male swimmer to turn professional.

It was about that time as well that, as I kept saying to Bob, why are all these people all of a sudden asking me about Mark Spitz?

Mark made himself legendary in Munich in 1972. But his excellence and potential had been apparent for years. In 1967, when he was seventeen, he won five gold medals at the Pan American Games in Mexico City. He then predicted he would win six golds at the 1968 Summer Games, again in Mexico City. He did win two golds, in the relays. But no more. In his last individual event, the 200 fly, he finished last.

Mark went to college at Indiana. In those days, there was no such thing as turning professional. There were no professionals at the Olympics then, and there had not been ever since the Games were revived in 1896, in Athens. In the ancient Games, way back when, at Olympia, winners got only an olive wreath; when the modern Olympics got started, it was with that ideal in mind. The rules of eligibility originally were driven by the notions of European aristocracy, in particular the idea that it would be cheap and undignified to play for pay. That's why Jim Thorpe was stripped of the medals he won in the pentathlon and the decathlon at the Olympics in 1912 in Stockholm; the year after the Games, he acknowledged he had earned $25 per week playing minor-league baseball in North Carolina in 1909 and 1910. By the strictest definition of the rules, he had been a professional athlete and therefore ineligible to compete at the Olympics.

The president of the IOC from 1952 through those Munich Olympics in 1972, Avery Brundage, an American, made the amateur code his official passion. It made no difference to Brundage that athletes in, say, the Soviet Union could get a commission in the army. If Spitz wanted to swim in Munich, to avenge his performance in 1968, he had to do so as an amateur. He could go to college, accept a scholarship, but that was it.

This story was all part of the lore of swimming.

And, as well, what happened in 1972.

First Mark won the 200 fly, beating, among others, Gary Hall, Sr. He anchored the winning 400 free relay. He won the 200 free, after which, waving to fans while holding a pair of tennis shoes, he got dragged before the IOC, and Brundage. Mark was accused by some of endorsing a product, which would have made him a professional. The IOC admonished Mark but did not ban him, the whole thing is a study in hypocrisy; on the Olympic grounds, the IOC was promoting the sale of special Games postcards bearing the images of Mark and other swim standouts.

He went back to the pool and got two more golds, in the 100 fly and 800 relay. He won the 100 free. The seventh gold came as he swam the butterfly leg of the medley relay.

Mark was not only the first to win seven golds.

He was the first to win six.

And then his career was over.

If he had been allowed to make money, it clearly would have been in his — not to mention, those hypothetical sponsors — interests to keep swimming. He could have gone to the 1976 Games in Montreal. Probably not swim seven events again. But he would have been only twenty-six, very much in his prime.

But he had no choice. He couldn't ponder the what-if, if I stayed in, how many more medals could I have won?

A few days after winning the seventh medal, Mark posed for a photo in his Speedo stars-and-stripes suit. It sold millions. That poster is probably one of those things that they'll find in one of those time capsules from the 1970s that got buried somewhere. Along with that one of Farrah Fawcett four years later.

Change to the Olympic eligibility code was very slow in coming. It didn't really happen until after 1981, when Juan Antonio Samaranch of Spain took over the IOC. It wasn't until 1985, the year I was born, that the international swimming federation — it's called FINA, after its French name, *Fédération Internationale de Natation* — began to allow swimmers to accept training stipends from their national federations. After the 1988 Seoul Olympics, under the direction of Samaranch, the IOC voted to accept professional athletes.

The IOC has since left eligibility rules up to the various international sports federations. Boxing chose to stick with amateurs. Soccer limits each team at the Olympics to three players over age twenty-three. The rest of the sports were only too glad to welcome professionals. Thus, for instance, the 1992 Olympics in Barcelona provided a worldwide stage for the Dream Team, the U.S. men's basketball all-star team that romped to the gold medal with Michael Jordan, Larry Bird, Magic Johnson, and the rest.

American swimmers who made the 1992 Olympic team were eligible to get a $1,500 monthly check from USA Swimming, plus a bonus of $1,250. The contrast with the Dream Teamers could not have been more dramatic.

That's why some swimmers set out to test the waters, so to speak.

I was very fortunate to be able to see an example of this first-hand. At North Baltimore, Anita Nall, who after winning those three medals in Barcelona was without question a star of our club, became the youngest American female swimmer to turn pro. But she did so without an agent. She maybe made $250,000 as a pro, mostly making speeches and working at swim clinics, and that was it.

Other swimmers did the college thing. Malchow went to Michigan. Jenny Thompson went to Stanford and starred at four Olympics, starting in 1992.

Bob, my mom, and I had started talking after Sydney about me turning pro; the world records in the 200 fly intensified the conversations; the records obviously increased my bargaining power. We all talked, too, about how important it would be to find not just an agent but the right agent, not just someone who would help find sponsors and negotiate contracts. The right agent would also be innovative and creative.

As we were having these discussions, I had not even begun my junior year of high school. I knew that if I turned pro I would be giving up the chance to compete for conference or NCAA championships, and might well not have the chance to experience the fraternity of college swimming. But what I was trying to do was bigger than conference or NCAA championships. I had already set a world record. I had already been to the Olympics. I had taken a hard look at my goals and realized I wanted more than college. Going pro would help me focus on meeting those goals.

I was on track to get my high school diploma in 2003. The Athens Olympics were in 2004. What was I going to do for that year? If I were a professional swimmer, the answer to that would be easy.

Yes, my high school classmates would be into and through their first year of college. Going pro would mean putting any formal education on the back burner. Then again, traveling the world because of swimming might offer me the equivalent of graduate-level courses in business, marketing, and international relations.

I have always done my swimming in a Speedo suit.

That first deal with Speedo, signed in 2001, went through 2005. It included a clause that would pay for my college education if my swimming career didn't work out.

Obviously, I had promise, but was still very much a work in progress. About a month after the news broke that I had turned pro, I traveled to the U.S. Open short-course meet in Long Island. Walking onto the deck to swim the 200 back, I realized I had forgotten my cap and goggles. I looked at my mom. She shrugged her shoulders. I shrugged mine. I looked at Bob. Same thing.

I had to learn to change from being a kid to a professional. They say you learn more from your mistakes than anything.

If it seemed obvious, it was no less imperative to find an agent with Olympic experience. But whom?

The Salt Lake City Winter Olympics took place in February 2002. Bob was watching the *Today* show one morning when Matt Lauer introduced an agent named Peter Carlisle. Two of his snowboarding clients, Ross Powers and Kelly Clark, had won the halfpipe events in Salt Lake; Peter was on the show explaining strategies to reach young people interested in action sports, music, computer games. Bob put down his coffee cup.

This, he thought, is the guy.

It took two months to hold a meeting, as Peter was just too busy looking after his stars from those Winter Games. He was director of Olympic sports for Octagon, an agency based outside Washington, D.C., that had acquired his independent agency the year before. His home base was in Maine, where he grew up.

"So," Peter said to me at that first meeting, "what do you want for your future, Michael? What are your goals?"

I said the first thing that came to mind: "I want to change the sport of swimming."

In Australia, swimmers were on billboards, in commercials. Kids grow up there wanting to be swimmers the way they grow up in the United States wanting to play quarterback. In Australia, swimming was often the lead topic on the nightly news — not just the sports segment, the entire news show. How often was swimming even shown on a sports highlight show in the United States?

I was still sixteen years old. I wasn't trying to be overbearing. I truly did not think I was that full of myself. I had been asked a question and was trying to answer it honestly.

"I want to change the sport of swimming, I want people to talk about it, think about it, and look forward to seeing it. I want them to want to jump in and do it. That's my goal."

I signed up with Peter that summer. He negotiated a deal with Visa that put me in line to make me one of the athletes it would feature in the run-up to the 2004 Olympics. And then he waited.

Peter has a guilty pleasure: reality television. He was fascinated by the dynamics of *Survivor*. What does the winner of *Survivor* get?

A $1 million check.

The first meet of mine that Peter saw in person came in the summer of 2002, the summer nationals in Fort Lauderdale, Florida. The meet, the U.S. qualifier for the 2003 Worlds in Barcelona, ended with me being the first man since Spitz to hold four American records. The next year, in Barcelona, I became the first swimmer to lower world records in different events on the same day.

While in Barcelona, the time had come. Peter asked to meet with Speedo's executives. He said, we need to renegotiate the contract, for all the right reasons.

What, they asked, do you want?

He said, a million bucks. If, in Athens, Michael matches Spitz's seven golds, you pay him a million bucks.

There were other details — a base salary, smaller bonuses for some lesser number of medals in Athens, and so on — but the million was the nut of the deal. Think, Peter told the company's executives, of the publicity this would bring not just Michael, but Speedo.

Incentive deals are common in pro football and baseball. You make the Pro Bowl, you get an extra $100,000. You make baseball's All-Star team, here's $50,000. Or whatever. This simply extended an idea that had become commonplace in other sports to swimming.

Carmelo Anthony went to high school a mile away from where I did. He spent one year in college, leading Syracuse to an NCAA championship. Then he was drafted by the Denver Nuggets. In July 2003, the Nuggets signed him to a four-year, $15.1 million contract. Five days later, I dove into the water for my first heat in the 200 fly at the Worlds in Barcelona. If I was in swimming solely to make money, I was in the wrong sport.

And this: Carmelo was going to be on television dozens of times that fall. Swimming wasn't going to be seen live on any American television network during all of 2003.

My Speedo deal, with the $1 million bonus, was announced in November 2003 and, from then on, I had to navigate a balance.

It wasn't until the Fort Lauderdale meet the year before that Bob had even allowed himself to think I might have the capability to reach for seven medals.

In fact, it had been such a nonstarter that, asked about it early in the meet by a reporter from the Colorado Springs newspaper — the U.S. Olympic Committee is based there, and so what's written by the local paper, the

Gazette, gets noticed by Olympic insiders everywhere — Bob almost snorted. "You can compare Michael to Mark Spitz in that he swims a lot of different events in different strokes at a high level," he said. "Now can he win seven events, seven gold medals? That's very difficult to do in this day and age.

". . . I can't imagine right now we'd try an event program that would be that ambitious."

Still, Bob said, "I'm not going to rule it out."

I had told the same reporter it might be fun to aim for. "It's harder now than it was back then. If you can do it, wow!"

Bob was having no more *wow* talk. As soon as the thought of seven came up, he shoved it right back down. The way to think about seven medals wasn't to talk about it. It was to train.

The bonus, predictably, generated enormous publicity. That was good. But complex.

It was essential never to be disrespectful of any of my teammates or rivals. Not that I ever would. I simply had to be aware of the dynamic. Each of them had goals, too.

It was key to be respectful in everything I said and did about Mark. That was easy. What he did was amazing. It deserves enormous respect. He has, always has had, mine.

It was also critical to separate myself from Mark. I wasn't trying to be him. I was me. And what I wanted, what I was after, was to do something no one else had done. That's what I set my mind to, and that's what I was going for.

It's not a lie that I wanted to beat the record. It's not a secret. I just wasn't going to come out and say it. Why would I? The only person who could help me accomplish my goals was Bob. No offense to anyone in the media, but is a reporter going to help me swim faster? A reporter going to help me win any medal of any kind? That's why I kept everything to myself. It wasn't necessary to share my goals with anyone but Bob. So I didn't do it.

If I was asked, can you beat Spitz? I might say, you never know what can happen. I would then go on to say, the only person I can worry about is myself. If I can prepare the best I can, that's all I can ask. If I go in and still get beat with my best time, that's all I can ask for. I can't say yes or no.

To answer, well, of course I want to beat him and I think I can, would be impolite and immodest. It would be trash-talking. Not my way.

My goals were my goals, and they were to

win as many as I could win. If everything broke right, I could win a number that, as it turns out, rhymes with the word "fate." Bob and I planned it. He said: You have the ability to swim these events at a high level. Show the world what you can do. Never mind the world. Show yourself.

We called it Plan A.

To see Plan A to its completion, I had to swim relays.

A major international swim meet lasts eight days. Even so, there are only so many individual events that it would be possible, even in theory, to swim, because race finals are sometimes scheduled one after the other, sometimes within minutes.

If I was to break into the 400 relay, that meant I had to, among other things, start swimming faster in the 100 free. I was told in Barcelona, and this was by one of the guys on our team, you'll never break 50 seconds.

I didn't say anything back. Everyone would learn, eventually, that, aside from losing itself, nothing made me more determined than when someone doubted me.

At the 2003 summer nationals in College Park, Maryland, just down the road from Baltimore, I won the 100 free in 49.19. Six months later, in Orlando, at the spring nationals, I won again, in 49.05, even though my reaction time off the blocks, 1.21 seconds, was awful, and I was dead last at the turn. In Santa Clara, California, in the spring of 2004, Jason and I raced head-to-head in the 100; I won.

I did not compete in the 100 free at the 2004 Trials. Jason won, in 48.41, ahead of Ian Crocker, in 49.06. Gary Hall, Jr. was just behind Ian, in 49.16. In fourth: Neil Walker, who for years had been one of the most reliable American relay guys.

In seventh place at those 2004 Trials: Garrett Weber-Gale.

Because I didn't swim in the 100 free at the Trials, of course there was some tension that revolved around whether I should get to swim in the 400 relay in Athens. It surfaced immediately in Long Beach.

I didn't swim the race at the Trials because I didn't have to. The fact is, any member of an Olympic team can be used in the relay. My 49.05 in Orlando was faster than Ian had gone at the Trials. I had beaten Jason in Santa Clara.

Obviously, though, if I swam, someone else was not going to.

At that point, Gary had eight Olympic medals. He had experience and pride. Having been beaten by Thorpe in the 400 relay final in Sydney, he was naturally seeking another chance. His point, as he told reporters, was, "Somebody swam the 100 free and earned a spot on that relay. You're talking about a lifetime of work. I'm supportive of Michael and his goals. I want to see the relay win gold. It's only fair for the individuals who earned a place on the relay to swim in the Olympics. Four of us are swimming for one spot if Michael's there."

The answer came from Eddie Reese, the U.S. men's coach. Our American men hadn't won a major international relay since 1998. Eddie, like Gary — like me, like all of us — wanted to win in Athens. When we got there, he said, somebody had to swim a split time of 48.2 or 48.3, roughly equivalent to a sub-49 time in an individual 100 free, to grab one of the spots in the final; a 48.2 or 48.3 relay split would trump the 49.05 I had done in Orlando. If fewer than two did so, I would swim with Ian and Jason, who by virtue of going one-two at the Trials had clinched two of the spots.

"I want Michael Phelps in as many events as possible," Eddie said, "and in as many as he can do well."

When we got to Athens, Neil swam a 48.16 split in the prelims. He got a spot in the finals. Gary went 48.73. He did not.

I know Gary didn't like not being on that relay in the finals, but you're not going to like everything that happens in life.

Ian, Neil, Jason and me, and I asked to swim leadoff. Bob asked that I swim leadoff. That's where I would feel the most comfortable.

Two reasons: I like being able to get an early lead, and I thought I could.

Also, for the guy going second, third, or fourth, the timing of leaving the blocks is an intricate thing. The ultimate goal is to time the dive so that you're horizontal to the water surface, but with your feet still in contact with the blocks, as the swimmer in the water is making his touch.

The coaching staff went with a different order: Ian, me, Neil, Jason.

Ian went first. He was fifth at the turn. And then he just didn't have it. He touched in 50.05, dead last, and what turned out to be the slowest time of any of the thirty-two guys in the field.

I swam 48.74. That got us into sixth. Neil went 47.97, the fastest split of his career, to get us to third. Jason swam furiously and for a moment we were in second. But he was passed in the closing meters by Pieter van den Hoogenband of the Netherlands.

The South Africans won in world-record

time, 3:13.17. The Dutch came in second, in 3:14.36. We finished third, in 3:14.62. It was the worst American showing ever in an Olympic 400 free relay.

"I'm sorry. It's my fault. It's my fault," Ian said.

"Dude, this is one race," I told him.

Gary did not even show up to watch. Word was that he stayed in the village.

Eddie, meanwhile, apparently did not know that Ian, who had swum in college for Eddie at the University of Texas, was sick, with a runny nose and a sore throat.

That race, which came on just the second day of the meet, abruptly ended any notions of going beyond seven gold medals in Athens. At the start of the Games, I had watched the movie *Miracle*, the story of the 1980 U.S. Olympic hockey team. Now, it looked as though I might need to call on a miracle of my own if I had any hope of seeing Plan A through; I would have to win all six of my remaining events, and in some of those events — the 200 free, in particular — I would not be the favorite.

But that's not why the walk off the pool deck that night was a long one. It would be a long four years until we could again claim that relay gold for the United States, where it belonged.

■ ■ ■ ■

The time I put up in Omaha in the 100 free prelims at the 2008 Trials, 47.92, tied Garrett's winning time in the Trials finals. This time around, there wasn't any question as to whether I was deserving; there would be no controversy about whether I ought to be one of the four swimming the 400 relay finals at the Olympics.

Garrett, after that seventh-place finish in the 2004 Trials, had steadily been improving, training in Texas with Eddie, whom Garrett's dad calls the "Zen master of swimming." For years, Eddie has been telling Garrett he has the gift of the kick. Eddie would keep telling Garrett: Kick! Kick! It wasn't until the Beijing Olympics were in sight, in the spring of 2008, that Garrett finally got it. Going into the Trials and then onto Beijing, you could tell Garrett was mentally just right there. Garrett is something of a foodie — he loves restaurants and collects recipes for dishes like smoky salmon jerky — but had been working all year with a nutritionist and had been on a low-sugar, low-protein diet. He kept saying that the rigorous diet was in part to help train his mind; he said it made him feel like he had an edge and was ready to go. If you don't expect to do well, he kept saying at the Trials, you're not going to swim fast. In Omaha, Garrett won both the 100 and the 50. He was swimming fast, even setting an American record of 21.47 in the 50, after which he treated himself to dessert for the first time in nearly three months: one raspberry sorbet.

Jason was swimming fast, too, going 47.58, also an American record, at the Trials in the 100 semifinals. And Jason was thirty-two years old. Just to compare: At the Trials, Garrett was twenty-two, I turned twenty-three during the meet, Cullen was twenty-four, and here was Jason, at thirty-two, still bringing it strong. Jason and I had been hanging out together on national teams since Sydney, but there was something different about him this time around. He was more relaxed and more social this year than I had ever seen him before. Not that he wasn't relaxed or social before, but it was obvious that he was appreciating what we had this time, an unbelievable sense of team and of camaraderie.

At the Olympic Village, I was put into a six-person suite with Lochte, Jones, Shanteau, Vendt, and Gil Stovall. Shanteau had made the 2008 team in the 200 breast; Vendt had made it for the prelims of the 800-meter free relay; Stovall was an up-and-comer in the 200 fly. Jason would come into our suite at the village and hang out while we were playing card games; Lochte and I would be taking on Cullen and Shanteau in spades. Jason would just soak it all in, would sit there, a big part of it all, all of us laughing and appreciating the moment and each other.

The sense of togetherness on this 2008 U.S. men's Olympic swim team will forever be one of my great memories from Beijing. In the pool, we had to compete. Outside of it, we were not just teammates but brothers. Every single one of us.

Before the Olympics started, we held an athletes-only meeting. No coaches. Some of us who had been at prior Games told the new guys about those memories. About how some of the best moments come away from the pool. About how being on the American swim team is one of the biggest honors anyone could ever have. About trying to savor not just the competition but the experience.

And about some of our goals for the Olympics, one of which was crystal clear: Take back the 400 relay gold.

Jason, in particular, was tired of losing. He swam the third leg on the 2000 relay, the anchor in 2004. Silver and bronze. He wanted gold.

And now comes Bob, the morning of the race, to say the French are trash-talking? They're going to smash us like guitars? Gary's words from 2000, now thrown in our face?

When I heard that, it was like a switch flipped in my body, like, you really want to do that? We didn't need any more motivation. But we had just gotten it.

I said to Jason at breakfast, you hear what the French are saying?

He just smiled.

Bob and I saw Garrett on his way back from breakfast. Hey, guess what the French said?

I don't want to hear it, Garrett said. We'll take care of business when we get out to the pool.

We got to the pool pretty fired up. And then we got fired up more.

In the hallway outside the ready room, the four of us got together in a football huddle. The talk immediately turned raw and emotional.

Jason said he had been on losing relays before. I'm not, he said, going to let it happen again. This, he said, is not a 4x100 relay, four guys each swimming a 100. There's nothing here about swimming a leg individually. This is a 400 relay; we're all together. We're all

151

going to be one. He said we have to prepare ourselves and go out there and kick it.

We were like: Yeah, yeah, yeah. Bouncing up and down. Ready to rock. Fired up.

Out on the deck, in introductions, nobody said a word. Nobody had to. We drew next to each other and raised our hands up in unison. A team. Together.

This was obviously going to be a super-fast race. Six of the eight teams in the final had gone faster in the 2008 prelims than the South Africans had done in winning the 2004 relay in Athens in a then-world record 3:13.17. Including the South Africans, who were back with the same four guys.

The Australians had Eamon Sullivan, the world-record holder in the 50 and a complete threat in the 100. They were for sure going to swim fast.

The French had three guys who had come on in the last year, one of them Bernard, the 100 world-record holder with that 47.5. He had broken the 100 record twice in March. They would swim fast.

Bring it on.

We were ready to rock, ready to swim fast, too.

Faster.

Until this moment, five guys in the entire world had gone under 48 seconds in an open

100 this year. Bernard, Sullivan, and three Americans: Garrett, Jason, and me.

The pressure had to be on the French. They had never won a medal in the event. They were trying to win France's first swimming relay gold.

I got up on the block, above Lane 4. My guys behind me were calling, come on, Mike! Come on, Phelps! Lead it off! Step it up! Let's go! I started to get chills.

The beep sounded.

I knew the French guy, Amaury Leveaux, second-fastest ever in the 50, was going to be out quick. The plan was to stay with him. He was in Lane 5, to my left. Sullivan, the Australian, was to my right, in Lane 3.

At 25 meters, halfway down the first length, I saw that Sullivan was already half a body length ahead of me. If I want to have a good split, I thought at the turn, I have got to win this leg.

Bang-bang-bang. In the relays, you're in the water and just that fast, you're out. I didn't win the leg. I had put us in second place, behind the Australians, and Sullivan. But I knew I had turned in a good leg. I had no idea about anyone's times, mine, anyone's. As soon as I touched I got out of the pool and got back behind our lane. I started cheering like no one has ever cheered before.

Garrett, in his first Olympic swim, moved us up to first. He overtook Australia's Andrew Lauterstein; the Aussies slipped back to third. Swimming second for the French was Fabien Gilot, who, going into the race, had put down the sixth-fastest time in the world that year in the 100; he moved France up into second at 200. Less than a second separated all three teams.

Cullen took off. So did France's Bousquet. We all knew about Bousquet. He spent four years, from 2001 to 2005, swimming for Auburn. He had an immense tattoo on his left shoulder. He was also no-doubt-about-it fast; with the flying starts the relays allow, he had gone 46.63 in the prelims the night before. That was the fastest relay split in history.

Bousquet poured it on. He took the lead going toward the far wall.

Cullen hung tough.

Bousquet touched. Bernard leaped into the water.

Cullen touched. Jason dove off after him. When they surfaced, Jason looked to be about half a body length behind.

Bernard, in his white cap, roared toward the far wall. Jason, to his right, hung to the left lane line. Technically perfect. So smart. He was riding in behind the wave that

Bernard, who is 6-feet-5, was making in Lane 5.

At the final turn, Bernard was 82-hundredths ahead, almost a full length.

If anyone else was starting to give up hope, Garrett, Cullen, and I were giving up nothing. We believed. Cullen, who had just finished his leg, was jumping up and down by the side of the pool. The noise level inside the Cube by now was furious. Garrett and I started screaming: Get this guy!

Behind the blocks, we could see that after his turn Bernard had made a stupid, and what would turn out to be colossal, mistake. After the flip, instead of swimming in the middle of his lane, he had drifted to the left. That meant that Jason, now to Bernard's left, could again tuck in behind him. Bernard was doing the hard work. Jason was cruising, preparing to slingshot by Bernard.

And Jason was starting to close. Jason would say later that when he turned and saw how far ahead Bernard was, he thought, no way; coming into the race, Bernard was the fastest guy in the world in the 100. But then, Jason said, he immediately thought, you know what, that is ridiculous. I'm here for my guys. I'm here for the United States of America. I don't care how bad it hurts. I'm just going to go out there and hit it. Jason thought all this in a split second. He got, as he described it, a super-charge, more adrenaline than he'd ever had. It was electric. The moment was electric.

Jason started swimming as if he were possessed. Bernard began to falter. He was suddenly tight. Overswimming it. Maybe his hellacious first 50 had left him without enough to finish.

Get this guy!

Garrett started pounding on the block.

We both were screaming. Big time.

Get this guy!

Jason closed some more. With each stroke, he was gaining. Clearly he was going to catch Bernard, if only he had enough pool left to do it.

With about 15 meters left, it suddenly looked like Jason would have enough pool.

Jason and Bernard churned toward the finish.

I was smacking the block. Smacking that block. Smacking it. Screaming. Garrett, to my right, was screaming.

Jason lunged toward the wall.

Garrett and I looked across the pool, at the big board.

Yes!

Next to the number 1, it said: United States.

Jason had touched first, in 3:08.24. The French were second, eight-hundredths behind. U-S-A! Victory!

I punched the air with my right fist. I threw both my arms up, touchdown style. Garrett put his arm around me for just a moment as I leaned back and screamed with everything I had. Garrett moved just a step away and flexed like he was Arnold Schwarzenegger in the 1970s.

I reached down and slapped Jason's hands in the water. I turned to the stands to my left, arched my back, and roared again. I had never been so excited in my entire life.

Cullen came over from the side of the pool. He and I had a fast hug. Jason climbed out of the water and hugged Garrett. All four of us got together and embraced, formed a huddle, like the one just a few minutes before in the hall outside the ready room. Way to go, guys, I said. We did it. That relay is ours again.

The huddle broke. "That's what I'm talking about!" I yelled.

Bernard was still in the pool. He had heaved his elbows onto the deck. He was just hanging there, heaving, exhausted, disappointed.

One of the French racers, Gilot, said afterward, *"C'est le sport,"* which means literally,

"It's sport," but in this context really meant, "That's why you race the race."

Jason had just thrown down the fastest relay split in history, 46.06 seconds. "America," Jason would say later, "has a great tradition of winning that relay. All of us knew what we're capable of, but to actually do it, to get that tradition back, it's a phenomenal feeling. Still, right now, I'm in disbelief."

All of us were. Later, when we ran the numbers, all we could say was: unbelievable, and incredible.

Our time, 3:08.24, was almost exactly four full seconds faster than the world record that Nathan, Cullen, Ben, and Matt had gone in the prelims. It had taken eighteen years, from the Seoul Olympics in 1988 until 2006, for the record to drop four seconds to the 3:12 range. Nathan, Cullen, Ben and Matt had cut another two-tenths of a second off the mark; now we had dropped it, the very next day, nearly four full seconds. Incredible.

Five of the eight teams in the relay final swam under the mark that Nathan, Cullen, Ben and Matt had set in the prelims. The Australians took bronze. The Swedes and Italians also went under what had been that world record time, and got nothing. No medal. Unbelievable.

My first-leg split, 47.51, was a new American record, just one-hundredth of a second off what had been the world record going into the race. That time was a personal best by 41-hundredths. It was just one-hundredth off my goal sheet time.

I had turned the race over to Garrett with us in second only because Sullivan, two lanes over, had set a new world record, 47.24. Two days later, Bernard would go 47.20, only to be outdone again, this time by Sullivan, 47.05.

The four of us Americans walked over to the NBC broadcast position on the deck. Andrea Kremer, the network's poolside reporter throughout the Olympics in Beijing, got us all together in front of the camera.

"Well," she said, "the French had said we're gonna smash the Americans. Who's talking now, guys?"

"We are," Garrett said. "United States of America."

This relay had loomed as one of the toughest races for me if I were to make it to eight. Thanks to my teammates, maybe, in Beijing in 2008, my dreams really could come true. There was a lot of swimming yet to go, an unforeseeable future. But maybe.

Jason couldn't have been more gracious. "I think Michael knows we didn't do this for him," he said. "He was just a part of it. We were a part of it."

Cullen, too. "He's on a mission to win eight and we're happy to be a part of it."

And Garrett. "And we wanted one of these, too," he said, meaning the gold medals they gave us when we had ascended the podium, arms together, to celebrate a race that the president of the United States had watched us win. President Bush had been back in the stands at the Cube.

The president told reporters that he had been watching me as Jason touched, watched my exuberance and joy. "The whole thing is genuine," President Bush said. "That's the good thing about the Olympics."

I have been asked many, many times since whether, because Jason's extraordinary effort kept alive my shot at the $1 million bonus, I said something to Jason about it, or his effort. The answer is no. There were no words, except for those Jason said himself: "People always step up and do things out of the ordinary at the Olympics."

3
REDEMPTION:
THE 200 FREESTYLE

When the $1 million bonus play was being studied and weighed, all of us knew that winning seven golds against world-class competition, much less eight, meant everything would have to break the right way.

That said, it was far from impossible.

Was I setting myself up for media hype? Absolutely.

Would I be perceived as a failure in some quarters if I didn't reach eight or seven? No doubt.

Would it nonetheless create unprecedented buzz for swimming? For sure, and that made the decision to go forward easy.

There are two ways to look at the hype and the attention. You can look at it as a negative, as pressure. Or you can look at it as a positive, as support.

I got those lines from Ian Thorpe. In response to any question about attention, those lines served as his standard response.

After a while, I learned to make the answer more my own. I'm glad people are interested, I would say. I don't look at it as pressure, only as expectations, but the only expectations I focus on are those I have for myself, because those are the only ones I can do something about.

In practice, I sometimes pass the time doing laps by singing in my head the last song I heard in the car on the way to the pool.

I got that from Ian Thorpe.

There was a lot I could learn from Ian Thorpe, the least of which had to do with swimming.

I have always looked up to Michael Jordan, the way he changed his sport, just the way I want to help change swimming. Ian, in Australia, was like Michael Jordan. The man.

When, in Fukuoka, Japan, in 2001, I won my first world title, in the 200 fly, Ian was in the midst of winning the 200, 400, and 800 freestyles, all in world-record time; he also anchored the Australian team to victory in all three relays. Ian's three world records came in four days; the six gold medals came in seven events — he finished fourth in the 100 free — and amounted to the most any male had won at a major international meet since Spitz, in 1972. My world record at that meet, in the 200 fly, had actually been the second one set on the night I swam; Ian had broken the record in the 400 free. At the Olympics in Sydney the year before, Ian had won five medals, three of them gold. In Fukuoka, he was even better. The day after I broke that mark in the 200 fly, a newspaper headline screamed, "Teenage Stars Thorpe, Phelps Break Records." Ian was eighteen, turning nineteen that October. I was barely sixteen. He was the star, the main attraction. And, at first, it was hard to think I had business being in the same headline — in some regards, at least at that point, even in the same pool. One day, warming up, Ian slipped into the water and blew by; he made up what seemed like 20 meters on me in two strokes.

Of all the records that Ian set in Fukuoka, the one that was without a doubt most impressive came in the 200 free. In Sydney, Ian had lost the 200 free to Pieter van den Hoogenband, Pieter touching in 1:45.35, which tied Pieter's own world record. At the Australian championships the next March, Ian went 1:44.69. In Fukuoka, he went 1:44.06. That time seemed ungodly fast, a record that might last for years, maybe a decade or more. At least that's what van den Hoogenband said, and most everyone who

163

knew anything about swimming, and the limits of human performance, agreed.

While Ian was magnificent in the pool, he was a study in how to behave out of it.

What composure. At a press conference in Fukuoka, he was asked if he could recite words he had learned in Japanese; he responded with a list of about thirty, the list including words and phrases that weren't related to each other. The follow-up question came: could he recite the same list in English? Ian did so, just as he had done in Japanese, not making even a single slip in the sequence.

Bob unabashedly used Ian as a model for my development. That made sense. There were remarkable parallels.

Ian had started swimming because his big sister did, like me with my older sisters. I didn't want to put my face in the water at first; he was initially thought to be allergic to chlorine. Ian's sister, Christina, and mine, Whitney, competed at the 1995 Pan Pacific Championships; neither made the 1996 Olympics. Ian's mom was a schoolteacher; mine was a teacher, later a principal. Ian was twelve when Doug Frost became his coach; I was eleven when Bob arrived at North Baltimore. He grew to be 6-feet-4; me, too. The 200 fly in Austin in 2001 made me the youngest male to set a world record; Ian had been the youngest before me. Moreover, Ian was the youngest world champion ever, just three months past his fifteenth birthday when he won the 400 free at the 1998 Worlds.

The pressure on Ian at the 2000 Olympics was intense; he was one of the country's biggest heroes in a nation where the majority of people live within a few miles of the water, seemingly everyone swims, and the Olympic effort in swimming is grossly out of proportion to its population. There are about 20 million people in Australia, compared to more than 300 million in the United States. Even so, going back decades, Australians have been winning swimming medals at the Olympics in bunches. At the 1956 Summer Games in Melbourne, Aussies won every event in freestyle, the Australian crawl. At the Sydney Games, with those five medals, Ian more than delivered; he was chosen to be the Australian flag-bearer in the closing ceremony.

An explosion of patriotic excitement enveloped Australia when Ian won the 400 at the Sydney Games. He was just seventeen; the 400 final was held on the first night of competition; the place was jammed with his countrymen; he led from start to finish; and he set a world record, 3:40.59. There's a photo of Ian touching at the finish, so far ahead of everyone, that Bob had framed. The moment was so moving for Bob that, in Ann Arbor, he hung the photo in a place of honor, over his piano.

Three nights after that 400, Ian came in second in the 200 free, behind van den Hoogenband. To all of Australia, this was a huge surprise. To Ian, too. Backstage at the Sydney Games, Bob had gone into a bathroom moments after that 200 free final; Ian walked in a moment later. For maybe a beat or two after he walked in, Ian looked totally in shock. But that's why he had gone into the bathroom, to compose himself, away from everyone and everything. It took just a moment. He and Bob saw each other, acknowledged each other's presence, and Bob said, "Hey, good job." Ian replied, "Thanks," and went out to meet the press.

Ian had been a public figure in Australia since he was fourteen. He was clever enough to copyright his nickname, "Thorpedo." He was active in charity work. He struck endorsement deals with major corporate interests. At the Sydney Olympics, you couldn't cross the street, it seemed, without seeing Ian's face on a billboard, couldn't watch television without seeing Ian in a commercial;

he had contracts with, among others, an airline and a bank. Later, he would have his own underwear line. Ian had interests in fashion and culture and moved easily within those circles everywhere in the world, especially in New York City; he was in New York on the morning of September 11, 2001, and had stopped at the World Trade Center on a morning run before going back to his hotel. He went on to help try to promote New York City's unsuccessful bid for the 2012 Summer Olympics.

In Australia, Ian was a star among stars. A couple of years after the Worlds in Fukuoka, a Sydney newspaper held a contest: Who would you like to invite to your home for Christmas? Russell Crowe finished fourth, Nicole Kidman third, then-Prime Minister John Howard second. Ian won.

Like many Aussies, Ian has always had a candor about him. In January 2008, in Beijing for the formal opening of the Water Cube, Ian was asked there by reporters whether that summer I could win eight gold medals.

"I don't think he will do it but I'd love to see it," Ian said. "There's a thing called competition. It won't just be one athlete that will be competing, and in a lot of events he has a lot of strong competition."

Bob, always sleuthing, knew I would be keen to read Ian's opinion.

At the Michigan pool, I had a collection of suits, caps, goggles, towels, and water bottles in my locker, all of it stashed around a big hook hanging from the locker top. After reading the sheet of paper with Ian's remarks, I took that paper and jammed it right onto that hook.

It stayed there all that winter, all that spring, into the summer, until we went to Omaha and the Trials. Every day when I'd open that locker, it was the first thing I'd see, that article, Ian's words, dangling there. Every day when I'd close that locker door, that fluttering piece of paper served as a reminder of the many doubters.

One of my early training tools consisted of videotape that Bob had picked up. It was of Ian overtaking Grant Hackett, another Australian, to win that 400 free at the 1998 Worlds. Ian's stokes, so fluid, managed somehow to combine economy and power. His freestyle kick, with his size-17 feet, was like a motor. Unreal. I started trying to make my kick more like his, to make it as powerful as I could. Then there was his dolphin kick, which was nothing less than revolutionary. At turns, instead of pushing off the wall and then surfacing, he would stay underwater, where there was less resistance than up top, for several meters, his feet and legs moving together instead of kicking separately, the motion creating an incredible whip through the water that mimicked the movements of a dolphin.

The videotape, a grainy VHS thing, veered from the race to a poolside interview that Ian conducted immediately afterward. I also studied the way Ian talked, the way he held his hands, where he looked.

It was all part of Bob's effort to get me to be serious. I got serious.

The rules say you're allowed to kick under-water off the turn for a full 15 meters. During the summer of 2002, Bob and I resolved to work that dolphin kick into my training, into my IM sets. If we did ten 400 IMs, for instance, I would dolphin kick on the last two, from breast to free; then work my way up to four, six, eight, and, finally, ten.

At those 2002 summer nationals in Fort Lauderdale, I saw for the first time at a big meet what a weapon that dolphin kick could be. A month beforehand, Vendt had beaten me in a 400 IM; that would be the last time I would lose, a streak I carried into and through the Olympics in Athens and Beijing. In Fort Lauderdale, Erik turned first at 350;

I stayed under for another 12 meters before breaking the surface. Watching a video of the race afterward, I could see that Erik had taken five full strokes before I even broke the surface. At the finish, I got the touch. Both of us finished in under world-record time, me in 4:11.09, Erik in 4:11.27.

Because I was naturally a butterflyer, the dolphin kick was relatively easy to pick up. In the IMs, it became an equalizer; even if other guys had a better breaststroke, I could use the dolphin on the turns. If they were getting tired on that final leg, I still had something to unleash.

Just three days after that meet ended, we went to the Pan Pacs, back in Japan, this time in Yokohama. I finished with three gold medals and two silvers. After the last race, I got on a bus, and there was Ian. We talked about this and that and, at one point, he said, if you ever want to train together, I'd be more than happy to have you in Australia. I was pumped. To be able to train with Ian Thorpe — cool. Think of what I'd learn. Hey, I said, and you can train with me in Baltimore, too.

When we got off the bus that night, no one paid any attention to me; those who had been waiting pushed by me to get a glimpse of Ian.

Bob spent a fair amount of time over the next six months trying to coordinate flights, pool times, training schedules, even an appearance at a training clinic in Australia. A week before we were to go, Ian's new coach, Tracy Menzies, e-mailed to say they were backing out. Something had come up, we were told.

This was a major disappointment.

There were other disappointments along the way as well.

We still went to Australia, where I trained with Hackett. Trained hard. For example, we raced each other over 50 meters, with and without fins, thirty times. We raced each other with pulleys. We raced freestyle; no wonder the Aussies were such great freestylers.

While there, Bob and I agreed to speak to what we were told would be a couple of reporters; there ended up being more than three dozen. We mentioned in passing that our morning practice the next day would be open to anyone who wanted to watch. We got to the pool at five-thirty in the morning. It was raining. We didn't expect to see a soul. The deck was jammed, a mass of people end to end. This was what swimming was all about in Australia. Why couldn't it be like this in the United States?

Grant, and Ian, and others had taken a sport that was already at the top in their country and moved it even farther along. As a sign of my profound respect, I wanted to measure myself against them even more after the trip Down Under than before. It was unlikely I would ever race against Grant; he was pursuing distance events, I was not. But to compete against Ian would be the ultimate. The 2003 Worlds in Barcelona would be coming up soon enough.

Bob's coaching philosophy can be distilled as follows:

Set your goals high. Work conscientiously, every day, to achieve them.

Among the many authors Bob has read, he likes to cite the motivational speaker Earl Nightingale, who survived the attack on Pearl Harbor on the USS *Arizona,* then went on to a career in broadcasting. The way Bob tells it, Nightingale's work revealed the one thing that's common to all successful people: They make a habit of doing things that unsuccessful people don't like to do.

That's it. That's Bob's game. His drill, while sometimes fabulously complex, is really quite simple — make a habit of doing things others weren't willing to do.

There are plenty of people with some

amount of talent. Are you willing to go farther, work harder, be more committed and dedicated than anyone else?

If others were inclined to take Sunday off, well, that just meant we might be one-seventh better.

For five years, from 1998 to 2003, we did not believe in days off. I had one because of a snowstorm, two more due to the removal of wisdom teeth. Christmas? See you at the pool. Thanksgiving? Pool. Birthdays? Pool. Sponsor obligations? Work them out around practice time.

On September 11, 2001, I reported to afternoon practice at Meadowbrook. Bob began the session, which ultimately ended early, with a defiant pep talk. We don't stop for snow, for rain, for a flood, and we for sure aren't going to stop for terrorists, he declared. Terrorists might kill innocent Americans but not our dreams. They want us to sit home and be scared. That, he said, is not us.

During those years, Bob figured, counting meets, that I could work in the pool about 550 times each year. In all, between Sydney and Athens, about 2,200 times, enough to swim somewhere around 9,000 miles.

I loved it when people who have no clue — mostly guys I knew from high school who had played other sports — would say to me, swimming can't be that hard. Okay, I would say, why don't you come do our workout for a day?

I knew I could get by in whatever workout anyone else might have. I could run. I could catch. I could play defense in football or lacrosse. I could kick a soccer ball, hit a baseball.

I guarantee you, I would say, there is not a chance you would make it through even my warm-up.

Yeah, right, dude, they'd say.

Then come, I'd say.

No one ever did.

To understand how much more difficult it is to move through water than it is through air, consider the time differences between world-class times in swimming events on one hand, track and field on the other. The difference is roughly four or five to one. In the pool, it takes about 47 seconds for the best swimmers now to cover 100 meters; it's under 10 on the track. In the water, it's about 1:43 now for 200 meters, under 20 seconds on the track. The Olympic 1500-meter champion goes about 14:45 in the pool, about 3:30 on the track.

In my workouts, I was determined not only to sustain versatility but to emphasize it. I thus had to develop both speed and endurance.

An endurance block of training might last for six or seven months. I would swim nearly 50 miles each week, about 80,000 meters. Each day's workouts would come in segments, those segments based on a particular base distance (50, 100, 200 meters) as well as on the number and intensity of repetitions of the distance, the stroke, and the interval, meaning the time I'd get to rest before starting the next repetition.

The speed block could mean roughly 37 miles each week, about 60,000 meters, but with 600 to 800 meters each day at race pace.

There were times when Bob pushed me even harder.

In the winter of 2002, after the success I'd had in Fort Lauderdale, pointing toward those 2003 Worlds in Barcelona, I averaged 85,000 meters per week in the pool. The next spring, Bob ratcheted it down to 75,000. Clearly, I was going to be in outlandishly good condition.

A few years beforehand, Bob had started using another saying, one that has come to define the way he and I approach these grueling blocks of training. When we practice long and hard, he would say, we're depositing money into the bank. We need to deposit enough so that, when we make a large withdrawal, we have enough funds to do so.

In April, we went to Indianapolis for back-to-back meets, first the spring nationals, which ran over several days, the latter a one-day event called "Duel in the Pool," Americans versus Australians. At the nationals, I became the first American swimmer to win races in three different strokes: in order, the 200 back, 200 free, and 100 fly. The anticipation for the duel, intense at first, had been considerably reduced when most of the Aussies declined to take part, among them Ian. Though I wished he and the others had come, I was nevertheless on a mission; in one afternoon, I would swim four races. In the first, I lowered the world record in the 400 IM to 4:10.73; forty minutes later, I just missed the chance to become the first male swimmer to set two individual world records in a single day, finishing outside the record in the 100 fly by three-hundredths of a second; ninety minutes after that I touched out Malchow to win the 200 fly; and then, in the last race of the day, went 51.61 on the butterfly leg as we beat the Aussies in the medley relay.

I had proven to myself that I could swim multiple events against a first-rate field. In the stands, my mom held up a sign. It read: "Actions Speak Louder than Words."

Three weeks before Barcelona, we went out to California, to Santa Clara. A Finnish journalist started pestering me about whether I really thought I could break the world record in the 200 IM, 1:58.16. It had been held since 1994, nine years, by Jani Sievinen of Finland.

I told him what I typically say, that anything is possible.

"Yes," the reporter said, "but then maybe you think it is too difficult. Nobody has done this for nine years so maybe it will not happen? Why do you think you can do it?"

Here was another doubter.

I love doubters. I love all doubters. I welcome all comments.

As much as I wanted that record, however, conditions did not seem optimal. I hadn't shaved and, with Barcelona still out there, hadn't tapered. Before the race, Bob and I ran over some projected split times; those splits had me just under Sievenen's time.

I said to Bob, you're thinking I should break a world record?

He said, why not?

With each stroke, I could hear the crowd going crazy. I could tell I was swimming hard. After I finished, I saw the board and threw my hands way, way up: 1:57.94. Too difficult? Nine years? Maybe it won't happen? Why do you think you can do it?

Because I believe in myself, because I reach for my goals, and because I work to get there.

To see just what I am, truly, capable of.

Barcelona and the 2003 Worlds would be unlike anything I had ever done before. In Sydney, I had only the one race. At the 2001 Worlds in Fukuoka, I had only the one race. In Barcelona, I was looking at multiple events.

Bob, meanwhile, unearthed a story that had run in the Australian papers. The article quoted Don Talbot, the former head coach of the Australian swim team who was then a team consultant. He said I had done "nothing in the world" and still had to prove myself on the world stage.

"We know that Phelps is a good boy, but people trying to say he's a greater swimmer than Ian — absolute nonsense," Talbot said. "He has showed promise in minor meets, no pressure. When he gets under the pressure with all the great swimmers around him, and each event he gets up will be a different one, he's got to master that.

"Ian Thorpe has got all the runs on the board right now. The promise with Phelps is there, but for people saying he's going to outdo Thorpie, I live to see that day."

I read that and hoped Don was going to keep living.

Ian weighed in, too. "I think he's one of the most talented swimmers in the world," he told an Australian newspaper reporter, talking about me, "and it's obvious from his results that he has to be up there on the list of the best swimmers. But he still has a lot more things that he needs to achieve before you put him in the category of being the best."

For my part, I made sure in talking to reporters to offer nothing about Ian but praise.

"In my opinion," I said, "Ian Thorpe is the number-one swimmer in the world. People have him on a pedestal and everyone is trying to get to him.

"But we will see who is the world's number-one swimmer after the world championships."

In Barcelona, I won six medals, four gold. I became the first swimmer to break five world records at a world championship as well as the first to break world records in two individual events on the same day. I became just the third swimmer — Spitz and West Germany's Michael Gross the others — to simultaneously hold world records in four individual events, and, in our first head-to-head matchup in a world or Olympic final, I defeated Ian by nearly two body lengths in the 200 IM.

Ian, meanwhile, won the 200 free. In Barcelona, I did not take part in that race. Maybe in Athens.

At the end of the Worlds, Talbot told an Australian reporter, "Greatness comes from longevity. Michael Phelps' potential is tremendous and he may come out as the most successful at this competition. He has hit that wave and he's going.

"And if he can do it at the Olympic Games and then the next world titles, and then the next Olympic Games, he will earn the mantle of greatness."

That December, Ian was honored at the Australian Swimmer of the Year Awards. The Speedo $1 million incentive had just been announced a few weeks before. Naturally, Ian was asked if he thought anyone could go seven or better.

"I think it is unattainable for me and unattainable for anyone," he said.

Nothing is unattainable.

Bob and I set about trying to fix some of my technical glitches. My turns needed work, my chin had to stay down when I was swimming the fly, my breathing during the free needed to come back farther to the left. We also tried during those months to figure out which events I would swim at the Trials and thus, if all went well, at the Games. The two flys, the two IMs, three relays if the coaches would let me, all that was easy enough to figure out. But between the 200 free and the 200 back, which? Just one? Or both? Or maybe the 100 free as well?

Before the 2004 spring nationals in Orlando, Bob and I were leaning toward the 200 free. There, though, I swam the 200 back in 1:55.30. Aaron Peirsol's world record at the time was 1:55.15. That same night, I won the 100 free in 49.05.

During the spring nationals, meantime, Bob struck up a conversation with Jon Urbanchek, the University of Michigan coach who had first seen me at the pool in Baltimore when I was eleven, and who had accurately predicted when I was fifteen that I would make the Sydney Olympic team. Jon had announced in January that after twenty-two years as Michigan coach he was planning to step aside. Would Bob have any interest in the job? Curious, Bob agreed to meet with Bill Martin, the Michigan athletic director who, at the time, was also the acting president of the U.S. Olympic Committee.

Jon was widely regarded as one of the premier coaches not just in the United States but the world. A star distance swimmer for Michigan in the late 1950s and early 1960s, he spent twenty years coaching in Southern California, then returned to Ann Arbor as the Michigan coach. His teams won thirteen Big Ten championships, ten straight from 1986 to 1995; the 1995 team won the NCAA title. Jon took good swimmers and made them great: Dolan and Malchow and, before them, Mike Barrowman. And others.

The culture Jon had created in Ann Arbor, that of a demanding pursuit of excellence, was Bob's culture. Michigan, with one of the nation's most successful athletic departments, with resources vastly different than those of a club team, even a highly successful club team, could be a dream job.

The more Bob thought about it, the more, indeed, it seemed like a dream job.

Even so, he told the people at Michigan, don't hire me thinking you're going to get Michael.

Bob and I reconnected in the Bahamas, where I'd gone to shoot a commercial, swimming next to a dolphin. Relax, the crew kept saying as the dolphin would bump up against me, swim away, come back a few minutes later, and pop up again. Just don't panic. Feel free to pet her.

On the flight home to Baltimore, Bob told me the Michigan job was his. If I go there, he said, what would you do?

I knew this had to be coming one day. Here it was. I'm going with you, I said.

After Athens, Bob knew, I would have to leave Baltimore for my own personal growth. Maybe, at some level, I knew, too, hard as it would be to leave my mother and sisters. There was no way I was leaving Bob. He was my coach, yes. But he was also much, much more. A friend, yes, but still more than that. Bob had changed not only how I swam but who I was as a person, reminding me constantly how much love and dedication he has for the sport and everyone in it. I don't think either one of us, to be honest, could do without the other for any length of time. I certainly wasn't about to try.

Bob accepted the Michigan job late in March of 2004. The news broke on April 1, as we — Bob, me, some others from North Baltimore — flew to Indianapolis. As soon as we landed, reporters from all over the world — even Xinhua, the Chinese news service — knew they had a story.

Of course, in a way, this was what I was after, drawing major attention to swimming.

There had been stories in the run-up to the Trials about the Olympic tattoo I had gotten on my right hip after Sydney, a cover story on *ESPN The Magazine* (as an answer to the *Sports Illustrated* swimsuit issue, I was described as "The Hottest Thing in a Swimsuit"), a photo on the cover of David Wallechinsky's *The Complete Book of the Summer Olympics,* and more.

The crush carried on all the way through the Trials, where I qualified for the team in six individual events, including both the 200 free and the 200 back. The night of the 200 free, the finals were moved up ten minutes so that the races could air on NBC, the network's first live prime-time broadcast of the swimming Trials since it had gotten the U.S. rights to broadcast the Games way back in 1988.

Having qualified for six, how much did I want to try to take on at the Games? Once the Trials wrapped, we had all of twenty-four hours to decide; USA Swimming needed to finalize its roster. The 200 back or 200 free?

The 200 free. I wanted a shot at Ian Thorpe.

There were days, perhaps even weeks, during the seven years after the IOC awarded the 2004 Olympics to Athens, when it wasn't at all clear that Athens was going to be ready.

Athens had lobbied for the 1996 Games, the centennial anniversary of the modern Olympics, but those went to Atlanta. In 1997, as something of a makeup, the IOC gave the 2004 Games to Greece despite very real economic and political concerns.

In 2000, the IOC said preparations in Athens were coming along so slowly that it was seriously considering its options, including the possibility of moving the Games somewhere else. Six months before the Games, the main Olympic park, which was called OAKA, remained a dusty construction zone. The Olympic pool, inside the OAKA zone, was going to go without a roof, officials finally announced. If it was hot and humid during the competitions, well, it was, after all, a pool.

Mostly, even before 2001, the buzz had to do over and again with security concerns. A radical anarchists' group called 17 November, who had assassinated U.S. officials and influential Greeks, had been on the loose for years. Then, of course, came 9/11. Osama bin Laden declared holy war on everything American. The IOC took out insurance against terrorism and other disasters. In the months before the Olympics, most American reporters who were going to be sent to Athens had to go through disaster training taught, in many cases, by former military specialists; the training was heavy on such notions as how to bandage up a wounded arm or leg in case a bomb went off. This was the atmosphere heading into Athens and, for those of us on the American team, there were additional concerns, which the U.S. Olympic Committee made clear in instructing us to be as low-key as possible. We were to avoid at all costs anything that might paint any one of us as ugly Americans.

I certainly wasn't going to do anything stupid. And I certainly felt secure.

"I feel extremely safe, extremely confident," I said in meeting reporters before the Olympics started. "The USA is doing a great job of supporting us and protecting us, especially the swim team. We wear the red, white, and blue proudly. We wear the stars and stripes."

I certainly was not going to comment on anything political. I understood that I was now a public figure, and that there might be interest in my take on such things, if I had one. That said, I was nineteen years old, a swimmer focused on swimming.

"Bush or Kerry?" I was asked at a pre-Olympics U.S. swim team training camp in

Mallorca, Spain. Who did I prefer in the 2004 U.S. presidential election?

"The objective at hand is swimming," I said. "That's what I'm worried about right now."

The sooner the attention shifted to sports, and to swimming, the better.

As it usually does at the Olympics, it did so as soon as the action got under way at that outdoor pool, enveloped by bleachers that slanted up and away into the sky, decorated by flags from countries near and far that fluttered in the breeze.

The 400 IM took place on a Saturday, the 400 free relay Sunday, the 200 free Monday.

Heading into that 200 free in Athens, then, I was one-for-two. The Spitz Watch was at full roar for what was being called the "Race of the Century," which seemed absurd given that the century's years could still be counted on one hand.

At these Olympics, Bob was one of Eddie Reese's three assistants. Entertaining the press before the 200 free, Bob was asked to equate it with a horse race. He brought up the 1938 classic when Seabiscuit challenged War Admiral. But this was not a match race, he emphasized.

Indeed not.

The first semifinal went to van den

Hoogenband. Ian and I went one-two in the other.

Klete Keller was also in the race; he finished second behind me at the Trials and had just two days before won his second straight Olympic bronze in the 400. Hackett was in, too; he'd held the world record in the 200 free for a few months in 1999.

Why, I kept getting asked, did I want into this race?

It's not your best event, I kept getting told. It's the one race in which you're not the favorite. Ian is the world-record holder, Hoogie the defending Olympic champion. Don't you get that?

I heard the murmurs: If you lose this race, it's over; you can't win seven golds at these Olympics.

Don't you understand?

Yes, I understood fully. I wanted to race in this race, against the guys who made up this field. And I especially wanted to race Ian Thorpe, the world-record holder, before either of us was done.

The point of competition is to compete. It's to take on the biggest challenge. When you compete against the very best, it makes you better; I don't care if someone is twenty times better, or one-tenth better. I want to race the best.

I hate to lose. But I was not afraid to lose. I am never afraid to lose.

There's a dry wind that's peculiar to Greece that's called the *meltemi*. It comes up in the late afternoons and early evenings. As we were called out onto the deck, the flags around the stadium were blowing straight out because of the *meltemi*.

I was in Lane 3, Hoogie in 4, Ian in 5.

There were cheers for me when I was introduced. There were more cheers for Hoogie. The cheers for Ian were deafening.

At the 50 wall, I was in fourth. No surprise there. Hoogie was under world-record pace. By the 100 wall, I had moved into third. We stayed in that order through the third wall: Hoogie, Ian, me. At the 150 wall, though, Ian came off the turn like a rocket. He overtook Hoogie and drove to the finish. I came on hard and, over that last 50, threw down the fastest last split in the pool. I made up more than a second on Hoogie, and touched in 1:45.32, an American record and a time that would have won gold at every prior Olympic Games, even in Sydney just four years before.

Here it was good for third. I was still third.

Hoogie touched nine-hundredths ahead of me, in 1:45.23. He got second.

Ian was first, in 1:44.71, an Olympic

record. As he touched, he ripped off his yellow cap, squinted at the board, saw the number "1" next to his name, pumped his right fist and yelled, "Yeah! Whoo!" He and Hoogie exchanged a handshake over the lane line, and a hug, and Ian, leaning in so Pieter could hear over the crowd noise, said, "Well, I guess that makes it one-all and I'd like to see you again in Beijing."

Later, talking to the press, Hoogie said, "I gave my best but Thorpe was better. He is the man in this distance. To be beaten by one of the best in my sport, well, that's the way it is."

Ian said, "You know, people kind of have their fate and their destiny and, you know, that was what it was tonight. I've worked damn hard for this. I've worked hard for all of my swims and, you know, it just happened for me tonight."

"Just the fact that Phelps wanted to step up and race Ian Thorpe, even though this isn't his best event, it's a testament to what kind of athlete he is," one of the television commentators said just moments after the finish. The commentator: Dara Torres, who was taking part in these Olympics from the broadcasting booth.

That effort in Athens was, at the time, the fastest I could go. I had made mistakes: My turns could have been so much better, particularly my third turn, which just killed me. Even so, I was closing fast and if the race had been 205 or 210 meters, I might have pulled it out. But it wasn't, of course, and so I didn't. I ran out of pool; that's the saying in swimming, and that's what happened.

But, I can see now, it's all part of how the puzzle was supposed to come together.

That loss in Athens has to be looked at as a — maybe *the* — defining moment in my swim career. I stepped up and raced the best. I found out I was good but, in the 200 free, not good enough. I had work to do. I was proud to stand on the podium with Pieter and Ian, with Ian in particular — it's competitive, never personal — but at the same time I felt immense resolve.

During the ceremony, as the gold medal was draped around his neck, I applauded in genuine respect, and I made sure afterward, in speaking with reporters, to praise him. "In my opinion, he has a perfect stroke," I said. "It's unbelievable how he moves through the water. It's pretty to watch."

He, in turn, said nice things about me: "Michael had a good race." But he also said, when asked, that seven golds might be too much for anyone. "It is a very difficult thing to do. I think people probably don't understand what goes on behind the scenes."

Spitz Watch was over, at least for 2004. I had tried to do something bold. I didn't quite get there, at least in Athens. But isn't the trying the thing that matters? I was taught to dream big. If you don't, don't you fall back?

When I was told, well after the Games, what was being said about me then, after I had won one gold medal and two bronzes, it was fascinating to learn that in some quarters I could be seen as a disappointment.

"Although Phelps could still win six gold medals in Athens," the Associated Press reported, "his audacious challenge fell short and could result in him being remembered as something of a failure at the Athens Games . . ."

I knew I was not a failure in any way, and so did those close to me. It doesn't matter if you fall short; it is never a failure to go after your goals with everything you've got. "'Will it crush him?' 'No,'" my mom said in that same AP story. "'He's already got a page in the history book.'"

To anyone who would listen in 2004, Bob would say, remember, Michael is only nineteen. We don't know how good he is yet. We're going to try to do whatever we can to get him to deliver his best performances. That's all I can do and that's all he can do.

After the 200 free in Athens, I could still win eight medals at those 2004 Games but only five more golds, which, as it turned out, I did. When those Olympics were over, I had become the second athlete in Olympic history to win eight total medals at a single Games; a gymnast from the Soviet Union, Alexander Ditiatin, won eight at the 1980 Games in Moscow.

That was immensely gratifying, of course. People would ask me, is it a disappointment not to win seven golds? I would say, I won eight medals, how is that a disappointment?

At the same time, I had a new measuring stick: that 200 free. I didn't yet know how good I could be. There was obviously more to do to get me to deliver my best. Between Athens and Beijing, as Bob and I mapped out the plan to get to 2008, we had three major meets that would test how far I could come: the 2005 world championships in Montreal; the 2006 Pan Pacs, again in Canada, this time out west, in Victoria; and the 2007 world championships in Melbourne.

I fully expected to get better. After Athens, as I grew into my twenties, I was bound to get bigger and stronger. In Ann Arbor, Bob could call on Jon's expertise as well; though Jon was formally stepping aside as Michigan's head coach, he was still going to be very much around. Jon knew a few things about how to get the world's best swimmers ready for the biggest meets, including the Olympics, where he had been an assistant coach at multiple editions of the Games.

Both Ian and Hoogie passed on the 2005 Worlds in Montreal, Ian saying he was taking the year off, Pieter recovering from back surgery. I won the 200 free there in 1:45.20, a personal best and a tenth of a second lower than the American record I had set in Athens. Hackett finished second, nearly a second behind. Halfway through the race, I was steaming along, ahead of Ian's world-record pace. But my last turn was still off. And then it was obvious, coming down the last 50, I was not in the most optimal condition. It was clear to Bob, and to me, that I had taken a major withdrawal from the account in Athens, and now needed to make significant deposits.

The most puzzling thing about that 200 final in Montreal is that it came two days after a disastrous 400 free prelim; I finished eighteenth of fifty-seven swimmers, and failed for the first time in years to advance to the final. In my 400 prelim, I had been third in my heat at the turn, then faded to seventh. Looking at the scoreboard, I couldn't believe it. I still can't. I am at a loss to explain why it happened. It just did.

It was a lesson I would rather not have been reminded of, that racing at a world-class level takes everything you've got, and you have to bring it each and every day. But I got reminded. I would be reminded of that time and again in Montreal, particularly later in that meet, in the 100 fly.

Every day thereafter, at the pool or in the weight room in Ann Arbor, I felt the sting. My response to that, the work that losing would spur me to put in, that was something I could control. Ian Thorpe's willingness to keep swimming: that I had no control over.

The work I was putting in jumped to a new level. Everything I accomplished in the pool leading up to and through Athens had been done without my doing any serious weightlifting. When I was growing, Bob had been particularly worried that weight work might do more harm than good, might well lead to serious injury. There was good reason for that, I am double-jointed in my knees, my ankles, and my elbows. I was, especially as a teenager, awkward out of the pool. Clumsy, even. Bob finally ordered me to stop jogging because I couldn't even do that without running the risk of tripping over my own feet.

After 2005, both of us understood the time had come. Yes, I had speed in the pool, but that was mostly because I could hold a steady pace over whatever distance was demanded. Now, I needed to build more sprint speed. One sure way would be producing ferocious drive off the wall in my turns. To do that, my legs needed to get much stronger.

I went from having never lifted so much as a barbell in my life to grueling workouts in the weight room three days a week, the weight work typically following two hours in the pool.

Because so much of the motion that's visible in the pool is with the arms, it's easy for most people in the stands or watching on television to think that swimming is all about the arms. Olympic swimming, like all long-course racing, is all in the legs.

Eight Olympic medals, six gold, and, when I started doing the box squat at Michigan, one of the most basic of strength-building exercises for the legs, I was lucky to be able to max out one rep at 300 pounds. I worked up to twenty.

To my disappointment, Ian did not show in Victoria, at the 2006 Pan Pacs. Word was he was living in Los Angeles. It was unclear to some whether swimming still motivated him.

With Ian out, I opted in Victoria not to swim the 200 free, pouring myself instead into the 200 fly (world record); that 400 relay with Neil, Cullen, and Jason (world record); and the 200 IM (world record). After no such records for almost two years, I suddenly had three.

The Pan Pacs were in August. That fall, I was at the condo I'd bought in Ann Arbor, just hanging around amid practices, messing around on the computer, and watching television, when I got a text message from a friend. It said, "Thorpe just retired." My first reaction was, no way. My second was, no way that could be true.

It was true.

Ian held a news conference in Sydney to say he simply was no longer motivated to keep swimming.

He had won eleven world titles, set thirteen long-course world records, and won five Olympic gold medals. And, just like that, it was over. He had never really gotten back into the pool after Athens and now he never would.

We issued a statement in which I called Ian "an inspiration and a terrific champion." The statement said Ian had "elevated the worldwide interest in swimming and was a great ambassador to our sport." It also said, because this was indisputably the right thing to do, "I wish him the best of luck in the future."

Which I wholeheartedly did. Even as I wished he were still swimming.

It took a while to sink in: I was never going to get the chance, ever again, to race him like we raced in Athens.

Just once more with the Aussie in the full-length black bodysuit, the man I considered the world's greatest freestyler. That's what I wanted. Head-to-head, he and I, to see what would happen now if he were at his best and me at mine.

A couple months before the 2007 Worlds, I went to Bob and asked him for video of all my swims from Athens. He didn't push this on me; this was me asking. I took those videos and watched them over and over. When I watched the 200 free from the 2004 Olympics, I understood clearly that I had gone out too slowly and that the third turn had left me at an impossible disadvantage. It was abundantly clear what I needed to fix. In Melbourne, I would have to swim the race aggressively from the start. Power through the turns, especially the third. The big mistake I could make would be to let van den

Hoogenband get ahead early, then have to reel him in, the way I'd tried to do in Athens, when he and Ian went out ahead.

At least I'd have the satisfaction of racing Hoogie, even if Ian was not going to be in this race.

And then Don Talbot opened his mouth. Again.

"Thorpe is still number one in my opinion, and Phelps doesn't outdo him yet," Talbot was quoted in Australian newspapers a few days before the meet got underway.

There was more: ". . . The Americans want to claim they invented Jesus Christ before he came, and the same thing with Phelps — they were saying he was the greatest in the world when Thorpey was the thing.

"I said he was a great swimmer but he's not there yet and they got into me about it . . . Certainly he's on the right track. If he wins at this meet what he's planning to do, then there is no doubt he'll be the best male swimmer of all time. He will supersede Thorpe.

". . . He doesn't want to be one of the greatest, he wants to be the greatest, and regardless of what I think, I think he has to outdo Spitz next year at the Olympics. Whether he can do that, I don't know."

I said nothing.

The day of the 200 free final, dipping into the warm-up pool, I felt it. My freestyle had never, ever felt that smooth. Right then and there, I thought, something special might happen here. Something really special.

No time on the books was even within a half-second of Ian's world-record 1:44.06, the swim from Fukuoka in 2001. The only other person to even break 1:45 had been van den Hoogenband.

Hoogie lined up for the finals in Melbourne in Lane 4; he'd had the fastest semifinal swim. I drew Lane 5. I turned first at the first wall, at 24.47, and again at the second, at 51-flat. Hoogie seemed to still be there with me, just off my shoulder, but, as I had planned, I was ahead. That third leg, I opened it up a bit, and after I turned and finally surfaced, I could hear the crowd noise getting louder and louder. The big video board in Melbourne was showing the race and, through a superimposed red line, it was also showing where I was in relationship to world-record pace. Obviously I was ahead, or at least close. In the water, I had no idea how far ahead. I just knew I had lost sight of Hoogie.

That last lap, Bob would say later, was perhaps the best lap he had ever seen. At least at the time. He knew the race was over at 50 meters, when I'd beaten everyone to that first wall. He had turned to Mark Schubert, the U.S. national coach, and said, this one's done. Mark would say later it looked like I was racing Ian even though Ian wasn't in the pool.

Bob had been hoping for 1:44-something.

I touched, turned, and looked at the clock. It read 1:43.86.

Not just a world record. A world record by two-tenths of a second. And better than I had ever done before in the 200 free by nearly a second and a half. I had erased Thorpe's name from the record books, in his own country.

I was so far ahead that I had time not only to touch but to spin to see the board, jam my left index finger into the air and grab the lane rope with my right arm before Hoogie, in the next lane over, touched the wall. He then turned, saw the board, which said that he was more than two seconds behind at 1:46.28, and came over to the lane line to exchange a handshake.

By then, I'd even had time to duck down, drink water, and spray some around in front of me. I have no idea why I do this. Just a quirk after big races.

Hoogie said to me, "Where did that come from?"

I answered honestly. "I don't know."

"What was your best time before that?"

"1:45.2."

"Off every wall," he said, "the only thing I could look at was your underwaters. I couldn't focus on any part of my race." And then he said, "I won't swim that next year," meaning in Beijing.

Ian arrived in Beijing on the eve of the Games, declared he admired my tenacity, and called me one of the greatest athletes in the world. And: "I have said before that I don't think he can do the eight, and still believe that. Mind you, if there is any person on the planet who is capable, it is him. It's sad, but I just don't think it will happen."

I said nothing.

Hoogie had been good to his word. He did not compete in the 200 free in Beijing. That meant the two swimmers most likely to chase after me were Peter Vanderkaay, one of my training partners in Ann Arbor, and Park Tae-Hwan of South Korea. Park was an excellent closer who, by the day of the 200 free final, had already won the 400 free; Peter hails from a family of top-notch University of Michigan swimmers and had, predictably, gotten even better under Bob and Jon's direction. He also was the centerpiece of what became one of Bob's favorite stories. Bob named a horse after the Vanderkaay family. The Vanderkaays instead of me? Well, Bob would say, first of all that's a lot of pressure to put on a horse. Second, and here came the punch line, this horse is too nice.

The one that bites, he said, that one I'll name Michael.

The 200 free prelims went down the night of the 400 IM final; the semifinals the morning of the 400 relay finals. I went an easy 1:46.48 in the prelims, 1:46.28 in the semis. I didn't care what time I got in the semifinal, really, as long as it got me a lane in the finals. The way the schedule worked, I had to swim the 200 semi at 10:13 Monday morning; the relay final took place just 71 minutes later. That Monday night, I swam in the prelims of the 200 fly.

The 200 free final, then, was the seventh of what was planned to be seventeen swims. Heading out to the deck, walking to Lane 6, where my semifinal time had placed me, I was already more than a third of the way done.

I was more than satisfied to be in Lane 6. It was not important to come in first in the preliminary or semifinal heats. If those times were, for me, ordinary, no worries, at least not on my part. Those were races to get into the final, that's all.

On my goal sheet, after that 1:43.86 in Melbourne, I had put down 1:43.5 as my target for 2008 and Beijing.

That turned out to be conservative. I felt good on the blocks that Tuesday morning. Very good.

I had thought the 200 free in Melbourne was pretty close to perfect.

This one: better.

The plan, as it was in Melbourne, was to go all out. No easy speed in the front half. Hard speed. Take it out and, in essence, dare the others to catch me. I wanted to be at 100 meters in a fraction over 50 seconds. Not 51. 50 point-something.

Immediately after the beep, I surged to the lead. When I popped up after the first turn, I could see I was already half a body length ahead. By the second of the four laps, I could tell I was way out in front. Studying the stat sheets later, I saw I hit the 100 wall in 50.29.

In this race, the weight work I'd done really showed. I had more endurance. I could hold a stronger kick longer. The dolphin kick had become more or less a fifth stroke. I now had developed incredible power off the turns and, in particular, that third turn. What once had been a vulnerability was now a killer asset, 12 or 13 meters underwater, enough to help reshape the contours of what was possible in the 200 free.

I hit that third turn in 1:16.84, almost two full seconds ahead of Peter.

I drove home. Four years before, in the Race of the Century, I was third, the one individual race in Athens I did not win. Now, in Beijing, untold hours of work in the pool and weight room later, I was going to take first.

In world-record time: 1:42.96.

Park finished second, in 1:44.85; Peter got bronze, in 1:45.14. Park had indeed closed fast, 26.17 over the final 50; I had gone even faster, 26.12.

"Phelps swims so fast," Park would say later. "It is my honor to compete with him."

A roar of applause and sound washed over me. My left elbow resting on the deck, I raised my right arm and pointed up, a number-one sign, a tribute to everyone who had helped me get to that moment.

This was history.

Indeed, so much history was made at the instant I touched that last wall in the 200 free.

Park finished 1.89 seconds behind me. That was by far the biggest margin of victory in an Olympic 200 free. West Germany's

Gross had won by 1.66 seconds in 1984.

In 1972, the 200 free was the race after which Spitz had exuberantly raised his shoes. Four years later, in Montreal, Bruce Furniss, John Naber, and Jim Montgomery went one-two-three in the 200 free; I had become the first American since then to win the event.

And, of course, I was three-for-three in Beijing; this third gold was the ninth of my Olympic career. I had just tied four legends of the Olympics: Spitz; another American, track star Carl Lewis; Paavo Nurmi of Finland, a distance-running star; and Larissa Latynina, a Soviet gymnast. Each of them had won nine Olympics golds.

I am honored to be in their company. To be listed in the same sentence is just incredible.

At the time, though, I didn't have time to contemplate history. Looking at the clock, I knew I was barely going to have time to get ready for the semifinals of the 200 fly, which would start in forty-six minutes from the instant I had made that number-one sign. That's mostly what I was thinking about. The 200 fly semis would be my eighth race of seventeen. None of the rest of it mattered, none of it would matter, unless I kept my focus on what was immediately at hand.

I warmed down for as many minutes as I

could. I changed into my red, white, and blue warm-up gear for the medal ceremony. On my way back to the backstage pool, intending to sneak in just a few minutes of warm-up for the 200 fly semis, my mind already thinking ahead to that race, seeing the ready room, the blocks, the dive into the water, I stopped for just a moment to reach into the stands and give the flowers presented to medal winners to my sister Hilary.

As I started to hustle off, she reached her hands up to her face. And wiped away tears.

4
DETERMINATION: THE 200 FLY

One thing that separates Michael from other swimmers, Bob likes to say, is that if they don't feel good they don't swim good.

That's not the way it is for Michael.

Michael, he says, performs no matter how he's feeling. He has practiced it a long time. He knows exactly what he wants to get done, and he's able to compartmentalize what's important.

Bob, with his seemingly endless collection of sayings, naturally has an acronym to describe the mental aspect to my racing. It's "W.I.N.: What's Important Now?"

It's true. When it comes down to it, when the time comes to focus and be mentally prepared, I can do whatever it takes to get there, in any situation.

I can because I know this, too: At the highest level of sports, and especially at the Olympics, you have to expect that everyone competing against you has physical talent.

So: How do you channel peak performance into championship performance? You have to be mentally tough, that's how.

How do you get to be mentally tough? You have to train your mind just like you train the body.

Unleash your imagination. Work hard. Embrace obstacles, difficulties, and mistakes.

Nothing in life is easy. You can't wake up one day, announce you're going to go do something, and expect it to be a success. At least not consistently. You have to put time and energy and whatever you've got into it. You have to want to do it, want it badly.

That's the point that perhaps some people who say they want something, whatever that something is, don't fully understand. A lot of swimmers I trained with said they wanted to achieve something great but didn't truly put time, energy, dedication, and heart into it.

I put time, energy, dedication, heart, and soul into it.

If I wasn't in the right mood to practice, I got myself into that right mood. I'm not saying that Bob and I didn't disagree, even argue with each other — of course we did — but I got myself into the place I needed to be to get the work done that I needed to get done.

When you're challenged: What's important now?

When it gets to be race day: What's important right now?

And when things don't go right on race day, and you absolutely have to take action: What's important this very instant? Sometimes there simply is no time to think. The situation demands action: What's it going to be?

As I lined up on the blocks for the finals of the 200 fly on Wednesday morning, the 13th of August, the first of two finals I would swim that morning — the second would be the leadoff leg of the 800 freestyle relay not even an hour later — I could not have been more ready to rock. The 200 fly was my race. This was the event in which I had first set a world record seven years before.

Thousands of miles away in Norway, Fernando Canales, an assistant Michigan swimming coach, and his wife, Mona Nyheim-Canales, were watching on television. Fernando is a former All-American swimmer at Michigan who represented his native Puerto Rico in three Olympics; Mona is a Norwegian swim champ, a swim coach in her own right, and a sports psychologist with an incredible eye for detail.

The television camera zoomed in on me

during introductions. Watching in Norway, Mona turned to Fernando. She said, you know what? His cap and goggles look really weird.

The back problems I had after Athens, the broken bone in 2005, and the broken wrist in 2007 were just some of the obstacles that had confronted me, and that I had to overcome, if I were to reach my goals at the 2008 Olympics.

Everyone has obstacles to overcome.

I learned that early in life.

But I also learned another essential truth early. Dedication, grit, and willpower could go a long way in meeting, and beating, whatever challenges I would face.

As a very little boy, I was not just always on the go; I simply could not sit still. I would twirl pens and pencils between my fingers. I made faces at cameras. I climbed on everything. I never shut up. Never. I had a question for everything, and wouldn't stop asking questions until I got the answer. If then. My energy level, my talkative nature, my restlessness; all this came as a complete surprise to a mother with two girls. Mom's girlfriends who were the mothers of boys would tell her all these stories about these young boys and she'd be confounded. "My girls don't do that," she would say.

And then I came along.

The baby brother in a house full of strong women. Even as little girls, Hilary and Whitney had dynamic personalities. Of course. They took after their mother.

Early in my elementary school years, my mom kept getting phone calls about what was routinely described as my "negative" behavior.

"Michael is not paying attention in class."

"Michael is having difficulty focusing in class."

"Michael is not doing his work the way he needs to be doing his work."

"Michael always hurries."

"Michael is agitating other children in the class."

Finally, my mom and the teacher held a meeting.

"Michael just can't focus," the teacher said.

"Well," Mom said, "maybe it's because Michael is bored with what he's being taught."

"Mrs. Phelps, are you saying that Michael is gifted? Michael is not gifted," the teacher said.

I was just seven when my parents split up. I didn't understand.

I had big ears. I was scrawny. I got picked on, a lot. Still in elementary school, I had a Mickey Mouse baseball hat. One day I got on the bus with the hat. I got off the bus without it. A bunch of older kids would pick on me and throw my hat around; one of them threw the hat out the window.

Another encounter: I was about eleven or twelve. We were at a swim meet. The older boys were about to dump my head in the toilet, give me a swirlie, as it was called, until someone came in, maybe Bob, maybe another group of kids, I don't remember, and I escaped. I do remember this: I ran out of that bathroom in tears.

My anger would build up inside and, while I wouldn't say anything about it to anyone, I would use that anger as motivation, especially at the pool.

At a swim meet in Princeton, New Jersey, a kid from Delaware beat me in a 200-yard freestyle race. This would have been just the sort of thing that typically would have sparked a first-class, goggles-throwing tantrum. Instead, I felt the burn inside, then let the emotion carry me through my next swims. At that meet, I had five more events. I won all five.

Looking back, I firmly believe these episodes taught me not just how to manage my emotions to my advantage. I also learned what was worth getting worked up about, what was meaningful and important in my life. And, it follows naturally, what was not.

I also saw firsthand, watching my mother, what family values and work ethic truly meant.

When I was in sixth grade, our family physician, Dr. Charles Wax, diagnosed me with attention deficit/hyperactivity disorder. ADHD is a relatively common childhood disorder; it can make it difficult for a child to do well in school or behave at home. The doctor prescribed the stimulant Ritalin.

Initially, the Ritalin program was three times a day during the school week: morning, lunchtime, dinner. I did not take Ritalin on weekends. Staying busy with sports, increasingly swimming, would burn off my energy. At school, the lunchtime dose meant I had to go to the school nurse's office. If I didn't remember, the nurse would come call me out of my next class. For a kid who was already being picked on, this was another reason to stand out. Why was the nurse coming to get me? Where was I going with the nurse all the time? What was going on?

Mom did not tell me at first what Ritalin was or what it was supposed to do. In class, I noticed I did seem less jumpy.

For her part, my mother, raising three kids by herself, pursuing her own career goals, just worked harder to make sure I was, indeed, not only focusing in class but was doing my homework.

So many times, it seemed, I would do my homework and bring it to her for a review, and she'd say, "Michael, your handwriting is so small, I can't read this." She'd rip it up, then and there.

"Mom!"

"You can't read this, Michael. You need to go back and do this again. And it has to be legible."

Doing it until I learned to do it right was one of my mom's many important lessons.

As I got into middle school, another teacher told mom in one of those parent-teacher conferences that I would never be successful at anything I did because I couldn't concentrate.

"So," my mom told this teacher right back, "what are you doing about it?"

At home, this was what she and I were doing about it. Okay, my mom would say, what's your topic?

I'd say, the Louisiana Purchase, or whatever it was, and she would say, okay, give me four main facts about your topic that you want to say.

215

I'd do that, and she'd say, great, now tell me about the first of those four points. It happened in 1803, I might say. And then the second. Lewis and Clark were assigned to explore the territory. And so on, until she had helped me work my way through the entire assignment.

There was no slacking off just because it might be difficult or because I didn't want to do it. I was expected to do the right thing.

Which is why, in seventh grade, I went to my mom and said, I wanted to stop taking Ritalin.

She said, "Are you sure?"

And, "How do you think you're going to be able to control yourself in the classroom?"

"Do you think you can get through your schoolwork without it?"

"Will you be able to accomplish everything you want to accomplish without the Ritalin?"

"Do you think you can get through not just your academics but manage your swim schedule, too?"

Yes, I said. I don't know if it was that I didn't want to go to the nurse's office, or that I thought I had beaten it. But I knew I didn't want to take Ritalin anymore. I viewed it as an unnecessary crutch. I was mentally tough enough to go without it, I was sure.

Okay, she said, Let's try it. Let's go talk to Dr. Wax, but let's not go cold turkey.

The doctor gradually weaned me off the medicine. The first to be cut out was that lunchtime dose. In short order, the frequency of the other doses was reduced, then eliminated entirely.

This was big. And not just because I was off the medicine. I had proven to myself that I could set a goal and, through willpower and being mentally tough, not only meet that goal but beat it.

And so: If I dedicated myself to my goals, if I worked as hard as I could — I could accomplish anything.

It was Dr. Wax who had suggested years before that Hilary and Whitney learn to swim. Every child should be water safe, he said.

Hilary turned out to be a very good swimmer. She set three school records at the University of Richmond.

Whitney turned out to be a very, very good swimmer, even though, a lot like me, she didn't want to get in the water at first. She had to be bribed with a Snickers bar. Once she got in, though, she didn't want to get out. And once she started to get better, she got really, really good. From 1990 to 1993, she was named Maryland's outstanding swimmer. The next year, when she was just thirteen, she finished second in the 200 fly at the spring nationals; that earned her a spot on her first world championship team. She went to Rome — she was fourteen by then — and finished ninth, and came back with all kinds of stories about being there. And a bunch of free stuff.

It was impossible not to hear the buzz: Whitney would be the next great American swim star. The gold medals were all but hers.

Of course everyone we knew was getting excited. The Christmas before those 1996 Games, an uncle, my mom's brother, B.J., gave Whitney a 1996 Atlanta mug. She said, I'm going to be there!

Whitney loved the routine, the discipline, the challenge of swimming. Up before dawn. If a coach told her to do ten laps, she would do twelve. If there was a blizzard and it wasn't safe to drive to practice, on went the parka and the boots, because it was time to walk there.

The pool was Whitney's passion, her outlet, her comfort. Even now, with a husband, two small children, and a job, she goes to the gym at five in the morning because it is what she has always done and is still a major part of who she is.

When Whitney was ten or eleven, her back started hurting. Halfway through her swim practices, her back would start feeling sore.

Whitney is not a quitter. She kept at it.

At thirteen, her back would hurt each time she'd do a flip turn. Her arms and legs would tingle. One day after practice, she bent down in the kitchen to pick up some fruit. She couldn't get back up.

Eventually, she did get back up, and at practice kept pushing through the stabbing pain. She was swimming in an elite NBAC group, seven girls, and the unspoken rule was: You don't get out.

Whitney is not the sort to show her emotions. For her to cry, she's got to be really hurting. She would swim through many a practice crying during the sets. No one knew because, after all, she was in a pool. Later, she would find out that two of the discs in her lower back had herniated; another disc in her neck was bulging.

If she couldn't actually gut out the swimming itself, Whitney still showed up at the pool. While the other girls were doing their sets, Whitney would hang in an outside lane, jogging in the water. She was not going to miss practice.

At the same time Whitney was confronted

with all this back pain, she was also wrestling with food-related issues. She was already doing all she could in the pool. Was there something else she could to make herself go faster? Lose weight, she thought. If she were skinnier, she'd have to go faster, right?

Whitney stopped eating snacks. Then she began to eat less at meals. Mom noticed and, every now and then, asked Whitney about it. Nothing's wrong, Mom, Whitney would say. Mom took Whitney to a nutritionist, who instructed her to keep a food diary and to post that diary on our mom's door. The entries went up; Whitney may or may not have been eating what she had written down she had eaten. The nutritionist gave our mother tips like this: Put butter in Whitney's potatoes. Whitney was too clever for that. She would come home from these grueling swim practices and do sit-ups in front of the TV.

Not surprisingly, Whitney's training began to suffer. After long sessions in the water, she would turn blue. She got good at staying under the water until her color came back.

Whitney came into the 1996 Trials, held in Indianapolis, with the best time in the nation in the 200 fly, 2:11.04. She finished sixth.

I knew nothing of any of Whitney's eating-related issues or her back problems. All I knew that day in Indianapolis was that Hilary and Mom were in tears after the race.

Several months after the Trials, Whitney confided that her back pain was worse than she had let on. She also sought help for her eating habits.

I saw her overcome all of that.

Then I saw her overcome her own heartache.

Before the Trials, college swim coaches were keenly interested in Whitney. Afterward, she was suddenly without that attention. She finally did get an offer, from the University of Nevada at Las Vegas. After time away from the pool, she came back, won her conference title, was named the conference's "newcomer of the year," and made the cut for the 2000 Trials. That spring, she came home and started training again at NBAC. But it didn't take long for her back to start hurting again. Rather than enter a race she knew she'd have no chance at winning and jeopardize her health over the long term, she withdrew.

These were the Trials at which I, at age fifteen, made my breakthrough, coming in second in the 200 fly.

Instead of chasing our Olympic dreams together, Whitney and I, it was just me.

Those 2000 Trials were back in Indianapolis, at the same pool where Whitney, favored to make the team just four years before, had not. It took extraordinary courage for Whitney to show up there again. After I had placed second to Malchow and made the Sydney team, she made her way down to the pool deck and threw her arms around me. I knew I had made that 2000 team in no small part because of Whitney; she had shown me what kind of dedication and commitment it took.

Whitney's heartache was far from over, however. She spent the next couple of years wrestling with her conflicting feelings. On the one hand, she had done great things in swimming; she'd earned her way to the top of the national rankings, she had represented the United States on the world stage. On the other, girls she had raced were now representing the United States at major meets, and it was too tough to watch. Something she had loved had been taken from her and it wasn't her fault. She had been injured; this was no fault of will.

I would go to meets, in Sydney, for instance, at the 2000 Games, and my mom and Hilary were in the stands, but Whitney was not.

It wasn't that she was spiteful.

Far from it. She was hurting. And being at meets felt even more hurtful. It was simply too frustrating for her to sit in the stands and think how fast she could have gone if she'd only been able to train.

Time is a great healer. One day, she realized that she had done amazing things, had accomplished a lot, should be proud of herself. That's when she started going to more of my meets.

One of the first back was in Indianapolis, in 2003, the Duel in the Pool; the one Ian and many of the other Australian swimmers declined to attend. I won four events that day, including the family legacy, the 200 fly.

Now, when I look into the stands, I see Whitney and Hilary on either side of my mom. Knowing what it took to get Whitney there, how could I not be even more motivated?

Everyone makes mistakes. In November 2004, I made a big one. I drove after drinking. I should not have gotten behind the wheel. It was wrong. Wrong for so many reasons.

By way of explanation, not excuse: After the Athens Games ended, I was, for the first time in my life, on my own. No Mom, no Bob telling me what to do.

Almost as soon as I got back from Greece, I went on a tour with Ian Crocker and another American Olympic swim star, Lenny Krayzelburg. We traveled around the United States on a bus that slept twelve and that used to belong to David Copperfield, the magician. We would visit schools and conduct swim shows at local pools; the three of us would demonstrate stroke techniques, then race each other, different strokes from show to show. We would also take turns as anchors on relays made up of local kids.

From the time I was fourteen, I had been sensitive to back pain, mindful of what had sidelined Whitney. As the post-Athens exhibition made its way through Oregon, I felt something sharp on my right side. It did not feel good.

The pain went away on the next leg of the trip, a six-hundred-mile bus ride down to Sacramento. All the way, however, I was obsessing about me, about Whitney, about back pain. I was unsettled. I felt insecure.

The tour ended in early October, in Anaheim. Mom and Bob met me there. We flew to Indianapolis, to the FINA short-course world championships, held at Conseco Fieldhouse, an event one of my sponsors was helping to underwrite. I won the 200 free in an American record time. But then I felt it in my back, again.

I withdrew from the meet and went to Baltimore. An MRI showed what's called a *pars fracture,* from repeated bending and stretching. Maybe I'd had it since I was a kid; maybe not. The doctors told me to wear a removable brace for six weeks and stay out of the pool.

I didn't know what to do with myself. I had no structure, no rhythm, no routine to my days or my nights.

One of my good friends was in college at a town on Maryland's Eastern Shore and so we decided, that first weekend of November, to go out there. Road trip. I had just gotten my new car, a silver 2005 Range Rover. One of my friends made sure to tell me before we left: no drinking and driving. I said, come on, that's not me.

We hung out at a party. I had three beers. We decided to go get some food. I got behind the wheel of the Range Rover. A few blocks away, I rolled through a stop sign. The car coming down the street, as it turned out, was a Maryland state patrol car.

As soon as the lights on the police car started whirling, I knew I was in trouble. I immediately understood I had made a seriously stupid mistake. The trooper gave me a Breathalyzer test. My blood-alcohol reading measured 0.08, precisely the state standard for driving under the influence.

I was thoroughly ashamed.

My decision to drink and drive could have hurt someone. I was lucky it had not.

I was not yet twenty-one, the legal drinking age. I had flouted the law.

I had embarrassed myself, my family, my coach, and my team, just for starters.

I would have to be held accountable.

Who to call first?

Should I call my mom, who would yell at me and worry? Bob, who would yell at me but help me? Or Peter, who I knew would help?

I called Peter. He said, let me figure out what we ought to do next, I'll get back to you.

When I called Bob, who was at a meet in Wisconsin, he was supportive, but he also gave me the hard truth: "Michael, just because you want to blow off some steam doesn't mean you can be an idiot."

Then, face to face, I had to tell my mom.

She knew I had made a mistake. But that's not how she had raised me, to make that kind of mistake. I was so, so sorry. I was immature and I'd been stupid. That didn't change anything but that was the reality.

I felt I'd gone from seemingly being on top of the world — the Olympics in Athens had ended a little over two months before — to being in the deepest black hole on the face of the earth.

Peter, Bob, my mom, and I met to talk about what to do. I said, it's on me to tell people what I had done. I called friends and extended family. I also called reporters I had come to know to tell them what I had done, that I made a mistake, and that I wanted each of them to hear it from me. I sat there for hours.

The look on Bob's face never changed; he was extremely disappointed.

Mom started crying. That hurt worse, maybe, than anything. I had never seen my mother that upset. I vowed it would never happen again.

We worried that my sponsors might abandon me. None did.

A week after my arrest, USA Swimming held a fundraiser, an awards dinner called the Golden Goggles, in New York City. Everyone makes mistakes, but I just want you to know — I've never seen anything handled the way you've been handling it, I was told by Dick Ebersol, the NBC Sports chairman. It meant a great deal to me that he said so.

In late December, I went to court in Salisbury to plead guilty to driving while impaired. It was humbling indeed to walk into court, my every step recorded by television cameras. Inside, after my guilty plea, the state dropped its other charges; I was ordered to pay $305 in fines and court costs, to attend a meeting of Mothers Against Drunk Driving, and to speak at a number of schools about drinking, driving, and decision making.

The next April, back in Salisbury, I spoke to the seniors at Parkside High School. It was a few days before their prom. Have fun, I said, but be responsible. You need to set goals and keep in mind that the decisions you make can determine whether you will achieve those goals, I said.

The night that I got behind the wheel after drinking, I said, I had lost sight of my goals. I was not thinking, as I should have been, about Beijing and 2008. "In order to make good decisions, you really have to see the whole picture," I said. "I guess you could say my head wasn't really on straight . . . my goals were not in order when I got behind the wheel."

I'd like to think that maybe I helped at least one person make a decision not to drive after drinking. Maybe at Parkside High School, maybe somewhere else. If even one person has looked at me, or heard about what I did, and shuddered, and thought, no, I don't want to go through that, then it was all worth it.

In no way would I wish the experience, any and all of it, on anyone, but it changed my life. It reminded me in the most direct way possible that no one is so important that he deserves to be, or will be, treated any differently than anybody else.

The experience also led me, in one of those connections in life that, after it happens, seems like one of those things that was all along somehow meant to be, to Greg Harden, who is an associate athletic director at Michigan and the school's director of athletic counseling. I went to check in with him after I'd moved to Ann Arbor. He knew what had occurred. Look, he said, one of the biggest things I'll tell you is this: Whenever you make a mistake, learn from it. As long as you can learn from every mistake, he said, you'll be fine. You can make a million mistakes, just not the same one twice.

Greg Harden gave me good advice. I am grateful.

Such good advice and yet, at least when it came to swimming, apparently just to swimming, I already knew not to be reckless.

I had learned that lesson the hard way, too, after my first Olympics, in the way I approached the 200 fly in particular.

Yes, I set the world record in Austin. Yes, I lowered it in Fukuoka.

But for a year after that?

At those 2002 Fort Lauderdale nationals, I had such a great meet except for the 200 fly, at least by the standards that mattered, mine and Bob's. I set out to break the record. I did not get there, and after the race I put my head in my hands. At that moment, I was only beginning to understand what not training diligently in the butterfly would yield. Bob directed my training sets, of course, but when it came to the fly he would every now and then give me a choice of doing extra butterfly sets at the close of practice. I usually said, no, thanks. It was, after all, my best stroke. At the end of a workout, I was genuinely tired.

Bob had let me learn the hard way that there was no substitute for the hard work it would always take to get better.

Later that summer, at the Pan Pacs in Yokohama, Malchow beat me in the 200 fly. If I needed an even more blunt reminder, now I had it.

I hated losing.

I also hated hearing Bob say, "I told you so."

After that, Bob gave me punishing butterfly sets. Through Athens, I devoured them. That is what Bob wanted — my best effort. There's a huge difference in not swimming well because of a technical glitch and not swimming well for lack of effort. Bob knows what's what. What he wants and expects are as many consecutive days of first-rate training as possible.

Bob also, quite deliberately, would arrange practices, schedules, workouts, drills, whatever he could think of, around the idea of being uncomfortable.

His thinking always has been to put his swimmers through every scenario possible. You're tired; you feel you can't move; you're truly hurting. That's when he would throw down especially hard sets. Bob wanted to gauge not only how I felt under pressure but, more important, how I responded under pressure. If I could deal with whatever it was when I was tired, I could deal with anything that came my way. Because that is the real definition of a champion, someone who can deal with any obstacle that comes his or her way, can deal with any situation at any given point.

Michael Jordan was so sick with the stomach flu before game five of the 1997 NBA Finals that he hardly slept the night before. He was exhausted and dehydrated. He played 44 minutes and scored 38 points, and his Chicago Bulls won the game by two points.

A champion can deal with any kind of pressure.

It wasn't just the intensity of the practices, however, that made up the Bowman approach to stress management. It was anything and everything. It was why, going all the way back to 1999 and the nationals in Minneapolis, we dragged back to the hotel to get me a swimsuit.

In Baltimore, I never had a lane to swim in by myself. I swam four or five to a lane, like everyone else. No special treatment, not after the 2000 Olympics, nothing.

That trip to the Bahamas, the same day I did a lengthy photo shoot with the dolphin? That day started off with a morning practice. The photo shoot followed. In the afternoon, instead of enjoying the island scenery or lounging poolside with a fruity drink, Bob ordered up practice. He knows that I shiver if I stay in cold water too long, and it was a cold, gray day in a pool warmed only by solar heat. Would I tough it out? Yes.

In Australia in 2003, Bob deliberately asked our driver to show up late. That way I had to spend more time waiting at the pool, and we missed dinner. I ordered pizza. That same trip, he stepped on my goggles, on purpose. I had to make do.

A power outage one day at the pool in Michigan meant nothing. We swam in the dark. That was good, Bob said. Made you swim by feel. Forced you to count your strokes.

Back in Australia in 2007, at the Worlds in Melbourne, my goggles started sliding down my face as I turned into the final 50, the freestyle leg, of the 200 IM. The goggles filled with water. I couldn't see Lochte or Cseh at all. I knew that I had turned about a half-second ahead and so I just drove for home. When I touched and turned, I blinked and blinked and blinked until I could see the board: 1:54.98, a new world record.

So what if I couldn't see? What's important now? Getting it done, no matter what.

The night before that 200 IM in Melbourne, I swam the finals of the 200 fly. This is how good that race was. Afterward, Bob just smiled at me.

I was timed in that 200 fly in Melbourne in 1:52.09, not just a world record but by 1.62 seconds. The runner-up in the race, Wu Peng of China, touched more than three seconds behind. Typically, when a record is broken, the line that gets superimposed on the television broadcast or on the arena big board runs just behind a swimmer's fingers; records are usually taken down by hundredths of tenths of a second. In this instance, the line was near my feet.

I felt like I was twelve again, in the sense that you break records by that much only when you're twelve.

It was the sort of thing that made newspapers and television around the world take notice of swimming, in a non-Olympic year, no less. On ESPN, they debated my place in sports history. The back page of the *Herald Sun,* Australia's largest newspaper, featured a photo of me rising out of the water in mid-stroke; the headline reached across the entire page of the tabloid, just one word: "Greatest." My hometown newspaper, the *Baltimore Sun,* called it "stunning" and offered comparisons to Bob Beamon's history-making long jump, 29 feet, 2 1/2 inches, two feet past what had been the world record, at the 1968 Mexico City Olympics. Mark Schubert, our U.S. team coach, told the Baltimore paper that what I did might have been even better. "I don't think it's comparable to Beamon's performance because that was a lifetime, out-of-body experience that we never saw again," he said, meaning Beamon never again jumped that far. "I think we're going to see an even better time from Michael. I just think he's that good."

Honestly, in the warm-ups before the 200 fly final in Melbourne I had felt crummy. My arms felt sore. I had gone 1:43.86 in the 200 free just the day before.

Once I got up on the blocks, I had to get over all that. How I felt then was not the least bit important to what was possible now. It was time to go out and race, the weight training obviously making a huge, huge difference in what I was now able to do.

The time in Melbourne surprised me, but not the record itself. I had realized the month before, at the annual midwinter meet in Missouri, that I was on the verge of something special. I showed up at the Missouri meet with a full goatee. My hair was hanging out of my cap. I was obviously not shaved and certainly not tapered. Even so, I had gone out that night and lowered my world record in the 200 fly. In Victoria, at the Pan Pacs in 2006, I had gone 1:53.80; in Missouri, I took nine-tenths of a second off that, dropping the record to 1:53.71.

To go under that in Melbourne by more than a second and a half is why I had enormous expectations for myself in this race in Beijing, why I put 1:51.1 on my 2008 goal sheet.

At the Olympic final, immediately before the starter called, "Take your marks," I pushed my goggles to my eyes. Not sure, even now, why.

I race in metallic Speedo goggles, a model called the "Speed Socket." I also race in two caps. The sequence goes like this: I put the goggles on, then one cap, then the other. That way the goggles are secure.

Nothing seemed amiss.

Obviously, however, something was wrong. Fernando and Mona could see that all the way from Norway.

At the beep, immediately after I dove in, the goggles started leaking. I couldn't tell whether the seal had broken on the top or bottom.

That wasn't important. What was important was to go.

When I turned at 50, the thought flashed through my mind that maybe the leak wouldn't be that bad. It seemed manageable.

At 100, though, things started getting more and more blurry. Just after that, as I made my way up the pool to the far wall, with perhaps 75 meters to go in the race, the cups of the goggles filled entirely. I could not see.

I could not see the line on the bottom of the pool. I could not see the black T that marks the coming of the wall. I could not see anybody else in any other lane. I could not see.

This wasn't football, or basketball. I didn't have the luxury of calling a time-out.

I couldn't take the goggles off and swim old school because the goggles were trapped under both caps.

This was an Olympic final. I had to go. At that instant, that's what was the most important thing. I had to go hard and fast.

There was no time to think about anything. But what was there to think about? I was the farthest thing from freaked out. This very thing had happened to me just the year before, in Melbourne, in the 200 IM finals. It happens sometimes in swimming. It was happening to me now.

In the 200 fly, there's a regular and predictable progression of strokes as the race goes along. That is, there are so many strokes per length of the pool, the number typically going up by one per lap because of the inevitable demands on the body and the fatigue.

The first length usually takes sixteen strokes. The second, eighteen; the gap is two because the race starts with a dive. The third length usually goes nineteen strokes. The final length, nineteen or twenty.

When my goggles filled, I was on the third length. Thus, the magic number to get to the far wall was nineteen, maybe twenty. Because my goggles were already leaking before the turn, anticipating the crisis, I had started a stroke count as soon as I made the turn into that third length.

Four or five strokes into that third length — that's where it all closed in and I could no longer see.

Sixteen. Seventeen. Eighteen. Nineteen. Where was that wall?

Twenty, and a glide; there, there it was.

Perfect. I had spaced it perfectly, the glide carrying me into the wall and a touch. I hadn't come into the wall in midstroke or hammered into it or jammed my fingers or bent back my wrist or any of the other things that could have gone wrong. In Omaha, Emily Silver had broken her right hand after swimming into the wall at the finish of the 50-meter free semis. It put her out of the pool for more than a week.

In the stands, Whitney was concerned. His stroke is tight, she said to Mom.

Bob was also wondering what was going on. The way we had planned it, I should have been much farther ahead, pushing for

1:51. Bob's mind had already started racing. Maybe, he figured, for some inexplicable reason I was looking ahead to the 800 relay, which both of us knew I was going to have to race later that morning, about fifty-six minutes after the end of the 200 fly, and was just going hard enough in the fly to get the job done.

Little did he know that I wasn't looking anywhere. I couldn't see. It was as bad as it could get.

Coming down the homestretch, I was just hoping I'd given myself enough of a lead so that nobody could run me down.

Seventeen. Eighteen.

I could hear the crowd roaring. For me? For someone else? Was it close?

Nineteen. Twenty. Wall, wall, wall, where was that last wall?

One more stroke. Give it one more stroke, twenty-one and reach for it, glide just a touch.

There, there it was! I felt it with my hands. Again, I had timed it just right. I didn't ram into the wall with my shoulder or, worse, my head. I reached for it, hands out in front, and got it with my fingers.

Just the way I would have tried to do it if I could have seen what I was doing.

With my right hand, I reached up and

ripped off my goggles. Both the caps came flying off, too, into the water with the goggles. I leaned on the lane line with my right arm, blinking hard. I tossed the caps behind me onto the deck with my left hand, picked up the goggles with my right and flung them behind me, too, then looked up, breathing hard, shaking my head from side to side, squinting at the scoreboard.

Next to my name it said, 1. It also said WR, a world record, 1:52.03. Incredible.

I was simultaneously thrilled and, candidly, frustrated as I got out of the pool and said to Bob, "I couldn't see anything."

I was not put out so much at the wardrobe malfunction — stuff happens — but frustrated at the opportunity lost. My fly had come on so strong in 2007 and 2008. I had extraordinary confidence I could go super-fast at the Olympics. I had, and yet I could have gone faster. There was no doubt in my mind that I could have gone faster. No doubt at all.

And it was natural, there in the pool, to wonder, would I have an opportunity ever again to swim this race so fast?

I shook it off.

What was important now was taking the briefest of moments to appreciate what I had just done.

Nine swims down, eight to go.

Four for four in gold-medal swims. Cseh had gone four seconds faster than he had ever gone before, and still come in second, in 1:52.70; Takeshi Matsuda of Japan went two seconds better than his prior best, and came in third, in 1:52.97. The field I had just beaten was so fast that bronze in Athens would not even have gotten a spot in the final eight in Beijing.

And now, of course I had ten gold medals over my three Olympics, more than anyone else in history. I thought, wow, the "greatest Olympian of all time," that's a pretty cool title.

It was too dizzying, way too much for me to appreciate right then and there. I had to go swim a relay. That relay was truly what was important now.

In the stands, meanwhile, Hilary said to Mom, it's ironic, isn't it? The 200 fly got Michael to the Olympics for the first time. The 200 fly is the event in which he got his first world record. It was the event that made him somebody in the international swim scene. Now that's the event that launched Michael into history with his tenth Olympic medal.

Mom thought about that for a moment amid the din there in the Water Cube. She looked at Hilary and said, where do you come up with these things?

5

CONFIDENCE: THE 800 FREE RELAY

My BlackBerry buzzed before I set out for the Water Cube the morning of the 200 fly and the 800 freestyle relay, a text message from back home: "Dude, it's ridiculous how many times I have to see your ugly face." Then came another message: "It's time to be the best ever."

I had to laugh.

I laughed a lot at the Beijing Games. It felt different than in Athens and that's because it was different. The 2008 Games were my third Olympics; I knew what to expect. I had been through the media storm in 2004, for instance, so I knew what was coming in 2008. That time, I was a deer in headlights; I had never gotten that much media attention. Also, in Athens, I was only nineteen. Maybe I was too young to appreciate fully what the Olympics were all about. It's like all the little lessons Bob and I had been working on for fully a dozen years; they were all there to see in Beijing, on display in particular in that 800 relay.

I knew, for example, how to conserve energy through a whole meet, whether it was seven, eight, or nine days. Related to that was the furious work I had put in during the hours in the pool and the weight room. If few people truly understood how hard I had worked, the grueling nature of the workouts Bob had put me and the others in our training group in Michigan through, the endurance that I had built would reveal itself in the relays.

Part of it, as well, was how I had grown up since Athens. I was now twenty-three. I had moved to Michigan, lived on my own, made mistakes, endured health scares. My relationship with Bob was forced to evolve, and it did. That maturity would be on ample display in the relays as well; we had to swim with passion but at the same time swim smart.

Then, too, there were the relationships with my teammates, which mattered to me immensely, and the opportunity to take all three relay titles back to the United States. That also mattered to me intensely. The 800 was not likely to be a replay of the 400 earlier in the week. What could be, after Jason had seemingly captivated the entire world with his anchor leg? But that didn't mean it could or should be taken for granted. And in this 800 we had a very definite goal, to do something no team of four guys swimming four laps apiece had ever done: break seven minutes.

We wanted to go six-something.

This relay had an incredible Olympic history. We wanted to make a little history of our own.

Before I found a place of my own in Michigan, I had to bunk with Bob. It was the most miserable month ever, for him and for me.

This arrangement occupied late November and early December 2004. Bob wanted to watch over me. I didn't want to be watched. The DUI had given him more reason to watch me more closely. I felt bad enough about it already.

"Are you eating enough?" Bob would ask. "Sleeping enough?"

Stop treating me like an eleven-year-old, I finally said after one too many of these sorts of questions.

The television was his television; we watched what he wanted to watch. I would retreat to my room to play video games or to hack around on my computer.

Finally, we got into it big time. I couldn't

stand even one more second.

"I'm out of here!" I said.

"Okay," Bob said. "Don't let the door hit you on your way out."

"Good," I said right back, ever so cleverly. "I'm going back to Baltimore."

I threw my things in the car and walked out, then called my mom.

"Now, Michael," she said, calmly, "what are the advantages of coming home? Of course you can come back, but would you train here? Are you going to find a new coach? What about school?"

I turned around. I even showed up at practice. But the feeling that he was making every decision in my life for me had hardly gone away. I had to get some space.

A few days later, I signed the papers to buy a condo near campus. I wanted out from Bob so badly that I slept there on an air mattress helpfully supplied by a Michigan assistant coach.

The dynamic was complicated further, and to be truthful, aggravated, by my back problems. At the very same time that I wanted the adult freedom of being on my own, I also needed Bob's reassurance. Little wonder things were edgy. Another MRI in early December offered clearer evidence of a stress fracture. I was given three options: stop training for six months; practice through the pain with uncertain short- and long-term consequences to my discs; surgery, with at least three months of no swimming. What was unsaid, of course, was that my entire career might be at risk — even if it was being thought by me and by anyone who knew Whitney and the family history.

More opinions were sought.

In the meantime, as I rested, my symptoms — just like that — went away. We began to incorporate cross-training and core work into my training, meaning push-ups, pull-ups, sit-ups, sessions with a medicine ball.

And I was left to figure out how to live this new life in Ann Arbor.

At first, I had no dishes. Having gone to the grocery store for milk and cereal, I did have something to eat. What to eat it in? A Gatorade container would have to do. I poured the cereal in there, sloshed the milk in on top, swirled it all around and drank it all down.

Soon enough, I had dishes. I put them in the dishwasher, then poured liquid hand soap in the soap tray. That led to a bubble bath all over the kitchen floor.

As time went along, I did become more accomplished in the house, sort of. At one point, the smoke detector started singing. I hadn't been cooking. I didn't smell anything burning. What could it be?

I called Bob. "Michael," he said, "when was the last time you changed the batteries in the smoke detector?"

"You need to do that?"

I took a handful of courses — at some point, I would like to get my college degree — and got the Michigan "M" tattooed on my left hip, a counterpoint to the Olympic rings on my right.

After getting a crash course after Athens in fame, I was mostly allowed to be alone in Ann Arbor. Nobody bothered the football players much; in the same way, I was mostly left to be myself and be by myself, if that's what I wanted. At the same time, I had to learn to juggle sponsor commitments around the country even as Peter and I weighed a seemingly relentless flood of invites from anyone and everyone interested in a piece of me, everything from the Miss USA pageant (yes) to bar mitzvahs (not really).

That winter, Bob and I wanted to be both cautious with my training, yet as aggressive as we could be. In March 2005, it was back to Indianapolis for the meet that would qualify swimmers for that year's Worlds in Montreal. I won the 200 IM, out-touched Ian Crocker in the 100 fly, and then, in the 100 free, set a personal-best, 49-flat, holding off Jason Lezak, who, like me, had not been training his hardest over that winter. At that Indy meet, my back felt fine; the times and the wins were not nearly as reassuring as that simple fact.

By the time we got to Montreal, I had for the year put in maybe half the miles in the pool I had done in years prior. I did win gold medals there. But it was clear after the 400 free prelim disaster, then that same week losing emphatically to Ian Crocker in the 100 fly, that I was not where I wanted to be. Montreal was a wake-up call.

"Phelps flop," screamed one newspaper headline. A columnist for the *Montreal Gazette* wrote, "Visitors to the World Aquatics Championships the past week have been wondering why the city of Montreal has lifeguards posted around the pools. Any chance you saw Michael Phelps struggle home over the final two lengths of his 400-metre freestyle heat yesterday? The U.S. superstar was breathtaking in the worst way imaginable, failing to make the eight-man final while looking like a weary age-grouper . . ."

The only thing I could do was use it as motivation.

Though I was taking some courses, loved

going to Michigan football games, said "Go Blue!" when I was honored with an ESPY for what I'd done in Athens, it took me a while to learn how to fit in at Michigan. I was never going to be just a regular college kid, not just another member of the high-performance training group — called Club Wolverine — at the pool.

Because I had turned professional years before, I was not representing Michigan at dual meets with the likes of Wisconsin or swimming for the Wolverines at the Big Ten or NCAA championships.

In its way, this was another challenge. If I didn't have the academic record of the college guys who were, for example, engineering majors, was it weirder for them to be in the same pool with me?

Then came the sudden death of Eric Namesnik in January 2006, which jolted everyone who'd ever had a connection to Michigan swimming and, for that matter, anyone with any connection of any kind to swimming, or even to the Olympics. Twice the Olympic silver medalist in the 400 IM, Snik, which is what everyone called him, died four days after being critically injured in an early-morning car crash on an icy road. I had first met Snik when I was eleven; he was only thirty-five, with a wife and two children, when he passed away. His favorite saying: "Dream no small dreams, for they have no power to move the hearts of men."

That April, meanwhile, Erik Vendt showed up in Ann Arbor, intent on resuming his racing career. I could not have been more thrilled. I needed, to use Bob's analogy, to make a considerable deposit into the fitness bank. And no one had ever trained harder than Erik Vendt.

Erik had taken time off after Athens. He'd gone backpacking around Europe, then moved to New York. There he worked at a swim school, teaching kids. The kids' attitude completely changed his. Before, he had looked at swimming as racing, placing, and medals. Working with the kids, he saw the success and pride of getting in the pool for the first time, getting their face in the water for that first time. Seeing their excitement and joy made him excited all over again about swimming. He was toying with the idea of coming back when, listening to the Olympic theme song from the telecast of the Winter Games from Torino, Italy, in February 2006, he literally got chills up and down his spine and thought to himself, I guess I'm not done yet. So he called Jon, and said, do you think I could get in with the Club Wolverine crew? Get back in here, Jon said.

Erik, who's from Massachusetts, had gone to college at USC, swimming under Mark Schubert. Mark had left USC to become the U.S. team national coach; with Bob and Jon, Erik figured he'd get punished in practice just like he would have with Mark but, at Michigan, he'd also get more of an emphasis on weight training, which I was aggressively starting to work on that year, too.

If I was willing to work hard in practice, Erik had perhaps an even greater appetite for it. He set out to remake himself into a freestyler instead of an all-arounder in the individual medleys, everything from the 200 free to 1500, no small thing because he was himself a two-time Olympic silver medalist in the 400 IM. And Erik just ate up whatever Bob threw at him. If, on a scale of one to ten, I was now turning in consistent eights at practice, very few sinking to a two, rising every now and then to a ten, Eric was maybe a nine each and every day. I had, and still have, never seen anyone work out so hard and be so competitive, both in workouts and in the racing itself.

Aside from that, Erik and I had history together, going back to the 2000 Olympic team and our one-two finish in the 400 IM in Athens. He was four years older, which suited me perfectly, because at North Balti-

252

more I was always the young kid hanging out with the older guys. He would motivate me when I needed motivation. He never held anything back, always told me exactly how it was. I sometimes didn't like to hear whatever it was Erik had for me, but better to hear it from him than one more time from Bob. Erik would also mediate when Bob and I had one of our periodic moments. On the road, Erik and I took to rooming together.

Without Erik Vendt, there was no way I could have gotten through the years from Athens to Beijing.

All of us in Club Wolverine pushed each other hard. In Baltimore, I had been used to winning every practice set, it seemed. Not here. Davis Tarwater had emerged as one of the best in the country in the butterfly. He and I would go at it in fly sets; I had never had anyone go with me in those sets but, literally, he and I would be swimming side by side in what seemed like every set. Peter Vanderkaay was a 2004 Olympic teammate of mine from Athens. Klete Keller, who trained in Ann Arbor until moving to Southern California, had been a teammate in both Sydney and Athens.

This was no boys-only club. Katie Carroll was a Big East swim champion at Notre

Dame. Kaitlin Sandeno won four Olympic medals, one in Sydney, three in Athens. As we got closer to the Trials in Omaha, we were joined by Michigan high school star Allison Schmitt. At first, there were some raised eyebrows in what was largely a group of post-grads, of older swimmers, about Allison's arrival. She was going to go on to college in the fall: Did she really belong? She quickly not only proved that she did belong, she brought immense life to the party. In truth, she brought all of us closer.

Jon may have sometimes affectionately referred to Kaitlin as "the Princess," but the girls got no breaks. No one wanted any. We were all there to train for the Trials and the Games, as the clock across the pool counted down the time, in days, hours, minutes, seconds, down to tenths of a second, before the start of the Beijing Olympics.

Morning practice at the Canham pool got started at either seven or seven-thirty, depending on the season, and went for roughly two hours.

If it was seven, my alarm would go off at six-twenty, maybe six-thirty. I still was not a morning person. I wouldn't be out of bed until six-forty-five. That gave me just enough time to grab something I could eat on the run, get to the pool, throw my suit on, walk onto the deck, get my equipment, and be ready to dive in. I would practice most mornings in a swimming brief, what the rest of the world might call a Speedo; they were Speedos, of course, often a model called the Flip Turn, and I particularly liked one with yellow moons and yellow unicorn heads set against a magenta background. It was so hideously ugly that it actually had tons of style. Same for a neon-green one plastered with red cherries.

There were afternoon practices as well, along with weights three times a week; and "dryland," push-ups, pull-ups, medicine ball or yoga, and, depending on the time of year, separate cardio work.

Bob spelled out in meticulous detail how each practice would go. He wrote the program out in longhand, then made copies for each of us and for the coaches. It was way too complicated to memorize. The trick was to dip your own copy in the pool water, which would give it just enough stick to get stuck to the metal guardrail at the end of each of our lanes. Each workout also included a notation in the corner: how many days to go until the Trials in Omaha as well as the Games in Beijing.

There were kicking drills. Work with kickboards, snorkels and paddles. With fins. Parachutes.

There were no bathroom breaks. At least for the guys. If you had to go, you went, right there in the pool.

Around all this working out there had to be resting, noon-time naps, especially.

And there had to be eating. Lots of eating. Thousands of calories. During the Olympics, that rumor got started that I was inhaling twelve thousand calories a day. It seemed to spread like wildfire. It's just not true.

Maybe eight to ten thousand calories per day. But not twelve thousand.

When I was in Baltimore, later in my high-school years, I used to go after practice every morning to a restaurant named Pete's. Breakfast there went like this: three sandwiches made of fried eggs, cheese, lettuce, tomato, fried onion, and mayonnaise. An omelet. A bowl of grits. Three slices of French toast with powdered sugar. And, as a kicker, three chocolate chip pancakes.

In Ann Arbor, my days started before that morning practice with a PowerBar, a bagel, a bowl of cereal, or a Pop-Tart. Just something quick and easy, some carbs before working out.

After the morning swim, I would go out for a real breakfast to places I soon discovered as I found my way around Ann Arbor.

If it was Benny's Family Dining, I liked to slide into a booth near the front, away from the cigarette smokers. Breakfast would start with a bowl of rice pudding. Then: three eggs over easy, hash browns, sausages, and wheat toast. Maybe a side of bacon. Sometimes, I'd go for the Mexican or Southern omelet. If I was off to Mr. Greek's, I would have a Greek's skillet: scrambled eggs, gyro meat, feta cheese, tomato, and onion, with bacon or sausage on the side. Plus a short stack of banana chocolate-chip pancakes. If I was really hungry, I might also get an order of cheese fries. At ten in the morning, cheese fries at the same meal with pancakes. Sounds so bad. Tasted so good.

The Maize and Blue Deli Delicatessen was another regular stop, for stuffed sandwiches, two or three. Maybe the No. 29, Jennifer's Dream: turkey, provolone, mayo, Dijon mustard, lettuce, tomato, and pickle on grilled white bread. Or the No. 30, Forever Turkey: turkey, provolone cheese, Dijon mustard, tomato, and onion on grilled sourdough rye. Or possibly the Maize 'N Blue Special, No. 69: roast beef, smoked turkey, cheddar, Jarlsberg cheese, mustard, lettuce, tomato, onion, and mild pepper on a sub roll.

If I didn't want to sit down, I'd hop by

Bruegger's, the bagel place, for two or three sausage, egg, and cream cheese bagels to go. Sausage, egg, and cream cheese. Tastes great.

Whether I ate at one of my favorite places or grabbed the bagels to go, the next destination was always home, to rest before the afternoon workout, usually four to six P.M. After I'd get up for that, I'd have something small to eat, maybe a sandwich, or leftover pizza, or a bowl of cereal.

At night, it was off to the Produce Station, one of those grocery stores that sells every different kind of fruit and vegetable as well as ready-made dinners like chicken or steak. If not there, to a Mexican restaurant called the Prickly Pear for the buffalo enchiladas. A place called Casey's had awesome burgers.

I had my few spots in Ann Arbor, and at those spots I had my selections on each of the menus. It got pretty quickly to the point where I didn't even bother looking at a menu. I got the same thing every time. It's always been like that with me: At that meet in Federal Way when I was not yet fifteen, I ate every single meal, twenty-one over seven days, at a place called Mitzell's, next to our hotel, and at every single meal I had clam chowder as an appetizer and cheesecake for dessert.

Erik, meanwhile, after moving to Ann Arbor, tried to go organic. When I wake up, he used to say, I feel it, I feel alive.

I felt alive, too, even if I wasn't going organic. I ate whatever I wanted, really. But I also ate my salads, my greens, making sure to give my body everything it needed.

But not twelve thousand calories per day. If I had done that, I would seriously have fit the funny headline in the New York Post during the Beijing Olympics that reported I was eating that much: "Boy Gorge."

As intense as the pace in Ann Arbor could be, swimming maybe 55 miles per week, it was a piece of cheesecake indeed when compared to our training sessions at the USOC base in Colorado Springs, altitude 6,100 feet. Those camps were, in a word, brutal.

We went there three times in the eighteen months preceding the 2008 Trials, once after the Melbourne Worlds, once as the calendar was turning from 2007 to 2008, then one last time, as April 2008 stretched into May.

The point of these excursions to Colorado was twofold: Swimming at altitude helps build endurance. And being at the USOC base makes you focus completely on swimming, because there is nothing else there to do. It's a place with absolutely no distractions. You swim, you eat, you sleep. Literally, that's all there is to do. Bob likes it that way. He has a captive audience.

The idea that you could ratchet up your endurance by training at altitude became widespread in track and field after Kip Keino, who had been born and raised at elevation in western Kenya, ran to Olympic glory in Mexico City at the 1968 Summer Games. From then on it was only a matter of time until it spread as well to other sports, including swimming.

It's easy to explain why altitude training works. Red blood cells carry oxygen; the cells in the muscles demand that oxygen. The more red blood cells you have, the more oxygen you can carry to the muscles. Training at altitude builds more red blood cells. Thus, back at sea level for competitions, the harder, faster, stronger — whatever — you should be able to go.

The trick at altitude is to ride the fine line between doing enough but not too much. Thus the coaching dilemma: How much to challenge each of us without anyone breaking down? The working theory for Bob and Jon was that we would do just as much work as if we were still in Michigan, but instead of two swims per day it would be spread over three — the shorter sessions being less of a challenge to the immune system. Even so, Bob would spend most of his time in Colorado worried about us going over the edge because once you're over, it's over. You don't come back, at least not quickly.

Bob's mentor, Paul Bergen, believed in the benefits of training at altitude; that led Bob to the altitude-training protocols developed by Gennady Touretsky, the former Soviet national sprint coach who, from a base in Australia, directed Alexander Popov, the Russian swimmer who won the sprints, both the 50 and 100, at both the 1992 Barcelona and 1996 Atlanta Olympics. Bob managed to get copies of what Touretsky had done. Using that as a starting point, then mixing in Jon's proven success in designing programs to hone middle-distance swimmers, Bob designed his own plan that pushed each one of us to our limits.

Each Colorado trip runs for three weeks and includes roughly seventy swimming, conditioning, or weightlifting workouts. Everything gets carefully plotted out on a Cambridge planning pad, on graph paper, that Bob buys at CVS drugstores, eight at a time; he always buys them in bulk because he's afraid one day they're going to stop selling them.

At the final camp, the one in April and

May, we swam, all in, about 200,000 meters, or just under 125 miles. If we were running on the roads, that would have been the equivalent of nearly five marathons.

The push is both in the mileage itself and in the intensity of the workouts. There were days of aerobic work, which for us meant a workout where we were not breathing hard and our pulse would average 120 to 140 beats per minute, alternating with days of anaerobic work, swims where we were breathing harder and our heart rates were pushed up to 175 to 200 beats. The area in between aerobic and anaerobic work, 150 to 175 beats, is called the "anaerobic threshold"; that threshold zone, according to Jon, provides the most optimal intensity for improving endurance. It was obviously critical to find that zone. Complicating things just a bit, that zone was different for each of us. How to find it? It was done in Ann Arbor the week before leaving for Colorado. Each of us was put through a timed swim, 300 meters ten times; the results were fed into a computer program of Jon's design; the program calculated the 100-meter threshold pace.

Altitude added a two-second difference. At sea level, my threshold before the last trip to Colorado was 1:05.7; at altitude, it then became 1:07.7. Peter and Erik were training for longer distances than I was. Erik's threshold at sea level, for instance, was 1:03.5; at altitude, it became 1:05.5.

When we got into the pool in Colorado, we would then each be assigned the same general workout but be expected to finish laps at times that were calculated from each individual threshold. So, for example, if it was Monday afternoon of the first week, the main swim would be called a rainbow set, when we progressed through a color code from the computer printout doing 4,000 meters, forty 100s. The 4,000 would be broken down into five groups of eight swims; after each 100 we earned a slight rest period, 12 to 19 seconds, depending on where it was in the sequence.

Each of us would be told to do two of those five groups below the threshold, what Bob and Jon called the white, then pink pace; then one at threshold pace, red; then two sets above threshold pace, blue and purple, the colors getting darker in the way your skin might show signs of hard work and lack of oxygen.

The white pace for me, then, would be eight laps holding a time of 1:08.3 per 100; pink, 1:06; red, 1:04.8; blue, 1:02.7; purple, 1:00.5. Erik and Peter would have their own times.

The red pace, 1:04.8, doesn't correlate exactly with the 1:07.7 threshold time because I wouldn't be asked to swim the set continuously; instead, I was doing it in intervals, the computer figuring out the difference.

It's physically demanding and perhaps even more so mentally.

Coming into Omaha, however, we knew we were in great shape. It showed in the 200 free finals. I won, and Peter came in second. Erik came in sixth, a finish that got him onto the 2008 U.S. team and meant he would be swimming, at the least, in the prelims of the 800 relay in Beijing. He was pumped. For everything he had done in his career, Erik had never been on an Olympic relay. Not even once, and when we were sitting around the hotel room in Omaha before the 200 free final, he asked me, what do you think it's going to take to make it?

1:46, I said.

I can do that, he said.

Hop a wave that first 100, then destroy it coming home, I said.

Erik finished in 1:46.95. At 150, he said after the race, he not only could hear the crowd roaring, he could feel the roar in the pool. The last 15 meters, he didn't risk even one breath; he just put his head down and went for it. He said afterward, "If I pass out,

I pass out." Better to have finished sixth and passed out afterwards than get seventh, he figured.

He did not pass out.

Klete came in fourth; he was in, too, along with two more up-and-coming talents from the University of Texas, Ricky Berens and Dave Walters, Ricky finishing third, Dave fifth.

As it turned out, Erik did not make the team in the 1500, to his, and pretty much everyone else's, surprise. Erik had come down from altitude and gone 14:46.78 at the Santa Clara meet in May, a U.S. Open record in the 1500; he finished an easy first, by 12 seconds, in the 1500 qualifying heat in Omaha. It seemed a foregone conclusion that he would not only win, he might set a record, especially when he told me the day before the finals, I'm feeling so good, so fresh.

That 1500 final was scheduled for the last day of the Trials, after I had finished my swims. Walking around the arena before the race, thinking Erik might finish in the low 14:40s, I ran into his parents, who said, well, how do you think he's going to do?

Really well, I said.

It just didn't turn out that way. Two-thirds of the way through the race, as Erik kept dropping farther and farther back, I found Bob and Jon poolside and I said, why is this happening?

No idea, each of them said. His warm-up was fine, his splits awesome.

After the race, Erik answered questions from the press for a long time. I waited for him. When he finished and got to me, I said, "You all right?"

"I don't know what it was," he said. "I felt so good today. But as soon as I dove in, I just didn't have it."

We stood there and hugged each other. Then he walked off. There wasn't anything more to say.

At least he was on the team. And in the relay pool. I was fired up about that. I was either going to be swimming with him, or for him.

Before the 400 free relay in Beijing, there is absolutely no question that the most exciting relay I had ever taken part in was the 800 free relay in Athens. There was also no question that this particular event had a special place in the tradition and culture of American swimming.

Before that Athens relay, for instance, Eddie showed us video of the 800 relay final from the 1984 Los Angeles Games. What a race. This was one of the few events at those Olympics unaffected by the Soviet-led boycott; everyone knew all along it was going to come down to the Americans and the West Germans, with Michael Gross. Coming into the Games, the Germans held the world record; in the prelims, a U.S. team broke it.

And then, for the finals, what strategy. The day before, Gross had won the 200 free in world-record time; American Michael Heath had come in second. An hour before the relay, Gross had to swim the 100 fly finals, which he won in another world record, out-touching Pablo Morales of the United States. Normally, the American coaches would have Heath, who had obviously just proven he was the fastest guy on the U.S. team at 200 meters, swim the anchor, matching him up against Gross. Given that Gross was so super-fast, though, the U.S. coaches switched it up. They put Heath first, with the idea that he would build up the biggest lead he could. The other two would try to push the lead. Then it was hold on and see what Gross had in him.

Bruce Hayes was told he'd be swimming the anchor leg; the year before, Hayes had anchored the winning 800 relay at the Pan American Games. Jeff Float, fourth in the 200 free behind Gross, swam the third leg;

David Larson pulled the second.

Float had lost most of the hearing in both ears after coming down with viral meningitis at the age of thirteen months. The crowd was so loud during his swim that even he — in the water, no less — could hear the roar.

The American strategy had been to give Hayes a lead of about three seconds at take-off. It was only about a second and a half. Gross made all of that up in the first 50. At 100 he passed Hayes. At 150, Gross had a lead of maybe two feet. But then, Hayes turned it on. At the Trials, Hayes had finished third in the 200 free; the 800 relay was thus the only event he had qualified for; he had spent training time since practicing his finishing touch. Practice paid off. Gross swam what was then the fastest 200 relay leg ever. But at the final wall, Hayes outtouched Gross by four-hundredths of a second. The Americans were Grossbusters, the new world-record holders by more than three seconds, in 7:15.69.

For his part, Gross couldn't have been more gracious, saying, "I just ran out of gas. That was a really hot race. It was an honorable defeat."

All of us on the Athens relay team knew about that 1984 relay. We also knew that, going into that 2004 Olympic 800 relay final, the Australians were riding a seven-year winning streak. They had won three straight world titles and had broken the world record five times. In Sydney, they had beaten our American team by more than five seconds.

In Sydney, Klete swam the anchor. He had slipped from second to fifth, then powered back in the final lap to second again, touching just six-hundredths ahead of van den Hoogenband and the Dutch, Hoogie swimming the fastest 200 relay leg ever, 1:44.88.

In Athens, Klete was going to swim the anchor again. The Aussie anchor: Thorpe. The Dutch hadn't qualified for the final. So, just as it was in 1984, everyone knew this was a two-team race, this time the Americans and the Aussies. And, as in 1984, our plan was to give our anchor as big a lead as we could. Klete had taken nearly three-quarters of a second off his lifetime best in the 200 the night before, in the Race of the Century, and still had come in fourth, behind Hoogie and me, 1.42 seconds behind Ian.

So Klete knew all too well what Ian could do. But we all knew from that Sydney relay what Klete could do, too.

I was named to swim the lead leg. Lochte pulled the second, Peter Vanderkaay the third. Just as we were set to walk out to the deck from the ready room, I said, "Wait. Come back." The four of us huddled together. "I don't know if you remember the scene in *Miracle* before the Soviet game where Brooks tells the team, 'This is your time.' Well, this is our time. I don't care what happened in the past. This is us. This is now."

I swam that first leg against Hackett. These were the Olympics, sure. But in a way it was just like it had been the year before at our little training camp in Australia. Just he and I. He turned one-hundredth ahead at 50; I moved ahead by a tenth at 100; then by three-tenths at 150; then I really turned it on. I swam that last lap in 26.78 and hit the wall in 1:46.49. The lead: 1.01 seconds. Ryan held the lead. Then Peter swam the best 200 time of his life to get us through 600 meters in 5:21.80. Klete dove in with a lead of 1.48 seconds.

Ian made it all up in the first 50. He and Klete seemed to be in a dead heat.

On the blocks, at the other end, Ryan, Peter, and I were jumping and screaming. Ian kept surging; Klete kept holding him off, barely. At 150, Klete turned first. I looked over at our team in the athlete seating area — there was Vendt on his feet, screaming, too. Jon and Bob were standing nearby. Jon knew it already even if the rest of us didn't. "If he didn't catch him there," Jon said, referring to Ian, "he's not catching him."

And he didn't. Klete got Ian at the final wall by thirteen-hundredths.

Leaning forward there on the deck, I couldn't tell immediately who had gotten whom at the wall. I had to look up at the scoreboard, and there it was, the 1 on the line that said United States. I had always been fairly reserved in my victory celebrations, especially on the world stage, but at that instant I couldn't help it and didn't want to; I raised both index fingers to the stars and let loose a scream of joy that seemed to have no end. Ryan was pumped, too. Peter, as reserved as they get, was bouncing up and down. I reached down to congratulate Klete. He, too, was usually a study in reserve. This was as excited as I'd ever seen him. He yelled, "Yeah, we did it! We kicked their butts!"

Ian, dejected, stayed in the pool a very long time. Finally, he hoisted himself up and came over to where the four of us Americans had huddled around each other in intense excitement and happiness. He waited patiently, then shook hands and walked away. It was his first 800 relay loss in international competition. The Aussie streak was done. We had finished in 7:07.33, the Aussies in 7.07.46.

It was, for me, until the 400 relay in Beijing, the most exciting moment I had ever been a part of on a pool deck. That night in Athens, I had trouble going to sleep. I kept playing the tape of the race in my head, over and over and over again.

In Melbourne in 2007, the four of us — me, Ryan, Peter, Klete — not only swam the 800 relay again, we lowered the world record the Aussies had set in 2001 in Fukuoka. They had gone 7:04.66. We went 7:03.24.

We knew the time in Beijing could be faster.

The thinking in most quarters was that it would be faster because of the suit: the Speedo LZR Racer. The suit that most of us on the American team raced in at the 2008 Olympics.

The suit was not the only reason we knew the time could be faster. But all of us spent untold hours answering questions about the suit beforehand, at the Trials and at the Games, because the suit had taken the swimming world by storm.

The full-body LZR was a major step forward in swimsuit design. It was made of special water-repellent fabrics. Built into it, to hold your stomach and lower back tight, was a corsetlike compression unit. To reduce drag, the suit had no stitches; instead, the pieces were ultrasonically bonded together. Even the zipper was bonded into the suit to help keep the surface as smooth as possible.

NASA scientists helped develop the LZR. So did, among others, Bob and I. We made a trip after those 2007 Worlds in Melbourne to the Australian capital, Canberra, to what's called the Australian Institute of Sport, to do some testing before it was introduced publicly, checking where the hot points were in the suit, what happened to it when you dove in, what it felt like in it.

It feels like wearing a girdle, or at least what I imagine wearing a girdle would have to feel like. It sucks everything in. It compresses everything. It's tight around your neck. You definitely had to get used to it, and you saw a lot of swimmers reach for the zipper in the back as soon as they were done racing because it was so tight.

The suit first got noticed in a big way at the 2008 short-course world championships in England. Swimmers wearing the LZR set seventeen world records.

Lochte, who set a handful of those records, then said, "When I put it on, people joke around about this, but I feel like I'm some kind of action hero, like ready to take on the world. That's just when I put it on. It makes me feel like when I dive in that water like I'm swimming downhill."

Then came controversy, with swimmers and coaches who were not tied to Speedo wondering whether it was unfair. It was not. The suit was available for anybody and everybody. Any single person in the world could wear the suit. Speedo made it available for anybody, and as the months went along some other companies said it would be okay if their swimmers wanted to wear the LZR at the Olympics, too.

Alberto Castagnetti, the coach of the Italian swim team, may have done more than anyone else to make the controversy what it was. He called the LZR "technological doping." Still, when he came several weeks later to the U.S. Trials, he was quietly exploring whether it might be possible for any of his swimmers to wear the LZR Racer.

I was watching ESPN's *Pardon the Interruption* on one of my breaks during the Trials, and laughed when I saw that one of the upcoming topics was the suit. It got to the point where, at every press conference, we were asked about the suit.

Even Spitz, who swam in a brief and without goggles, the way it was done back in the day, got asked about the suit. Working in a reference to me, he said at the Trials, "I said this sort of tongue-in-cheek, that if that suit had hair on it, Michael would set world records in it and everyone else would get in the same type of suit. I don't really think it's the swimming suit, and if it was the suit then I am going out and buying Tiger Woods' golf clubs, because it means no matter who the swinger is, I am going to be able to score like that."

Maybe the best line of all came from Markus Rogan of Austria, a 2004 two-time silver medalist in the backstroke. Markus went to high school in suburban Washington, D.C., then to college at Stanford. He said, "I tested it. I threw it in the pool and it didn't move at all. So I'll still have to swim."

A lot of hard work went into the suit. But the suit helped make a difference of a hundred or a tenth of a second. That was not going to get our relay team under seven minutes.

This was, though: It was an Olympic year. Everyone everywhere was training for the Games. That's why times were dropping and records falling.

The Olympic record, going into the prelims, stood at 7:07.05, set by the Aussies in Sydney in 2000. That lasted as long as it took for Walters, Berens, Vendt, and Keller to swim. They finished in 7:04.66.

As it was within the 400 relay prelims, there was a competition within the competition itself in the 800 prelims — the fastest guy of the four would get to swim in the finals.

Here's how it broke down:

Walters, swimming the first leg, went 1:46.57.

Berens, second, 1:45.47.

Vendt, 1:47.11.

Keller, 1:45.51.

Erik, at that time, was definitely not going to swim in the finals. It was disappointing for him, I'm sure, because it was for me. But what was there to say? Nothing. If we won gold in the final, he would get a gold, too. That would speak volumes.

The coaches had a tough decision to make. Ricky was four-hundredths faster than Klete. But Klete had abundantly proven himself, especially in that Athens 800 relay.

Swimming is a tough sport. There's little if any room for sentiment. All anyone looking at the situation had to do was to think back to what the U.S. coaches faced in Sydney, when Chad Carvin swam in the 800 relay prelims. If anyone was deserving of extra consideration, it had to be Chad. Before Atlanta and 1996, he was considered a virtual lock for a gold medal or two; then, though, his times began to creep up. He couldn't figure out why. He became so depressed he attempted suicide by swallowing sleeping pills. In the hospital afterward, doctors discovered why he had gotten slower — a heart condition. Chad watched the first day of the 1996 Trials in tears. He rededicated himself and was diagnosed with a degenerative back problem. Again, he came back. At the 2000 Trials, finally, he earned his spot on the team in the 400 free and in the 800 relay. In Sydney, he didn't have it the way he had hoped. He finished sixth in the 400 free, seven seconds back. And then he could not convince the U.S. coaches that he deserved one of the spots in the relay finals.

One of those spots, instead, went to an incoming college freshman who in the prelims had gone faster than Chad: Klete Keller.

Ricky had gone fastest in the 2008 prelims. So, just as it was for Klete eight years ago, now it was for Ricky. Ricky got the spot in the finals.

The rest of us knew Klete, sure. But we also knew Ricky was swimming fast and, if you swim a time, you're going to be on the relay. Just as I deserved to be on that 400 free relay in Athens, Ricky had earned his spot. Klete handled it this time around with graciousness.

Not to sound cocky by any means but, as a team, we knew going into the 800 relay finals that we were going to win. We had won this relay easily in Melbourne; no single country was close at that meet to our times, and no evidence had surfaced since that anyone was going to be close; this was not a situation like Athens in any way. The only way we weren't going to win was if someone was disqualified for a false start.

But could we break seven minutes?

I knew going into this final that I was going to swim fast. For one thing, I had not gone as fast in the 200 fly as I'd wanted to because of the equipment malfunction; this relay was the next place to prove what I still had in me. For another, when I lead off a relay, I want to help my teammates by giving them open water; if they have open water, they're going to swim faster. Thirdly, I had not done what I'd wanted in my leadoff leg in the 800 relay at the Melbourne Worlds; I had wanted to back up the 1:43.86 I'd had there in the open 200 with a similar swim but, instead, went a full second and a half slower, 1:45.36.

I was still mad about that.

And then, looking up into the stands, we saw several of the stars of the U.S. Olympic basketball team, including Kobe Bryant, LeBron James, Chris Paul, Jason Kidd, and Carmelo Anthony. No way were we giving it anything less than 100 percent with those guys on hand to watch. On deck, we could even hear them cheering. That was cool, those guys cheering for us.

I was fired up when I dove in. It showed, too. I went 1:43.31, the second-fastest time of all time. We had a lead of more than two seconds when I touched, Ryan — then Ricky, then Peter — looking at nothing but open water ahead.

I swam in the relay with the same pair of goggles that hadn't worked in the 200 fly. They didn't work right in the relay, either; one side filled up a little bit. But this time I could still see.

Back on the deck through Ryan's swim, I was encouraging Ricky to step it up. "When you have a guy like that yelling at you, you better do what he says," Ricky said later.

As Peter made the final turn of his four laps, we had already thrown down such a dominating performance that the camera had to pan back to the left just to get the other swimmers in the picture. "Come on!" I yelled at him. "Let's go!" And go he did.

When he touched, the scoreboard said 6:58.56.

We had not just gone under seven minutes; we had gone a full second under seven. We had put four guys together who wanted to achieve a common goal, who had the talent and the confidence to achieve that goal, and this race showed what we could do together. Of all the records broken in Beijing, this race was the one in which we lowered the record by the largest margin, 4.28 seconds.

Inevitably, the reporters afterward wanted to know whether the other guys were swimming in part for me. Peter put it best. He said, "I think it's special to be a part of that, but there's still a ton of pressure on us to win, anyway. We want to win. We want to do it for the U.S.A. and for the team. I don't think there's much more pressure than there already was."

The gold medal was my fifth in Beijing, the eleventh of my career. The media crews naturally wanted to know what I had to say about that. "You're always an Olympic gold medalist," I said. "Birthdays happen every year. Christmas happens every year. You only go to be an Olympic gold medalist so many times and it definitely never, ever gets old — you know, listening to the national anthem play with a gold medal around your neck, it's one of the greatest feelings I've ever had in the sport of swimming."

To keep it going, meanwhile, I was clearly going to have to get a new pair of Speedo Speed Socket metallic goggles. I borrowed a pair from Ricky. He was done competing. As for me: six swims still to go, three of the six finals: the 200 IM, the 100 fly, and the medley relay. Eleven swims were in the books. And I still felt very, very solid.

6

COURAGE:
THE 200 INDIVIDUAL
MEDLEY

Whether it was at the pool or in the village, my teammates would not and did not talk to me about eight gold medals, in much the same way that a pitcher's teammates avoid talking to him during a no-hitter or a perfect game.

At night, in our suite in the village, we would play cards or the board game Risk. We'd talk about anything but swimming. Just guy stuff. The games were supercompetitive. One night Lochte and I, playing spades against Cullen and Eric Shanteau, found ourselves down 385–5. The game was to 500; we came back to win. There was lots of hollering and carrying on.

You would never have known that Shanteau had been diagnosed with testicular cancer. Which is just the way he wanted it.

At the 2004 Trials, Eric had finished third in both the 200 and 400 IMs. He hung in there. In Omaha, he made it onto the 2008 team, in the 200 breaststroke. At training camp in Palo Alto, he told us he had competed at the Trials knowing he had been diagnosed; the tests had come back on June 19, about a week before the start of the Trials. Eric had talked it over with the doctors and they had given him their okay, he could go to Beijing. Surgery could wait until after the Games.

Eric told us all these things at a team meeting after we had finished dinner, taken a team photo, and filed back into a meeting room. Everyone was getting drowsy. Then Eddie stood up and said Eric had something to say. And then we were all, like, oh, my God, what do you say? Fortunately, Eric had the words: "I've been going through this for a while now and it's not the easiest thing. But I've been able to get the okay for being here, and trying to accomplish my goals and dreams."

That wasn't all to the story, either. Eric's dad, Rick, had been diagnosed with lung cancer the year before.

I hadn't known Eric that well before Beijing. He is an awesome guy. The whole time we were at the Olympics, he was fully alive, fully living his dream. Ultimately, he didn't win a medal, but who cared?

I admired the way Eric was handling the

challenge. Just as I was motivated by Dara Torres, who proved over and over again that age was no barrier to anything, winning three silver medals in Beijing, and by her coach, Michael Lohberg, who had been diagnosed with a rare blood disorder, aplastic anemia, after the Trials but before we flew to Asia. Just as I had been deeply affected by the fight against cancer of a boy in Baltimore who had become a good friend, Stevie Hansen.

The day after the 200 fly and the 800 relay, I had no finals — I swam the 200 IM semifinals in the morning, the 100 fly prelims at night — and so I had, for the first time since the Games had begun, a moment or two to reflect on the struggles, the journeys, and the courage of people I knew and what it meant to be a hero.

The five gold medals I had won had already prompted so much talk about me being a hero. After the fifth medal, the president of the International Olympic Committee, Dr. Rogge, had called me "the icon of the Games." He also said, "The Olympic Games live around super-heroes. You had Jesse Owens. You had Paavo Nurmi, Carl Lewis, and now you have Phelps. And that's what we need to have."

Castagnetti, the Italian coach who had

stirred so much talk about the LZR, said I was "undisputedly the greatest swimmer of all time." He had a unique perspective; like Spitz, he had competed at the 1972 Olympics in Munich.

There was funny talk about science fiction. After the 800 free relay, Alexander Sukhorukov of Russia, with a silver medal around his neck, said, "He is just a normal person but maybe from a different planet." Cornel Marculescu, the executive director of FINA, said something very similar: "The problem is, we have an extraterrestrial. No one else can win." British swimmer Simon Burnett said something much like that, too, talking with Eddie Reese when they ran into each other in the cafeteria. "He was saying to me, 'I think I've figured out Michael Phelps,'" Eddie said later. "'He is not from another planet. He is from the future. His father made him and made a time machine. Sixty years from now, he is an average swimmer but he has come back here to mop up.'"

I would find out later that there were other stories in which I would be described as the greatest American athlete of our generation, or comparing me to the likes of Michael Jordan or Tiger Woods. On NBC, Dan Hicks, who called the swim races from the Water

Cube, had described me as "Tiger in a Speedo."

All these comparisons were humbling. To even be mentioned in the same sentence with some of the greatest, most dominating athletes in the world was overwhelming, especially because I was just doing what I love to do. My goal was never to become the best athlete ever; it was simply to become the best athlete I could be.

If what I was doing was helping inspire someone else to stand up and take on a challenge, I was honored by that.

But a hero?

Stevie Hansen was a hero.

Stevie was only seven when he was diagnosed with a brain tumor, in October 2002. He was a promising age-group swimmer; at six, he was not only already swimming but winning awards.

The day before Stevie's surgery, I brought over a flag, some shirts, and a poster. We shot hoops in the driveway at his house and we just talked about how each of us loved to eat junk food. The day of the surgery, I made sure to send balloons to the hospital. Stevie's dad, Steve Hansen, later told me that meant the world to Stevie.

It made me happy to try to make Stevie happy, that's all. This is the way my mom raised me. This is the way I am. If Stevie had wanted to meet me because he thought I was a cool swimmer, I quickly came to learn that he was a cool swimmer, too, and a brave, even fearless, young man.

Over the next year, Stevie seemed to get better. That next summer, I sent a note saying I wanted to come watch Stevie swim at a local meet. Which I did. I showed up unannounced. When he saw me, Stevie sprinted over, leapt into my arms, and said, "Wow, you came!" I got to watch Stevie that afternoon as he raced in the free, the fly, and the relay. We had lunch together and I signed autographs for the other kids, including Stevie's sister, Grace, who never lets me forget that I used a red Sharpie on her forehead. I then got persuaded to swim a relay leg myself in a parents' and coaches' race, even though I had to borrow a suit. Stevie was thrilled. I was thrilled for him.

Throughout the 2004 Olympics, and after I came back and moved to Ann Arbor, I made sure to stay in touch with Stevie and the Hansens as he underwent three more surgeries. So, in April 2007, when Stevie's mom, Betsy, called my mom, to say, "We have a disaster here . . . he wants to see Michael," there was no question.

I rearranged my schedule to get to Baltimore. Then I had one of those days traveling that everyone seems to have at one point. The plane was late. Bags were lost. So, by the time Mom and I got to the Hansens' house it was already after midnight.

We stayed there for two hours, maybe longer. Stevie was only eleven and so desperately ill. But his fighting spirit, that's what had always impressed me about him. I sat there on Stevie's bed, holding his hand, just talking. He was sound asleep and didn't wake up. Even so, I was sure he could hear, which is just what Stevie told his mom the next morning: "I wish I had woken up. But I know he was here."

The next day, I posted a note to Stevie's personal page on an Internet site for people confronting serious illnesses. I said, "Stevie, it was great to see you last night. I'm really glad I got to visit. You are very brave. You really are an inspiration to us all. Talk to you soon — Michael."

"Yours was a gift like none other," Betsy posted back.

Stevie died on May 29, 2007. The memorial service took place a few days later. I sent purple flowers — purple was Stevie's favorite color — and I was honored to be asked to stand with the Hansens as they greeted friends and family.

I was sure Stevie was looking down on us. I was just as sure that, when I went to Beijing, Stevie was cheering from above.

Stevie had told his parents he wanted me to try to win an Olympic medal for him. At his bedside that night, just a few weeks before Stevie passed away, I made Stevie this promise: I'd try to get a medal. Hopefully, it would be gold.

I owed Stevie my very best effort in everything I did at these Olympics. And the 200 IM was going to take every bit of that effort. Just like the 400, it demands consistency and endurance across all four strokes. And just like the 400, it exposes flaws or weaknesses, only faster.

I had not lost in the 200 IM, at least in a 50-meter pool, in a major competition. Lochte had gotten me at the end of 2007, at the short-course nationals, but that was just weeks after I'd broken my wrist.

I had no intention of losing at the Olympics.

The top four seeds in the Beijing final were the same top four going into the final in Athens: me, Lochte, Laszlo Cseh, and Thiago Pereira of Brazil. In 2004, though I got the gold, my winning time was well off the world record; I pushed the pace but simply didn't have the physical strength to get home over the final 100 meters. By that point in my Athens schedule, I was probably more worn down than I knew, and you could see that the polish and pop in my stroke was just not there.

This time I had no doubt. It would be there. I was going to take it out hard early, like the 200 free, and dare the other guys to match what I could do.

Laszlo sat on my shoulder through the first 100, through the fly and the back, and even into the turn for the breast. Maybe I would flinch? No chance. I reeled off far and away the fastest breast split of the top four, 33.5, a second faster than Laszlo, more than a half-second faster than Ryan. Coming off the 150 turn, I was already a body length ahead of Laszlo.

This time, I could drive hard for the finish. My last lap: 27.33. Nobody else even broke 28.

I touched in 1:54.23, 57-hundredths of a second better than the 1:54.8 world record I had gone in Omaha.

Laszlo was second, Ryan third. Both those guys went faster in Beijing than I went for gold in Athens; even so, I had touched more than two seconds ahead of each of them. When the results went up on the big board,

I reached over to Ryan's lane; we shook hands and patted each other on the head.

Ryan's bronze has, in some quarters, been overlooked, too. No way should it be — and this is no knock on Laszlo, who earned the silver. Laszlo, in fact, was the definition of sportsmanship after the 200 IM, saying, "It's not a shame to be beaten by a better one." Ryan, meanwhile, tackled one of the toughest doubles imaginable that morning. At 10:19 that morning, he swam the 200 backstroke final, winning gold and setting a world record in defeating Aaron Peirsol, among others. The 200 IM final went off at 10:48. Ryan only had twenty-seven minutes in between the two races. For him to medal in both races was just amazing. Only he and another American, John Naber, have ever done it, John in 1976 in Montreal.

Later, on the medals stand for the 200 IM, Ryan and I got to smile and enjoy what we'd done, but just for the briefest of moments. Now, it was my turn to double, twenty-nine minutes from the end of the IM until the semifinals of the 100 fly. As soon as the anthem was over and some photos taken, I switched from my dress sweats to my parka and shoes, I threw my cap and goggles on, and then they pushed us out there. The medal from the 200 IM — I was now six-for-

six, twelve career golds, fourteen overall —
was in my warmup jacket.

After I won that sixth gold, I was asked in a
news conference, "What do you say to those
who think you may be too good to be true?"

I wasn't surprised by the question.

If anything, I was only surprised that the
issue of doping hadn't come up until this
point in the Games.

"Anyone can say whatever they want," I
replied. "I know, for me, I am clean. I purposely wanted to do more tests to prove it.
People can say what they want, but the facts
are the facts."

I knew going into Beijing that anything I
might do there, any medals I might win,
would without doubt be viewed by some
with skepticism. Doping scandals will do
that, and, in recent years, there had been far
too many doping scandals in sports. Since I
had won my medals in Athens, the Mitchell
Report had fallen upon baseball. Floyd
Landis had failed a doping test and had his
2006 Tour de France victory taken away.
Marion Jones, who had won five Olympic
medals in track and field in Sydney, was
sentenced to federal prison at the beginning
of 2008 for lying to federal agents about her
use of performance-enhancing substances.

So, I understood why there might well be skepticism. Somebody somewhere does something and immediately the first reaction now is, well, he or she is on the juice. It might be unfair, but it's reality.

I wanted to help do something to help change that reality.

I understand that kids look up to athletes. If any kid anywhere was looking up to me, I never, ever would want to let that young person down. Growing up, I watched the Olympics. I watched Cal Ripken, Jr., play baseball. I looked up to Michael Jordan, too. I watched all these great athletes compete for the love of the game, because they were having fun. That's what I wanted to do, too.

When I was younger, I proved I could do without Ritalin. Then, in ninth grade, I did a school project on drug cheats, at about the time I started to be tested myself, when I was fourteen and just onto the national radar. Then, later in high school, I saw how devastating it could be for someone to be accused of doping. When Beth Botsford, the North Baltimore swimmer, grew up, she became engaged to Kicker Vencill, another swimmer. In January 2003, an out-of-competition doping test found evidence in Kicker's system of a by-product of the banned steroid nandrolone. Kicker told everyone he was innocent. A nutritional supplement he was taking, a multivitamin, must have been tainted, he said, and there was good reason to believe this was very likely what had happened. In 2001, an IOC-financed study had found that 15 percent of the hundreds of products tested contained steroid precursors, a building block that the body turns into steroids, even though the precursors weren't listed anywhere on the label. The contamination might happen during the manufacturing process, might be the fault of tainted ingredients. Doesn't matter. The rules of international sports are that if something is in your system, it doesn't matter how it got there; it doesn't matter in the slightest whether you intended to cheat. All that matters is if it's there. Ignorance is never an excuse. Kicker was banned from competition for two years. Later he went to trial, and in a California court won a jury verdict against the vitamin manufacturer; after that, the case settled. But Kicker's Olympic dream was ended.

There are two kinds of doping tests. Some you take at a competition; you know you're going to get tested if you're at a big meet and, usually, one of the top finishers. Other tests are unannounced. That is, if you're on the testing lists, which are kept by the U.S. Anti-Doping Agency and by FINA, a tester can show up at the pool or even at your house — anywhere, really — and order you to take a test, right then and there. You have to keep USADA and FINA notified at all times of your whereabouts. If you don't agree to take the test, it counts as a positive.

The rules are strict, but they have to be.

The rules for Olympic athletes are much, much stricter than they are for NFL players or Major League Baseball players. That's not fair, but those of us who are not cheating, who would never cheat, have learned to embrace the double standard, not get mad about it.

In fact, we have tried to make the contrast even more clear. At the start of 2008, USADA was putting together a project in which twelve U.S. Olympic athletes would volunteer for extra testing: not just urine tests but blood as well, six weeks of tests, once a week, to establish a baseline. If USADA asked, your entire medical history would have to be provided. It all went toward going as far as possible to answering the common-sense question: What would you do if you knew you were clean?

I heard about this project from Dara, who said she was going to do it.

I wanted in, too. I wanted to prove to everybody that I was 100 percent clean.

Ultimately, USADA picked three of us swimmers among the twelve — Dara, Natalie Coughlin, and me. The others included track and field stars such as Bryan Clay, who would go on to win gold in the decathlon at Beijing.

I willingly provided the extra samples, even though the first time, when they took five vials of blood from me, I confess I felt a little woozy afterward. Five vials is a lot of blood.

From early June through the end of the Olympics, I was tested probably twenty-five to thirty times. I was tested every day at the Trials and at the Games. The day I checked into the Olympic Village, I was tested.

I'm clean. Always have been, always will be. Facts are facts.

7
WILL:
THE 100 FLY

Of the seven medals that Matt Biondi won at the 1988 Olympics in Seoul, five were gold, one was silver, and one bronze.

Matt's silver came in the 100 fly. Matt was first at the turn and with 10 meters to go was still in the lead. As he neared the wall, though, Matt got caught between strokes. What to do? He opted to glide instead of taking an extra stroke with his arms, even if that extra stroke might have been nothing more than a half stroke. The problem: Matt was father away from the wall and the touch pad than he thought.

At 99 meters Matt was in first.

At 100 meters he was in second. Matt's glide allowed Anthony Nesty to sneak past. Anthony was timed in 53 seconds flat, Matt in 53.01.

Anthony was a sophomore at the University of Florida who was swimming for the country in which he had grown up, Suriname, a small nation on the northeast coast of South America. The entire country had one 50-meter pool. For three years prior to those 1988 Games, Anthony had been training in the United States, first at a private school in Jacksonville, then in college in Gainesville.

Suddenly, Anthony was indisputably Suriname's first-ever Olympic medalist. He was also the first black man to win an Olympic swimming medal. In Suriname, they would go on to issue a stamp in Anthony's honor, as well as commemorative gold and silver coins.

Initially, Matt could not believe what had happened. "One one-hundredth of a second," he said afterward. "What if I had grown my fingernails longer?"

In 2002, at the nationals in Fort Lauderdale, after I out-touched Ian Crocker for my first major victory in the 100 fly, Anthony came up to me and said, "That's how I beat Matt Biondi in the 100 fly that day. It was the touch."

That day was the first time I truly understood how important the finish of the 100 fly could be. Among all the events on my race schedule, the 100 fly was always going to be one of the hardest, if not outright the most difficult, of the individual races. Why? Because, compared to the others, it is much shorter, a simple up-and-back sprint. And because my habit of swimming the first 50 at easy speed and then coming on hard was always going to leave me fighting at the end.

When I was twelve, Bob shocked me one day. We were at a meet and he said, Michael, you know what my job is?

No, I said.

It's to get you in the ballpark.

You know what your job is?

It's to get your freaking hand on the wall. And he didn't say freaking.

Bob was trying, even then, to drill into my head that a finish was important, that you swim aggressively all the way to the wall. He would not tolerate lazy finishes in practices, ever.

It all came together that day in 2002. Just hearing Anthony say it made real what Bob had been preaching. If I nailed the touch, it could make all the difference.

I thought about all of that in Beijing after hustling through my semifinal swim in the 100 fly.

Milorad Cavic of Serbia looked strong. He and I had been in the same preliminary heat the day before. In that prelim, he had turned first and finished in 50.76, an Olympic record; I was sixth at the turn, a body length behind, but predictably surged the last 50, closing to finish second in 50.87. In the semis, Cavic got through with the fastest time; I was second-fastest; Crocker, since 2003 the world-record holder in the event, was tied for third, with Andrew Lauterstein of Australia, and said, "People point at me, but Cavic is looking good and it'll be a tight race."

The final was indeed going to be tough. I needed to try to be faster in the first 50 and come on even stronger at the finish. The touch might make all the difference.

"On this planet," a Korean journalist had asked me in a news conference in the middle of my week of racing in Beijing, "is there anybody who can defeat you? And if so, who is it?"

I laughed and shrugged: "I don't know."

A moment or two later, I said, "I'm not un-beatable. No one's unbeatable. Everyone can be beaten."

Ian Crocker had beaten me before in the 100 fly. And though we had become good friends, he wouldn't be all broken up if he were to beat me in Beijing. Not in the slight-est.

"Sports is all about one person trying to derail the other person's dreams," Crock said. "It's kind of the dog-eat-dog part of sports. Michael has his goals and I have mine. I'm not going to feel bad if I race my heart out and end up winning."

Crock is one of the greatest athletes ever to come out of the state of Maine. And Maine didn't even have it as good as Suriname when Crock was growing up; in the entire state, there wasn't one Olympic-sized pool. Instead, Crock spent his first training years swimming in a four-lane, 25-yard pool attached to an elementary school; the pool was also used to provide therapy for the developmentally disabled. As Crock tells the story, their diapers didn't always work.

Crock, like me, was diagnosed with a learning disability, in his case attention-deficit disorder. In high school, moreover, he began developing signs of depression; when he went away to college, to Texas, he sought help and was prescribed the antidepression medication Zoloft. Then he was able to kick the medication cold turkey.

Crock has always been one of the most thoughtful guys out there, a guy with insight and perspective. He has for years had a thing for classic cars; one of the first cars he bought was a 1971 Buick Riviera. He got his first guitar in the eighth grade, for Christmas. Asked to name his favorite Bob Dylan tune, he says it's like asking him to choose among which of the breaths he has taken over the past twenty-five years. His blog quotes from Steve Earle's "Fort Worth Blues," its lines about the highway:

*It's just the only place a man can go
When he don't know where he's travelin' to.*

Not surprisingly, Crock has a certain way with words. "The 100 fly is the gift I was given," he said. "So, you shake your money-maker . . . and you see what happens."

Crock won the 100 fly at the 2000 Trials. In Sydney, he finished fourth, 22-hundredths of a second away from bronze; he also swam the final of the gold medal-winning, world record-setting medley relay. By 2002, I had added the 100 fly to my program; in Fort Lauderdale, I beat him and went under his American record. That set the stage for the next year, and the Worlds in Barcelona.

In the first of the two semifinals in Spain in 2003, Andriy Serdinov of the Ukraine went 51.76, lowering a world record that had stood for five years. He got to hold the record for as long as it took me to swim the second semi. I went 51.47.

In the final, I went 51.10. I had lowered the record again. But Crock went 50.98. He was the first man under 51.

In the warm-down pool, Bob offered a two-part lesson: Let the loss go. And think fast now about how, having come up just short, you're going to present yourself to reporters. Are you a sore loser? Or are you gracious? Remember, he said, better here than next summer.

"I hate to lose and I think it's going to drive me even more," I said when I met the press. "It definitely makes me hungrier for next year leading into Athens. I have a lot of goals for that meet and I think the 100 fly is a big part of that."

There was more to winning in the 100 fly, meanwhile, than just that race. The fastest American in the 100 fly also earns a spot in the finals of the medley relay. Second-best got the prelim, and I was suddenly in the prelim. Bob was adamant: I was going to swim in that prelim. It was my responsibility.

I went home from Barcelona with five gold medals but, as well, the image in my mind of Crock and the three other guys on top of the podium after winning the medley in record time.

Crock had prepared better for the 100 fly in Barcelona than I had. He had executed better than I had. If I was going to turn that around in Athens, I had to do better.

The morning after the 100 final, a local paper ran the headline, "Phelps es Humano." Translation: "Phelps is Human."

The headline on the cover of the October 2003, issue of *Swimming World,* in bright yellow letters, shouted, "Super Flyer." That would be Crock, guitar in hand, leaned up against that 1971 Buick. Inside was a lengthy feature that included a centerfold of Crock swimming the fly. I ripped out that centerfold and plastered it on the wall above my bed. Every morning, the first thing I'd see when I woke up was that photo. Every morning that photo was a kick in the backside. It drove me. It pushed me. It punished me.

At the 2004 Trials, Crock not only beat me again, he lowered his world record, to 50.76. The Olympic final was shaping up to be a classic.

By then, thanks to numerous stories about what I'd done with the poster, he knew full well that he was motivating me. But, it turned out, I was motivating him, too. He had in his head the image of me rushing by him on the final 50, and he didn't like that one bit.

We were, in the best spirit of what sports is supposed to be all about, pushing each other to be the best each of us could be.

The 100 fly semis in Athens turned out to be a rerun of sorts of Barcelona. Serdinov won the first semi, in an Olympic record, 51.74. In the next semifinal, I went him one better, 51.61. Crock went 51.83.

The medley relay heats took place before the 100 fly final. Thus, the coaches had to make a decision that ended with me swimming in the heats. Crock had beaten me at the Trials and in Barcelona; he had to be considered a slight favorite for the 100 fly finals. Plus, earlier in the week he hadn't been at his best physically, and that had showed in the 400 free relay; better to rest him for the 100 final.

Did I want to swim in the medley finals? "Big time," I told the press. "Everybody wants to swim in the finals of a relay. I missed out on that last year, and I really want to do it here."

As I was warming up before the finals, Bob looked me over. He liked what he saw, liked the look in my eyes. Michael's going to win, he thought.

At the turn, however, it looked like I was doomed. Crock got off the blocks like a rocket. At the turn he was under world-record place; I was in fifth, 77-hundredths of a second behind him.

As I hit the wall, I turned the power on. I

surged into third, Serdinov and Crock still ahead.

In the stands, Bob had stopped looking at the pool at 50 meters, figuring I was too far back. At 20 meters, I had pulled up to Crock's shoulder. At 15 meters, Bob looked down again at the water. Well, he thought, second isn't that bad.

The three of us churned toward the wall. Serdinov, though, bobbed too high and Crock got caught in midstroke while I timed my strokes perfectly. I reached for the wall at full extension, at the end of my stroke, just as I was supposed to do.

My goggles came off so I could see the scoreboard.

Serdinov, it said, had touched in 51.36.

Crocker: 51.29.

Me: 51.25.

Seventeen races into my program in Athens, and I still had enough in me to reach for the wall and my dreams. Four-hundredths of a second — the touch could, indeed, make all the difference.

Crock said on television, "Michael is just pure tough. That's like just the only word for it. So, I mean, I knew he was going to be tough. And I just got out there and gave it my best shot. And I'm real proud of both of us."

Later, on a victory lap, in the stands I saw Spitz. He waved to me, his thumb down, the other four fingers up, a sign he knew full well what I had done. The 100 fly was my fourth individual gold in Athens, the same number of individual medals he had won in Munich.

I also had the two bronze medals, of course, in the 200 free and the 400 relay. And I still had the medley relay to go, which, assuming the American team won, would make it eight overall.

Crock, on the other hand, came to Athens anticipating three golds. If I swam the medley final, he would go home with none.

Before I started swimming the 100 fly, Crock had been the undisputed best in that event. Now I was Olympic champion. But, because of me, he was now the world-record holder.

Crock had a silver and a bronze at the Olympics. How could that seem like failure? And yet, somehow, it did. Why did he have to have gotten a sore throat at the Olympics, of all times? It wasn't right. It just didn't seem fair for a guy who, for as many times as I had looked at his photo, was someone for whom I had developed abundant and profound respect. He was rival and competitor, yes. But also my teammate and my friend.

I thought about this some more, then told

Bob that Crock could have my spot in the medley final. He deserved it, I said.

Okay, he said. He understood. Go tell Eddie, Bob said.

"Michael," Eddie said, "are you sure this is what you want? It has to come from you."

"It is."

Someone else went to tell Crock, who was coming out of drug testing, to get back in the pool for another warm-down swim. But I'm done, Ian said. No, he was told, no, you're not.

Now it was his turn to say no. I didn't earn it, he said. But you deserve it, we said.

Eventually, he agreed. We let Eddie make the announcement to the press. I said, and I meant every word, "We came in as a team and we're going to go out as a team." Crock said, "I'm kind of speechless. I feel like it's a huge gift that is difficult to accept but it makes me want to just go out and tear up the pool."

Which, of course, he and the other three guys — Peirsol, Hansen, Lezak — did. Crock turned in the fastest butterfly split ever in the medley and the American team took nearly a second off the world record. I got to wear baggy shorts and flip-flops and lead the cheers from the stands.

After the medal ceremony, Crock came

over to where I was sitting. We hugged each other.

"Congratulations," I said.

"Thank you," he said.

Later, Crock told everyone, "I thanked him because he was one of the main reasons I had the opportunity to do that. He gave me a gift."

It was an easy call, really. It was the right thing to do.

After those Games, of course, Crock and Krayzelburg and I criss-crossed the country on our tour. We were with each other twenty-four hours a day for several weeks. Crock opened up and we had a good time in each other's company. A documentary film, *Unfiltered,* shot in the months between Athens and the 2005 Worlds in Montreal, chronicled it all.

When the tour ended, Crock got back to serious training. Me? I endured the ferocious anxiety of my back problems, got arrested for drinking and driving, moved to Ann Arbor, and had to learn how to live life away from home. Other distractions abounded as well. I made the rounds of various talk shows. I judged a beauty pageant.

At the 2005 Worlds in Montreal, Crock thrashed me in the 100 fly. Absolutely dominated. He not only beat me by more than a second, he lowered the world record — his — to 50.4.

When I saw Bob afterward, I said, "I want to put a bag over my head."

He looked at me and said, "Me, too."

Immediately after those Worlds, I was off to China, on a promotional tour arranged by some of my sponsors. Finally, in September, Bob had had enough.

"Michael," he said, "what is it you want to do? What are we doing here?"

"I want to swim all my events," I said. "And I want to win."

"You know what needs to happen?"

"I know."

I did, in fact, know. I just needed to hear myself say it.

The 2007 Worlds in Melbourne were not all that far away, in late March of that year, after a long Australian summer. I knew what needed to happen.

In all of 2006, Crock and I went head to head only once, at the summer nationals. I won, touching in 51.51, Crock in 51.73. The nationals served as the qualifier for the Pan Pacs; I passed in Victoria on the 100 fly, Crock going on to an easy win, 51.47, in the finals.

The 100 fly final at the 2007 Worlds took

310

place on a Saturday night. By the time we stepped onto the blocks, I had already won five golds at the meet. This race could be six. The 400 IM, seven. The medley relay, eight. Crock got to the turn first, with me third. We tore for the final wall and, again, I caught him at the end, if just barely, touching in 50.77, Crock in 50.82.

Five-hundredths of a second.

In Athens, I'd won by four-hundredths.

"Knowing that he's having the meet of his life, I expected him to go very fast and he did," Crock said afterward. "I'm just glad I still hold the world record."

"That's how I won the Olympic medal," I told the reporters. "You have to nail the finish as best you can."

The very next morning, Sunday, April 1, brought the medley relay prelims. Crock, as the silver medalist in the 100 fly, was up third on the blocks for the butterfly leg, swimming with Lochte, Scott Usher, and Neil Walker. Those guys put up what would have been the fastest time overall by more than two seconds. Except, on the board next to United States, it said DSQ. Disqualified. Crock had left the starting block too soon.

The rules allow a relay swimmer the leeway to start three-hundredths of a second early. Crock, according to the timing device, had gone off four-hundredths before Neil touched, meaning his feet had left the blocks one-hundredth of a second too fast. When the judges ruled against him, Crock slapped his hands to his face in disbelief.

A few hours later, he stood up at a team meeting in our hotel and apologized. I didn't mean it, he said. I feel horrible. He kept talking about how bad he felt.

I knew Crock didn't purposely false-start. It was a mistake; people make mistakes. There was nothing I could do. It happened. I could win seven medals in Melbourne, not eight. Crock apologized. It was over.

At least from my perspective, it was.

But as 2007 rolled into 2008, Crock didn't seem himself.

At the U.S. nationals in Indianapolis in the summer of 2007, Crock false-started again, in the 100 fly; I ended up winning the event. A photographic strobe had mistakenly been fired after the "take your mark" command but before the beep; Crock flinched.

In Omaha, in the prelims of the 100 free, Crock false-started yet again.

It wasn't only that I won the 100 fly at the Trials, Crock coming in second. It's that I beat him by 73-hundredths of a second. He wasn't, for whatever reason, himself. In the prelims in Beijing, he inexplicably wore a jammer, a suit that runs from the waist to just above the knees; his time was so poor he almost didn't make the semifinals. He switched back to a legsuit for the semifinals and swam much faster, tied for the third-best time with Lauterstein, the Australian.

You could tell when Crock was on and when he was not, and I wanted him on. When he was on, he had speed, he had tempo. I like racing people at their best, and I knew that through the Trials and even into the prelims and semis of the Games he was not at his best.

Then again, he might have that one special race still left in him.

And then there was Cavic, Milorad on the scoreboard, Mike to all of us who had known him for years, a guy who had been born in Southern California, went to high school there, then to college at Berkeley. Cavic had been training in South Florida with Mike Bottom, who used to be the coach at Cal and had proven himself time and again as one of the best anywhere at developing sprinters; Bottom was in Florida with a bunch of guys — Gary Hall, Jr., Nathan Adrian, and others — that was called "The Race Club."

At the Olympics, Cavic was swimming for

Serbia in part because he could. Each country gets two entrants per event. To qualify at the U.S. Trials in the 100 fly, Cavic would have had to have gotten by me, Crocker, Stovall, Tarwater, and others.

Not to say that he didn't have talent. Cavic had ability. He finished sixth in the 100 fly in Melbourne, for instance. In Beijing, he had put up the sixth-fastest time in the prelims of the 100 free, proving he was on his game, then scratched out of the semifinal to concentrate on the 100 fly.

Before 2008, though, Cavic had never shown that he was a breakthrough talent on the Olympic stage. His Olympic run in Athens had ended in the semifinals of the 100 fly when water had flooded the inside of his racing suit. After that, he dealt with back problems, even taking several months off in 2006.

He did, however, have a talent for getting noticed.

In the prelims at big meets, the fastest swimmers are seeded into the last three heats. The early heats, and at a meet like the 2007 Worlds there are sixteen heats, are for swimmers who are expected to go much slower. In heat number one of the sixteen 100 fly heats in Melbourne, however, there was Cavic; the start list didn't show a qualifying time next to his name. The only two others due to swim in that heat were a guy from Ghana and another from Malaysia. And then the guy from Ghana didn't go. So, Cavic essentially had open water, which is always an advantage. The three fastest times from all 16 heats in those prelims: Crocker, 51.44; Cavic, 51.7; me, 51.95.

At the European swimming championships in March 2008, Cavic was suspended for wearing a T-shirt that proclaimed, in the Serbian language, "Kosovo is Serbia," as he was awarded his gold medal for winning the 50-meter butterfly. After that, he went to Belgrade, where he was greeted by hundreds of fans and met with the prime minister, who called him a "hero."

Because of that suspension, Cavic didn't get to swim the 100 fly at the European championships. Thus he came to Beijing slightly under the radar.

After setting the top time in the semifinals in Beijing, Cavic did not simply allow the time to speak for itself. Instead, he said:

"I've got nothing against Michael Phelps. The guy's the king. Do I want to make a rivalry of this? Of course. Why not?"

And: "It would be kind of nice that one day, historically, we'll speak of Michael Phelps maybe winning seven gold medals, and having lost an opportunity to win eight gold medals. When they talk about that, they'll talk about whoever that guy is that took it away from him. I'd love to be that guy.

"I think it'd be good for the sport, and it'd be good for him if he lost once. Just once.

"Let's be honest about that. It's true. It's good to lose sometimes. I know because I've lost a lot. For him, what would it mean? I would hope that he would cut down on his events for the next year and start training more for the 100 fly. There's no doubt in my mind that he's the best. Will he be the best here? I don't know. He's got a lot on his plate. Hopefully, that will work out for me."

Gary Hall, Jr. — the same Gary Hall, Jr., who made so much noise in 2004 about me being on the relay — predicted in the *Los Angeles Times* that Cavic would beat me. After training with Cavic at The Race Club for a year and a half, Gary said, Cavic had "worked harder than anyone," had "endured taunt and torment from his teammates, myself included, for being overzealous with his training," adding, "We caught him sneaking in extra workouts."

Gary also said in that article that Cavic had "matured a lot, had somehow mellowed in the right ways and matured in others," had "become something of a champion and a team leader," adding, "He never faltered."

Gary closed his piece by recounting a toast he had made in Cavic's honor: " 'Here's to the guy that is going to upset Michael Phelps in the 100-meter butterfly,' I said, handing him his Race Club–embroidered terry cloth robe at the team dinner at the end of the season before heading off to the Olympic Trials.

"It looks like for once I might be right."

During the heats, Cavic made a shooting motion, as though his hand were a gun. He was asked if he had been "shooting" at me over in the next lane. "That's ridiculous," he said. "If you were there, you would have seen I was firing above him, at my manager."

I had no idea at the time that any of this was going on. I didn't know the first thing about it until, at breakfast the morning of the final, Bob said to me, hey, Cavic says it would be good for swimming if you got beat and he'd love to be the guy who took the gold medal away from you.

I perked right up. What?!

We walked out onto the deck with the Water Cube roaring with noise. In the stands, just up off the blocks, my mom sat between my sisters, Hilary on her right, Whitney on her left. They were holding hands, tense.

I was in Lane 5, Crocker 6, Cavic 4. As I went through my prerace routine, stretching, I turned in Cavic's direction; he was turned to face me. It looked to a lot of people, including Bob, as if he was trying to stare me down, which, later, Cavic denied, saying of me, "Maybe he was able to see the reflection of himself and he's like, 'Hey, I look pretty good.' I saw myself in his reflection and was keeping things under control."

Bob absolutely, positively thought Cavic was trying to play mind games with me. I had no idea. I saw him looking in my direction, and looked away. I was looking out through my metallic goggles in his direction, but not at him. I was paying no attention to what he was doing. Why would I? Bob had always instilled in me this notion: What does Tiger Woods do? What did Michael Jordan do? The great champions — there's nobody on their level, he used to tell me, and so when they're competing they're competing against themselves, and only themselves. You hear Woods talk after a great round, Bob would say, and what does he say? Something like, "I had good control of my game today," or, "I managed the last five holes really well." Never anything like, "Gee, I was really worried whether I was going to beat Vijay, or Ernie, or Phil." You be

318

like that, Michael, Bob would say.

The goal in this Olympic final that Bob and I had sketched out was for me to turn at 50 meters at 23-point-something seconds. If you turn at 24.2, Bob said, you're dead. At 24-flat, he made plain, well, you'd be making it very difficult on yourself but you might still have a chance.

My goal sheet for this race had me finishing at 49.5. No one had ever gone under 50 seconds. Crock's world record had been at 50.4 since 2005.

The goal sheet, it turned out, was perhaps too aggressive. Everything else about this race, though, was unbelievable.

"Take your marks," the big voice boomed out over the Cube.

Beep!

The dive. The underwater. Just as I had visualized it.

I popped up and launched into the fly. Fluid, strong, easy. Cavic, I knew, would be going out faster than I was. Crocker, too. I wasn't particularly worried. They had their style, going out harder on the front half; I had mine.

Hilary couldn't stand it any longer. She stood up on her chair. Behind her was a woman from Holland; the Dutch woman kept pulling at her shirt and yelling, "Sit down! Sit down!" Hilary turned and yelled back "I'm watching my brother and I'm going to stand. He's a good swimmer and you're going to have to tackle me if you want me to sit down!"

Bob, over on the other side of the stands, was imploring me to go faster: "Come on! Come on!"

At 50, I wanted to be half a body length back. I looked at the turn and saw Crocker and thought, okay, Cavic's not too far ahead.

What I didn't know was that I was seventh at the turn, in 24.04.

Cavic had turned first, at 23.42; Crock was right behind him, at 23.7.

Halfway down the backstretch, as I passed Crock to my right, I moved up on Cavic, to my left.

The Dutch woman was still pulling on Hilary's shirt: "Sit down!" Mom was fretting out loud, talking to Hilary, to Whitney, to no one and everyone, hoping against hope that what she was saying wasn't really going to come true, that just saying it might make it not happen: "He's going to get second. He's going to get second."

With 15 to go, Cavic knew I was coming hard. He said later he saw "kind of a shadow by the side of my goggle," adding, "The last 15 meters, the last eight meters, I just put my head down. I did not breathe the last eight meters. I was just hoping for the best."

In the coach's box, Bob was swaying like he was at a church service. Left, right, left, right.

In the water, Cavic and I hurtled toward the wall together.

Cavic opted to glide in.

I chopped my last stroke. It was short and fast, a half-stroke, really. I still can't fully explain why. Maybe it was experience. Absolutely competitive will. There wasn't time, really, to form a complete thought. It was an impulse. I knew I had to do something. The situation demanded action. Gliding was not going to win gold. It didn't for Matt Biondi and it for sure wasn't going to for me.

The Omega timing pads take roughly 6.5 pounds of pressure — 3 kilograms — to trigger. Anything less and the pad thinks it's just waves and won't respond. Anything that much or more, you turn off the clock.

Both Cavic and I touched, turned, and looked at the scoreboard.

Next to my name, it said: 1.

I looked over to where Bob had to be, pointed that way with my left hand, slapped the water with both hands and roared in victory, Olympic champion again, four years ago by four-hundredths of a second, now by one-hundredth, the smallest margin there was or ever could be. Mark Spitz had won seven medals at a single Olympics; now, with stupendously hard work, ferocious willpower, and a little luck, so had I.

In that instant, I had just matched the great Spitz.

At the finish, Bob initially thought I had lost. He muttered, a note of dejection in his voice, referring first to Cavic, then to me, "Oh, he got him." Then Bob swiveled to his right, to take in the board. In that instant he went from the lowest of lows to the highest of highs: "Oh! Oh, my God! Oh, my God!"

As Cavic and I had driven toward the wall, my mom had put up two fingers, for second. As we hit the wall, Hilary, still standing, still screaming, had her left arm around Mom. The two of them looked up at the board and Hilary started shouting, "Oh, my God! Oh, my God! Oh, my God! He won, he won, he won!" Mom just stared in disbelief. Hilary said, again, "He won!"

Mom sunk down into the chair as if she didn't have any bones. She was numb. Stunned.

Hilary and Whitney and everyone around them were going nuts, jumping up and down, shaking, freaking out, Hilary yelling over and again, "I can't believe it!"

In the pool, I said to Cavic, "Nice job."

Then I turned to Crocker. He and I shook hands and hugged. I leaned back, right elbow on the deck and lifted my left hand in the air, wagging just one finger high above me.

First, in 50.58 seconds, a flash of history in the present tense and proof that no matter what you set your imagination to, anything can happen if you dream as big as you can dream.

Cavic touched in 50.59. Lauterstein was third, in 51.12. Crocker was fourth, out of the medals, in 51.13, by one-hundredth of a second.

The close finish drew a formal protest from the Serbian team. Officials from FINA, the international swimming federation, said video replay confirmed what the scoreboard said.

The issue was never going to be whether Cavic ought to be the winner and me the runner-up, according to Cornel Marculescu, executive director of FINA. It was, he told reporters afterward, whether the race ought to be called a tie. FINA officials reviewed the video evidence frame by frame, and the race referee, Ben Ekumbo of Kenya, said, "It was very clear the Serbian swimmer had second, after Michael Phelps. It is evident from the video that it was an issue of stroking. One was stroking, the other was gliding." To make sure everyone was on the same page, FINA officials shared with the Serbian team the video evidence; if the Serbs had not been satisfied, they could have taken the protest to an appeal jury. Instead, Marculescu said, they were satisfied that I'd won and Cavic had come in second.

Cavic wore his silver medal to a news conference and said, referring to the race, "I'm stoked with what happened. I'm very, very happy."

Before the race, as Bob told me, Cavic had a lot to say. Afterward, Cavic had a lot more to say. At that news conference, he said, "Perhaps I was the only guy at this competition who had a real shot at beating Phelps one-on-one. This is completely new to me; I've never been in such a position with so much pressure, and I am very proud of how I handled that whole race and how I was able to keep myself under control emotionally and the stress level. It is a frightening thing to know that you're racing Michael Phelps, but I think that it's even more frightening to know that it's going to be a very, very close race and that nobody knows the outcome.

"... I read a lot of articles online. I like to read — it encourages me and I knew a lot of people had their money against me. That was totally understandable. Michael has been breaking world records here by seconds. This is something that no other swimmer in swimming really does, so what do you expect from a man who breaks world records by seconds in the 100 fly? You know, I expected that he'd go a world-record time — maybe something close, like 50.2. But it was a real honor for me to be able to race with Michael Phelps and be in this situation where all eyes were on me as the one man that would possibly be able to do it. It was just great.

"Pieter van den Hoogenband talked to me yesterday and I told him, 'Pieter, this is pretty stressful. I'm scared. I don't know what to expect.' And he just said, 'Just enjoy the experience, just have fun, and don't get too nervous. This is a beautiful thing.' Just hearing this from a legend such as Pieter — it really kind of calmed me down and I was like, 'He was right, the best races I've swum, I've swum when I was relaxed.'

"I believe I just did that here."

Asked about the appeal, he said, "You know, people will be asking me this for years, and I am sure people will be bringing this up for years, saying that, 'You won that race.' Well, you know, this is just what the results showed. This is what the electronic board showed. I guess I kind of have mixed emotions about it, you know. This could be kind of the where — if I had lost by a tenth of a second or two-tenths of a second, I could probably be a lot cooler about this but with a hundredth of a second I'll have a lot more people really saying that, 'You know, you won that race.' That kind of makes me feel good, but I'm gonna be happy with where I am."

The very last question of Cavic's news conference went like this:

"In your mind, was Michael Phelps the gold-medal winner?"

"Uh, is Michael Phelps the gold-medal winner? He — I think if we got to do this again, I'd win."

My style, as ever, was to let my swimming do the talking for me. Besides, there would never, ever be an "again." The time to seize that moment was right then, right there.

When I chopped the last stroke, I thought at first that it cost me the race. But it turned out to be just the exact opposite. If I had glided, I would have been way too long, caught in what swimmers call just that, a long finish, the way Cavic was. Instead, I turned a long finish into a short finish. I knew that little extra half stroke had to be a quick stroke, fast as I could do it.

I did some highly technical little things right at the very end, too, which Cavic did not, and those bought me time and made a difference. My head was down; his came up. My feet were straight; his, again, came up. Swimming fast is, generally speaking, a horizontal proposition; vertical movements slow you down. It typically pays to be in as straight and horizontal a line as possible. I was. He wasn't.

After the race, my mom and my sisters got to come on deck for just a moment.

"We're so proud of you!" came the chorus. Mom had that glowing, adoring look that only mothers looking at their children can have. That look doesn't change when the kids get to be big kids.

I let them in on a secret: "I didn't realize I was that far behind."

Still on the deck, I was put on the phone with Spitz, who was back in the States. "Epic," he told me. "What you did tonight was epic. It was epic for the whole world to see how great you are." He also said, "When I look at Michael and I think of the lore of what he has done over the last four years — it's more remarkable than myself."

The two others with nine gold medals over an Olympic career were, as it turned out, in Beijing. Carl Lewis said, "The reality is, congratulations." Larisa Latynina, the Soviet-era gymnast, wrote me a note that said, "You have shattered all sort of records with truly inspiring Olympic character." It also said, "In ceding my record for most Olympic gold medals, I do it with little regret. I am sure we share the joy of competition and a timeless joy for excellence."

Earlier in the week, I had said when asked about being "the greatest athlete in Olympic history," that I was "kind of at a loss for words." I explained, "Growing up, I always wanted to be an Olympian, and now to be the most decorated Olympian of all time, it just sounds weird saying it. I have absolutely nothing to say. I'm speechless." Now I had won seven and, no matter how many times I was asked, I still felt as if I was at a loss for just the right thing to say. I tried to explain my feelings this way: "I knew that in my dreams I always wanted it, and thought that under perfect circumstances I could do it. Just believing all along that you can do it goes a long way."

Maybe a little something extra helps, too — what Crock told me after the race. I'll never forget it. He said, marveling that I had somehow pulled it off, "You have to have angels with you, or something."

8

COMMITMENT: THE MEDLEY RELAY

No one could have been more supportive of my swimming for Mark Spitz's records than Mark Spitz.

Mark showed up in Omaha near the end of the 2008 Trials to take in the scene, and to tell anyone who would listen his emphatic prediction: I would win eight gold medals in Beijing.

"This is going to be history," he declared. "He's going to do — what we say — a little schooling to the rest of the world, and it's going to be exciting for those that will see it in person and for those who watch it on TV."

Mark also said that he had only good feelings about the possibility of seeing someone else in the record books on the line that says, "Most Golds Won at One Edition of Olympic Games, Individual." He said, "Records are made to be broken," adding, "Thirty-six years is a long time."

He also said, sitting at the head table in a

room off the warm-down pool in the Qwest Center, dozens of journalists scribbling down everything he had to say, "It just dawned on me that it was forty years ago that I was at training camp, and I was going, wow, that is almost twice as old as Michael Phelps is now! Wow, I swam a long time ago and, it's okay, it's okay."

I first met Mark in 2004, at the Trials in Long Beach, not until then, as improbable as that may seem in hindsight. I knew he was likely to show up at some point at those Trials — Mark is based in Southern California — but didn't know until after I won the 200 fly that Mark would be presenting nineteen-year-old me with the medal for the victory. At the podium, Mark shook my hand and leaned in to say a few words: "I'll be over in Athens to watch you, and I'm behind you all the way. I know what you're going through. I went through it once before. Enjoy it. Have fun with it. Go get 'em." Mark has always had a gift for the dramatic and at that point he hopped onto the podium, grabbed my right wrist with his left hand and raised both of our arms to the sky. He then pointed to me with his right finger, as if to say, here's your new champion. It was, and is still, one of the most exciting memories swimming could ever have given me.

When I won six golds in Athens, Mark remained steadfastly encouraging. It was hardly a failure to win six gold medals, he would remind anyone who asked. Just wait, he would say. Michael is going to be better in 2008 than he was in 2004.

Through the years, Mark could also not have been more gracious in pointing out how swimming had changed from his time to mine. In 1972, swimming featured a semifinal round only for 100-meter events; in each of Mark's 200-meter events, he had to swim twice for a gold medal. I had to swim three times for each individual gold, with the exception of the 400 IM, an event with no semifinal. Over the course of the meet in Munich, Mark swam thirteen times in eight days, in all about 1,800 meters of racing, just over a mile; in Beijing, I would swim seventeen times over nine days for 3,400 meters, or just over two miles. In Mark's day, American swimmers had very little international competition, and the relays, in particular, were all but guaranteed United States wins; by 2008, swimming was definitely global. The proof: In Beijing, swimmers from twenty-one countries would ultimately win medals. Moreover, Mark was not only the first to win seven golds; he was the first to win six. Going into Munich, he didn't have to deal with the same sort of media attention — not to mention that the media world in 1972 was not one filled with cable channels, Internet outlets, newspapers, magazines, all of which had a never-ending need for copy and outtakes. "I can unequivocally say he has shown a different type of courage than perhaps I did," Mark said of me. "I was not chasing Mark Spitz's record."

In Omaha, it was hardly surprising to see that Mark would show extraordinary insight about what awaited me in Beijing, his remarks almost foretelling the challenges in races such as the 100 fly: "There were so many things that had to go right with my story with each one of my events, and there is something that had to go wrong with someone else. So they didn't get that one flash of the greatest swim of their life to beat me. And it is kind of scary when you think about it, because it could have happened in any of the events."

He also ticked off three concerns that might stop me from getting to eight:

I obviously had to win the first event, the 400 IM. That I had done.

I had to continue my "winning ways" in the 100 fly, which he, like most observers, had tagged as the single toughest individual event on my calendar, in part because it was the one event in Beijing I would be racing in which I was not the world-record holder.

I had won the 100 fly.

Finally, Mark said, Michael can't control the relays, adding, "Anything can happen."

On paper, the medley relay, the final race of the Games at the Water Cube, looked like we should — repeat, should — win. But the Aussies had improved enough in their individual 100s to make a lot of people nervous. When you added up their best flat-start times in the four disciplines and compared them to ours, the Aussies were within 43-hundredths of a second, even if their best times had come in the semifinals, ours in the finals. Bob told my mom before the race that he thought our chances of winning were 60–40, maybe 70–30.

This was a relay the United States had never lost at the Olympics (not counting the Games in 1980 in Moscow, when the U.S. team didn't take part). The four of us in the finals — Peirsol, Hansen, me, Lezak — had been swimming medleys together since the 2002 Pan Pacs in Yokohama, when we set a world record. The 2004 team, with Crock swimming the butterfly leg in the finals, had won gold; Crock took the butterfly leg in the prelims of the medley in Beijing, so he stood to win gold again if we won in the finals.

And I was going for an eighth gold.

But that last element was not the be-all, end-all. "We absolutely respect and admire Michael's goals but the feeling on the team is that by no means does one man come first," Aaron told the *New York Times* before the medley final.

"Honestly, when Lezak pushed out that relay, the next day guys were bringing up the fact that if Lezak didn't touch out, Mike might not have had his eight golds. It's not something Mike talks about. No one here is racing for second place, even the guys racing Mike. The feeling on our team is, we're all racing to win. He's doing exceptionally well; we're all rooting for him. But by no means is he the only one we're rooting for."

All the U.S. coaches were nervous. Everyone knew how much was at stake.

Safe starts, they kept saying. Safe starts. If we heard it once we heard it a dozen times: If your start is a tenth too slow, you can make it up; if it's a tenth too fast, you're done. It's an awful feeling, we kept hearing, to swim wondering if you'd false-started.

Crock made sure in the preliminary to start safely, if cautiously. "When Phelps is done, I don't want to stand in the way, to do something stupid like '07," he told a reporter later. "I want him to have every shot he's got."

Grevers, who swam the backstroke leg in the prelim, acknowledged everyone's anxiety: "I don't think we were going to leave China if anyone DQ'd us," he said.

The morning of the final, the Cube was so jam-packed, with attendance way past the announced capacity of about 17,000, that people were crammed four and five deep in the aisles. Kobe Bryant and LeBron James came back to root us on. Our teammates and coaches were there. My family, of course — Whitney in a gold-colored top, Hilary a gold jacket, both in gold on purpose. Mom opted for black, nervous as always before the start of the race. On deck, there wasn't much to say; we'd do any talking afterward.

I was more than fired up. I'd gotten a text message that morning from back home, from Troy Pusateri. When I was just starting out at North Baltimore, Troy was one of the older boys; he used to call me "Little Phelps." Troy was always himself mentally tough, too; he went on to become a Navy SEAL. Of all the messages I got from home during the course of the 2008 Olympics, Troy's is the only one I saved so that I could read it afterward, get fired way, way up time and again. This is what it said:

"All right, brother man!! Last race!! This one is NOT for you . . . it's for your fans, like me, who you inspire every day for the past six years . . . it's for Bob and your mom. . . . for without them none of this would be possible . . . it's for the United States . . . the best damn country on the face of the earth . . . it's for history!! It's for you making this sport what it is today!! It's for all the people who talked smack and doubted you ever!! It's for being the best Olympic athlete ever to grace this planet!!! Go get 'em!! Don't hold back!! You can do it, buddy!! I'm so damn proud of ya!! Give 'em hellllllllll !!!!!"

On the deck, we got ourselves ready as Aaron and the other backstrokers got into the water and got set to go. The individual medley starts with the butterfly; the medley relay starts with the backstroke, which only makes sense. If backstroke were not first, the starting backstroke swimmer and the finishing previous swimmer might well crash into each other.

Beep! Aaron and the others dove backwards, arms above their heads, and the race was on. The quiet of the start gave way to an immediate wall of sound all around us.

Aaron had won gold in the 100 back in both Athens and Beijing. His backstroke is elegant. And yet still so powerful. He got us off to a solid start, though, as it turned out, he was 62-hundredths of a second slower than his gold-medal swim earlier in the week. Fortunately, Australia's Hayden Stoeckel was 83-hundredths slower than the lifetime best he went in the 100 back semifinals.

Brendan went next. His time was respectable, 59.27, but he was passed by both Kosuke Kitajima of Japan — his 58-flat split the fastest of all time — and by Australia's Brenton Rickard. We were in third when it was my turn. The Japanese didn't have the speed in the third and fourth legs, so they were not much of a worry. So it was now me and Lauterstein — a rematch of sorts from the 100 fly the day before.

My start was deliberately super-slow. It was, in fact, so slow I actually saw Brendan's hands touch the wall. I was taking no chances.

Lauterstein got to the wall first but I just hammered hard on the turn. When I came up from underwater, I was in front. This was my last swim of the Games. I gave it everything I had. Everything. I drove so hard that my finish was ugly. Caught between strokes again. This time I did glide. Had to.

When I touched, though, Jason had a cushion of 81-hundredths of a second.

In the seventeenth of my seventeen swims, even with that glide slowing me down, I laid down the fastest 100 fly leg in history, 50.15; Lauterstein's split of 51.03 was even faster than his 51.12 flat-swim for bronze the day before — but factoring in a relay flying start, not as fast as we had thought he might go. No way Jason was going to let himself, us, the United States down. He dug hard to the far wall. He turned and dug harder for home.

As soon as I touched, I sprinted out of the pool to watch the race from behind our block. The noise level in the building was now out of control. Except for the guys in the water, it seemed everyone in the building was yelling. I was excited beyond words but also calmly confident. About halfway through Jason's final lap, it became clear, even obvious — we were going to win. Standing there on the deck, I knew it. In the stands, Bob knew it, too. Eamon Sullivan was coming hard, but Jason was holding him off.

With 15 meters to go, Bob thought to him-self — you know what, this is actually going to happen. They're going to win and Michael is going to have eight medals. He's not going to have seven; he's really going to have eight.

"Come on, Jason!" Mom was yelling.

"Come on, Jason! Come on, Jason! Come on, Jason! Come on, Jason!"

Jason came home strong, and as he touched with his left hand, the roar of history enveloping all of us, my mom yelling, "Yes!" long and loud, holding the note as if she would never let it end, I pumped my fist in triumph, then grabbed Aaron and shouted, "Let's go! Let's go!"

Jason pulled himself up out of the water and we huddled, just the four of us. "We're part of history," he said. Jason had gone 46.76 to Sullivan's 46.65; we had won by seven-tenths of a second; we had set a new world record, 3:29.34. I said, "Without what you guys just did for me as a team this whole week, none of this would have been possible. We worked as a team and we worked really well together. I want to thank you guys for the opportunity you gave me."

In the stands, fate had put Ian Thorpe in the row immediately ahead of Mom and my sisters. He turned around and wished them congratulations, saying graciously and sincerely, "Good job. That was great."

Mom cried and cried, tears of joy and relief and amazement.

We were honored after the race to be able to carry around an American flag that had flown in Iraq; it had been sent to one of our teammates, Larsen Jensen, a bronze medalist in Beijing in the 400 free. It made a special moment that much more special.

When the medals ceremony ended, walking along the side of the pool, I saw Mom and the girls and started climbing through the photographers to get to them. The photographers parted, allowed me to get to my mother and sisters, then, as if on cue, immediately closed in around us. Surrounded there by dozens if not hundreds of cameras, by thousands of fans still packed into the Water Cube, it nonetheless seemed as if we were in our own little bubble.

I said, "I'm so tired."

Brendan won two breaststroke medals in Athens. In 2006, he set three world records in breaststroke events in three weeks. In Omaha at the 2008 Trials, he won the 100 breast. Then, to the surprise of many of us, he finished fourth in the 200 breast, failing to qualify in that event. What he did thereafter speaks to the kind of guy Brendan is. He immediately said he would try to help the two guys who beat him in the 200, Shanteau and Scott Spann. And then, when he could have begged off, Brendan went to sign autographs and pose for photos at a session USA Swimming had organized.

The 100 breast final came early in the week in Beijing, on Monday, overshadowed completely by the 400 free relay final an hour later. Brendan, who is not related to my friend Stevie's family, finished fourth. What Brendan did after that underscored again what kind of guy he is. He ran into my mom at the Beijing version of USA House, a gathering spot for the USOC and for American athletes and guests at every Olympics, and vowed, "I'll be ready for the relay."

Brendan was not at his greatest in the medley. But, as he promised, he was ready. He did his part. And what he said after the race made plain why anyone would be proud to call Brendan a teammate.

"It's one of the greatest things sport in general has ever seen," Brendan said when asked about the eight medals. "I mean, coming from a swimmer, looking at what he did, there's an immeasurable amount of respect for what he did. The shame of it is other athletes are not going to realize how hard what he did is.

"The world is fast at swimming now. The world was not fast when Mark Spitz did his seven. Everybody is stepping up. Michael got on the blocks for every final against seven different people and denied them every single time. That just goes to show —

it's every part of sport. It's endurance, it's strength, it's pressure.

"... He made the pressure putt in the U.S. Open, he won the Tour de France, and he knocked out the best fighter in the world in the sixteenth round with an uppercut. He did absolutely everything sport is supposed to be and he did it with a smile on his face, and he's a good kid."

Brendan had another great line that, when I read it later, I also truly enjoyed. He said he had been amazed that I could separate myself so seemingly completely from the pool when I wasn't at the Cube. Brendan said, "I'd be like, 'Do you realize what you're doing?' And he'd be like, 'Man, the pizza is good today.'"

Aaron and Jason had great words, too.

Aaron said, "He's coined a new term: the Phelpsian feat. We've all heard of the Spitzian feat. I think there's a new one now." Jason said, "Before the race, I saw Kobe and LeBron, the two best players in the world in basketball. I love basketball; there is no way I was going to let these guys down. They came out here to watch this — it was awesome."

Seemingly everyone around the pool, in the moments after the race, was suddenly fair game: What do you think of what

Michael did? Some of the answers were hugely, hugely flattering. Like Leisel Jones, the Australian breaststroke champion, who won two gold medals in Beijing: "I couldn't care less about my swims. To swim the same era as him has been awesome." Or the Australian coach, Alan Thompson: "We've been talking about Mark Spitz for thirty-six years now. I don't know if I'm going to be alive when they stop talking about this bloke. You wonder if we are going to see someone as good as this again."

I got whisked to a news conference in the basement of the Water Cube. In those moments after we'd won the medley, it dawned on me that my life had abruptly moved into a new and completely different phase. President Bush called, and said, "If you can handle eight gold medals, you can handle anything." I'd been told that our medley swim had been shown on the big screens at M&T Bank Stadium in Baltimore after the Ravens faced the Minnesota Vikings in a preseason NFL game; more than 10,000 people stayed to watch us win. The Associated Press had filed a "flash" onto the wire when the medley ended with us winning; the AP uses a "flash" only for what it believes is a "transcendent development," which through the years has meant such occasions as the shooting of President Kennedy, the first moon landing, the falling of the Twin Towers.

And now — for swimming.

I was, as I said in my first comments at this news conference — held in a basement of the Water Cube, the room hot and sweaty, packed beyond full with reporters and cameras — "fairly speechless." I tried to explain: "This is all a dream come true," seeing as my main goal was to raise the sport of swimming as "high as I can get it." Besides the Ravens game, I said, I'd heard they had made an announcement at Yankee Stadium when I'd won the 100 fly. The St. Louis Cardinals had held up their team bus back to the hotel in Cincinnati so the players and coaches could watch us win the medley. "People all over the place are saying it's crazy. They're out to eat, the TV is on and swimming is on. I think the goal that I have and I'm working toward is in progress . . . I think it's really just starting to get more of an awareness for the sport in the United States. By far, it's already starting. It started four years ago. With the help of my team and the coaching staff, I think this sport can take off even more than it is. That's a goal that isn't going to happen overnight. It's going to happen over time and that's something I'm going to be in the long run for."

I tried, too, to explain why my emotions surfaced so much more in Beijing, there for everybody to see on live television, than they had in Athens: "I've dreamed of a lot of things. I've written down a lot of goals; this was the biggest one I ever really wrote down. Sort of thinking of all the memories I've had through my career to get here, with my family, my friends, my coaches — my coach, I've really only had one coach — everything I've gone through. It's — I guess my mom and I still joke about it, I was in middle school and I had a teacher say I'd never be successful. It's little things like that. It's stuff like that you think back to and it's just fun. I saw my mom for a minute and we just hugged. She started to cry. I started crying. My sisters started crying. It has been a really fun week and I'm really glad to accomplish everything I wanted to."

After that news conference, Bob and I were whisked away to another one, to a much bigger room at what was called the Main Press Center a few minutes away from the Water Cube. By then, Darryl Seibel, the USOC's chief communications officer, had joined us. He had been through these kinds of media get-togethers a time or two before and knew just what to say.

"Are you hungry?" he asked me.

"God, yes."

"Cheeseburgers?"

"God, yes."

Darryl sent a USOC volunteer to the McDonald's in the press center for four cheeseburgers and fries, pronto. When the burgers arrived, Bob knocked back one in world-record time and I wolfed two.

Before we went out to meet the press again, I cleared my BlackBerry again of yet another avalanche of e-mails and text messages. I would clear it; it would fill up immediately; I would try to clear it; I'd get a new batch. I couldn't keep up.

When we walked out onto the stage of the room at the press center for this next news conference, it was even clearer to me just how my life was changed. This room was enormous. It was crowded beyond capacity, too.

One reporter wanted to know if I had stayed in the Olympic Village or a fancy hotel. The village, of course, I said. I got to meet Rafael Nadal; he was one of my favorite tennis players to watch on television. I saw Roger Federer. I saw Dirk Nowitzki, I said.

What about Spitz? "Being able to have something like that to shoot for made those days when I was tired and I didn't want to be there — you wanted to go home and sleep instead of work out — you look at him and you say, 'I want to do this.' It has been something I wanted to do and I'm just thankful for having him do what he did."

Mostly, I said, I was just thankful.

For the way it had all worked out: "Seeing 8/8/08 and the opening ceremonies starting at eight, I guess it was maybe meant to be. I don't know. For this to happen, everything had to fall into perfect place."

For my teammates. For all the games of spades and Risk at night. The laughs we shared. "I just wanted to make sure I took every single moment in and every single swim in, every single moment with my teammates, so I would remember them. I don't want to forget anything that happened."

For my family, and for Bob. Bob said, "Clearly, an accomplishment of this magnitude doesn't happen with just one or two people. There are a lot of people who have been involved in this process, from Michael's family, my family for that matter, everyone back at NBAC where we started and will soon return, all our fans in Ann Arbor and Baltimore, Club Wolverine — I'd like to thank them for everything they've done. And particularly this amazing Olympic swimming team, the best group of guys I've ever been around — and it has just been an honor to be a part of it."

For sure, I planned to be back at the Games in 2012, I said, but probably doing different events.

When that press conference wrapped up, we went across the street to the NBC compound at what was called the International Broadcast Center, to Dick Ebersol's office. There, for the first time since arriving in Beijing, I got to spend more than just a moment with my family. President Bush had given me a message for my mom: Hug her for me, he had said. I made sure I followed the president's orders.

Bob was in the room. So was Mike Unger of USA Swimming. Peter Carlisle, Drew Johnson, and Marissa Gagnon of Octagon were there, too, along with Dan Hicks, Rowdy Gaines, Andrea Kremer, Tommy Roy, Drew Esocoff, and a few others from NBC, and, of course, Ebersol, whose office had banks of TV screens. He asked, what do you want to see? The 400 free relay, I said before he could even really get the question out.

I could watch that relay 100 times and I think I'd still have the same reaction — wow, that really happened.

We watched that relay and some other

races. We saw my mom cry watching me. Hilary, too.

Dick and I had come to occupy a special place in each other's lives that had nothing to do with how many medals I won or how the broadcasts of the Olympics did in the ratings. He had supported me, stood up for my character, when I'd been called to account for drinking and driving; just a few weeks later, he was badly hurt in the plane crash near Telluride in which his son, Teddy, who was just fourteen, was killed. Mom and I were honored to be invited to the funeral. Dick had followed me as I had grown up after Athens and I had learned so much from him about what strength in the face of adversity looked like. In his eighth-grade graduation speech, Teddy had said, "The finish line is only the beginning of a whole new race."

Watching the replays, Dick cried, too.

That half hour in that office was one of the few moments of quiet and calm in what quickly became a whirlwind.

No complaints. None at all. The opportunities that were extended to me from around the world were unbelievably thrilling. And every single one might be the one that would encourage some little boy or girl somewhere to get to the pool to start swimming for nine medals.

Bob and I had, before the Games, come to an understanding. I would be back in the pool, just not immediately. The 2009 World Championships, in Rome, weren't until the summer; my mom had always wanted to see Rome, so I had to be back in time to try to make the team. Bob said, fine, see you in early 2009 back at the pool, back in Baltimore. He announced several months before the Olympics that he was going back to NBAC, to become chief executive officer. Starting in Rome, you might see me focus on different events: more of the sprints, for instance, maybe the 100 free, perhaps the 200 back. Both of us were excited, me to have new goals, Bob to see whether a guy more naturally suited for longer distances could make the switch. Beyond that, I fully intended to compete at the 2012 Summer Games in London, assuming I qualified for the U.S. team. My plan all along has been to be retired from swimming by the time I'm thirty; London, when I will be twenty-seven, figures to be my last go-round.

Enjoy whatever it is you're going to do, Bob made plain before we left Beijing. He didn't have to say the rest — make good decisions.

From Beijing, it was off to London, where I took part in the ceremony that marked the end of the Games and the handover from the 2008 to 2012 Summer Olympics. In Orlando, I rode in a convertible down Main Street at Disney World with Mickey Mouse. In Chicago, more than 150 of us from the 2008 U.S. Olympic team got to be on *The Oprah Winfrey Show;* I also was privileged to add my support to Chicago's bid for the 2016 Summer Olympics.

In Los Angeles, I got to be a presenter at MTV's Video Music Awards and a guest on shows such as *Jimmy Kimmel Live* and *The Tonight Show with Jay Leno.* In New York, I rang the bell, along with Lochte and Natalie Coughlin, at the New York Stock Exchange and hosted *Saturday Night Live.* On *SNL,* I got to joke that being on the show was "like, the ninth greatest moment of my life." In the audience that night was Bruce Springsteen; at a concert a couple weeks before in St. Louis he had, before launching into "Thunder Road," given me a shoutout: "Eight golds, man — whoo!" The *SNL* musical guest — the one and only Lil Wayne, whose music had gotten me in the mood before getting on the blocks in Beijing — he gave me a signed iPod that held forty unreleased tracks, one of them called "Michael Phelps," about me. I hardly knew what to say besides — thank you.

Everywhere I went I was flattered to have touched so many people. A driver in Cleveland told me, "You honored the entire country with your effort." At the baggage check-in in Newark, one of the skycaps said, "Congrats, Michael — you killed it out there."

Everywhere, it seemed, swimming had become part of the national conversation. When the Los Angeles Angels clinched the American League West title in early September, one of their outfielders, Torii Hunter, put on goggles, got down on the floor in a pool of champagne and beer, and shouted out, "I love it. I'm Michael Phelps!"

In late September, I went back to Ann Arbor for the Wisconsin-Michigan football game and had one of those experiences that gave me chills. I saw Bob for the first time since Beijing; we got to go into the Michigan locker room before the game, where I told them to beat the Badgers. The players were all fired up and so was I, and then Bob and I walked down to the field through this long tunnel under the stadium. The Michigan band was in there, and as soon as they saw me at the top of the tunnel, they all started going nuts. As we walked toward the field, the cheers echoed in front of us and rolled out into the great bowl, and then the people outside heard what was going on, and they started applauding, and so by the time we got to the light, the entire stadium was cheering. And that was way before we were introduced, when we got another thunderous ovation.

In Baltimore the next weekend, the city formally welcomed me home with both a parade, which also honored Katie Hoff, as well as Paralympic athletes and Special Olympians, and then a fireworks show at Fort McHenry, birthplace of "The Star Spangled Banner."

All of it was amazing. It sometimes seemed surreal, especially because I never set out to be a celebrity. I set out to be the best I could be and then to do something no one else had ever done, and as we zipped from one city to the next, it was never far from my mind that, for sure in my case, celebrity comes with a certain responsibility. I was privileged enough that people wanted to hear me and see me. What was it I could tell them?

The answer, in part, came with the establishment of a foundation we set up immediately after the Games that bears my name with the aim to get kids into swimming and to help teach healthier lifestyles. I donated the entire $1 million Speedo bonus. Then Speedo and its North American licensee, The Warnaco Group, Inc., announced another $200,000 donation, and Kellogg's, which put my picture on boxes of Frosted Flakes and other products, donated another $250,000. One of the foundation's first initiatives: visits to a number of cities to launch an educational program that helps kids achieve their goals. The program is based on what my mom and Bob, in particular, helped me learn when I was younger: to set goals, take responsibility, and practice discipline.

Maybe we're onto something. By the fall, USA Swimming announced that record numbers of kids were signing up at local clubs. In Mount Laurel, New Jersey, enrollment in the learn-to-swim program doubled; in Chicago, the Lyons Swim Club saw a 28 percent increase in their team size from the beginning of August through the end of September; in Farmington, New Mexico, the Four Corners Aquatic team grew by 40 percent; in Sarasota, Florida, the YMCA Sharks added 135 new members, a 36 percent increase.

Through all the glitz and the glitter after the Games, some of my best memories will always be the quieter moments, especially those I was lucky enough to spend with kids, particularly at Boys & Girls Clubs across the country. In Burbank, California, at the Boys & Girls Club, a seven-year-old named Javier Silva gave me a handmade leather bracelet; he had put eight little gold rings on it. He told me that he had watched me swim a lot at the Olympics and that he was my number-one fan. I told him I would wear it; I was true to my word. A few days later, at the Dunlevy Milbank Community Center in Harlem, I watched a group of about two dozen boys and girls swim laps. Never, I said, let anyone tell you that anything is impossible. "There were people who said no way anyone could win eight medals," I said. "When people say that, I want to prove them wrong. I was able to prove them wrong this year. And one of the best things about the most exciting time in my life was looking up and seeing my mom there."

All over the country — really, the world — people have gravitated toward my mom. As many people, maybe more, have come up to say, "We love your mom," as have said, "Congratulations." At the close of *Saturday Night Live,* the female cast members kept saying, we love your mom — she's awesome!

She is awesome.

In early October, President Bush welcomed more than five hundred members of the 2008 U.S. Olympic and Paralympic teams to the White House. We gathered on the South Lawn and, as part of his remarks, the president said, "People say, did you ever get to meet Michael Phelps? I said I did. So that was the highlight? I said, not really. Meeting his mother was more of a highlight. She reminded me of my mother — plain-spoken and full of love."

Everywhere my mom went after the Olympics, people would stop her and say, "Hey, Debbie," hundreds, maybe thousands, of people she had never before met calling her by her first name as if they were old friends. People wanted just a moment with my mom — to say thank you, to say wow, to say what a great family we are. Mom had people tell her that the love she had for me and my sisters, and all of us for her, was something that America needed, that it was evidence of American values at their best. Mom had people stop her at the store and say, "Debbie, outstanding job — we are so proud of you and your son."

Mom also starred in one of the best stories that came out of the 2008 Summer Olympics. Mom likes to shop at a clothing store named Chico's. After she got back from Beijing, she went to her favorite Chico's and, after some parking difficulties, was approached by a security guard in the parking lot. He started talking to her. Then a flash of recognition lit his face.

"Hey," he said, "I know you. You — you're the seven-medal mama."

Mom didn't miss a beat. She said, "Eight."

ABOUT THE AUTHORS

Michael Phelps is an American swimmer. He holds the record for winning the most gold medals (eight) in a single Olympics (2008). He has won sixteen Olympic medals, fourteen gold and two bronze. He holds seven world records and has more than twenty World Championship medals.

After returning home from Beijing in 2008, Michael used the well-publicized $1 million Speedo bonus he received to start the Michael Phelps Foundation, through which he hopes to encourage children to lead healthy, active lives and to continue to grow the sport of swimming. He now resides in Baltimore, Maryland, with his dog, Herman.

Alan Abrahamson is an award-winning sportswriter and a recognized authority on the Olympics. In 2006, he left the *Los Angeles Times,* where he had been a staff writer for seventeen years, to write for the NBC suite of online properties, which now includes NBCOlympics.com, NBCSports.com, and UniversalSports.com. Since 2003, Alan has also served as a sports and Olympic analyst for the NBC television networks. Among other honors, Alan won the 2002 National Headliner Award for sports writing and was named the Los Angeles Press Club's 2004 sports journalist of the year. Alan, his wife, Laura, and their three children live in Southern California.